ACCA

PRACTICE & REVISION KIT

PAPER F8

AUDIT AND ASSURANCE (INTERNATIONAL)

In this January 2010 new edition

- We discuss the **best strategies** for revising and taking your ACCA exams
- We show you how to be **well prepared** for your exam
- We give you **lots of great guidance** on tackling questions
- We show you how you can **build your own exams**
- We provide you with **three** mock exams including the **December 2009 exam**
- We provide the **ACCA examiner's answers** as well as our own to the June and December 2009 exams as an additional revision aid

Our **i-Pass** product also supports this paper.

FOR EXAMS IN 2010

BPP LEARNING MEDIA

First edition 2007
Fourth edition January 2010

ISBN 9780 7517 8056 7
(previous ISBN 9780 7517 6663 9)

British Library Cataloguing-in-Publication Data
A catalogue record for this book
is available from the British Library

Published by

BPP Learning Media Ltd
BPP House, Aldine Place
London W12 8AA

www.bpp.com/learningmedia

Printed in the United Kingdom

We are grateful to the Association of Chartered Certified Accountants for permission to reproduce past examination questions. The suggested solutions in the exam answer bank have been prepared by BPP Learning Media Ltd, except where otherwise stated.

Your learning materials, published by BPP Learning Media Ltd, are printed on paper sourced from sustainable, managed forests.

Contents

Page

Finding questions

Using your BPP Learning Media Practice and Revision Kit

Revising F8

Planning your question practice

Questions and answers

Exam practice

Review form & free prize draw

Question index

The headings in this checklist/index indicate the main topics of questions, but questions are expected to cover several different topics.

Questions set under the old syllabus *Audit and Internal Review* (AIR) paper are included because their style and content are similar to those which appear in the F8 exam. The questions have been amended to reflect the current exam format.

Planning your question practice

Our guidance from page xxvi shows you how to organise your question practice, either by attempting questions from each syllabus areas or **by building your own exams** – tackling questions as a series of practice exams.

ACCA's examiner's answers

The ACCA examiner's answers to questions marked '**Pilot paper**', **'12/07'**, **'6/08'**, or **'12/08'** can be found on the BPP website at the following link:

www.bpp.com/acca/examiner-solutions

Additional question guidance

Additional guidance to certain questions can be found on the BPP website at the following link:

www.bpp.com/acca/extra-question-guidance

Using your BPP Learning Media products

This Kit gives you the question practice and guidance you need in the exam. Our other products can also help you pass:

- **Learning to Learn Accountancy** gives further valuable advice on revision
- **Passcards** provide you with clear topic summaries and exam tips
- **Success CDs** help you revise on the move
- **i-Pass CDs** offer tests of knowledge against the clock

You can purchase these products by visiting www.bpp.com/mybpp.

You can view demonstrations of i-Learn and i-Pass products by visiting www.bpp.com/acca/study-materials/#ilearn. Scroll down the page until you find the sections for i-Learn and i-Pass and click on the appropriate 'View demo' button.

Topic index

Listed below are the key Paper F8 syllabus topics and the numbers of the questions in this Kit covering those topics.

If you need to concentrate your practice and revision on certain topics or if you want to attempt all available questions that refer to a particular subject, you will find this index useful.

Syllabus topic	Question numbers
Accounting estimates	43, 50
Analytical procedures	24, 30, 40, 43, 46, 47, 62, ME2 Q3
Audit appointment	ME1 Q1
Audit evidence	24, 27, 40, 44, 53, 55, 71, 80, ME3 Q2
Audit planning	17, 20, 21, 22, 26, 30, ME3 Q1
Audit regulation	1
Audit reporting	44, 80, 81, 82, 83, 84, 85, ME1 Q5
Audit risk	17, 18, 22, 23, 27, 29, 30, 62, ME1 Q1, ME2 Q3
Audit sampling	28, 43, 44, 46, 68
Auditing standards	5
CAATs	25, 26, 37, 46, 60, 67, 68
Cash and bank	38, 45, 51, 52, 58, 62
Confidentiality	3, 10
Corporate governance	2, 6, 7, 8, 11, 31, ME3 Q2
Engagement letters	49, 80, ME1 Q1
Ethics	3, 9, 10, 11, 12, 49, 72, 74, 78, ME1 Q3, ME1 Q5
Expert	41, 42, 66
External audit	4
External confirmations	45, 52, 58
Fraud	35, 74, ME2 Q2
Going concern	22, 72, 78, 79, 82
Independence	3, 10, 11, ME1 Q3
Internal audit	7, 8, 12, 13, 14, 15, 16, 26, 38, 41, 61, ME1 Q3, ME2 Q1, ME2 Q2
Internal controls	18, 23, 32, 39, 69, 84, ME1 Q4, ME3 Q3
Inventory	49, 56, 61, 64, 65, 66, 70, 74, ME2 Q1, ME3 Q1
Materiality	28
Negative assurance	27, 79, 83, ME3 Q4
Non-current assets	42, 46, 48, 56, 63, ME3 Q3
Not-for-profit organisations	23, 36, 59
Payables	53, 54, 67, ME3 Q5
Provisions	53, 54, 56, ME1 Q5
Purchases systems	34, 67, 70
Receivables	30, 45, 50, 68, 69
Removal from office	73, 75
Report to management	39
Review reports	81
Sales systems	31, 32, 33
Subsequent events	75, 76, 77, 78, 85, ME2 Q4, ME2 Q5

Syllabus topic	Question numbers
Wages systems	35, 40, 55, 60, ME1 Q4
Working papers	17, 19
Written representations	57, 71, ME1 Q2

Using your BPP Learning Media Practice and Revision Kit

Tackling revision and the exam

You can significantly improve your chances of passing by tackling revision and the exam in the right ways. Our advice is based on feedback from ACCA examiners.

- We look at the dos and don'ts of revising for, and taking, ACCA exams
- We focus on Paper F8; we discuss revising the syllabus, what to do (and what not to do) in the exam, how to approach different types of question and ways of obtaining easy marks

Selecting questions

We provide signposts to help you plan your revision.

- A full **question index**
- A **topic index** listing all the questions that cover key topics, so that you can locate the questions that provide practice on these topics, and see the different ways in which they might be examined
- **BPP's question plan** highlighting the most important questions and explaining why you should attempt them
- **Build your own exams**, showing how you can practise questions in a series of exams

Making the most of question practice

At BPP Learning Media we realise that you need more than just questions and model answers to get the most from your question practice.

- Our **Top tips** included for certain questions provide essential advice on tackling questions, presenting answers and the key points that answers need to include
- We show you how you can pick up **Easy marks** on some questions, as we know that picking up all readily available marks often can make the difference between passing and failing
- We include **marking guides** to show you what the examiner rewards
- We include **examiners' comments** to show you where students struggled or performed well in the actual exam
- We refer to the **BPP Study Text** (for exams in 2010) for detailed coverage of the topics covered in questions
- In a bank at the end of this Kit we include the **examiner's answers** to the June and December 2009 papers. Used in conjunction with our answers they provide an indication of all possible points that could be made, issues that could be covered and approaches to adopt.

Attempting mock exams

There are three mock exams that provide practice at coping with the pressures of the exam day. We strongly recommend that you attempt them under exam conditions. **Mock exams 1 and 2** reflect the question styles and syllabus coverage of the exam; **Mock exam 3** is the December 2009 paper.

Revising F8

General exam support from BPP Learning Media

BPP Learning Media is committed to giving you the best possible support in your quest for exam success. With this in mind, we have produced **guidance** on how to revise and techniques you can apply to **improve your chances of passing** the exam. This guidance can be found on the BPP Learning Media web site at the following link:

www.bpp.com/acca/examtips/Revising-for-ACCA-exams.doc

A paper copy of this guidance is available by emailing learningmedia@bpp.com

Topics to revise

Any part of the syllabus could be tested in the F8 exam because all of the questions are compulsory, therefore it is essential that you learn the **entire syllabus** to maximise your chances of passing.

The F8 paper assumes knowledge of Paper F3 *Financial Accounting*. It is important, therefore, that candidates can apply the knowledge they have gained in this paper to the audit and assurance context of Paper F8.

All questions will require a written response but there may be questions requiring the calculation and interpretation of some basic ratios in the context of audit planning or review.

The following table summarises the expected format of the F8 exam.

Question	*Format/indicative subject area*	*Marks available*
1	This will always be a question on audit procedures and their application to a specific scenario.	30
2	Short factual questions based on ISAs and other key areas of the Study Guide.	10
3	Risk and audit approach.	20
4	More specialised audit areas.	20
5	Collection of audit evidence, closedown, reporting.	20

In short, remember that **all** the questions in this paper are compulsory. Therefore, we **strongly advise** that you do not selectively revise certain topics – any topic from the syllabus could be examined. Selective revision will limit the number of questions you can answer and hence reduce your chances of passing this paper.

Question practice

You should use the Passcards and any brief notes you have to revise the syllabus, but you mustn't spend all your revision time passively reading. **Question practice is vital;** doing as many questions as you can in full will help develop your ability to analyse scenarios and produce relevant discussion and recommendations. The question plan on page xxvi tells you what questions cover so that you can choose questions covering a variety of syllabus areas.

Make sure you leave enough time in your revision schedule to practise 30 mark, 10 mark and 20 mark questions that will comprise the F8 exam. The F8 paper will have one 30 mark question, one 10 mark question and three 20 mark questions. They are all compulsory and different in style so you must be comfortable with approaching them. Also ensure that you attempt all three of the mock exams under exam conditions.

Passing the F8 exam

Displaying the right qualities and avoiding weaknesses

In order to pass this paper it is important that you get some of the basics right. These include the following:

Reading time

You have 15 minutes of reading time – make sure you use it wisely.

Consider the following:

- Speed read through the question paper, jotting down any ideas that come to you about any of the questions
- Decide the order in which you would prefer to tackle questions
- Spend the reminder of the reading time reading the question(s) you'll do first in detail, analysing scenarios, jotting down plans
- When you can start writing, get straight on with the questions you've planned in detail

Read the question

Again this sounds obvious but is absolutely critical. When you are reading the question think about the following:

- Which technical area is being tested?

  This should let you identify the relevant areas of technical knowledge to draw on.
- What am I being asked to do?

  (We will take a more detailed look at the wording of requirements later.)
- Are there any key dates?

  This is important in questions on inventory. If the inventory count takes place at a time other than the year-end you need to be aware of this.
- What is the status of your client?

  For example is it large or small, is it a new or existing client? This might affect issues such as risk.
- What is the nature of the business?

  This is particularly relevant in planning questions as it will have an impact on risk areas.
- How many marks are allocated to each part of the question so approximately how many points do I need to make?

  When you think about the number of points you need to achieve you need to consider this in relation to the requirement. If you are asked for explanation it is likely that you will score more marks per point than if you are simply asked for a list of points.

You also need to think about the order in which you read information in the question. If the question is scenario based it is important that you read the requirement first so that as you read through the rest of the information you are aware of the key matters/issues which you are looking out for. For example if you are asked for risks in a scenario you can try to identify as many risk factors as possible as you read the detailed information.

You should also try to read the question as 'actively' as possible. Underline key words, annotate the question and link related points together. These points can often serve as the basis for an outline plan.

Understand the requirements

It is important that you can understand and differentiate between the requirements that the examiner typically uses. Here are some examples:

Requirement	Meaning
Explain	Make a point clear, develop basic point, justify a point of view
Discuss	Critically examine an issue
List	Normally punchier points than 'explain' or 'discuss'
Illustrate	Explain by using examples
Audit procedures/audit tests	Actions
Enquiries	Questions
Evidence	Source (eg document) and what it proves

Think and plan

No matter how well prepared you are you are going to have to do some thinking in the exam. Obviously you will be under time pressure, but if used effectively thinking and planning time should not be seen as a waste of time.

Generating ideas can often be a problem at this stage. Remember that your knowledge of key ISAs can serve as a good starting point.

In audit evidence questions you may think about the financial statement assertions (completeness, accuracy, valuation etc). You could also think about the different types of procedures listed in ISA 500 (inspection, observation, inquiry, confirmation, recalculation/reperformance and analytical procedures).

In risk questions it might be helpful to think about the different elements of risk (inherent risk, control risk, detection risk).

Repeating this knowledge will not be sufficient in most cases to pass the question but these ideas can form a very sound basis for developing a good answer.

One particular issue you need to consider at this stage is the problem of repetition. In many auditing questions it is possible that the same point may be relevant in more than one part of the answer. Candidates will only get credit once so repeating the same point several times is a waste of time. Decide where you want to make the point, make it once and move on.

Keep going back to the requirement and make sure that you really are answering the question. One of the most common errors in auditing papers is identifying the correct point but using it in the wrong way. Make sure that your answer is focused on the requirements. It may be tempting to write everything you know about a particular point but this will not help you to pass the exam. This 'scattergun' approach will attract few, if any, marks.

Producing your answer

Although much of the hard work has been done by the time you get to this stage you need to think carefully about how you put down each point on paper. The way you make the point can make a difference to the number of marks scored. The main criticism from the examiner in the previous syllabus was the lack of clarity and precision. This is particularly the case regarding questions on audit evidence. For example lists of tests stating 'check this' and 'check that' without explaining what is being checked and why is likely to score few marks. If you find it difficult to gauge the right level of detail try to imagine that you are explaining the procedure to a junior member of staff. Would they be able to perform the procedure based on your description?

Think about your style. A well structured answer with clearly identifiable points is generally preferable to long paragraphs of text. However, do not fall into the trap of producing note-form answers. This is rarely sufficiently detailed to score marks.

Tackling questions

In summary, you'll improve your chances by following a step-by-step approach along the following lines.

Step 1 **Read the requirement**

Identify the knowledge areas being tested and see precisely what the examiner wants you to do. This will help you focus on what's important in the scenario.

Step 2 **Check the mark allocation**

This shows the depth of answer anticipated and helps you allocate time.

Step 3 **Read the scenario/preamble**

Identify which information is relevant to which part. There are lots of clues in the scenario so make sure you identify those that you should use in your answer.

Step 4 **Plan your answer**

Consider the formats you'll use and discussion points you'll make.

Step 5 **Write your answer**

Gaining the easy marks

Stick carefully to the time allocation for each question, and for each part of each question. All questions in this paper are compulsory so you need to attempt them all in order to improve your chances of passing. Easier marks are available in Question 2, a 10 mark question based on factual elements of the syllabus. Such knowledge-based requirements could also feature in parts of the scenario questions in this paper. However, do not be tempted to write down everything you know about a particular topic – stick to the time allocation and answer the question set.

Exam information

Important information regarding the F8 examiner

From the **June 2010** exam sitting onwards, the F8 examiner will be **Pami Bahl**. The current syllabus exams in this kit have been written by Alan Lewin, but you should be aware of the change in examiner and look out for any articles that may be written by Pami Bahl in *Student Accountant*.

The exam paper

The F8 exam is a three-hour paper with 15 minutes of reading time and consists of five compulsory questions.

Question 1 will comprise a 30 mark case study style question, split into several parts, perhaps including *one* knowledge-based part. Question 2 will be a 10 mark knowledge-based question from across the syllabus. The remaining three questions will be worth 20 marks each and scenario-based.

The pass mark is 50%.

December 2009

1	Audit planning; audit procedures; risk assessment; auditing inventory
2	Audit evidence (reliability); communication with those charged with governance
3	Understanding the entity and its environment; non-current assets (control environment and completeness)
4	Interim and final audit; reliance on internal audit work; other assurance engagements
5	Assertions relevant to accounts payable; internal controls (purchases); contingent liabilities and reporting

The December 2009 exam is Mock Exam 3 in this Kit.

June 2009

		Question in this kit
1	Audit planning; audit risk; analytical procedures; audit procedures (receivables)	30
2	Audit sampling; audit evidence (assertions); audit report term	44
3	CAATs; evaluating internal audit work	26
4	Internal audit; corporate governance	8
5	Inventory; fraud; professional ethics	74

Examiner's comments. Many candidates presented a high standard of answer for all five questions. Question 1 (a) and (c) appeared to be the most challenging as the subject matter appeared to be less well understood.

The inadequate performance of many candidates was once again exacerbated by a clear failure to carefully read the requirements of questions and note the time allocation indicated by the marks to be awarded. Of significant concern was the lack of clear time allocation in question 2. Many candidates answered this question first and wrote a significant amount of detail on each section (in many cases more than question 1). Given that question 2 had only 10 marks available and question 1, 30 marks, there was a clear lack of examination technique in using the time available to maximise mark earning potential.

Many candidates continue to display their answers inadequately, with a lack of clear labelling to indicate which questions are being attempted. Each question should be started on a new page and candidates must give more thought to the layout and organisation of their answers. Many scripts were also presented quite inadequately, with lengthy paragraphs of writing "hiding" many individual relevant points.

December 2008

		Question in this kit
1	Wages system; analytical procedures; audit evidence	40
2	Expert; rights of auditors; assertions relating to tangible non-current assets	42
3	Professional ethics; internal audit	12
4	Audit risk; inherent risk; control environment	23
5	Events after the reporting period	77

Examiner's comments. Many candidates presented a high standard of answer for all five questions. Question 4 appeared to be the most challenging as this was based on a charity. However, not for profit entities are within the syllabus and candidates who applied their auditing knowledge to this question did obtain a pass standard.

The inadequate performance of many candidates was once again exacerbated by a clear failure to carefully read the content and requirements of questions. Of significant concern was the lack of understanding of the meaning of requirement verbs such as "list" particularly in relation to question 2. Rather than "list", many candidates provided a detailed discussion in their answers.

As in previous diets, many candidates continue to display their answers inadequately, with a lack of clear labelling to indicate which questions are being attempted.

June 2008

		Question in this kit
1	Internal control questionnaires; tests of controls on sales system; receivables' confirmation	69
2	Audit evidence; representations; tests of controls	71
3	Analytical procedures; bank confirmation letter	62
4	Internal audit and outsourcing	16
5	Going concern; negative assurance	79

Examiner's comments. Performance on this paper highlighted the following key issues:

- Failure to read the content and requirement of questions
- Poor presentation of answers
- Lack of technical knowledge
- Lack of breadth of answers
- Lack of sufficient explanation where required
- Repetition of points already made

December 2007

		Question in this kit
1	Purchases system; inventory system and count	70
2	ACCA's *Code of Ethics and Conduct*; going concern	72
3	Internal audit; petty cash	38
4	CAATs; auditing around the computer	37
5	Non-compliance with accounting standards; audit reports	85

Examiner's comments. Performance on this paper highlighted the following key issues:

- Failure to read the content and requirement of questions
- Poor presentation of answers
- Lack of technical knowledge
- Lack of breadth of answers
- Lack of sufficient explanation where required
- Repetition of points already made

Pilot paper

		Question in this kit
1	Substantive procedures on trade payables and purchases; use of CAATs	67
2	Engagement letter, audit evidence; audit reports	80
3	Threats to independance; corporate governance and audit committees	11
4	Weaknesses in wages system; fraud; use of an external consultant	35
5	Events after the year-end and impact on audit report	75

Analysis of past papers – F8 Audit and Assurance

The table below provides details of when each element of the syllabus has been examined and the question number and section in which each element appeared.

Covered in Text chapter		Dec 2009	June 2009	Dec 2008	June 2008	Dec 2007	Pilot Paper
	AUDIT FRAMEWORK AND REGULATION						
1	Audit and other assurance engagements	4d			5d		
2	Statutory audit and regulation			2b			
3	Corporate governance	2b	4b				3b, c
4	Professional ethics		5b	3a		2a	2a, 3a
	INTERNAL AUDIT						
5	Internal audit		4a	3b	4	3a	4b, c
	PLANNING AND RISK ASSESSMENT						
6	Risk assessment	3a	3, 5b	4		4c	
7	Audit planning and documentation	1a, 4a	1a				
8	Introduction to audit evidence	1b, c, 2a	2b	1d	2a, c		
	INTERNAL CONTROL						
9	Internal control	3b			1a	1c, d	1c, 4a
10	Tests of controls	3b, 5b	1b	1a, b	1b	1c	1c, 4a
	AUDIT EVIDENCE						
11	Audit procedures and sampling	4b, c	1c, 2a, 3	1c, 2a	3a, b	1d, 4	1d, 2b
12	Non-current assets	3c		2c			
13	Inventory	1d, e				1b	
14	Receivables		1d		1c, d	4a	
15	Cash and bank				3c	3b	
16	Liabilities and capital	5a, c				1a	1a, b
17	Not-for-profit organisations			4b, c			
	REVIEW						
18	Audit review and finalisation	5c	5a	5	2b, 5	2b, 5a	5
	REPORTING						
19	Reports	5d	2c			5	2c, 5

Study guide for exams in 2010

The F8 study text for exams in 2010 contains the study guide relating to the December 2009 exam because the study guide for the 2010 exams was unavailable at the date the study text was published. The 2010 study guide is now available and is included below.

A AUDIT FRAMEWORK AND REGULATION

1. The concept of audit and other assurance engagements

(a) Identify and describe the objective and general principles of external audit engagements.[2]
(b) Explain the nature and development of audit and other assurance engagements.[1]
(c) Discuss the concepts of accountability, stewardship and agency.[2]
(d) Discuss the concepts of materiality, true and fair presentation and reasonable assurance.[2]
(e) Explain reporting as a means of communication to different stakeholders.[1]
(f) Explain the level of assurance provided by audit and other review assignments.[1]

2. Statutory audits

(a) Describe the regulatory environment within which statutory audits take place.[1]

(b) Discuss the reasons and mechanisms for the regulation of auditors.[2]

(c) Explain the statutory regulations governing the appointment, rights, removal and resignation of auditors.[1]

(d) Discuss the types of opinion provided in statutory audits.[2]

(e) State the objectives and principle activities of statutory audit and assess its value (e.g. in assisting management to reduce risk and improve performance).[1]

(f) Describe the limitations of statutory audits.[1]

3. The regulatory environment and corporate governance

(a) Explain the development and status of International Standards on Auditing.[1]

(b) Explain the relationship between International Standards on Auditing and national standards.[1]

(c) Discuss the objective, relevance and importance of corporate governance.[2]

(d) Discuss the need for auditors to communicate with those charged with governance.[2]

(e) Discuss the provisions of international codes of corporate governance (such as OECD) that are most relevant to auditors.[2]

(f) Describe good corporate governance requirements relating to directors' responsibilities (e.g. for risk management and internal control) and the reporting responsibilities of auditors.[1]

(g) Analyse the structure and roles of audit committees and discuss their benefits and limitations.[2]

(h) Explain the importance of internal control and risk management.[1]

(i) Compare the responsibilities of management and auditors for the design and operation of systems and controls.[2]

4. Professional ethics and ACCA's Code of Ethics and Conduct

(a) Define and apply the fundamental principles of professional ethics of integrity, objectivity, professional competence and due care, confidentiality and professional behaviour.[2]

(b) Define and apply the conceptual framework.[2]

(c) Discuss the sources of, and enforcement mechanisms associated with, ACCA's Code of Ethics and Conduct.[2]

(d) Discuss the preconditions, requirements of professional ethics and other requirements in relation to the acceptance of new audit engagements.[2]

(e) Discuss the process by which an auditor obtains an audit engagement.[2]

(f) Explain the importance of engagement letters and state their contents.[1]

B INTERNAL AUDIT

1. Internal audit and corporate governance

(a) Discuss the factors to be taken into account when assessing the need for internal audit.[2]

(b) Discuss the elements of best practice in the structure and operations of internal audit with reference to appropriate international codes of corporate governance.[2]

2. Differences between the external auditor and the internal audit function

(a) Compare and contrast the role of external and internal audit regarding audit planning and the collection of audit evidence.[2]

(b) Compare and contrast the types of report provided by internal and external audit.[2]

3. The scope of the internal audit function

(a) Discuss the scope of internal audit and the limitations of the internal audit function.[2]

(b) Explain the types of audit report provided in internal audit assignments.[1]

(c) Discuss the responsibilities of internal and external auditors for the prevention and detection of fraud and error.[2]

4. Outsourcing the internal audit function

(a) Explain the advantages and disadvantages of outsourcing internal audit.[1]

5. Internal audit assignments

(a) Discuss the nature and purpose of internal audit assignments including value for money, IT, best value and financial.[2]

(b) Discuss the nature and purpose of operational internal audit assignments including procurement, marketing, treasury and human resources management.[2]

C PLANNING AND RISK ASSESSMENT

1. Objective and general principles

(a) Identify and describe the need to plan and perform audits with an attitude of professional scepticism.[2]

(b) Identify and describe engagement risks affecting the audit of an entity.[1]

(c) Explain the components of audit risk.[1]

(d) Compare and contrast risk based, procedural and other approaches to audit work.[2]

(e) Discuss the importance of risk analysis.[2]

(f) Describe the use of information technology in risk analysis.[1]

2. Understanding the entity and its environment

(a) Explain how auditors obtain an initial understanding of the entity and its environment.[2]

3. **Assessing the risks of material misstatement and fraud**

(a) Define and explain the concepts of materiality and performance materiality.[2]
(b) Compute indicative materiality levels from financial information.[2]
(c) Discuss the effect of fraud and misstatements on the audit strategy and extent of audit work.[2]

4. **Analytical procedures**

(a) Describe and explain the nature and purpose of analytical procedures in planning.[2]
(b) Compute and interpret key ratios used in analytical procedures.[2]

5. **Planning an audit**

(a) Identify and explain the need for planning an audit.[2]
(b) Identify and describe the contents of the overall audit strategy and audit plan.[2]
(c) Explain and describe the relationship between the overall audit strategy and the audit plan.[2]
(d) Develop and document an audit plan.[2]
(e) Explain the difference between interim and final audit.[1]

6. **Audit documentation**

(a) Explain the need for and the importance of audit documentation. [1]
(b) Describe and prepare working papers and supporting documentation.[2]
(c) Explain the procedures to ensure safe custody and retention of working papers.[1]

7. **The work of others**

(a) Discuss the extent to which auditors are able to rely on the work of experts.[2]
(b) Discuss the extent to which external auditors are able to rely on the work of internal audit.[2]
(c) Discuss the audit considerations relating to entities using service organisations.[2]
(d) Discuss why auditors rely on the work of others.[2]
(e) Explain the extent to which reference to the work of others can be made in audit reports.[1]

D **INTERNAL CONTROL**

The following transaction cycles and account balances are relevant to this capability:

- Revenue,
- Purchases,
- Inventory,
- Revenue and capital expenditure,
- Payroll,
- Bank and cash.

1. **Internal control systems**

(a) Explain why an auditor needs to obtain an understanding of internal control activities relevant to the audit.[1]

(b) Describe and explain the key components of an internal control system.[1]

(c) Identify and describe the important elements of internal control including the control environment and management control activities. [1]

(d) Discuss the difference between tests of control and substantive procedures. [2]

2. **The use of internal control systems by auditors**

(a) Explain the importance of internal control to auditors.[1]

(b) Explain how auditors identify weaknesses in internal control systems and how those weaknesses limit the extent of auditors' reliance on those systems.[2]

3. **Transaction cycles**

(a) Explain, analyse and provide examples of internal control procedures and control activities.[2]
(b) Provide examples of computer system controls.[2]

4. **Tests of control**

(a) Explain and tabulate tests of control suitable for inclusion in audit working papers.[2]
(b) List examples of application controls and general IT controls.[2]

5. **The evaluation of internal control components**

(a) Analyse the limitations of internal control components in the context of fraud and error.[2]

(b) Explain the need to modify the audit strategy and audit plan following the results of tests of control.[1]

(c) Identify and explain management's risk assessment process with reference to internal control components.[1]

6. **Communication on internal control**

(a) Discuss and provide examples of how the reporting of internal control deficiencies and recommendations to overcome those deficiencies are provided to management.[2]

E AUDIT EVIDENCE

1. **The use of assertions by auditors**

(a) Explain the assertions contained in the financial statements.[2]

(b) Explain the principles and objectives of transaction testing, account balance testing and disclosure testing.[1]

(c) Explain the use of assertions in obtaining audit evidence.[2]

2. **Audit procedures**

(a) Discuss the sources and relative merits of the different types of evidence available.[2]

(b) Discuss and provide examples of how analytical procedures are used as substantive procedures.[2]

(c) Discuss the problems associated with the audit and review of accounting estimates.[2]

(d) Describe why smaller entities may have different control environments and describe the types of evidence likely to be available in smaller entities.[1]

(e) Discuss the quality of evidence obtained.[2]

3. **The audit of specific items**

For each of the account balances stated in this sub-capability:

- Explain the purpose of substantive procedures in relation to financial statement assertions,
- Explain the substantive procedures used in auditing each balance, and
- Tabulate those substantive procedures in a work program.

(a) Receivables: [2]

(i) Direct confirmation of accounts receivable
(ii) Other evidence in relation to receivables and prepayments, and
(iii) The related income statement entries.

(b) Inventory: [2]

  (i) Inventory counting procedures in relation to year-end and continuous inventory systems
  (ii) Cut-off
  (iii) Auditor's attendance at inventory counting
  (iv) Direct confirmation of inventory held by third parties,
  (v) Other evidence in relation to inventory.

(c) Payables and accruals: [2]

  (i) Supplier statement reconciliations and direct confirmation of accounts payable,
  (ii) Obtain evidence in relation to payables and accruals, and
  (iii) The related income statement entries.

(d) Bank and cash: [2]

  (i) Bank confirmation reports used in obtaining evidence in relation to bank and cash
  (ii) Other evidence in relation to bank and cash, and
  (iii) The related income statement entries.

(e) Tangible non-current assets and long-term liabilities: [2]

  (i) Evidence in relation to non-current assets and
  (ii) Non-current liabilities and
  (iii) The related income statement entries.

4. Audit sampling and other means of testing

(a) Define audit sampling and explain the need for sampling.[1]

(b) Identify and discuss the differences between statistical and non-statistical sampling.[2]

(c) Discuss and provide relevant examples of, the application of the basic principles of statistical sampling and other selective testing procedures. [2]

(d) Discuss the results of statistical sampling, including consideration of whether additional testing is required.[2]

5. Computer-assisted audit techniques

(a) Explain the use of computer-assisted audit techniques in the context of an audit.[1]

(b) Discuss and provide relevant examples of the use of test data and audit software for the transaction cycles and balances mentioned in sub-capability 3.[2]

(c) Discuss the use of computers in relation to the administration of the audit.[2]

6. Not-for-profit organisations

(a) Apply audit techniques to small not-for-profit organisations.[2]

(b) Explain how the audit of small not-for-profit organisations differs from the audit of for-profit organisations.[1]

F REVIEW

1. Subsequent events

(a) Explain the purpose of a subsequent events review.[1]
(b) Discuss the procedures to be undertaken in performing a subsequent events review.[2]

2. Going concern

(a) Define and discuss the significance of the concept of going concern.[2]
(b) Explain the importance of and the need for going concern reviews.[2]
(c) Explain the respective responsibilities of auditors and management regarding going concern.[1]
(d) Discuss the procedures to be applied in performing going concern reviews.[2]
(e) Discuss the disclosure requirements in relation to going concern issues.[2]
(f) Discuss the reporting implications of the findings of going concern reviews.[2]

3. Written representations

(a) Explain the purpose of and procedure for obtaining written representations.[2]

(b) Discuss the quality and reliability of written representations as audit evidence.[2]

(c) Discuss the circumstances where written representations are necessary and the matters on which representations are commonly obtained. [2]

4. Audit finalisation and the final review

(a) Discuss the importance of the overall review of evidence obtained.[2]
(b) Explain the significance of unadjusted differences.[1]

G REPORTING

1. Audit reports

(a) Describe and analyse the format and content of unmodified audit reports.[2]
(b) Describe and analyse the format and content of modified audit reports.[2]

2. Reports to management

(a) Identify and analyse internal control and system deficiencies and their potential effects and make appropriate recommendations to management.[2]

3. Internal audit reports

(a) Describe and explain the format and content of internal audit review reports and other reports dealing with the enhancement of performance.[1]

(b) Explain the process for producing an internal audit report.[1]

Notes:

The specific capabilities within the detailed syllabuses and study guides are assessed at one of three intellectual or cognitive levels:

Level 1: Knowledge and comprehension
Level 2: Application and analysis
Level 3: Synthesis and evaluation

Very broadly, these intellectual levels relate to the three cognitive levels at which the Knowledge module, the Skills module and the Professional level are assessed.

Each subject area in the detailed study guide above is given a 1, 2, or 3 superscript, denoting intellectual level, marked at the end of each relevant line. This gives an indication of the intellectual depth at which an area could be assessed within the examination.

Useful websites

The websites below provide additional sources of information of relevance to your studies for *Audit and Assurance*.

- www.accaglobal.com

  ACCA's website. The students' section of the website is invaluable for detailed information about the qualification, past issues of *Student Accountant* (including technical articles) and even interviews with the examiners.

- www.bpp.com

  Our website provides information about BPP products and services, with a link to the ACCA website.

- www.ifac.org

  This website provides information on international accounting and auditing issues.

- www.ft.com

  This website provides information about current international business. You can search for information and articles on specific industry groups as well as individual companies.

Planning your question practice

We have already stressed that question practice should be right at the centre of your revision. Whilst you will spend some time looking at your notes and Paper F8 Passcards, you should spend the majority of your revision time practising questions.

We recommend two ways in which you can practise questions.

- Use **BPP Learning Media's question plan** to work systematically through the syllabus and attempt key and other questions on a section-by-section basis
- **Build your own exams** – attempt questions as a series of practice exams

These ways are suggestions and simply following them is no guarantee of success. You or your college may prefer an alternative but equally valid approach.

BPP Learning Media's question plan

The BPP Learning Media plan below requires you to devote a **minimum of 40 hours** to revision of Paper F8. Any time you can spend over and above this should only increase your chances of success.

Step 1 **Review your notes** and the chapter summaries in the Paper F8 **Passcards** for each section of the syllabus.

Step 2 **Answer the key questions** for that section. These questions have boxes round the question number in the table below and you should answer them in full. Even if you are short of time you must attempt these questions if you want to pass the exam. You should complete your answers without referring to our solutions.

Step 3 **Attempt the other questions** in that section. For some questions we have suggested that you prepare **answer plans** rather than full solutions. Planning an answer means that you should spend about 40% of the time allowance for the questions brainstorming the question and drawing up a list of points to be included in the answer.

Step 4 Attempt **Mock exams 1, 2 and 3** under strict exam conditions.

Syllabus section	Passcards chapters	Questions in this Kit	Comments	Done ☑
Revision period 1				
Audit framework and regulation				
Statutory audit	1/2	4	Answer in full. The regulatory context of auditing is extremely important and could be examined in a compulsory question. It is key that you can explain the basic purpose of an audit as it is the basis of the rest of the syllabus. This question also looks at the distinction between the interim and final audits.	☐
Other Assurance engagements	1	79	Do part (d)	☐
Regulatory environment	2	5	Answer in full. This question is a good one to practise to confirm your understanding of the regulatory environment that governs external audits. This topic could potentially come up in Question 2 of the paper.	☐
Corporate governance	3	6	Answer in full. This is an excellent scenario-based question on corporate governance and the requirements of international codes. It tests both your knowledge of international codes and your ability to apply that knowledge to a given scenario.	☐
Internal audit	3/5	7	Do part (a).	☐
Revision period 2				
Professional ethics				
Confidentiality	4	10	Answer in full. It is important to remember that whilst independence is a key ethical issue it is not the only one. This tests your basic knowledge of when the auditor can/cannot reveal information to third parties. Part (b) focuses on independence issues.	☐
Corporate governance and independence	3/4	11	Answer in full. This pilot paper question demonstrates the links between corporate governance and independence. You need to show how the audit committee can strengthen the external auditors' position.	☐
Ethical threats and safeguards	4	12	Do part (a).	☐
Revision period 3				
Internal audit				
Internal audit objectives	5	13	Answer parts (a) and (c).	☐
Internal audit and corporate governance	3/5	8	Answer in full. This question tests your knowledge of how the role of internal and external auditors differs and requires you to apply your knowledge of the benefits of audit committees to a company described in a scenario.	☐

Syllabus section	Passcards chapters	Questions in this Kit	Comments	Done ☑
Internal audit assignments	5	15	Answer in full. This is a good question because it looks at the sort of work internal auditors would carry out within an organisation. It is scenario-based so you must be able to apply your knowledge to the circumstances in the question.	☐
Internal audit	5	16	Do part (b).	☐
Planning and risk assessment				
Business risk	6/7	18	Answer in full. Run through this past exam question from the old syllabus to ensure that you can differentiate between audit risk and business risk. Although many of the issues will be common to both, business risk tends to involve a broader range of topics.	☐
Revision period 4				
Audit risk and planning	6/7	20	Answer in full. Risk is a key topic in this syllabus and may be examined from the auditor's perspective or from the point of view of the business. Being able to identify risks will only come with practice, so this is a question on which to practise this important skill. Notice that in this case your identification of risk is based on an analysis of financial information. This makes it a demanding question but it is something which you need to be prepared to deal with.	☐
Audit risk	6/7	22	Do parts (a) and (b)(i).	☐
Planning, CAATS	6/7/11	26	Answer in full. The scenario in this question describes an auditor at the planning stage and includes a part which asks you to identify problems based on information given about the entity and its environment. It then requires you to suggest how these problems may be overcome, which you would need to do in practice as part of the planning process. It also tests application and knowledge of the benefits of using CAATs and includes a question which requires you to explain how you would evaluate a specific piece of internal audit work.	☐
Planning and risk assessment	7	30	Do parts (a) and (b). Part (a) involves listing and explaining the purpose of the main sections of an audit strategy document and providing relevant examples for the company described in the scenario. Part (b) includes looking at risk assessment relating to the area of cash and sales receipts.	☐
Documentation	7/8	19	Answer in full. This question is a comprehensive test of your knowledge of what good working papers should contain. It also asks you to consider how client documentation can provide audit information.	☐

Syllabus section	Passcards chapters	Questions in this Kit	Comments	Done ☑
Revision period 5				
Audit evidence				
Sufficiency of audit evidence	8	71	Do part (a).	☐
Evidence, sampling and documentation	8/11	24	Answer in full. This is an excellent revision question as it covers a number of different methods of obtaining evidence. It demonstrates the importance of being able to explain key audit principles and techniques.	☐
Sampling and assertions	8/11	44	Do parts (a) and (b).	☐
CAATs	8/11	25	Answer in full. This is a challenging question on CAATs. Part (a) is straightforward but parts (b) and (c) are more complex as they relate to the use of test data and audit software in a particular scenario.	☐
Using the work of others	8/11	41	Plan an answer to this question.	☐
Sampling	11	68	Answer in full. This is a good question to test your knowledge of sampling. It includes both knowledge-based and scenario-based requirements.	☐
Sampling	11	28	Attempt part (b).	☐
Revision period 6				
Internal control				
Internal control	9	39	Answer in full. Internal controls is a key topic area and is very likely to come up. You need to be aware of the problems which result from poor controls and you need to be able to make recommendations that are useful and relevant to the organisation in question.	☐
Purchases system	10	34	Answer in full. Although this question covers purchases it also looks at controls over capital expenditure. Controls questions covering more than one business cycle are possible.	☐
Sales system	10	32	Answer in full. This question considers controls in specific aspects of the sales cycle. It also deals with procedures which auditors should perform if they wish to rely on internal controls. This makes it a very good all-round revision question.	☐
Sales system	10	69	Do part (b).	☐
Wages system	10/19	40	Do part (b).	☐
Wages system	6/10/11	35	Answer in full. This wideranging pilot paper question requires you to apply your knowledge of wages systems to a company with a number of deficiencies in its system. The question also covers detection of fraud and use of external consultants.	☐

Syllabus section	Passcards chapters	Questions in this Kit	Comments	Done ☑
Revision period 7				
Audit of inventories				
Valuation and existence	13	66	Answer in full. This question looks at the issues of inventory counts and valuation and using an external valuer.	☐
Perpetual inventory, ethical concepts, engagement letters	4/13	49	Answer in full. This question tests your understanding of perpetual inventory systems, which many businesses use. It is also a quick test of your knowledge of key ethical concepts, and your ability to provide a solution to a tricky problem – directors not signing an engagement letter.	☐
Inventory, ethical concepts and fraud	4/6/13/18/19	74	Answer in full. This question tests a range of topics related to an inventory valuation issue arising towards the end of an audit. You will need to draw on the appropriate knowledge for each requirement and keep your answer relevant to the scenario.	☐
Revision period 8				
Audit of other assets				
External confirmations	14/15	45	Answer in full. This question is a good one as it tests both your knowledge of external confirmations and your ability to answer the 10 mark question in the time available.	☐
Audit of income and receivables balances	11/14	30	Do parts (c) and (d). Part (c) involves listing analytical procedures to give assurance on total income for the company described in the scenario. Part (d) is concerned with the audit of credit card receivables balances.	☐
Bad and doubtful receivable balances	12	50	Plan an answer to this question.	☐
Bank	15	51	Answer in full. This question covers a bank reconciliation and controls over cash and bank, so is a good one to practise.	☐
Bank confirmations	15	62	Do part (c).	☐
Audit of non-current assets				
Assertions and audit work	12	42	Do part (c).	☐
Audit work	12/14	48	Plan an answer to this question.	☐
Audit risk	12	47	Answer in full. This is a good question to test the application of your knowledge of auditing non-current assets to a specific company in a scenario. It includes identifying and explaining issues with a non-current asset note before explaining how these issues could be resolved.	☐

Syllabus section	Passcards chapters	Questions in this Kit	Comments	Done ☑
Revision period 9				
Audit of payables				
Liabilities	16	53	Answer in full. This is a good all-round question on liabilities audit and tests your application skills.	☐
Payables, CAATs	10/11/16	67	Answer in full. This pilot paper question gives a lot of information about a payables system, so is a good test of your ability to analyse that information and use your analysis to suggest audit tests. It also covers computerised data and CAATs.	☐
Payroll	16	55	Answer in full. This question considers the audit of payroll balances	☐
Provisions/ subsequent events	16/18	56	Answer in full. This question tests your knowledge of IAS 37 and your ability to apply it to a particular situation during an audit.	☐
Revision period 10				
Review				
Subsequent events	18/19	75	Answer in full. This pilot paper question tests your ability to distinguish different kinds of subsequent events, decide what the auditor should do and assess the impact on the accounts and report.	☐
Subsequent events	18	77	Do part (a).	☐
Going concern	4/18	78	Answer in full. Going concern can be examined in a number of different contexts eg in a planning question. Here it is combined with audit ethics. As well as considering the audit procedures, you also need to consider issues affecting the preparation of financial statements on a going concern basis.	☐
Written representations	18	57	Plan an answer to this question.	☐
Representation letter	18	71	Do part (b).	☐
Going concern and audit reports	18/19	82	Answer in full. Going concern is often combined with audit reports as it is here. You need to be able to identify going concern risk factors and describe the potential impact on the audit report.	☐

Syllabus section	Passcards chapters	Questions in this Kit	Comments	Done ☑
Revision period 11 *Reporting*				
Engagement letters, audit evidence and audit reports	4/8/19	80	Answer in full. This pilot paper question is a quick test of knowledge of a number of important areas, and is a good question to do in the last few days before your exam.	☐
Audit reports	19	84	Answer in full. This question provides a hopefully easy test of your knowledge of audit reports; however the majority of marks are available for discussing what the auditors need to do about controversial issues in a set of financial statements.	☐
Audit reports	19	44	Do part (c) relating to term 'modified' in the context of audit reports.	☐
Audit reports	19	83	Do part (b).	☐
Audit and other reports	19	85	Answer in full. This past exam question looks at audit reports in the context of outstanding audit issues.	☐

Build your own exams

Having revised your notes and the BPP Passcards, you can attempt the questions in the Kit as a series of practice exams. You can organise the questions in the following ways.

- Either you can attempt complete past exam papers; recent papers are listed below:

	Pilot paper Question in kit	*December 07 Question in Kit*	*June 08 Question in kit*	*December 08 Question in Kit*	*June 09 Question in Kit*
1	67	70	69	40	30
2	80	72	71	42	44
3	11	38	62	12	26
4	35	37	16	23	8
5	75	85	79	77	74

- Or you can make up practice exams, either yourself or using the suggestions we have listed below.

	Practice exams						
	1	2	3	4	5	6	7
1	39	67	69	70	66	64	68
2	41	43	46	17	71	72	80
3	61	60	62	58	59	16	11
4	37	38	35	31	7	25	27
5	78	84	83	73	75	79	85

- Whichever practice exams you use, you must attempt **Mock exams 1, 2 and 3** at the end of your revision.

Questions

ACCA's examiner's answers

The ACCA examiner's answers to questions marked '**Pilot paper**', '**12/07**', '**6/08**' or '**12/08**' can be found on the BPP website at the following link:

www.bpp.com/acca/examiner-solutions

Additional question guidance

Remember that you can find additional guidance to certain questions at the following link:

www.bpp.com/acca/extra-question-guidance

AUDIT FRAMEWORK AND REGULATION

Questions 1 – 12 cover Audit framework and regulation, the subject of Part A of the BPP Study Text for F8.

1 Audit regulation **18 mins**

(a) Explain how ISAs are developed by the International Auditing and Assurance Standards Board (IAASB). **(5 marks)**

(b) Explain the role of the professional bodies in the regulation of auditors. **(5 marks)**

(Total = 10 marks)

2 Corporate governance **18 mins**

(a) The UK's Combined Code on Corporate Governance is an established code of best practice and is mandatory only for UK listed companies.

Required

List the advantages and disadvantages of voluntary codes of corporate governance. **(3 marks)**

(b) List four requirements for the board of directors as recommended by the UK's Combined Code. **(4 marks)**

(c) Briefly explain the function of an audit committee. **(3 marks)**

(Total = 10 marks)

3 Ethical issues **18 mins**

(a) List and briefly explain the main threats to independence and objectivity as identified in the ACCA's *Code of ethics and conduct.* **(5 marks)**

(b) Briefly explain the fundamental principle of confidentiality and list the circumstances in which obligatory and voluntary disclosure of information may be applicable. **(5 marks)**

(Total = 10 marks)

4 External audit (AIR 12/04) **36 mins**

The purpose of an external audit and its role are not well understood. You have been asked to write some material for inclusion in your firm's training materials dealing with these issues in the audit of large companies.

Required

(a) Draft an explanation dealing with the purpose of an external audit and its role in the audit of large companies, for inclusion in your firm's training materials. **(10 marks)**

(b) The external audit process for the audit of large entities generally involves two or more recognisable stages. One stage involves understanding the business and risk assessment, determining the response to assessed risk, testing of controls and a limited amount of substantive procedures. This stage is sometimes known as the interim audit. Another stage involves further tests of controls and substantive procedures and audit finalisation procedures. This stage is sometimes known as the final audit.

Describe and explain the main audit procedures and processes that take place during the interim and final audit of a large entity. **(10 marks)**

(Total = 20 marks)

5 International Standards on Auditing (AIR 6/06) **36 mins**

International Standards on Auditing (ISAs) are produced by the International Auditing and Assurance Standards Board (IAASB), which is a technical committee of the International Federation of Accountants (IFAC). In recent years, there has been a trend for more countries to implement the ISAs rather than produce their own auditing standards.

A school friend who you have not seen for a number of years is considering joining ACCA as a trainee accountant. However, she is concerned about the extent of regulations which auditors have to follow and does not understand why ISAs have to be used in your country.

Required

Write a letter to your friend explaining the regulatory framework which applies to auditors.

Your letter should cover the following points:

(a) The due process of the IAASB involved in producing an ISA. **(4 marks)**
(b) The overall authority of ISAs and how they are applied in individual countries. **(8 marks)**
(c) The extent to which an auditor must follow ISAs. **(4 marks)**
(d) The extent to which ISAs apply to small entities. **(4 marks)**

(Total = 20 marks)

6 Jumper (AIR 6/06) **36 mins**

You are the audit manager of Tela & Co, a medium sized firm of accountants. Your firm has just been asked for assistance from Jumper & Co, a firm of accountants in an adjacent country. This country has just implemented the internationally recognised codes on corporate governance and Jumper & Co has a number of clients where the codes are not being followed. One example of this, from SGCC, a listed company, is shown below. As your country already has appropriate corporate governance codes in place, Jumper & Co have asked for your advice regarding the changes necessary in SGCC to achieve appropriate compliance with corporate governance codes.

Extract from financial statements regarding corporate governance

Mr Sheppard is the Chief Executive Officer and board chairman of SGCC. He appoints and maintains a board of five executive and two non-executive directors. While the board sets performance targets for the senior managers in the company, no formal targets or review of board policies is carried out. Board salaries are therefore set and paid by Mr Sheppard based on his assessment of all the board members, including himself, and not their actual performance.

Internal controls in the company are monitored by the senior accountant, although detailed review is assumed to be carried out by the external auditors; SGCC does not have an internal audit department.

Annual financial statements are produced, providing detailed information on past performance.

Required

Write a memo to Jumper & Co which:

(a) Explains why SGCC does not meet international codes of corporate governance
(b) Explains why not meeting the international codes may cause a problem for SGCC, and
(c) Recommends any changes necessary to implement those codes in the company.

(20 marks)

7 ZX (AIR 6/05) **36 mins**

You are a recently qualified Chartered Certified Accountant in charge of the internal audit department of ZX, a rapidly expanding company. Turnover has increased by about 20% pa for the last five years, to the current level of $50 million. Net profits are also high, with an acceptable return being provided for the four shareholders.

The internal audit department was established last year to assist the board of directors in their control of the company and to prepare for a possible listing on the stock exchange. The Managing Director is keen to follow the principles of good corporate governance with respect to internal audit. However, he is also aware that the other board members do not have complete knowledge of corporate governance or detailed knowledge of International Auditing Standards.

Required

Write a memo to the board of ZX that:

(a) Explains how the internal audit department can assist the board of directors in fulfilling their obligations under the principles of good corporate governance. **(10 marks)**

(b) Explains the advantages and disadvantages to ZX of an audit committee. **(10 marks)**

(Total = 20 marks)

8 Conoy (6/09) 36 mins

(a) Contrast the role of internal and external auditors. **(8 marks)**

(b) Conoy Co designs and manufactures luxury motor vehicles. The company employs 2,500 staff and consistently makes a net profit of between 10% and 15% of sales. Conoy Co is not listed; its shares are held by 15 individuals, most of them from the same family. The maximum shareholding is 15% of the share capital.

The executive directors are drawn mainly from the shareholders. There are no non-executive directors because the company legislation in Conoy Co's jurisdiction does not require any. The executive directors are very successful in running Conoy Co, partly from their training in production and management techniques, and partly from their 'hands-on' approach providing motivation to employees.

The board are considering a significant expansion of the company. However, the company's bankers are concerned with the standard of financial reporting as the financial director (FD) has recently left Conoy Co. The board are delaying provision of additional financial information until a new FD is appointed.

Conoy Co does have an internal audit department, although the chief internal auditor frequently comments that the board of Conoy Co do not understand his reports or provide sufficient support for his department or the internal control systems within Conoy Co. The board of Conoy Co concur with this view. Anders & Co, the external auditors have also expressed concern in this area and the fact that the internal audit department focuses work on control systems, not financial reporting. Anders & Co are appointed by and report to the board of Conoy Co.

The board of Conoy Co are considering a proposal from the chief internal auditor to establish an audit committee. The committee would consist of one executive director, the chief internal auditor as well as three new appointees. One appointee would have a non-executive seat on the board of directors.

Required

Discuss the benefits to Conoy Co of forming an audit committee. **(12 marks)**

(Total = 20 marks)

9 Ethical dilemma (AIR 6/02) 36 mins

(a) You are a Chartered Certified Accountant and the newly appointed internal auditor of a company that is experiencing financial difficulties. As a condition for obtaining bank loans, the company has agreed to maintain specified liquidity ratios, asset to liability ratios, and gross profit margins. The draft financial statements for the period-end appear to show that the company has not succeeded in complying with some of these requirements. The profit figures are significantly affected by the calculation of bad debt and depreciation charges. There has been a suggestion to the effect that these could be changed, in order to meet the bank's conditions. There is a real danger that if the bank withdraws its funding, the company will become insolvent and will have to cease trading. The chief financial accountant has asked you to sign certain internal records that have been altered in order to show that the bank's conditions have been met.

Required

Explain the courses of action open to you in these circumstances. **(10 marks)**

(b) You are the external auditor of the company in financial difficulties described in (a) above. You have noted that the calculations of the bad debt allowance and depreciation provisions have been altered in the current year and that as a result, the bank's requirements have been met. You also note that certain accounting policy changes have been made in relation to accounting for leases and that as a result, the profit targets expected by certain investment analysts have now been met. If the changes had not been made, the targets would not have been met. You have asked to speak to the internal auditor but you have been told that he is on long-term sick leave. The chief financial accountant is away on holiday and will not be back until shortly before the audit is due to be completed.

Required

In relation to the facts above, explain the:

(i) Implications for the audit of the financial statements;
(ii) Potential effect, if any, on the auditor's report on the financial statements;
(iii) Implications for the continuing relationship between the audit firm and the client. **(10 marks)**

(Total = 20 marks)

10 Confidentiality and independence (AIR 6/06) 36 mins

(a) Explain the situations where an auditor may disclose confidential information about a client. **(8 marks)**

(b) You are an audit manager in McKay & Co, a firm of Chartered Certified Accountants. You are preparing the engagement letter for the audit of Ancients, a public limited liability company, for the year ending 30 June 20X6.

Ancients has grown rapidly over the past few years, and is now one of your firm's most important clients. Ancients has been an audit client for eight years and McKay & Co has provided audit, taxation and management consultancy advice during this time. The client has been satisfied with the services provided, although the taxation fee for the period to 31 December 20X5 remains unpaid.

Audit personnel available for this year's audit are most of the staff from last year, including Mr Grace, an audit partner and Mr Jones, an audit senior. Mr Grace has been the audit partner since Ancients became an audit client. You are aware that Allyson Grace, the daughter of Mr Grace, has recently been appointed the financial director at Ancients.

To celebrate her new appointment, Allyson has suggested taking all of the audit staff out to an expensive restaurant prior to the start of the audit work for this year.

Required

Identify and explain the risks to independence arising in carrying out your audit of Ancients for the year ending 30 June 20X6, and suggest ways of mitigating each of the risks you identify. **(12 marks)**

(Total = 20 marks)

11 NorthCee (Pilot Paper) 36 mins

You are the audit manager in the audit firm of Dark & Co. One of your audit clients is NorthCee Co, a company specialising in the manufacture and supply of sporting equipment. NorthCee have been an audit client for five years and you have been audit manager for the past three years while the audit partner has remained unchanged.

You are now planning the audit for the year ending 31 December 20X7. Following an initial meeting with the directors of NorthCee, you have obtained the following information.

(i) NorthCee is attempting to obtain a listing on a recognised stock exchange. The directors have established an audit committee, as required by corporate governance regulations, although no further action has been taken in this respect. Information on the listing is not yet public knowledge.

(ii) You have been asked to continue to prepare the company's financial statements as in previous years.

(iii) As the company's auditors, NorthCee would like you and the audit partner to attend an evening reception in a hotel, where NorthCee will present their listing arrangements to banks and existing major shareholders.

(iv) NorthCee has indicated that the fee for taxation services rendered in the year to 31 December 20X5 will be paid as soon as the taxation authorities have agreed the company's taxation liability. You have been advising NorthCee regarding the legality of certain items as 'allowable' for taxation purposes and the taxation authority is disputing these items.

Finally, you have just acquired about 5% of NorthCee's share capital as an inheritance on the death of a distant relative.

Required

(a) Identify, and explain the relevance of, any factors which may threaten the independence of Dark & Co's audit of NorthCee Co's financial statements for the year ending 31 December 20X7. Briefly explain how each threat should be managed. **(10 marks)**

(b) Explain the actions that the board of directors of NorthCee Co must take in order to meet corporate governance requirements for the listing of NorthCee Co. **(6 marks)**

(c) Explain why your audit firm will need to communicate with NorthCee Co's audit committee for this and future audits. **(4 marks)**

(Total = 20 marks)

12 Stark (12/08) — 36 mins

You are a manager in the audit firm of Ali & Co; and this is your first time you have worked on one of the firm's established clients, Stark Co. The main activity of Stark Co is providing investment advice to individuals regarding saving for retirement, purchase of shares and securities and investing in tax efficient savings schemes. Stark is regulated by the relevant financial services authority.

You have been asked to start the audit planning for Stark Co, by Mr Son, a partner in Ali & Co. Mr Son has been the engagement partner for Stark Co, for the previous nine years and so has excellent knowledge of the client. Mr Sonhas informed you that he would like his daughter Zoe to be part of the audit team this year; Zoe is currently studying for her first set of fundamentals papers for her ACCA qualification. Mr Son also informs you that Mr Far, the audit senior, received investment advice from Stark Co during the year and intends to do the same next year.

In an initial meeting with the finance director of Stark Co, you learn that the audit team will not be entertained on Stark Co's yacht this year as this could appear to be an attempt to influence the opinion of the audit. Instead, he has arranged a balloon flight costing less than one-tenth of the expense of using the yacht and hopes this will be acceptable. The director also states that the fee for taxation services this year should be based on a percentage of tax saved and trusts that your firm will accept a fixed fee for representing Stark Co in a dispute regarding the amount of sales tax payable to the taxation authorities.

Required

(a) (i) Explain the ethical threats which may affect the auditor of Stark Co. **(6 marks)**

(ii) For each ethical threat, discuss how the effect of the threat can be mitigated. **(6 marks)**

(b) Discuss the benefits of Stark Co establishing an internal audit department. **(8 marks)**

(Total = 20 marks)

INTERNAL AUDIT

Questions 13 – 16 cover Internal audit, the subject of Part B of the BPP Study Text for F8.

13 Internal audit function — 18 mins

(a) List the types of activity normally carried out by internal audit departments. **(3 marks)**

(b) Briefly explain the main differences between internal and external auditors in respect of objectives, scope of work and reporting responsibilities. **(3 marks)**

(c) Explain the term 'outsourcing' and list three advantages and three disadvantages of outsourcing an internal audit department. **(4 marks)**

(Total = 10 marks)

14 Internal audit (AIR 6/03) — 36 mins

Your firm is the newly appointed external auditor to a large company that sells, maintains and leases office equipment and furniture to its customers. You have been asked to co-operate with internal audit to keep audit costs down. The company wants you to rely on some of the work already performed by internal audit.

The internal auditors provide the following services to the company:

(i) A cyclical audit of the operation of internal controls in the company's major functions (operations, finance, customer support and information services);

(ii) A review of the structure of internal controls in each major function every four years;

(iii) An annual review of the effectiveness of measures put in place by management to minimise the major risks facing the company.

During the current year, the company has gone through a major internal restructuring in its information services function and the internal auditors have been closely involved in the preparation of plans for restructuring, and in the related post-implementation review.

Required

(a) Explain the extent to which your firm will seek to rely on the work of the internal auditors in each of the areas noted above. **(6 marks)**

(b) Describe the information your firm will seek from the internal auditors in order for you to determine the extent of your reliance. **(6 marks)**

(c) Describe the circumstances in which it would *not* be possible to rely on the work of the internal auditors. **(4 marks)**

(d) Explain why it will be necessary for your firm to perform its own work in certain audit areas in addition to relying on the work performed by internal audit. **(4 marks)**

(Total = 20 marks)

15 Value for money audit (AIR 12/06) (amended) — 36 mins

(a) Explain the purpose of the three 'Es' in relation to a value for money audit. **(4 marks)**

(b) You are an audit manager in the internal audit department of KLE Co. The internal audit department is auditing the company's procurement system in the company. Extracts from your system notes, which are correct and contain no errors, are provided below.

Details on ordering department:

– Six members of staff – one buyer and five purchasing clerks.
– Receives about 75 orders each day, many orders for duplicate items come from different departments in the organisation.
– Initial evaluation of internal controls is high.

Procurement systems

Ordering department

All orders are raised on pre-numbered purchase requisitions and sent to the ordering department.

In the ordering department, each requisition is signed by the chief buyer. A purchasing clerk transfers the order information onto an order form and identifies the appropriate supplier for the goods.

Part one of the two part order form is sent to the supplier and part two to the accounts department. The requisition is thrown away.

Goods inwards department

All goods received are checked for damage. Damaged items are returned to the supplier and a damaged goods note completed.

For undamaged items a two-part pre-numbered Goods Received Note (GRN) is raised.

- Part one is sent to the ordering department with the damaged goods notes.
- Part two is filed in order of the reference number for the goods being ordered (obtained from the supplier's goods despatched documentation), in the goods inwards department.

Ordering department

GRNs are separated from damaged goods notes, which are filed. The GRN is forwarded to the accounts department.

Accounts department

GRNs matched with the order awaiting the receipt of the invoice.

Required

Using the system notes provided

(i) Identify and explain the internal control deficiencies and provide a recommendation to overcome each deficiency. **(10 marks)**

(ii) Identify and explain the additional deficiencies that should be raised by a value for money audit and provide a suitable recommendation to overcome each deficiency. **(6 marks)**

(Total = 20 marks)

16 MonteHodge (6/08) — 36 mins

(a) Discuss the advantages and disadvantages of outsourcing an internal audit department. **(8 marks)**

(b) MonteHodge Co has a sales income of $253 million and employs 1,200 people in 15 different locations. MonteHodge Co provides various financial services from pension and investment advice to individuals, to maintaining cash books and cash forecasting in small to medium-sized companies. The company is owned by six shareholders, who belong to the same family; it is not listed on any stock-exchange and the shareholders have no intention of applying for a listing. However, an annual audit is required by statute and additional regulation of the financial services sector is expected in the near future.

Most employees are provided with on-line, real-time computer systems, which present financial and stock market information to enable the employees to provide up-to-date advice to their clients. Accounting systems record income, which is based on fees generated from investment advice. Expenditure is mainly fixed, being salaries, office rent, lighting and heating, etc. Internal control systems are limited; the directors tending to trust staff and being more concerned with making profits than implementing detailed controls.

Four of the shareholders are board members, with one member being the chairman and chief executive officer. The financial accountant is not qualified, although has many years experience in preparing financial statements.

Required

Discuss the reasons for and against having an internal audit department in MonteHodge Co. **(12 marks)**

(Total = 20 marks)

PLANNING AND RISK ASSESSMENT

Questions 17 – 30 cover Planning and risk assessment, the subject of Part C of the BPP Study Text for F8.

17 Audit risk and planning **18 mins**

(a) Explain the meaning of audit risk in the context of the audit risk model. **(4 marks)**

(b) ISA 315 *Identifying and assessing the risks of material misstatement through understanding the entity and its environment* sets out matters that should be documented during the planning stage of an audit.

Required

List six matters that should be documented during audit planning. **(3 marks)**

(c) ISA 230 *Audit documentation* provides guidance to auditors in respect of audit working papers.

Required

List six factors which affect the form and content of audit working papers. **(3 marks)**

(Total = 10 marks)

18 Twinkletoes (AIR 6/04) **36 mins**

Required

(a) Explain how the classification of risks into categories such as 'high', 'medium' or 'low', helps entities manage their businesses. **(4 marks)**

You are the internal auditor of a large private company, Twinkletoes. Twinkletoes manufactures a high volume of reasonably priced shoes for elderly people. The company has a trade receivables ledger that is material to the financial statements containing four different categories of account. The categories of account, and the risks associated with them, are as follows:

(i) Small retail shoe shops. These accounts represent nearly two thirds of the accounts on the ledger by number, and one third of the receivables by value. Some of these customers pay promptly, others are very slow;

(ii) Large retail shoe shops (including a number of overseas accounts) that sell a wide range of shoes. Some of these accounts are large and overdue;

(iii) Chains of discount shoe shops that buy their inventory centrally. These accounts are mostly well-established 'high street' chains. Again, some of these accounts are large and overdue; and

(iv) Mail order companies who sell the company's shoes. There have been a number of large **new** accounts in this category, although there is no history of bad debts in this category.

Receivables listed under (ii) to (iv) are roughly evenly split by both value and number. All receivables are dealt with by the same managers and staff and the same internal controls are applied to each category of receivables. You do not consider that using the same managers and staff, and the same controls, is necessarily the best method of managing the receivables ledger.

Twinkletoes has suffered an increasing level of bad debts and slow payers in recent years, mostly as a result of small shoe shops becoming insolvent. The company has also lost several overseas accounts because of a requirement for them to pay in advance. Management wishes to expand the overseas market and has decided that overseas customers will in future be allowed credit terms.

Management has asked you to classify the risks associated with the receivables ledger in order to manage trade receivables as a whole more efficiently. You have been asked to classify accounts as high, medium or low risk.

Required

(b) Classify the risks relating to the four categories of trade receivables as *high*, *medium* or *low* and explain your classification. **(8 marks)**

Note. More than one risk classification may be appropriate within each account category.

(c) Describe the internal controls that you would recommend to Twinkletoes to manage the risks associated with the receivables ledger under the headings: *all customers*, *slow paying customers*, *larger accounts*, and *overseas customers*. **(8 marks)**

(Total = 20 marks)

19 Specs4You (AIR 6/07) 36 mins

ISA 230 *Audit documentation* establishes standards and provides guidance regarding documentation in the context of the audit of financial statements.

Required

(a) List the purposes of audit working papers. **(3 marks)**

(b) You have recently been promoted to audit manager in the audit firm of Trums & Co. As part of your new responsibilities, you have been placed in charge of the audit of Specs4You Co, a long established audit client of Trums & Co. Specs4You Co sells spectacles; the company owns 42 stores where customers can have their eyes tested and choose from a range of frames.

Required

List the documentation that should be of assistance to you in familiarising yourself with Specs4You Co. Describe the information you should expect to obtain from each document. **(8 marks)**

(c) The time is now towards the end of the audit, and you are reviewing working papers produced by the audit team. An example of a working paper you have just reviewed is shown below.

Client Name **Specs4You Co** Year end **30 April** Page **xxxxx**

Working paper **Payables transaction testing**

Prepared by Date
Reviewed by **CW** Date **12 June 20X7**

Audit assertion: To make sure that the purchases day book is correct.

Method: Select a sample of 15 purchase orders recorded in the purchase order system. Trace details to the goods received note (GRN), purchase invoice (PI) and the purchase day book (PDB) ensuring that the quantities and prices recorded on the purchase order match those on the GRN, PI and PDB.

Test details: In accordance with audit risk, a sample of purchase orders were selected from a numerically sequenced purchase order system and details traced as stated in the method. Details of items tested can be found on another working paper.

Results: Details of purchase orders were normally correctly recorded through the system. Five purchase orders did not have any associated GRN, PI and were not recorded in the PDB. Further investigation showed that these orders had been cancelled due to a change in spectacle specification. However, this does not appear to be a system weakness as the internal controls do not allow for changes in specification.

Conclusion: Purchase orders are completed recorded in the purchase day book.

Required

Explain why the working paper shown above does not meet the standards normally expected of a working paper.

Note. You are not required to reproduce the working paper. **(9 marks)**

(Total = 20 marks)

20 Tempest (AIR 12/05) 36 mins

(a) International Standard on Auditing 300 *Planning an audit of financial statements*, states that an auditor must plan the audit.

Explain why it is important to plan an audit. **(5 marks)**

(b) You are the audit manager in charge of the audit of Tempest, a limited liability company. The company's year end is 31 December, and Tempest has been a client for seven years. The company purchases and resells fittings for ships including anchors, compasses, rudders, sails etc. Clients vary in size from small businesses making yachts to large companies maintaining large luxury cruise ships. No manufacturing takes place in Tempest.

Information on the company's financial performance is available as follows:

	20X7 Forecast	*20X6 Actual*
	$'000	$'000
Revenue	45,928	40,825
Cost of sales	(37,998)	(31,874)
Gross profit	7,930	8,951
Administration costs	(4,994)	(4,758)
Distribution costs	(2,500)	(2,500)
Net profit	436	1,693
Non-current assets (at net book value)	3,600	4,500
Current assets		
Inventory	200	1,278
Receivables	6,000	4,052
Cash and bank	500	1,590
Total assets	10,300	11,420
Capital and reserves		
Share capital	1,000	1,000
Accumulated profits	5,300	5,764
Total shareholders' funds	6,300	6,764
Non-current liabilities	1,000	2,058
Current liabilities	3,000	2,598
	10,300	11,420

Other information

The industry that Tempest trades in has seen moderate growth of 7% over the last year.

- Non-current assets mainly relate to company premises for storing inventory. Ten delivery vehicles are owned with a net book value of $300,000.
- One of the directors purchased a yacht during the year.
- Inventory is stored in ten different locations across the country, with your firm again having offices close to seven of those locations.
- A computerised inventory control system was introduced in August 20X7. Inventory balances are now obtainable directly from the computer system. The client does not intend to count inventory at the year-end but rely instead on the computerised inventory control system.

Required

Using the information provided above, prepare the audit strategy for Tempest for the year ending 31 December 20X7. **(15 marks)**

(Total = 20 marks)

21 Bridgford Products **36 mins**

Your firm has been the auditor of Bridgford Products, a listed company, for a number of years. The engagement partner has asked you to describe the matters you would consider when planning the audit for the year ended 31 January 20X9.

During a recent visit to the company you obtained the following information.

(a) The management accounts for the 10 months to 30 November 20X8 show a revenue of $130 million and profit before tax of $4 million. Assume sales and profits accrue evenly throughout the year. In the year ended 31 January 20X8 Bridgford Products had sales of $110 million and profit before tax of $8 million.

(b) The company installed a new computerised inventory control system which has operated from 1 June 20X8. As the inventory control system records inventory movements and current inventory quantities, the company is proposing:

   (i) To use the inventory quantities on the computer to value the inventory at the year-end
   (ii) Not to carry out an inventory count at the year-end

(c) You are aware there have been reliability problems with the company's products, which have resulted in legal claims being brought against the company by customers, and customers refusing to pay for the products.

(d) The sales increase in the 10 months to 30 November 20X8 over the previous year has been achieved by attracting new customers and by offering extended credit. The new credit arrangements allow customers three months credit before their debt becomes overdue, rather than the one month credit period allowed previously. As a result of this change, trade receivables age has increased from 1.6 to 4.1 months.

(e) The financial director and purchasing manager were dismissed on 15 August. A replacement purchasing manager has been appointed but it is not expected that a new financial director will be appointed before the year end of 31 January 20X9. The chief accountant will be responsible for preparing the financial statements for audit.

Required

(a) Describe the reasons why it is important that auditors should plan their audit work. **(5 marks)**

(b) Describe the matters you will consider in planning the audit and the further action you will take concerning the information you obtained during your recent visit to the company. **(15 marks)**

(Total = 20 marks)

22 Parker (AIR 6/05) (amended) **36 mins**

(a) Explain the term 'audit risk'. **(4 marks)**

(b) You are the audit manager for Parker, a limited liability company which sells books, CDs, DVDs and similar items via two divisions: mail order and on-line ordering on the Internet. Parker is a new audit client. You are commencing the planning of the audit for the year ended 31 May 20X7. An initial meeting with the directors has provided the information below.

   The company's turnover is in excess of $85 million with net profits of $4 million. All profits are currently earned in the mail order division, although the Internet division is expected to return a small net profit next year. Turnover is growing at the rate of 20% pa Net profit has remained almost the same for the last four years.

   In the next year, the directors plan to expand the range of goods sold through the Internet division to include toys, garden furniture and fashion clothes. The directors believe that when one product has been sold on the Internet, then any other product can be as well.

   The accounting system to record sales by the mail order division is relatively old. It relies on extensive manual input to transfer orders received in the post onto Parker's computer systems. Recently errors have been known to occur, in the input of orders, and in the invoicing of goods following dispatch. The directors maintain that the accounting system produces materially correct figures and they cannot waste time in identifying relatively minor errors. The company accountant, who is not qualified and was appointed because he is a personal friend of the directors, agrees with this view.

The directors estimate that their expansion plans will require a bank loan of approximately $30 million, partly to finance the enhanced web site but also to provide working capital to increase inventory levels. A meeting with the bank has been scheduled for three months after the year end. The directors expect an auditor's report with an unmodified audit opinion to be signed prior to this time.

Required

(i) Identify and describe the matters that give rise to audit risks associated with Parker. **(10 marks)**

(ii) Explain the enquiries you will make, and the audit procedures you will perform to assist you in making a decision regarding the going concern status of Parker in reaching your audit opinion on the financial statements. **(6 marks)**

(Total = 20 marks)

23 EuKaRe (12/08) — 36 mins

(a) Explain the term 'audit risk' and the three elements of risk that contribute to total audit risk. **(4 marks)**

The EuKaRe charity was established in 1960. The charity's aim is to provide support to children from disadvantaged backgrounds who wish to take part in sports such as tennis, badminton and football.

EuKaRe has a detailed constitution which explains how the charity's income can be spent. The constitution also notes that administration expenditure cannot exceed 10% of income in any year.

The charity's income is derived wholly from voluntary donations. Sources of donations include:

(i) Cash collected by volunteers asking the public for donations in shopping areas,

(ii) Cheques sent to the charity's head office,

(iii) Donations from generous individuals. Some of these donations have specific clauses attached to them indicating that the initial amount donated (capital) cannot be spent and that the income (interest) from the donation must be spent on specific activities, for example, provision of sports equipment.

The rules regarding the taxation of charities in the country EuKaRe is based are complicated, with only certain expenditure being allowable for taxation purposes and donations of capital being treated as income in some situations.

Required

(b) Identify areas of inherent risk in the EuKaRe charity and explain the effect of each of these risks on the audit approach. **(12 marks)**

(c) Explain why the control environment may be weak at the charity EuKaRe. **(4 marks)**

(Total = 20 marks)

24 BearsWorld (AIR 6/05) — 36 mins

You are the auditor of BearsWorld, a limited liability company which manufactures and sells small cuddly toys by mail order. The company is managed by Mr Kyto and two assistants. Mr Kyto authorises important transactions such as wages and large orders, one assistant maintains the payables ledger and orders inventory and pays suppliers, and the other assistant receives customer orders and despatches cuddly toys. Due to other business commitments Mr Kyto only visits the office once per week.

At any time, about 100 different types of cuddly toys are available for sale. All sales are made cash with order – there are no receivables. Customers pay using credit cards and occasionally by sending cash. Turnover is over $5.2 million.

You are planning the audit of BearsWorld and are considering using some of the procedures for gathering audit evidence recommended by ISA 500 as follows:

(i) Analytical Procedures
(ii) Inquiry
(iii) Inspection
(iv) Observation
(v) Recalculation

Required

(a) For EACH of the above procedures:

(i) Explain its use in gathering audit evidence. **(5 marks)**
(ii) Describe one example for the audit of BearsWorld. **(5 marks)**

(b) Discuss the suitability of each procedure for BearsWorld, explaining the limitations of each. **(10 marks)**

(Total = 20 marks)

25 Porthos (AIR 12/05) — 36 mins

(a) Computer-Assisted Audit Techniques (CAATs) are used to assist an auditor in the collection of audit evidence from computerised systems.

Required

List and briefly explain four advantages of CAATs. **(4 marks)**

(b) Porthos, a limited liability company, is a reseller of sports equipment, specialising in racquet sports such as tennis, squash and badminton. The company purchases equipment from a variety of different suppliers and then resells this using the Internet as the only selling media. The company has over 150 different types of racquets available in inventory, each identified via a unique product code.

Customers place their orders directly on the Internet site. Most orders are for one or two racquets only. The ordering/sales software automatically verifies the order details, customer address and credit card information prior to orders being verified and goods being despatched. The integrity of the ordering system is checked regularly by ArcherWeb, an independent Internet service company.

You are the audit manager working for the external auditors of Porthos, and you have just started planning the audit of the sales system of the company. You have decided to use test data to check the input of details into the sales system. This will involve entering dummy orders into the Porthos system from an online terminal.

Required

List the test data you will use in your audit of the financial statements of Porthos to confirm the completeness and accuracy of input into the sales system, clearly explaining the reason for each item of data. **(6 marks)**

(c) You are also considering using audit software as part of your substantive testing of the data files in the sales and inventory systems of Porthos Ltd.

(i) List and briefly explain some of the difficulties of using audit software. **(4 marks)**

(ii) List the audit tests that you can program into your audit software for the sales and inventory system in Porthos, explaining the reason for each test. **(6 marks)**

(Total = 20 marks)

26 Tirrol (6/09) **36 mins**

Following a competitive tender, your audit firm Cal & Co has just gained a new audit client Tirrol Co. You are the manager in charge of planning the audit work. Tirrol Co's year end is 30 June 20X9 with a scheduled date to complete the audit of 15 August 20X9. The date now is 3 June 20X9.

Tirrol Co provides repair services to motor vehicles from 25 different locations. All inventory, sales and purchasing systems are computerised, with each location maintaining its own computer system. The software in each location is the same because the programs were written specifically for Tirrol Co by a reputable software house. Data from each location is amalgamated on a monthly basis at Tirrol Co's head office to produce management and financial accounts.

You are currently planning your audit approach for Tirrol Co. One option being considered is to re-write Cal & Co's audit software to interrogate the computerised inventory systems in each location of Tirrol Co (except for head office) as part of inventory valuation testing. However, you have also been informed that any computer testing will have to be on a live basis and you are aware that July is a major holiday period for your audit firm.

Required

(a) (i) Explain the benefits of using audit software in the audit of Tirrol Co; **(4 marks)**

(ii) Explain the problems that may be encountered in the audit of Tirrol Co and for each problem, explain how that problem could be overcome. **(10 marks)**

(b) Following a discussion with the management at Tirrol Co you now understand that the internal audit department are prepared to assist with the statutory audit. Specifically, the chief internal auditor is prepared to provide you with documentation on the computerised inventory systems at Tirrol Co. The documentation provides details of the software and shows diagrammatically how transactions are processed through the inventory system. This documentation can be used to significantly decrease the time needed to understand the computer systems and enable audit software to be written for this year's audit.

Required

Explain how you will evaluate the computer systems documentation produced by the internal audit department in order to place reliance on it during your audit. **(6 marks)**

(Total = 20 marks)

27 Serenity (AIR 12/06) (amended) **36 mins**

(a) ISA 315 *Identifying and assessing the risks of material misstatement through understanding the entity and its environment* requires the auditor to perform risk assessment procedures which include obtaining an understanding of the entity and its environment, including its internal control.

Required

(i) Explain the purpose of risk assessment procedures. **(3 marks)**

(ii) Outline the sources of audit evidence the auditor can use as part of risk assessment procedures. **(3 marks)**

(b) Mal & Co, an audit firm, has seven partners. The firm has a number of audit clients in different industrial sectors, with a wide range of fee income.

An audit partner of Mal & Co has just delegated to you the planning work for the audit of Serenity Co. This company provides a range of mobile communication facilities and this will be the second year your firm has provided audit services.

You have just met with the financial controller of Serenity prior to agreeing the engagement letter for this year. The controller has informed you that Serenity has continued to grow quickly, with financial accounting systems changing rapidly and appropriate control systems being difficult to maintain. Additional services in terms of review and implementation of control systems have been requested. An internal audit department has recently been established and the controller wants you to ensure that external audit work is limited by using this department.

You have also learnt that Serenity is to market a new type of mobile telephone, which is able to intercept messages from law enforcement agencies. The legal status of this telephone is unclear at present and development is not being publicised.

The granting of the licence to market the mobile telephone is dependent on the financial stability of Serenity. The financial controller has indicated that Mal & Co may be asked to provide a report to the mobile telephone licensing authority regarding Serenity's cash flow forecast for the year ending December 20X7 to support the licence application.

Required

As part of your risk assessment procedures for the audit of Serenity Co for the year ending 31 December 20X6, identify and describe the issues to be considered when providing services to this client.

(10 marks)

(c) When reporting on a cash flow forecast, explain the term 'negative assurance' and why this is used.

(4 marks)

(Total = 20 marks)

28 Tam (AIR 12/06) (amended) — 36 mins

(a) (i) In the context of ISA 530 *Audit Sampling*, explain and provide examples of the terms 'sampling risk' and 'non-sampling' risk. **(4 marks)**

(ii) Briefly explain how sampling and non-sampling risk can be controlled by the audit firm. **(2 marks)**

(b) Tam Co, is owned and managed by two brothers with equal shareholdings. The company specialises in the sale of expensive motor vehicles. Annual revenue is in the region of $70,000,000 and the company requires an audit under local legislation. About 500 cars are sold each year, with an average value of $140,000, although the range of values is from $130,000 to $160,000. Invoices are completed manually with one director signing all invoices to confirm the sales value is correct. All accounting and financial statement preparation is carried out by the directors. A recent expansion of the company's showroom was financed by a bank loan, repayable over the next five years.

The audit manager is starting to plan the audit of Tam Co. The audit senior and audit junior assigned to the audit are helping the manager as a training exercise.

Comments are being made about how to select a sample of sales invoices for testing. Audit procedures are needed to ensure that the managing director has signed them and then to trace details into the sales day book and sales ledger.

'We should check all invoices' suggests the audit manager.

'How about selecting a sample using statistical sampling techniques' adds the audit senior.

'Why waste time obtaining a sample?' asks the audit junior. He adds 'taking a random sample of invoices by reviewing the invoice file and manually choosing a few important invoices will be much quicker.'

Required

Briefly explain each of the sample selection methods suggested by the audit manager, audit senior and audit junior, and discuss whether or not they are appropriate for obtaining a representative sample of sales invoices. **(9 marks)**

(c) Define 'materiality' and explain why the auditors of Tam Co must form an opinion on whether the financial statements are free from material misstatement. **(5 marks)**

(Total = 20 marks)

29 Ajio (AIR 12/03) **36 mins**

Ajio is a charity whose constitution requires that it raises funds for educational projects. These projects seek to educate children and support teachers in certain countries. Charities in the country from which Ajio operates have recently become subject to new audit and accounting regulations. Charity income consists of cash collections at fund raising events, telephone appeals, and bequests (money left to the charity by deceased persons). The charity is small and the trustees do not consider that the charity can afford to employ a qualified accountant. The charity employs a part-time bookkeeper and relies on volunteers for fund raising. Your firm has been appointed as accountants and auditors to this charity because of the new regulations. Accounts have been prepared (but not audited) in the past by a volunteer who is a recently retired Chartered Certified Accountant.

Required

(a) Describe the risks associated with the audit of Ajio under the headings inherent risk, control risk and detection risk and explain the implications of these risks for overall audit risk. **(10 marks)**

(b) List and explain the audit tests to be performed on income and expenditure from fund raising events. **(10 marks)**

Note. In part (a) you may deal with inherent risk and control risk together. You are not required to deal with the detail of accounting for charities in either part of the question.

(Total = 20 marks)

30 B-Star (6/09) **54 mins**

Background information

B-Star is a theme park based on a popular series of children's books. Customers pay a fixed fee to enter the park, where they can participate in a variety of activities such as riding roller-coasters, playing on slides and purchasing themed souvenirs from gift shops.

The park is open all year and has been in operation for the last seven years. It is located in a country which has very little rainfall – the park is open-air so poor weather such as rain results in a significant fall in the number of customers for that day (normally by 50%). During the last seven years there have been on average 30 days each year with rain.

B-Star is now very successful; customer numbers are increasing at approximately 15% each year.

Ticket sales

Customers purchase tickets to enter the theme park from ticket offices located outside the park. Tickets are only valid on the day of purchase. Adults and children are charged the same price for admission to the park. Tickets are preprinted and stored in each ticket office.

Tickets are purchased using either cash or credit cards.

Each ticket has a number comprising of two elements – two digits relating to the ticket office followed by six digits to identify the ticket. The last six digits are in ascending sequential order.

Cash sales

1 All ticket sales are recorded on a computer showing the amount of each sale and the number of tickets issued. This information is transferred electronically to the accounts office.

2 Cash is collected regularly from each ticket office by two security guards. The cash is then counted by two accounts clerks and banked on a daily basis.

3 The total cash from each ticket office is agreed to the sales information that has been transferred from each office.

4 Total cash received is then recorded in the cash book, and then the general ledger.

Credit card sales

1 Payments by credit cards are authorised online as the customers purchase their tickets.

2 Computers in each ticket office record the sales information which is transferred electronically to the accounts office.

3 Credit card sales are recorded for each credit card company in a receivables ledger.

4 When payment is received from the credit card companies, the accounts clerks agree the total sales values to the amounts received from the credit card companies, less the commission payable to those companies. The receivables ledger is updated with the payments received.

You are now commencing the planning of the annual audit of B-Star. The date is 3 June 20X9 and B-Star's year end is 30 June 20X9.

Required

(a) List and explain the purpose of the main sections of an audit strategy document and for each section, provide an example relevant to B-Star. **(8 marks)**

(b) (i) For the cash sales system of B-Star, identify the risks that could affect the assertion of completeness of sales and cash receipts; **(4 marks)**

(ii) Discuss the extent to which tests of controls and substantive procedures could be used to confirm the assertion of completeness of income in B-Star. **(6 marks)**

(c) (i) List the substantive analytical procedures that may be used to give assurance on the total income from ticket sales for one day in B-Star;

(ii) List the substantive analytical procedures that may be used to give assurance on the total income from ticket sales in B-Star for the year. **(8 marks)**

(d) List the audit procedures you should perform on the credit card receivables balance. **(4 marks)**

(Total = 30 marks)

INTERNAL CONTROL

Questions 31 – 40 cover Internal control, the subject of Part D of the BPP Study Text for F8.

31 Rhapsody (AIR 6/07) (amended) 36 mins

Rhapsody Co supplies a wide range of garden and agricultural products to trade and domestic customers. The company has 11 divisions, with each division specialising in the sale of specific products, for example, seeds, garden furniture, agricultural fertilizers. The company has an internal audit department which provides audit reports to the audit committee on each division on a rotational basis.

Products in the seed division are offered for sale to domestic customers via an internet site. Customers review the product list on the internet and place orders for packets of seeds using specific product codes, along with their credit card details, onto Rhapsody Co's secure server. Order quantities are normally between one and three packets for each type of seed. Order details are transferred manually onto the company's internal inventory control and sales system, and a two part packing list is printed in the seed warehouse. Each order and packing list is given a random alphabetical code based on the name of the employee inputting the order, the date, and the products being ordered.

In the seed warehouse, the packages of seeds for each order are taken from specific bins and despatched to the customer with one copy of the packing list. The second copy of the packing list is sent to the accounts department where the inventory and sales computer is updated to show that the order has been despatched. The customer's credit card is then charged by the inventory control and sales computer. Bad debts in Rhapsody are currently 3% of total sales.

Finally, the computer system checks that for each charge made to a customer's credit card account, the order details are on file to prove that the charge was made correctly. The order file is marked as completed confirming that the order has been despatched and payment obtained.

Required

(a) In respect of sales in the seeds division of Rhapsody Co, prepare a report to be sent to the audit committee of Rhapsody Co which:

(i) identifies and explains FOUR deficiencies in that sales system;
(ii) explains the possible effect of each deficiency; and
(iii) provides a recommendation to alleviate each deficiency.

(Note. Up to 2 marks will be awarded for presentation.) **(14 marks)**

(b) Explain the advantages to Rhapsody Co of having an audit committee. **(6 marks)**

(Total = 20 marks)

32 Risk assessment and internal control (AIR 12/02) 36 mins

(a) There are a number of key procedures which auditors should perform if they wish to rely on internal controls and reduce the level of substantive testing they perform. These include:

(i) Documentation of accounting systems and internal control;
(ii) Walk-through tests;
(iii) Audit sampling;
(iv) Testing internal controls;
(v) Dealing with deviations from the application of control activities.

Required

Briefly explain each of the procedures listed above. **(10 marks)**

(Note. (i) – (v) above carry equal marks.)

(b) Flowers Anytime sells flowers wholesale. Customers telephone the company and their orders are taken by clerks who take details of the flowers to be delivered, the address to which they are to be delivered, and account details of the customer. The clerks input these details into the company's computer system (whilst the order is being taken) which is integrated with the company's inventory control system. The company's standard credit terms are payment one month from the order (all orders are despatched within 48 hours) and most customers pay by bank transfer. An accounts receivable ledger is maintained and statements are sent to customers once a month. Credit limits are set by the credit controller according to a standard formula and are automatically applied by the computer system, as are the prices of flowers.

Required

Describe and explain the purpose of the internal controls you might expect to see in the sales system at Flowers Anytime over the:

(i) Receipt, processing and recording of orders **(6 marks)**

(ii) Collection of cash **(4 marks)**

(Total = 20 marks)

33 Atlantis Standard Goods (AIR 6/06) 36 mins

(a) State the control objectives for the ordering, despatch and invoicing of goods. **(5 marks)**

(b) Atlantis Standard Goods (ASG) Co has a year end of 30 June 20X6. ASG is a retailer of kitchen appliances such as washing machines, fridges and microwaves. All sales are made via the company's Internet site with dispatch and delivery of goods to the customer's house made using ASG's vehicles. Appliances are purchased from many different manufacturers.

The process of making a sale is as follows:

(1) Potential customers visit ASG's website and select the kitchen appliance that they require. The website ordering system accesses the inventory specification file to obtain details of products ASG sells.

(2) When the customer chooses an appliance, order information including price, item and quantity required are stored in the orders pending file.

(3) Online authorisation of credit card details is obtained from the customer's credit card company automatically by ASG's computer systems.

(4) Following authorisation, the sales amount is transferred to the computerised sales day book. At the end of each day the total from this ledger is transferred to the general ledger.

(5) Reimbursement of the sales amount is obtained from each credit card company monthly, less the appropriate commission charged by the credit card company.

(6) Following authorisation of the credit card, order details are transferred to a goods awaiting despatch file and allocated a unique order reference code. Order details are automatically transferred to the dispatch department's computer system.

(7) In the despatch department, goods are obtained from the physical inventory, placed on ASG vehicles and the computerised inventory system updated. Order information is downloaded on a hand held computer with a writable screen.

(8) On delivery, the customer signs for the goods on the hand held computer. On return to ASG's warehouse, images of the customer signature are uploaded to the orders file which is then flagged as 'order complete'.

This year's audit planning documentation states that a substantive approach will be taken on the audit.

Required

Tabulate the audit tests you should carry out on the sales and despatch system, explaining the reason for each test. **(15 marks)**

(Total = 20 marks)

34 Cosmo (AIR 12/01) (amended) 36 mins

(a) Internal control is designed, amongst other things, to prevent error and misappropriation.

Required

Describe the errors and misappropriations that may occur if purchases and capital expenditure are not properly controlled. **(5 marks)**

(b) Cosmo is a high-quality, private motor manufacturing company. It has recently joined a consortium for the purchase of parts. Cosmo's purchases and capital expenditure systems are not integrated.

Purchases and capital expenditure

There are complex internal rules relating to what constitutes a purchase, and what constitutes capital expenditure and the budgets for both are tightly controlled. Problems associated with the internal rules result in a significant number of manual adjustments to the management accounts which take up an excessive amount of management time.

The system for authorising capital expenditure is not well controlled which results in some capital items being acquired without proper consideration, at the monthly meetings of the capital expenditure committee.

Purchase orders

Purchase orders are generated automatically by the computerised inventory system when inventories levels fall below a given level in the context of scheduled production. This system does not work well because the system uses outdated purchasing and production patterns and many manual adjustments are required. The orders are reviewed by the production controller and her junior managers and changes are made informally by junior clerical staff in the production controller's department.

Some of the purchases are input into the buying consortium system which shows the optimum supplier for any combination of cost, delivery time and specification. This system has only been in operation for a few months. The system takes up a substantial amount of disk space on the company's computers and is suspected of causing problems in other systems. It is difficult to use and so far, only two of the production controller's junior managers are able to use it. As a result, the parts ordered through the system are sometimes of the incorrect specification or are delivered late. The remaining purchases are ordered directly from manufacturers, as before, through a reasonably well-controlled buying department.

Required

Set out, in a form suitable for inclusion in a report to management, the deficiencies, potential consequences and your recommendations relating to the purchases and capital expenditure systems of Cosmo.

(15 marks)

(Total = 20 marks)

35 SouthLea (Pilot Paper) (amended) 36 mins

SouthLea Co is a construction company (building houses, offices and hotels) employing a large number of workers on various construction sites. The internal audit department of SouthLea Co is currently reviewing cash wages systems within the company.

The following information is available concerning the wages systems:

(i) Hours worked are recorded using a clocking in/out system. On arriving for work and at the end of each days work, each worker enters their unique employee number on a keypad.

(ii) Workers on each site are controlled by a foreman. The foreman has a record of all employee numbers and can issue temporary numbers for new employees.

(iii) Any overtime is calculated by the computerised wages system and added to the standard pay.

(iv) The two staff in the wages department make amendments to the computerised wages system in respect of employee holidays, illness, as well as setting up and maintaining all employee records.

(v) The computerised wages system calculates deductions from gross pay, such as employee taxes, and net pay. Finally a list of net cash payments for each employee is produced.

(vi) Cash is delivered to the wages office by secure courier.

(vii) The two staff place cash into wages packets for each employee along with a handwritten note of gross pay, deductions and net pay. The packets are given to the foreman for distribution to the individual employees.

Required

(a) (i) Identify and explain deficiencies in SouthLea Co's system of internal control over the wages system that could lead to mis-statements in the financial statements;

(ii) For each deficiency, suggest an internal control to overcome that deficiency. **(8 marks)**

(b) Compare the responsibilities of the external and internal auditors to detect fraud. **(6 marks)**

The computer system in the wages department needs to be replaced. The replacement will be carried out under the control of a specialist external consultant.

Required

(c) Explain the factors that should be taken into consideration when appointing an external consultant. **(6 marks)**

(Total = 20 marks)

36 Burton Housing 36 mins

Your firm is the auditor of Burton Housing, which is a small charity and housing association. Its principal asset is a large freehold building which contains a restaurant, accommodation for 50 young people, and recreational facilities.

The charity is controlled by a management committee which comprises the voluntary chairman and treasurer, and other voluntary members elected annually. However, day-to-day management is by a chief executive who manages the full-time staff who perform accounting, cleaning, maintenance, housing management and other functions.

You are auditing the company's financial statements for the year ended 31 October 20X5. Draft accounts have been prepared by the treasurer from accounting records kept on a microcomputer by the bookkeeper. The partner in charge of the audit has asked you to consider the audit work you would perform on income from rents, and the income and expenditure account of the restaurant.

For income from rents:

(a) The housing manager allocates rooms to individuals, and this information is sent to the bookkeeper.

(b) Each week the bookkeeper posts the rents to each resident's account on the sales ledger. All rooms are let at the same rent.

(c) Rents are received from residents by reception staff who are independent of the housing manager and bookkeeper. Reception staff give the rents to the bookkeeper.

(d) The bookkeeper posts cash received for rents to the sales ledger, enters them in the cash book and pays them into the bank.

(e) The housing manager reports voids (that is, rooms unlet) to the management committee.

The restaurant comprises the manager and four staff, who prepare and sell food to residents and other individuals.

Cash takings from the restaurant are recorded on a till and each day's takings are given to the bookkeeper who records and pays them into the bank. Details of cash takings are recorded on the till roll.

The system for purchasing food comprises the following:

(a) The restaurant manager orders the food by sending an order to the supplier.

(b) Food received is checked by the restaurant manager.

(c) The restaurant manager authorises purchase invoices, confirming the food has been received.

(d) The bookkeeper posts the purchase invoices to the payables ledger.

(e) The bookkeeper makes out the cheques to pay the suppliers, which the chief executive signs. The cheques are posted to the payables ledger and cash book.

The bookkeeper is responsible for paying the wages of staff in the restaurant. The restaurant manager notifies the bookkeeper of any absences of staff.

You should assume that the income and expenditure account of the restaurant includes only:

(a) Income from customers who purchase food
(b) Expenditure on purchasing food and wages of restaurant staff

Required

Consider the control activities which should be in operation and the audit procedures you will carry out to verify:

(a) For rents received:

(i) Recording of rental income on the sales ledger
(ii) Receipt and recording of rents received from residents
(iii) Posting of adjustments, credit notes and write off of bad debts on the sales ledger **(11 marks)**

(b) The income and expenditure account of the restaurant. **(9 marks)**

(Total = 20 marks)

37 Delphic (12/07) 36 mins

Delphic Co is a wholesaler of furniture (such as chairs, tables and cupboards). Delphic buys the furniture from six major manufacturers and sells them to over 600 different customers ranging from large retail chain stores to smaller owner-controlled businesses. The receivables balance therefore includes customers owing up to $125,000 to smaller balances of about $5,000, all with many different due dates for payments and credit limits. All information is stored on Delphic's computer systems although previous audits have tended to adopt an 'audit around the computer' approach.

You are the audit senior in charge of the audit of the receivables balance. For the first time at this client, you have decided to use audit software to assist with the audit of the receivables balance. Computer staff at Delphic are happy to help the auditor, although they cannot confirm completeness of systems documentation, and warn that the systems have very old operating systems in place, limiting file compatibility with more modern programs.

The change in audit approach has been taken mainly to fully understand Delphic's computer systems prior to new internet modules being added next year. To limit the possibility of damage to Delphic's computer files, copy files will be provided by Delphic's computer staff for the auditor to use with their own audit software.

Required

(a) Explain the audit procedures that should be carried out using audit software on the receivables balance at Delphic Co. For each procedure, explain the reason for that procedure. **(9 marks)**

(b) Explain the potential problems of using audit software at Delphic Co. For each problem, explain how it can be resolved. **(8 marks)**

(c) Explain the concept of 'auditing around the computer' and discuss why this increases audit risk for the auditor. **(3 marks)**

(Total = 20 marks)

38 Matalas (12/07) (amended) 36 mins

Matalas Co sells cars, car parts and petrol from 25 different locations in one country. Each branch has up to 20 staff working there, although most of the accounting systems are designed and implemented from the company's head office. All accounting systems, apart from petty cash, are computerised, with the internal audit department frequently advising and implementing controls within those systems.

Matalas has an internal audit department of six staff, all of whom have been employed at Matalas for a minimum of five years and some for as long as 15 years. In the past, the chief internal auditor appoints staff within the internal audit department, although the chief executive officer (CEO) is responsible for appointing the chief internal auditor.

The chief internal auditor reports directly to the finance director. The finance director also assists the chief internal auditor in deciding on the scope of work of the internal audit department.

You are an audit manager in the internal audit department of Matalas. You are currently auditing the petty cash systems at the different branches. Your initial systems notes on petty cash contain the following information:

1. The average petty cash balance at each branch is $5,000.
2. Average monthly expenditure is $1,538, with amounts ranging from $1 to $500.
3. Petty cash is kept in a lockable box on a bookcase in the accounts office.
4. Vouchers for expenditure are signed by the person incurring that expenditure to confirm they have received re-imbursement from petty cash.
5. Vouchers are recorded in the petty cash book by the accounts clerk; each voucher records the date, reason for the expenditure, amount of expenditure and person incurring that expenditure.
6. Petty cash is counted every month by the accounts clerk, who is in charge of the cash. The petty cash balance is then reimbursed using the 'imprest' system and the journal entry produced to record expenditure in the general ledger.
7. The cheque to reimburse petty cash is signed by the accountant at the branch at the same time as the journal entry to the general ledger is reviewed.

Required

(a) Explain the issues which limit the independence of the internal audit department in Matalas Co. Recommend a way of overcoming each issue. **(8 marks)**

(b) Explain the internal control deficiencies in the petty cash system at Matalas Co. For each deficiency, recommend a control to overcome that deficiency. **(12 marks)**

(Total = 20 marks)

39 Cliff (AIR 12/04) (amended) — 54 mins

Day-to-day internal controls are important for all businesses to maximise the efficient use of resources and profitability.

Your firm has recently been appointed as auditor to Cliff, a private company that runs a chain of small supermarkets selling fresh and frozen food, and canned and dry food. Cliff has very few controls over inventory because the company trusts local managers to make good decisions regarding the purchase, sales and control of inventory, all of which is done locally. Pricing is generally performed on a cost-plus basis.

Each supermarket has a stand-alone computer system on which monthly accounts are prepared. These accounts are mailed to head office every quarter. There is no integrated inventory control, sales or purchasing system and no regular system for inventory counting. Management accounts are produced twice a year.

Trade at the supermarkets has increased in recent years and the number of supermarkets has increased. However, the quality of staff that has been recruited has fallen. Senior management at Cliff are now prepared to invest in more up-to-date systems.

Required

(a) Describe the problems that you might expect to find at Cliff resulting from poor internal controls. **(10 marks)**

(b) Make four recommendations to the senior management of Cliff for the improvement of internal controls, and explain the advantages and disadvantages of each recommendation. **(12 marks)**

(c) Explain the impact that the internal control environment at Cliff is likely to have on your audit approach. **(5 marks)**

(d) Briefly discuss the benefits of a report to management at the interim stage of an audit. **(3 marks)**

(Total = 30 marks)

40 Blake (12/08) (amended) **54 mins**

Introduction

Blake Co assembles specialist motor vehicles such as lorries, buses and trucks. The company owns four assembly plants to which parts are delivered and assembled into the motor vehicles.

The motor vehicles are assembled using a mix of robot and manual production lines. The 'human' workers normally work a standard eight hour day, although this is supplemented by overtime on a regular basis as Blake has a full order book. There is one shift per day; mass production and around the clock working are not possible due to the specialist nature of the motor vehicles being assembled.

Wages system – shift workers

Shift-workers arrive for work at about 7.00 am and 'clock in' using an electronic identification card. The card is scanned by the time recording system and each production shift-worker's identification number is read from their card by the scanner. The worker is then logged in as being at work. Shift-workers are paid from the time of logging in. The logging in process is not monitored as it is assumed that shift-workers would not work without first logging in on the time recording system.

Shift-workers are split into groups of about 25 employees, with each group under the supervision of a shift foreman. Each day, each group of shift-workers is allocated a specific vehicle to manufacture. At least 400 vehicles have to be manufactured each day by each work group. If necessary, overtime is worked to complete the day's quota of vehicles. The shift foreman is not required to monitor the extent of any overtime working although the foreman does ensure workers are not taking unnecessary or prolonged breaks which would automatically increase the amount of overtime worked. Shift-workers log off at the end of each shift by re-scanning their identification card.

Payment of wages

Details of hours worked each week are sent electronically to the payroll department, where hours worked are allocated by the computerised wages system to each employee's wages records. Staff in the payroll department compare hours worked from the time recording system to the computerised wages system, and enter a code word to confirm the accuracy of transfer. The code word also acts as authorisation to calculate net wages. The code word is the name of a domestic cat belonging to the department head and is therefore generally known around the department.

Each week the computerised wages system calculates:

(i) gross wages, using the standard rate and overtime rates per hour for each employee,
(ii) statutory deductions from wages, and
(iii) net pay.

The list of net pay for each employee is sent over Blake's internal network to the accounts department. In the accounts department, an accounts clerk ensures that employee bank details are on file. The clerk then authorises and makes payment to those employees using Blake's online banking systems. Every few weeks the financial accountant reviews the total amount of wages made to ensure that the management accounts are accurate.

Termination of employees

Occasionally, employees leave Blake. When this happens, the personnel department sends an e-mail to the payroll department detailing the employee's termination date and any unclaimed holiday pay. The receipt of the e-mail by the payroll department is not monitored by the personnel department.

Salaries system – shift managers

All shift managers are paid an annual salary; there are no overtime payments.

Salaries were increased in July by 3% and an annual bonus of 5% of salary was paid in November.

Required

(a) List FOUR control objectives of a wages system. **(2 marks)**

(b) As the external auditors of Blake Co, write a management letter to the directors in respect of the shift-workers wages recording and payment systems which:

(i) Identifies and explains FOUR deficiencies in that system;

(ii) Explains the possible effect of each deficiency;

(iii) Provides a recommendation to alleviate each deficiency. Note up to two marks will be awarded within this requirement for presentation. **(14 marks)**

(c) List THREE substantive analytical procedures you should perform on the shift managers' salary system. For each procedure, state your expectation of the result of that procedure. **(6 marks)**

(d) Audit evidence can be obtained using various audit procedures, such as inspection. APART FROM THIS PROCEDURE, in respect of testing the accuracy of the time recording system at Blake Co, explain FOUR procedures used in collecting audit evidence and discuss whether the auditor will benefit from using each procedure. **(8 marks)**

(Total = 30 marks)

AUDIT EVIDENCE

Questions 41 – 70 cover Audit evidence, the subject of Part E of the BPP Study Text for F8.

41 Using the work of others — 18 mins

(a) ISA 610 *Using the work of internal auditors* provides guidance to external auditors on the use of internal audit work.

Required

List and briefly explain the various criteria that should be considered by external auditors when assessing whether to take reliance from work performed by internal audit. **(4 marks)**

(b) List four examples of audit evidence that might be obtained from the use of an auditor's expert. **(2 marks)**

(c) ISA 620 *Using the work of an auditor's expert* provides guidance to auditors on relying on work carried out by an expert.

Required

List the factors that should be considered by the auditor when evaluating the work carried out by the expert and briefly explain what actions the auditor should take if he concludes that the results of the expert's work do not provide sufficient, appropriate audit evidence or if the results are inconsistent with other audit evidence. **(4 marks)**

(Total = 10 marks)

42 Expert (12/08) (amended) — 18 mins

(a) ISA 620 *Using the work of an auditor's expert* explains how an auditor may use an expert to obtain audit evidence.

Required

Explain THREE factors that the external auditor should consider when assessing the competence and objectivity of the auditor's expert. **(3 marks)**

(b) Auditors have various duties to perform in their role as auditors, for example, to assess the truth and fairness of the financial statements.

Required

Explain THREE rights that enable auditors to carry out their duties. **(3 marks)**

(c) List FOUR assertions relevant to the audit of tangible non-current assets and state one audit procedure which provides appropriate evidence for each assertion. **(4 marks)**

(Total =10 marks)

43 Audit techniques and sampling — 18 mins

(a) ISA 520 *Analytical procedures* provides guidance on the use of analytical procedures during the course of the external audit. Analytical procedures can be used as substantive audit procedures during audit fieldwork, as well as during planning and review.

Required

List six factors that should be considered by the external auditor when using analytical procedures as substantive audit procedures. **(3 marks)**

(b) ISA 540 *Auditing accounting estimates, including fair value accounting estimates, and related disclosures* provides guidance on the audit of estimates contained in the financial statements.

Required

Explain what an accounting estimate is and list four examples of situations where accounting estimates might be used in the financial statements. **(4 marks)**

(c) ISA 530 *Audit sampling* states that the objective of the auditor, when using audit sampling, is to provide a reasonable basis for the auditor to draw conclusions about the population from which the sample is selected.

Explain the difference between statistical and non-statistical sampling and list three examples of methods of sample selection. **(4 marks)**

(Total = 10 marks)

44 Sampling methods (6/09) (amended) 18 mins

(a) List and explain FOUR methods of selecting a sample of items to test from a population in accordance with ISA 530 *Audit Sampling* **(4 marks)**

(b) List and explain FOUR assertions from ISA 315 *Identifying and assessing the risks of material misstatement through understanding the entity and its environment* that relate to classes of transactions and events. **(4 marks)**

(c) In terms of audit reports, explain the term 'modified'. **(2 marks)**

(Total = 10 marks)

45 External confirmations 18 mins

(a) ISA 505 *External confirmations* considers a number of different types of external confirmations including accounts receivables' confirmations.

Required

Explain the difference between a positive and negative confirmation. **(4 marks)**

(b) List six examples, other than the confirmation of receivables, of situations where external confirmations may be used by the auditor to obtain audit evidence. **(3 marks)**

(c) List six items of information that could be requested in a bank confirmation letter. **(3 marks)**

(Total = 10 marks)

46 Analytical procedures, sampling and CAATs 18 mins

(a) ISA 520 *Analytical procedures* provides guidance to auditors on the use of analytical procedures during the course of the external audit.

Required

When using analytical procedures as substantive audit procedures, list and briefly explain with examples three factors to consider when determining the extent of reliance that can be placed on the results of such procedures. **(3 marks)**

(b) Explain the meaning of the terms 'sampling risk' and 'non-sampling risk', including how these risks can be reduced. **(3 marks)**

(c) Computer-assisted audit techniques (CAATs) are the use of computers for audit work and comprise mainly audit software and test data.

Required

Explain the terms 'audit software' and 'test data' and list the advantages of using CAATs in an audit. **(4 marks)**

(Total = 10 marks)

47 Wear Wraith (AIR 6/06) 36 mins

Wear Wraith (WW) Co's main activity is the extraction and supply of building materials including sand, gravel, cement and similar aggregates. The company's year end is 31 May and your firm has audited WW for a number of years. The main asset on the statement of financial position relates to non-current assets. A junior member of staff has attempted to prepare the non-current asset note for the financial statements. The note has not been reviewed by the senior accountant and so may contain errors.

	Land and buildings	*Plant and machinery*	*Motor vehicles*	*Railway trucks*	*Total*
COST	$	$	$	$	$
1 June 20X5	100,000	875,000	1,500,000	–	2,475,000
Additions	10,000	125,000	525,000	995,000	1,655,000
Disposals	–	(100,000)	(325,000)	–	(425,000)
31 May 20X6	110,000	900,000	1,700,000	995,000	3,705,000
Depreciation					
1 June 20X5	60,000	550,000	750,000	–	1,360,000
Charge	2,200	180,000	425,000	199,000	806,200
Disposals	–	(120,000)	(325,000)	–	(445,000)
31 May 20X6	62,200	610,000	850,000	199,000	1,721,200
Net Book Value					
31 May 20X6	47,800	290,000	850,000	796,000	1,983,800
Net Book Value					
31 May 20X5	40,000	325,000	750,000	–	1,115,000

- Land and buildings relate to company offices and land for those offices.
- Plant and machinery includes extraction equipment such as diggers and dumper trucks used to extract sand and gravel etc.
- Motor vehicles include large trucks to transport the sand, gravel etc.
- Railway trucks relate to containers used to transport sand and gravel over long distances on the railway network.

Depreciation rates stated in the financial statements are all based on cost and calculated using the straight line basis.

The rates are:

Land and buildings	2%
Plant and machinery	20%
Motor vehicles	33%
Railway trucks	20%

Disposals in the motor vehicles category relates to vehicles which were five years old.

Required

(a) List the audit work you should perform on railway trucks. **(10 marks)**

(b) You have just completed your analytical procedures of the non-current assets note.

Required

(i) Excluding railway trucks, identify and explain any issues with the non-current asset note to raise with management.

(ii) Explain how each issue could be resolved. **(10 marks)**

Note. You do not need to re-cast the schedule.

(Total = 20 marks)

48 Tracey Transporters (AIR 6/05) 36 mins

You are the external auditor of Tracey Transporters, a public limited company (TT). The company's year end is 31 March. You have been the auditor since the company was formed 24 years ago to take advantage of the increase in goods being transported by road. Many companies needed to transport their products but did not always have sufficient vehicles to move them. TT therefore purchased ten vehicles and hired these to haulage companies for amounts of time ranging from three days to six months.

The business has grown in size and profitability and now has over 550 vehicles on hire to many different companies. At any one time, between five and 20 vehicles are located at the company premises where they are being repaired; the rest could be anywhere on the extensive road network of the country it operates in. Full details of all vehicles are maintained in a non-current asset register.

Bookings for hire of vehicles are received either over the telephone or via e-mail in TT's offices. A booking clerk checks the customer's credit status on the receivables ledger and then the availability of vehicles using the Vehicle Management System (VMS) software on TT's computer network. E-mails are filed electronically by customer name in the e-mail programme used by TT. If the customer's credit rating is acceptable and a vehicle is available, the booking is entered into the VMS and confirmed to the customer using the telephone or e-mail. Booking information is then transferred within the network from the VMS to the receivables ledger programme, where a sales invoice is raised. Standard rental amounts are allocated to each booking depending on the amount of time the vehicle is being hired for. Hard copy invoices are sent in the post for telephone orders or via e-mail for e-mail orders.

The main class of asset on TT's statement of financial position is the vehicles. The net book value of the vehicles is $6 million out of total shareholders' funds of $15 million as at 31 March 20X5.

Required

(a) List and explain the reason for the audit tests you should perform to check the completeness and accuracy of the sales figure in TT's financial statements. **(10 marks)**

(b) List and describe the audit work you should perform on the figure in the statement of financial position for vehicles in TT's financial statements for the year ended 31 March 20X5. **(10 marks)**

(Total = 20 marks)

49 MistiRead (AIR 6/07) 36 mins

You are an audit manager in Ron & Co. One of your audit clients, MistiRead Co, is a specialist supplier of crime fiction with over 120,000 customers. The company owns one large warehouse, which contains at any one time about 1 million books of up to 80,000 different titles. Customers place orders for books either over the internet or by mail order. Books are despatched on the day of receipt of the order. Returns are allowed up to 30 days from the despatch date provided the books look new and unread.

Due to the high inventory turnover, MistiRead maintains a perpetual inventory system using standard 'off the shelf' software. Ron & Co has audited the system for the last five years and has found no errors within the software. Continuous inventory checking is carried out by MistiRead's internal audit department.

You are currently reviewing the continuous inventory checking system with an audit junior. The junior needs experience in continuous inventory checking systems and some basic knowledge on ACCA's Code of Ethics and Conduct.

Required

(a) Explain the advantages of using a perpetual inventory system. **(4 marks)**

(b) List the audit procedures you should perform to confirm the accuracy of the continuous inventory checking at MistiRead Co. For each procedure, explain the reason for carrying out that procedure. **(6 marks)**

(c) Explain the fundamental principles set out in ACCA's *Code of Ethics and Conduct* of integrity, objectivity and independence to accountants. **(6 marks)**

(d) During your preliminary audit planning you note that the engagement letter has been returned un-signed by the directors of MistiRead. When asked to explain their action, the directors indicate that they cannot allow you access to information on the company's new website development as this contains various trade secrets. You will not, therefore, be able to perform audit procedures on the research and development expenditure incurred on the website and included in non-current assets.

Briefly explain the actions you should take as a result of the directors not signing the engagement letter. **(4 marks)**

(Total = 20 marks)

50 Coogee — 36 mins

Coogee is a medium sized, privately owned and incorporated engineering company with an annual revenue of $23 million. Most of its sales are on credit. At its financial year end 31 December 20X8 its accounts receivable ledger contained 2,000 accounts with balances ranging from $50 to $10,000 and totalling $2,300,000. As a staff member of Coogee's external auditors you have been assigned to the audit of the allowance for bad and doubtful debts which has been set as $120,000. Your initial enquiries established that $80,000 relates to the allowance against specific bad and doubtful debts and $40,000 is a general allowance determined as a percentage of overdue debts with an increasing percentage being applied against the longest overdue accounts.

Required

(a) Explain the approaches adopted by auditors in obtaining sufficient appropriate audit evidence regarding accounting estimates. **(3 marks)**

(b) Describe the procedures you would apply in verifying the general allowance for bad and doubtful debts. **(9 marks)**

(c) Describe the procedures you would apply in verifying the specific allowance for bad and doubtful debts. **(8 marks)**

(Total = 20 marks)

51 Duckworth Computers — 36 mins

The firm of Chartered Certified Accountants you are employed by is the external auditor of Duckworth Computers, a privately owned incorporated business.

Accounting records are maintained on a computer using proprietary software.

You have worked on the audit for three years and this year you are in charge of the audit. Your assistant is a newly recruited business graduate who has done an accounting course but has no practical experience.

Because of the small size of the company there is limited opportunity for segregation of duties. You decide, as in previous years, that the appropriate audit strategy is to obtain evidence primarily through the performance of substantive procedures. You also plan to perform the audit around the computer as the proprietary software is known to be reliable and details of all transactions and balances can be readily printed out.

On arriving at the company's premises in December 20X9 to perform the final audit on the 31 October 20X9 financial statements, you obtain a copy of the year end bank reconciliation prepared by the bookkeeper and checked by the managing director. This is reproduced below.

Duckworth Computers
Bank Reconciliation 31 October 20X9

	$	$
Balance per bank statement 31 October 20X9		18,375.91
Deposits outstanding		
30 October	1,887.00	
31 October	1,973.00	3,860.00
		22,235.91
Outstanding cheques		
2696	25.00	
2724	289.40	
2725	569.00	
2728	724.25	
2729	1,900.00	
2730	398.00	
2731	53.50	
2732	1,776.00	
2733	255.65	5,990.80
		16,245.11
Cheque returned 'not sufficient funds' 29 October		348.00
Bank charges October		90.00
Balance per books 31 October 20X9		16,683.11

You have already obtained the bank confirmation and lists of cash (and cheque) receipts and payments printed out from the computer. These lists have been added and the totals agreed with ledger postings. You decide the first task to set for your assistant is the verification of the bank reconciliation.

Required

(a) (i) List the audit procedures to be followed by your assistant in verifying the bank reconciliation in sufficient detail for an inexperienced staff member to follow. **(6 marks)**

(ii) Explain the purpose of each procedure in terms of audit objectives. **(5 marks)**

(b) Discuss the reliability of bank statements as audit evidence. What steps can be taken if it is considered desirable to increase their reliability? **(3 marks)**

(c) (i) Distinguish between 'auditing around the computer' and 'auditing through the computer'. **(3 marks)**

(ii) Explain the circumstances when it would be inappropriate for the auditor to rely on auditing around the computer. **(3 marks)**

(Total = 20 marks)

52 Cash audit (AIR 6/02) 36 mins

(a) Internal control is designed, amongst other things, to prevent error and misappropriation.

Required

Describe the errors and misappropriations that may occur if the following are not properly controlled:

(i) Receipts paid into bank accounts; **(2 marks)**
(ii) Payments made out of bank accounts; **(3 marks)**
(iii) Interest and charges debited and credited to bank accounts. **(2 marks)**

(b) A book selling company has a head office and 25 shops, each of which holds cash (banknotes, coins and credit card vouchers) at the year-end date. There are no receivables. Accounting records are held at shops. Shops make returns to head office and head office holds its own accounting records. Your firm has been the external auditor to the company for many years and has offices near to the location of some but not all of the shops.

Required

List the audit objectives for the audit of cash and state how you would gain the audit evidence in relation to those objectives at the year end. **(8 marks)**

(c) The external auditors of companies often write to companies' bankers asking for details of bank balances and other matters at the year end.

Required

Explain why auditors write to companies' bankers and list the matters you would expect banks to confirm. **(5 marks)**

(Total = 20 marks)

53 Metcalf (AIR 6/07) (amended) — 36 mins

ISA 500 *Audit evidence* states that the auditors objective 'is to design and perform audit procedures in such a way as to enable the auditor to obtain sufficient appropriate audit evidence to be able to draw reasonable conclusions on which to base the auditor's opinion'.

Required

(a) List and explain the factors which will influence the auditor's judgement concerning the sufficiency of audit evidence obtained. **(4 marks)**

(b) You are the audit senior in charge of the audit of Metcalf Co, a company that has been trading for over 50 years. Metcalf Co manufactures and sells tables and chairs directly to the public. The company's year end is 31 March.

Current liabilities are shown on Metcalf Co's statement of financial position as follows.

	20X7	*20X6*
	$	$
Trade payables	884,824	816,817
Accruals	56,903	51,551
Provision for legal action	60,000	-
	1,001,727	868,368

The provision for legal action relates to a claim from a customer who suffered an injury while assembling a chair supplied by Metcalf Co. The directors of Metcalf Co dispute the claim, although they are recommending an out of court settlement to avoid damaging publicity against Metcalf Co.

Required

List the substantive audit procedures that you should undertake in the audit of current liabilities of Metcalf Co for the year ended 31 March 20X7. For each procedure, explain the purpose of that procedure.

Marks are allocated as follows.

(i) Trade payables **(9 marks)**
(ii) Accruals **(3 marks)**
(iii) The provision for legal action **(4 marks)**

(Total = 20 marks)

54 Liabilities (AIR 12/02) — 36 mins

(a) Company A has a number of long and short-term payables, accruals and provisions in its statement of financial position.

Required

Describe the audit procedures you would apply to each of the three items listed below, including those relating to disclosure.

(i) A 10-year bank loan with a variable interest rate and an overdraft (a bank account with a debit balance on the bank statement), both from the same bank. **(5 marks)**

(ii) Expense accruals **(4 marks)**

(iii) Trade payables and purchase accruals **(6 marks)**

(b) Company B has a provision in its statement of financial position for claims made by customers for product defects under 1 year company warranties.

Required

Describe the matters you would consider and the audit evidence you would require for the provision.

(5 marks)

(Total = 20 marks)

55 Boulder (AIR 12/04) (amended) — 36 mins

ISA 315 *Identifying and assessing the risks of material misstatement through understanding the entity and its environment* states that management implicitly or explicitly makes assertions relating to the various elements of financial statements including related disclosures. Auditors may use three categories of assertions to form a basis for risk assessments and the design and performance of further audit procedures. The three categories suggested by ISA 315 relate to (i) classes of transactions, (ii) account balances, and (iii) presentation and disclosure. One assertion applicable to all three categories is completeness: that all transactions, events, assets, liabilities, equity interests and disclosures that should be included, are included in the financial statements.

Required

(a) List and describe six financial statement assertions, other than completeness, used by auditors in the audit of financial statements. **(6 marks)**

(b) Boulder is a small company that manufactures hosiery products. It employs approximately 150 staff, all of whom are paid by bank transfer.

Temporary factory staff are hired through an agency and are paid on piece rates (ie for the number of items that they produce or process) on a weekly basis. Supervisors at Boulder authorise documentation indicating the number of items produced or processed by agency staff. The agency is paid by bank transfer and it, not Boulder, is responsible for the deduction of tax and social insurance.

Permanent factory staff are paid on a weekly basis on the basis of hours worked as evidenced by clock cards. Administration and sales staff are paid a monthly salary. The two directors of the company are also paid a monthly salary.

Sales staff are paid a quarterly bonus calculated on the basis of sales. Directors are paid an annual bonus based on profits.

You will be performing the audit of the financial statements for the year ending 31 December 20X4 and you will be responsible for the figures in the financial statements relating to payroll.

Required

Describe the substantive audit procedures you will perform on:

(i) the payroll balances in the statement of financial position of Boulder; **(10 marks)**

(ii) the payroll transactions in the income statement of Boulder. **(4 marks)**

(Total = 20 marks)

56 Newthorpe — 36 mins

You are auditing the financial statements of Newthorpe Engineering Co, a listed company, for the year ended 30 April 20X7.

(a) In March 20X7 the Board decided to close one of the company's factories on 30 April 20X7. The plant and equipment and inventories will be sold. The employees will either be transferred to another factory or made redundant.

At the time of your audit in June 20X7, you are aware that:

(i) Some of the plant and equipment has been sold
(ii) Most of the inventories have been sold
(iii) All the employees have either been made redundant or transferred to another factory

The company has provided you with a schedule of the closure costs, the realisable values of the assets in (i) and (ii) above and the redundancy cost.

Details of the plant and machinery are maintained in a non-current asset register.

A full inventory count was carried out at 30 April 20X7. Audit tests have confirmed that the inventory counts are accurate and there are no purchases or sales cut-off errors.

You are aware the redundancy payments are based on the number of years service of the employee and their annual salary (or wage). Most employees were given redundancy of one week's pay for each year's service. A few employees have a service contract with the company and were paid the amount stated in their service contract which will be more than the redundancy pay offered to other employees. Employees who are transferred to another factory were not paid any redundancy.

As part of the audit of the closure cost, you have been asked to carry out the audit work described below.

Required

For the factory being closed, describe the audit procedures you will carry out to verify the company's estimates of:

(i) The net realisable value of plant and equipment, and inventories **(7 marks)**
(ii) The redundancy cost **(4 marks)**

Notes

(1) In auditing inventories you are required only to verify that the price per unit is correctly determined.
(2) For the redundancy cost, you should ignore any national statutory rules for determining redundancy procedures and minimum redundancy pay.

(b) In February 20X7 the directors of Newthorpe Engineering suspended the managing director. At a disciplinary hearing held by the company on 17 March 20X7 the managing director was dismissed for gross misconduct, and it was decided the managing director's salary should stop from that date and no redundancy or compensation payments should be made.

The managing director has claimed unfair dismissal and is taking legal action against the company to obtain compensation for loss of his employment. The managing director says he has a service contract with the company which would entitle him to two years' salary at the date of dismissal.

The financial statements for the year ended 30 April 20X7 record the resignation of the director. However, they do not mention his dismissal and no provision for any damages has been included in the financial statements.

Required

(i) State how contingent losses should be disclosed in financial statements according to IAS 37 *Provisions, contingent liabilities and contingent assets.* **(3 marks)**
(ii) Describe the audit procedures you will carry out to determine whether the company will have to pay damages to the director for unfair dismissal, and the amount of damages and costs which should be included in the financial statements. **(6 marks)**

Note. Assume the amounts you are auditing are material. **(Total = 20 marks)**

57 Crighton-Ward (AIR 6/05) (amended) 36 mins

(a) Explain the purpose of a representation letter. **(5 marks)**

(b) You are the manager in charge of the audit of Crighton-Ward, a public limited liability company which manufactures specialist cars and other motor vehicles for use in films. Audited turnover is $140 million with profit before tax of $7·5 million.

All audit work up to, but not including, the obtaining of written representations has been completed. A review of the audit file has disclosed the following outstanding points:

Lion's Roar

The company is facing a potential legal claim from the Lion's Roar company in respect of a defective vehicle that was supplied for one of their films. Lion's Roar maintains that the vehicle was not built strongly enough while the directors of Crighton-Ward argue that the specification was not sufficiently detailed. Dropping a vehicle 50 metres into a river and expecting it to continue to remain in working condition would be unusual, but this is what Lion's Roar expected. Solicitors are unable to determine liability at the present time. A claim for $4 million being the cost of a replacement vehicle and lost production time has been received by Crighton-Ward from Lion's Roar. The director's opinion is that the claim is not justified.

Depreciation

Depreciation of specialist production equipment has been included in the financial statements at the amount of 10% pa based on reducing balance. However the treatment is consistent with prior accounting periods (which received an auditor's report with an unmodified audit opinion) and other companies in the same industry and sales of old equipment show negligible profit or loss on sale. The audit senior, who is new to the audit, feels that depreciation is being undercharged in the financial statements.

Required

For each of the above matters:

(i) Discuss whether or not a paragraph is required in the representation letter; and
(ii) *If appropriate*, draft the paragraph for inclusion in the representation letter. **(10 marks)**

(c) A suggested format for the letter of representation has been sent by the auditors to the directors of Crighton-Ward. The directors have stated that they will not sign the letter of representation this year on the grounds that they believe the additional evidence that it provides is not required by the auditor.

Required

Discuss the actions the auditor may take as a result of the decision made by the directors not to sign the representation letter. **(5 marks)**

(Total = 20 marks)

58 Jayne (AIR 12/06) (amended) 36 mins

(a) ISA 505, *External confirmations*, states that 'the objective of the auditor, when using external confirmation procedures is to design and perform such procedures to obtain relevant and reliable audit evidence'.

Required

(i) List four examples of external confirmations. **(2 marks)**
(ii) For each of the examples in (i) above explain:

One audit assertion that the external confirmation supports, and
One audit assertion that the external confirmation does NOT support. **(8 marks)**

(b) Jayne Co has a significant number of cash transactions and recent non-current asset purchases have been financed by a bank loan. This loan is repayable in equal annual instalments for the next five years.

Required

(i) Explain the procedures to obtain a bank report for audit purposes from Jayne Co's bank and the substantive procedures that should be carried out on that report. **(5 marks)**

(ii) List the further substantive procedures that should be carried out on the bank balances in Jayne Co's financial statements. **(5 marks)**

(Total = 20 marks)

59 FireFly Tennis Club (AIR 12/06) — 36 mins

The FireFly Tennis Club owns 12 tennis courts. The club uses 'all weather' tarmac tennis courts, which have floodlights for night-time use. The club's year end is 30 September.

Members pay an annual fee to use the courts and participate in club championships. The club had 430 members as at 1 October 20X5.

Income is derived from two main sources:

1. Membership fees. Each member pays a fee of $200 per annum. Fees for the new financial year are payable within one month of the club year end. Approximately 10% of members do not renew their membership. New members joining during the year pay 50% of the total fees that would have been payable had they been members for a full year. During 20X6, 50 new members joined the club. No members pay their fees before they are due.
2. Court hire fees: Non-members pay $5 per hour to hire a court. Non-members have to sign a list in the club house showing courts hired. Money is placed in a cash box in the club house for collection by the club secretary. All fees (membership and court hire) are paid in cash. They are collected by the club secretary and banked on a regular basis. The paying-in slip shows the analysis between fees and court hire income. The secretary provides the treasurer with a list of bankings showing member's names (for membership fees) and the amount banked. Details of all bankings are entered into the cash book by the treasurer.

Main items of expenditure are:

1. Court maintenance including repainting lines on a regular basis.
2. Power costs for floodlights.
3. Tennis balls for club championships. Each match in the championship uses 12 tennis balls.

The treasurer pays for all expenditure using the club's debit card. Receipts are obtained for all expenses and these are maintained in date order in an expenses file. The treasurer also prepares the annual financial statements.

Under the rules of the club, the annual accounts must be audited by an independent auditor. The date is now 13 December 20X6 and the treasurer has just prepared the financial statements for audit.

Required

(a) Describe the audit work that should be performed to determine the completeness of income for the FireFly Tennis Club. **(10 marks)**

(b) Describe the audit procedures that should be performed to check the completeness and accuracy of expenditure for the FireFly Tennis Club. **(5 marks)**

(c) Discuss why internal control testing has limited value when auditing not-for-profit entities such as the FireFly Tennis Club. **(5 marks)**

(Total = 20 marks)

60 Walsh (AIR 12/06) **36 mins**

Walsh Co sells motor vehicle fuel, accessories and spares to retail customers. The company owns 25 shops.

The company has recently implemented a new computerised wages system. Employees work a standard eight hour day. Hours are recorded using a magnetic card system; when each employee arrives for work, they hold their card close to the card reader; the reader recognises the magnetic information on the card identifying the employee as being 'at work'. When the employee leaves work at the end of the day the process is reversed showing that the employee has left work.

Hours worked are calculated each week by the computer system using the magnetic card information. Overtime is calculated as any excess over the standard hours worked. Any overtime over 10% of standard hours is sent on a computer generated report by e-mail to the financial accountant. If necessary, the accountant overrides overtime payments if the hours worked are incorrect.

Statutory deductions and net pay are also computer calculated with payments being made directly into the employee's bank account. The only other manual check is the financial accountant authorising the net pay from Walsh's bank account, having reviewed the list of wages to be paid.

Required

(a) Using examples from Walsh Co, explain the benefits of using Computer-Assisted Audit Techniques to help the auditor to obtain sufficient appropriate audit evidence to be able to draw reasonable conclusions on which to base the audit opinion. **(8 marks)**

(b) List six examples of audit tests on Walsh Co's wages system using audit software. **(6 marks)**

(c) Explain how using test data should help in the audit of Walsh Co's wages system, noting any problems with this audit technique. **(6 marks)**

(Total = 20 marks)

61 ZPM (AIR 6/06) (amended) **36 mins**

ISA 610 *Using the Work of Internal Auditors* states that 'in order for the external auditor to use specific work of the internal auditors, the external auditor shall evaluate and perform audit procedures on that work to determine its adequacy for the external auditor's purposes.'

Required

(a) In relation to ISA 610, explain the factors the external auditor will consider when evaluating the work of the internal auditor. **(5 marks)**

(b) ZPM is a listed limited liability company with a year end of 30 June. ZPM's main activity is selling home improvement or 'Do-It-Yourself' (DIY) products to the public. Products sold range from nails, paint and tools to doors and showers; some stores also sell garden tools and furniture. Products are purchased from approximately 200 different suppliers. ZPM has 103 stores in eight different countries.

ZPM has a well-staffed internal audit department, who report on a regular basis to the audit committee. Areas where the internal and external auditors may carry out work include:

(1) Attending the year end inventory count in 30 stores annually. All stores are visited rotationally.

(2) Checking the internal controls over the procurement systems (eg ensuring a liability is only recorded when the inventory has been received).

(3) Reviewing the operations of the marketing department.

Required

For each of the above three areas, discuss

(i) The objectives of the internal auditor; **(5 marks)**

(ii) The objectives of the external auditor; and **(5 marks)**

(iii) Whether the external auditor will rely on the internal auditor, and if reliance is required, the extent of that reliance. **(5 marks)**

(Total = 20 marks)

62 Zak (6/08) (amended) **36 mins**

(a) With reference to ISA 520 *Analytical Procedures* and ISA 315 *Identifying and assessing the risks of material misstatement through understanding the entity and its environment* explain

(i) what is meant by the term 'analytical procedures'; **(2 marks)**
(ii) the different types of analytical procedures available to the auditor; and **(3 marks)**
(iii) the situations in the audit when analytical procedures can be used. **(3 marks)**

Zak Co sells garden sheds and furniture from 15 retail outlets. Sales are made to individuals, with income being in the form of cash and debit cards. All items purchased are delivered to the customer using Zak's own delivery vans; most sheds are too big for individuals to transport in their own motor vehicles. The directors of Zak indicate that the company has had a difficult year, but are pleased to present some acceptable results to the members.

The income statements for the last two financial years are shown below:

Income statement

	31 March 2008	*31 March 2007*
	$'000	$'000
Revenue	7,482	6,364
Cost of sales	(3,520)	(4,253)
Gross profit	3,962	2,111
Operating expenses		
Administration	(1,235)	(1,320)
Selling and distribution	(981)	(689)
Interest payable	(101)	(105)
Investment income	145	–
Profit/(loss) before tax	1,790	(3)
Financial statement extract		
Cash and bank	253	(950)

Required

(b) As part of your risk assessment procedures for Zak Co, identify and provide a possible explanation for unusual changes in the income statement. **(9 marks)**

(c) Confirmation of the end of year bank balances is an important audit procedure.

Required

Explain the procedures necessary to obtain a bank confirmation letter from Zak Co's bank. **(3 marks)**

(Total = 20 marks)

63 Springfield Nurseries (AIR Pilot Paper) (amended) **54 mins**

Your firm is the auditor of Springfield Nurseries, a company operating three large garden centres which sell plants, shrubs and trees, garden furniture and gardening equipment (such as lawnmowers and sprinklers) to the general public. You are involved in the audit of the company's non-current assets. The main categories of non-current assets are as follows:

(i) Land and buildings (all of which are owned outright by the company, none of which are leased)
(ii) Computers (on which an integrated inventory control and sales system is operated)
(iii) A number of large and small motor vehicles, mostly used for the delivery of inventory to customers
(iv) Equipment for packaging and pricing products.

The depreciation rates used are as follows:

(i)	Buildings	5% each year on cost
(ii)	Computers and motor vehicles	20% each year on the reducing balance basis

(iii) Equipment 15% each year on cost

You are concerned that these depreciation rates may be inappropriate.

Required

(a) List and explain the main financial statements assertions tested for in the audit of non-current assets. **(5 marks)**

(b) Explain the main risks associated with the assertions relating to non-current assets. **(4 marks)**

(c) List the sources of evidence available to you in verifying the ownership and cost of:

(i) The land and buildings
(ii) The computers and motor vehicles. **(10 marks)**

(d) List the audit procedures you would perform to check the appropriateness of the depreciation rates on each of the three categories of non-current asset. **(6 marks)**

(e) Describe the action you would take if you disagreed with any of the depreciation rates used and explain the potential effect of the disagreement on your audit report. **(5 marks)**

(Total = 30 marks)

64 Snu (AIR 6/03) (amended) 54 mins

Some organisations conduct inventory counts once a year and external auditors attend those counts. Other organisations have perpetual systems (continuous inventory counting) and do not conduct a year-end count.

Snu is a family-owned company which retails beds, mattresses and other bedroom furniture items. The company's year-end is 31 December 20X3. The only full inventory count takes place at the year-end. The company maintains up-to-date computerised inventory records.

Where the company delivers goods to customers, a deposit is taken from the customer and customers are invoiced for the balance after the delivery. Some goods that are in inventory at the year-end have already been paid for in full – customers who collect goods themselves pay by cash or credit card.

Staff at the company's warehouse and shop will conduct the year-end count. The shop and warehouse are open seven days a week except for two important public holidays during the year, one of which is 1 January. The company is very busy in the week prior to the inventory count but the shops will close at 15.00 hours on 31 December and staff will work until 17.00 hours to prepare the inventory for counting. The company has a high turnover of staff. The following inventory counting instructions have been provided to staff at Snu.

(i) The inventory count will take place on 1 January 20X4 commencing at 09.00 hours. No movement of inventory will take place on that day.

(ii) The count will be supervised by Mr Sneg, the inventory controller. All staff will be provided with pre-printed, pre-numbered inventory counting sheets that are produced by the computerised system. Mr Sneg will ensure that all sheets are issued, and that all are collected at the end of the count.

(iii) Counters will work on their own, because there are insufficient staff for them to work in pairs, but they will be supervised by Mr Sneg and Mrs Zapad, an experienced shop manager who will make checks on the work performed by counters. Staff will count inventory with which they are most familiar in order to ensure that the count is completed as quickly and efficiently as possible.

(iv) Any inventory that is known to be old, slow-moving or already sold will be highlighted on the sheets. Staff are required to highlight any inventory that appears to be soiled or damaged.

(v) All inventory items counted will have a piece of paper attached to them that will show that they have been counted.

(vi) All inventory that has been delivered to customers but that has not yet been paid for in full will be added back to the inventory quantities by Mr Sneg.

Required

(a) Explain why year-end inventory counting is important to the auditors of organisations that do not have perpetual inventory systems. **(5 marks)**

(b) Describe audit procedures you would perform in order to rely on a perpetual inventory system in a large, dispersed organisation. **(6 marks)**

(c) Briefly describe the principal risks associated with the financial statements assertions relating to inventory. **(4 marks)**

(d) Describe the deficiencies in Snu's inventory counting instructions and explain why these deficiencies are difficult to overcome. **(15 marks)**

(Total = 30 marks)

65 Textile Wholesalers **54 mins**

Your firm is the auditor of Textile Wholesalers, a limited liability company, which buys textile products (eg clothing) from manufacturers and sells them to retailers. You attended the inventory count at the company's year-end of Thursday 31 October 20X6. The company does not maintain book inventory records, and previous years' audits have revealed problems with purchases cut-off.

Your audit procedures on purchases cut-off, which started from the goods received note (GRN), have revealed the following results:

	Date of GRN	*GRN Number*	*Supplier's Invoice No*	*Invoice value* $	*On purchase ledger before year end*	*In purchase accruals at year end*
1	28.10.X6	1324	6254	4,642	Yes	No
2	29.10.X6	1327	1372	5,164	Yes	Yes
3	30.10.X6	1331	9515	7,893	No	Yes
4	31.10.X6	1335	4763	9,624	No	No
5	1.11.X6	1340	5624	8,243	Yes	No
6	4.11.X6	1345	9695	6,389	No	Yes
7	5.11.X6	1350	2865	7,124	No	No

Assume that goods received before the year-end are in inventories at the year-end, and goods received after the year-end are not in inventories at the year-end.

A purchase accrual is included in payables at the year-end for goods received before the year-end when the purchase invoice has not been posted to the trade payables ledger before the year-end.

Required

(a) At the inventory count:

(i) Describe the procedures the company's staff should carry out to ensure that inventories are counted accurately and cut-off details are recorded

(ii) Describe the procedures you could carry out and the matters you would record in your working papers. **(12 marks)**

(b) Briefly explain why cut-off is an important issue in the audit of inventory. **(4 marks)**

(c) From the results of your purchases cut-off test, described in the question:

(i) Identify the cut-off errors and produce a schedule of the adjustments which should be made to the reported profit, purchases and payables in the financial statements to correct the errors **(5 marks)**

(ii) Comment on the results of your test, and state what further action you would take. **(4 marks)**

(d) Where a company uses a perpetual inventory counting system, describe the audit work that auditors would carry out to satisfy themselves that inventory was fairly stated. **(5 marks)**

(Total = 30 marks)

66 Rocks Forever (AIR 12/05) (amended) — 54 mins

You are the audit manager in the firm of DeCe & Co, an audit firm with ten national offices.

One of your clients, Rocks Forever, purchases diamond jewellery from three manufacturers. The jewellery is then sold from Rocks Forever's four shops. This is the only client your firm has in the diamond industry.

You are planning to attend the physical inventory count for Rocks Forever. Inventory is the largest account on the statement of financial position with each of the four shops holding material amounts. Due to the high value of the inventory, all shops will be visited and test counts performed.

With the permission of the directors of Rocks Forever, you have employed UJ, a firm of specialist diamond valuers who will also be in attendance. UJ will verify that the jewellery is, in fact, made from diamonds and that the jewellery is saleable with respect to current trends in fashion. UJ will also suggest, on a sample basis, the value of specific items of jewellery.

Counting will be carried out by shop staff in teams of two using pre-numbered count sheets.

Required

(a) Describe the main risks associated with the financial statement assertions relating to inventory. **(3 marks)**

(b) Briefly describe the main risks associated with inventory in a company such as Rocks Forever. **(4 marks)**

(c) List and explain the reason for the audit procedures used in obtaining evidence in relation to the inventory count of inventory held in the shops. **(12 marks)**

(d) Explain the factors you should consider when placing reliance on the work of UJ. **(6 marks)**

(e) Describe the audit procedures you should perform to ensure that jewellery inventory is valued correctly. **(5 marks)**

(Total = 30 marks)

67 Westra (Pilot Paper) — 54 mins

Westra Co assembles mobile telephones in a large factory. Each telephone contains up to 100 different parts, with each part being obtained from one of 50 authorised suppliers.

Like many companies, Westra's accounting systems are partly manual and partly computerised. In overview the systems include:

(i) Design software

(ii) A computerised database of suppliers (bespoke system written in-house at Westra)

(iii) A manual system for recording goods inwards and transferring information to the accounts department

(iv) A computerised payables ledger maintained in the accounts department (purchased off-the-shelf and used with no program amendments)

(v) Online payment to suppliers, also in the accounts department

(vi) A computerised nominal ledger which is updated by the payables ledger

Mobile telephones are assembled in batches of 10,000 to 50,000 telephones. When a batch is scheduled for production, a list of parts is produced by the design software and sent, electronically, to the ordering department. Staff in the ordering department use this list to place orders with authorised suppliers. Orders can only be sent to suppliers on the suppliers' database. Orders are sent using electronic data interchange (EDI) and confirmed by each supplier using the same system. The list of parts and orders are retained on the computer in an 'orders placed' file, which is kept in date sequence.

Parts are delivered to the goods inwards department at Westra. All deliveries are checked against the orders placed file before being accepted. A hand-written pre-numbered goods received note (GRN) is raised in the goods inwards department showing details of the goods received with a cross-reference to the date of the order. The top copy of the GRN is sent to the accounts department and the second copy retained in the goods inwards department. The orders placed file is updated with the GRN number to show that the parts have been received.

Paper invoices are sent by all suppliers following dispatch of goods. Invoices are sent to the accounts department, where they are stamped with a unique ascending number. Invoice details are matched to the GRN, which is then attached to the invoice. Invoice details are then entered into the computerised payables ledger. The invoice is signed by the accounts clerk to confirm entry into the payables ledger. Invoices are then retained in a temporary file in number order while awaiting payment.

After 30 days, the payables ledger automatically generates a computerised list of payments to be made, which is sent electronically to the chief accountant. The chief accountant compares this list to the invoices, signs each invoice to indicate approval for payment, and then forwards the electronic payments list to the accounts assistant. The assistant uses online banking to pay the suppliers. The electronic payments list is filed in month order on the computer.

Required

(a) List the substantive audit procedures you should perform to confirm the assertions of completeness, occurrence and cut-off for purchases in the financial statements of Westra Co. For each procedure, explain the purpose of that procedure. **(12 marks)**

(b) List the audit procedures you should perform on the trade payables balance in Westra Co's financial statements. For each procedure, explain the purpose of that procedure. **(8 marks)**

(c) Describe the control procedures that should be in place over the standing data on the trade payables master file in Westra Co's computer system. **(5 marks)**

(d) Discuss the extent to which computer-assisted audit techniques might be used in your audit of purchases and payables at Westra Co. **(5 marks)**

(Total = 30 marks)

68 Strathfield **54 mins**

The recorded value of Strathfield's accounts receivable as at 31 October 20X9, was $2,350,000.

Out of the 5,350 accounts receivable, Sarah Jones selected 120 accounts for confirmation as part of the external audit of the company.

In selecting accounts for confirmation Sarah picked the 10 largest accounts totalling $205,000 and 110 other accounts selected haphazardly. Her working paper states that she rejected any accounts that were less than $100 as not being worth confirming and accounts with government bodies since she knew they never bother replying to confirmation requests.

Each of the 10 largest accounts was satisfactorily confirmed. Sarah analysed the responses to confirmation of the other 110 accounts as follows:

Result of confirmation	*Number of accounts*	*Recorded amount*	*Amount confirmed*
		$	$
Satisfactorily confirmed	75	245,000	245,000
Confirmation returned marked 'gone away – address unknown'	4	950	0
Cut-off differences due to cash or goods in transit	8	6,800	5,750
Invoicing errors	4	2,800	2,200
Invoices posted to the wrong customer's account	2	1,300	980
Disputed as to price or quantity or quality of goods	3	2,800	1,300
Not confirmed – verified by alternative procedures	14	5,800	5,800
Totals	110	265,450	261,030

Sarah is about to draw up her working paper in which she reaches a conclusion as to whether the results of the confirmation of accounts receivable enables her to conclude that the recorded balance is not materially misstated. She is aware that ISA 530 *Audit sampling* requires her to:

(1) Consider the qualitative aspects of errors and whether any of these relate to a sub-population and not to accounts receivable as a whole

(2) Project the error results of the sample to the population from which the sample was selected.

Required

(a) Briefly explain the principal risks associated with the financial statement assertions for trade receivables. **(3 marks)**

(b) Discuss Sarah's method of selecting items to be confirmed. Your answer should:

   (i) Identify any aspects of her approach that might be considered inconsistent with sampling

   (ii) Suggest alternative means of selecting a sample ensuring that the more material balances stand the greatest chance of selection

   (iii) Compare and contrast the haphazard method of selection with random selection and systematic selection. **(10 marks)**

(c) Consider qualitative aspects of each of the five categories of error or other reported differences analysed by Sarah. Suggest which of them should be included in arriving at an estimate of population error. **(7 marks)**

(d) Calculate the projected error in accounts receivable based on the results of the sample test consistent with the qualitative considerations in your answer to (b). **(5 marks)**

(e) Discuss the extent to which Sarah could use computer-assisted audit techniques in her work. **(5 marks)**

(Total = 30 marks)

69 Seeley (6/08) — 54 mins

Introduction – audit firm

You are an audit senior in Brennon & Co, a firm providing audit and assurance services. At the request of an audit partner, you are preparing the audit programme for the income and receivables systems of Seeley Co.

Audit documentation is available from the previous year's audit, including internal control questionnaires and audit programmes for the despatch and sales system. The audit approach last year did not involve the use of computer-assisted audit techniques (CAATs); the same approach will be taken this year. As far as you are aware, Seeley's system of internal control has not changed in the last year.

Client background – sales system

Seeley Co is a wholesaler of electrical goods such as kettles, televisions, MP3 players, etc. The company maintains one large warehouse in a major city. The customers of Seeley are always owners of small retail shops, where electrical goods are sold to members of the public. Seeley only sells to authorised customers; following appropriate credit checks, each customer is given a Seeley identification card to confirm their status. The card must be used to obtain goods from the warehouse.

Despatch and sales system

The despatch and sales system operates as follows:

1. Customers visit Seeley's warehouse and load the goods they require into their vans after showing their Seeley identification card to the despatch staff.
2. A pre-numbered goods despatch note (GDN) is produced and signed by the customer and a member of Seeley's despatch staff confirming goods taken.
3. One copy of the GDN is sent to the accounts department, the second copy is retained in the despatch department.
4. Accounts staff enter goods despatch information onto the computerised sales system. The GDN is signed.
5. The computer system produces the sales invoice, with reference to the inventory master file for product details and prices, maintains the sales day book and also the receivables ledger. The receivables control account is balanced by the computer.
6. Invoices are printed out and sent to each customer in the post with paper copies maintained in the accounts department. Invoices are compared to GDNs by accounts staff and signed.

7. Paper copies of the receivables ledger control account and list of aged receivables are also available.

8. Error reports are produced showing breaks in the GDN sequence.

Information on receivables

The chief accountant has informed you that receivables days have increased from 45 to 60 days over the last year.

The aged receivables report produced by the computer is shown below:

Number of receivables	*Range of debt*	*Total debt $*	*Current $*	*1 to 2 months old $*	*More than 2 months old $*
15	Less than $0	(87,253)	(87,253)		
197	$0 to $20,000	2,167,762	548,894	643,523	975,3545
153	$20,000 to 50,000	5,508,077	2,044,253	2,735,073	728,751
23	$50,001 or more	1,495,498	750,235	672,750	72,513
388		9,084,084	3,256,129	4,051,346	1,776,609

In view of the deteriorating receivables situation, a direct confirmation of receivables will be performed this year.

Required

(a) Explain the steps necessary to check the accuracy of the previous year's internal control questionnaires. **(4 marks)**

(b) Using information from the scenario, list six tests of control that an auditor would normally carry out on the despatch and sales system at Seeley Co and explain the reason for each test. **(12 marks)**

(c) State and explain the meaning of four assertions that relate to the direct confirmation of receivables. **(4 marks)**

(d) (i) Describe the procedures up to despatch of letters to individual receivables in relation to a direct confirmation of receivables. **(5 marks)**

(ii) Discuss which particular categories of receivables might be chosen for the sample. **(5 marks)**

(Total = 30 marks)

70 DinZee (12/07) (amended) — 54 mins

DinZee Co assembles fridges, microwaves, washing machines and other similar domestic appliances from parts procured from a large number of suppliers. As part of the interim audit work two weeks prior to the company year-end, you are testing the procurement and purchases systems and attending the inventory count.

Procurement and purchases system

Parts inventory is monitored by the stores manager. When the quantity of a particular part falls below re-order level, an e-mail is sent to the procurement department detailing the part required and the quantity to order. A copy of the e-mail is filed on the store manager's computer.

Staff in the procurement department check the e-mail, allocate the order to an authorised supplier and send the order to that supplier using Electronic Data Interchange (EDI). A copy of the EDI order is filed in the order database by the computer system. The order is identified by a unique order number.

When goods are received at DinZee, the stores clerk confirms that the inventory agrees to the delivery note and checks the order database to ensure that the inventory were in fact ordered by DinZee. (Delivery is refused where goods do not have a delivery note.)

The order in the order database is updated to confirm receipt of goods, and the perpetual inventory system updated to show the receipt of inventory. The physical goods are added to the parts store and the paper delivery note is stamped with the order number and is filed in the goods inwards department.

The supplier sends a purchase invoice to DinZee using EDI; invoices are automatically routed to the accounts department. On receipt of the invoice, the accounts clerk checks the order database, matches the invoice details with the database and updates the database to confirm receipt of invoice. The invoice is added to the purchases database, where the purchase day book (PDB) and suppliers individual account in the payables ledger are automatically updated.

Required

(a) List six audit procedures that an auditor would normally carry out on the purchases system at DinZee Co, explaining the reason for each procedure. **(12 marks)**

(b) List four audit procedures that an auditor will normally perform prior to attending the client's premises on the day of the inventory count. **(2 marks)**

(c) On the day of the inventory count, you attended depot nine at DinZee. You observed the following activities:

1. Prenumbered count sheets were being issued to client's staff carrying out the count. The count sheets showed the inventory ledger balances for checking against physical inventory.
2. All count staff were drawn from the inventory warehouse and were counting in teams of two.
3. Three counting teams were allocated to each area of the stores to count, although the teams were allowed to decide which pair of staff counted which inventory within each area. Staff were warned that they had to remember which inventory had been counted.
4. Information was recorded on the count sheets in pencil so amendments could be made easily as required.
5. Any inventory not located on the pre-numbered inventory sheets was recorded on separate inventory sheets – which were numbered by staff as they were used.
6. At the end of the count, all count sheets were collected and the numeric sequence of the sheets checked; the sheets were not signed.

Required

(i) List the deficiencies in the control system for counting inventory at depot nine. **(3 marks)**

(ii) For each deficiency, explain why it is a deficiency and state how that deficiency can be overcome. **(9 marks)**

(d) (i) State the aim of a test of control and the aim of a substantive procedure.

(ii) In respect of your attendance at DinZee Co's inventory count, state one test of control and one substantive procedure that you should perform.

(4 marks)

(Total = 30 marks)

REVIEW

Questions 71 – 79 cover Review, the subject of Part F of the BPP Study Text for F8.

71 Evidence and written representations (6/08) (amended)

18 mins

(a) List and explain four factors that will influence the auditor's judgement regarding the sufficiency of the evidence obtained. **(4 marks)**

(b) ISA 580 *Written Representations* provides guidance on the use of written representations as audit evidence.

Required

List six items that could be included in a representation letter. **(3 marks)**

(c) After performing tests of controls, the auditor is of the opinion that audit evidence is not sufficient to support the audit opinion; in other words many control errors were found.

Required

Explain three actions that the auditor may now take in response to this problem. **(3 marks)**

(Total = 10 marks)

72 Ethics and going concern (12/07)

18 mins

(a) Explain each of the five fundamental principles of ACCA's *Code of Ethics and Conduct.* **(5 marks)**

(b) ISA 570 *Going Concern* provides guidance to auditors in respect of ensuring that an entity can continue as a going concern.

Required

Explain the actions that an auditor should carry out to try and ascertain whether an entity is a going concern. **(5 marks)**

(Total = 10 marks)

73 LALD (AIR 12/05)

36 mins

You are the auditor of LALD, a limited liability company. The main activity of the company is the construction of buildings ranging in size from individual houses to large offices and blocks of flats.

Under the laws of the country LALD operates in, LALD must add sales tax to all buildings sold and they pay this tax to the government at the end of each month.

The largest non-current asset on LALD's statement of financial position is the plant and machinery used in the construction of buildings. Due to the variety of different assets used, four different sub-classes of plant and machinery are recognised, each with its own rate of depreciation.

You are now reaching the end of the audit work for the year ended 30 September 20X5. There are two specific matters where additional audit work is required:

(i) The sales tax for the month of August was not paid to the government. This appears to have been an accidental error and the amount involved is not material to the financial statements.

(ii) The complicated method of calculating depreciation for plant and machinery appears to have resulted in depreciation being calculated incorrectly, with the result that depreciation may have been under-provided in the financial statements.

Required

(a) Explain the additional audit procedures you should take regarding the accidental underpayment of sales tax. **(7 marks)**

(b) Explain the additional audit procedures you should take regarding the possible underprovision of depreciation. **(7 marks)**

You have determined that the under-provision is material to the financial statements and therefore need to qualify the audit report. The directors have informed you that they do not intend to take any action regarding the underprovision of depreciation. They also disagree with your action and have threatened to remove your company as the auditors of LALD unless you agree not to qualify your report.

Required

(c) Explain the procedures that the directors must follow in order to remove your company as the auditors of LALD. **(6 marks)**

(Total = 20 marks)

74 Tye (6/09) — 36 mins

One of your audit clients is Tye Co a company providing petrol, aviation fuel and similar oil based products to the government of the country it is based in. Although the company is not listed on any stock exchange, it does follow best practice regarding corporate governance regulations. The audit work for this year is complete, apart from the matter referred to below.

As part of Tye Co's service contract with the government, it is required to hold an emergency inventory reserve of 6,000 barrels of aviation fuel. The inventory is to be used if the supply of aviation fuel is interrupted due to unforeseen events such as natural disaster or terrorist activity.

This fuel has in the past been valued at its cost price of $15 a barrel. The current value of aviation fuel is $120 a barrel. Although the audit work is complete, as noted above, the directors of Tye Co have now decided to show the 'real' value of this closing inventory in the financial statements by valuing closing inventory of fuel at market value, which does not comply with relevant accounting standards. The draft financial statements of Tye Co currently show a profit of approximately $500,000 with net assets of $170 million.

Required

(a) List the audit procedures and actions that you should now take in respect of the above matter. **(6 marks)**

(b) *For the purposes of this section assume from part (a) that the directors have agreed to value inventory at $15/barrel.*

Having investigated the matter in part (a) above, the directors present you with an amended set of financial statements showing the emergency reserve stated not at 6,000 barrels, but reported as 60,000 barrels. The final financial statements now show a profit following the inclusion of another 54,000 barrels of oil in inventory. When queried about the change from 6,000 to 60,000 barrels of inventory, the finance director stated that this change was made to meet expected amendments to emergency reserve requirements to be published in about six months time. The inventory will be purchased this year, and no liability will be shown in the financial statements for this future purchase. The finance director also pointed out that part of Tye Co's contract with the government requires Tye Co to disclose an annual profit and that a review of bank loans is due in three months. Finally the finance director stated that if your audit firm qualifies the financial statements in respect of the increase in inventory, they will not be recommended for re-appointment at the annual general meeting. The finance director refuses to amend the financial statements to remove this 'fictitious' inventory.

Required

(i) State the external auditor's responsibilities regarding the detection of fraud; **(4 marks)**

(ii) Discuss to which groups the auditors of Tye Co could report the 'fictitious' aviation fuel inventory; **(6 marks)**

(iii) Discuss the safeguards that the auditors of Tye Co can use in an attempt to overcome the intimidation threat from the directors of Tye Co. **(4 marks)**

(Total = 20 marks)

75 Eastvale (Pilot Paper) **36 mins**

EastVale Co manufactures a range of dairy products (for example, milk, yoghurt and cheese) in one factory. Products are stored in a nearby warehouse (which is rented by EastVale) before being sold to 350 supermarkets located within 200 kilometres of EastVale's factory. The products are perishable with an average shelf life of eight days. EastVale's financial statements year-end is 31 July.

It is four months since the year-end at your audit client of EastVale and the annual audit of EastVale is almost complete, but the auditor's report has not been signed.

The following events have just come to your attention. Both events occurred in late November.

(a) A fire in the warehouse rented by the company has destroyed 60% of the inventory held for resale.

(b) A batch of cheese produced by EastVale was found to contain some chemical impurities. Over 300 consumers have complained about food poisoning after eating the cheese. 115 supermarkets have stopped purchasing EastVale's products and another 85 are considering whether to stop purchasing from EastVale. Lawyers acting on behalf of the consumers are now presenting a substantial claim for damages against EastVale.

Required

In respect of each of the events at EastVale Co mentioned above:

(i) Describe the additional audit procedures you will carry out; **(8 marks)**

(ii) State, with reasons, whether or not the financial statements for the year-end require amendment; and **(6 marks)**

(iii) Discuss whether or not the audit report should be modified. **(6 marks)**

(*Note*. The total marks will be split equally between each event.)

(Total = 20 marks)

76 OilRakers (AIR 12/05) **36 mins**

(a) ISA 560 *Subsequent Events* explains the audit work required in connection with subsequent events.

Required

List the audit procedures that can be used prior to the auditors' report being signed to identify events that may require adjustment or disclosure in the financial statements. **(5 marks)**

(b) You are the auditor of OilRakers, a limited liability company which extracts, refines and sells oil and petroleum related products.

The audit of OilRakers for the year ended 30 June 20X5 had the following events:

Date	**Event**
15 August 20X5	Bankruptcy of major customer representing 11% of the trade receivables on the statement of financial position.
21 September 20X5	Financial statements approved by directors.
22 September 20X5	Audit work completed and auditors' report signed.
1 November 20X5	Accidental release of toxic chemicals into the sea from the company's oil refinery resulting in severe damage to the environment. Management had amended and made adequate disclosure of the event in the financial statements.
23 November 20X5	Financial statements issued to members of OilRakers.
30 November 20X5	A fire at one of the company's oil wells completely destroys the well. Drilling a new well will take ten months with a consequent loss in oil production during this time.

Required

For each of the following three dates:

- 15 August 20X5;
- 1 November 20X5; and
- 30 November 20X5.

(i) State whether the events occurring on those dates are adjusting or non-adjusting according to IAS 10 *Events after the reporting period*, giving reasons for your decision. **(6 marks)**

(ii) Explain the auditor's responsibility and the audit procedures that should be carried out. **(9 marks)**

(*Note:* Marks are allocated evenly across the three dates.) **(Total = 20 marks)**

77 ZeeDiem (12/08) — 36 mins

The date is 3 December 20X8. The audit of ZeeDiem Co is nearly complete and the financial statements and the audit report are due to be signed next week. However, the following additional information on two material events has just been presented to the auditor. The company's year end was 30 September 2008.

Event 1 – Occurred on 10 October 20X8

The springs in a new type of mattress have been found to be defective making the mattress unsafe for use. There have been no sales of this mattress; it was due to be marketed in the next few weeks. The company's insurers estimate that inventory to the value of $750,000 has been affected. The insurers also estimate that the mattresses are now only worth $225,000. No claim can be made against the supplier of springs as this company is in liquidation with no prospect of any amounts being paid to third parties. The insurers will not pay ZeeDiem for the fall in value of the inventory as the company was underinsured. All of this inventory was in the finished goods store at the end of the year and no movements of inventory have been recorded post year-end.

Event 2 – Occurred 5 November 20X8

Production at the ShamEve factory was halted for one day when a truck carrying dye used in colouring the fabric on mattresses reversed into a metal pylon, puncturing the vehicle allowing dye to spread across the factory premises and into a local river. The Environmental Agency is currently considering whether the release of dye was in breach of environmental legislation. The company's insurers have not yet commented on the event.

Required

(a) For each of the two events above:

(i) Explain whether the events are adjusting or non-adjusting according to IAS 10 *Events After the Reporting Period.* **(4 marks)**

(ii) Explain the auditors' responsibility and the audit procedures and actions that should be carried out according to ISA 560 *Subsequent Events.* **(12 marks)**

(b) Assume that the date is now 20 December 20X8, the financial statements and the audit report have just been signed, and the annual general meeting is to take place on 10 January 20X9. The Environmental Agency has issued a report stating that ZeeDiem Co is in breach of environmental legislation and a fine of $900,000 will now be levied on the company. The amount is material to the financial statements.

Required

Explain the additional audit work the auditor should carry out in respect of this fine. **(4 marks)**

(Total = 20 marks)

78 Green (AIR 6/07) **36 mins**

Green Co grows crops on a large farm according to strict organic principles that prohibit the use of artificial pesticides and fertilizers. The farm has an 'organic certification', which guarantees its products are to be organic. The certification has increased its sales of flour, potatoes and other products, as customers seek to eat more healthily.

Green Co is run by two managers who are the only shareholders. Annual revenue is $50 million with a net profit of 5%. Both managers have run other businesses in the last 10 years. One business was closed due to suspected tax fraud (although no case was ever brought to court).

Green Co's current auditors provide audit services. Additional assurance on business controls and the preparation of financial statements are provided by a different accountancy firm.

Last year, a neighbouring farm, Black Co started growing genetically modified (GM) crops, the pollen from which blows over Green Co's fields on a regular basis. This is a threat to Green Co's organic status because organic crops must not be contaminated with GM material. Green Co is considering court action against Black Co for loss of income and to stop Black Co growing GM crops.

You are an audit partner in Lime & Co, a 15 partner firm of auditors and business advisors. You have been friends with the managers of Green Co for the last 15 years, advising them on an informal basis. The managers of Green Co have indicated that the audit will be put out to tender next month and have asked your audit firm to tender for the audit and the provision of other professional services.

Required

(a) Using the information provided, identify and explain the ethical threats that could affect Lime. **(8 marks)**

(b) In respect of the going concern concept:

(i) Define 'going concern' and state two situations in which it should NOT be applied in the preparation of financial statements; **(3 marks)**

(ii) Explain the directors' responsibilities and the auditors' responsibilities regarding financial statements prepared on the going concern principle. **(4 marks)**

(c) List the audit procedures that should be carried out to determine whether or not the going concern basis is appropriate for Green Co. **(5 marks)**

(Total = 20 marks)

79 Smithson (6/08) **36 mins**

Smithson Co provides scientific services to a wide range of clients. Typical assignments range from testing food for illegal additives to providing forensic analysis on items used to commit crimes to assist law enforcement officers.

The annual audit is nearly complete. As audit senior you have reported to the engagement partner that Smithson is having some financial difficulties. Income has fallen due to the adverse effect of two high-profile court cases, where Smithson's services to assist the prosecution were found to be in error. Not only did this provide adverse publicity for Smithson, but a number of clients withdrew their contracts. A senior employee then left Smithson, stating lack of investment in new analysis machines was increasing the risk of incorrect information being provided by the company.

A cash flow forecast prepared internally shows Smithson requiring significant additional cash within the next 12 months to maintain even the current level of services. Smithson's auditors have been asked to provide a negative assurance report on this forecast.

Required

(a) Define 'going concern' and discuss the auditor's responsibilities in respect of going concern. **(4 marks)**

(b) State the audit procedures that may be carried out to try to determine whether or not Smithson Co is a going concern. **(8 marks)**

(c) Explain the audit procedures the auditor may take where the auditor has decided that Smithson Co is unlikely to be a going concern. **(4 marks)**

(d) In the context of the cash flow forecast, define the term 'negative assurance' and explain how this differs from the assurance provided by an audit report on statutory financial statements. **(4 marks)**

(Total = 20 marks)

REPORTING

Questions 80 – 85 cover Reporting, the subject of Part G of the BPP Study Text for F8.

80 Terms, evidence and modified reports (Pilot Paper) (amended) — 18 mins

(a) ISA 210 *Agreeing the terms of audit engagements* explains the content and use of engagement letters.

Required

State six items that could be included in an engagement letter. **(3 marks)**

(b) ISA 500 *Audit evidence* explains types of audit evidence that the auditor can obtain.

Required

State, and briefly explain, four types of audit evidence that can be obtained by the auditor. **(4 marks)**

(c) ISA 705 *Modifications to the opinion in the independent auditor's report* sets out the different types of modified opinions.

Required

State three ways in which an auditor's opinion may be modified and briefly explain each modification. **(3 marks)**

(Total = 10 marks)

81 Reporting — 18 mins

(a) ISA 720 *The auditor's responsibilities relating to other information in documents containing audited financial statements* provides guidance in relation to other information.

Required

List six examples of other information in documents containing audited financial statements. **(3 marks)**

(b) ISA 700 *Forming an opinion and reporting on financial statements* explains the form and content of external audit reports.

Required

List the main elements of the external audit report. **(3 marks)**

(c) ISRE 2400 *Engagements to review financial statements* provides guidance on reports for review engagements.

Required

Briefly explain the types of modified report that can be produced when matters have come to the attention of the auditor who has undertaken a review engagement. **(4 marks)**

(Total = 10 marks)

82 Corsco (AIR 12/03) (amended) — 36 mins

(a) Describe external auditor's responsibilities and the work that the auditor must perform in relation to the going concern status of companies. **(5 marks)**

(b) Describe the possible audit reports that can be issued where the going concern status of a company is called into question; your answer should describe the circumstances in which they can be issued. **(5 marks)**

Corsco is a large telecommunications company that is listed on a stock exchange. It is highly geared because, like many such companies, it borrowed a large sum to pay for a licence to operate a mobile phone network with technology that has not proved popular. The company's share price has dropped by 50% during the last three years and there have been several changes of senior management during that period. There has been considerable speculation in the press over the last six months about whether the company can survive without being taken over by a rival. There have been three approaches made to the company by other companies regarding a possible takeover but all have failed, mainly because the bidders pulled out of the deal as a result of the drop in share prices generally.

The company has net assets, but has found it necessary to severely curtail its capital investment program. Some commentators consider this to be fundamental to the future growth of the business, others consider that the existing business is fundamentally sound. It has also been necessary for the company to restructure its finances. Detailed disclosures of all of these matters have always been made in the financial statements. No reference has been made to the going concern status of the company in previous auditor's reports on financial statements and the deterioration in circumstances in the current year is no worse than it has been in previous years.

Required

(c) On the basis of the information provided above, describe the audit report that you consider is likely to be issued in the case of Corsco, giving reasons. **(4 marks)**

(d) Explain the difficulties that would be faced by Corsco and its auditors if Corsco's audit report made reference to going concern issues. **(6 marks)**

(Total = 20 marks)

83 Hood Enterprises (AIR 6/05) (amended) 36 mins

You are the audit manager of Hood Enterprises a limited liability company. The company's annual turnover is over $10 million.

Required

(a) Compare the responsibilities of the directors and auditors regarding the published financial statements of Hood Enterprises. **(6 marks)**

(b) Extracts from the draft audit report produced by an audit junior are given below:

'We have audited the accompanying financial statements of Hood Enterprises Limited which comprise........We have also evaluated the overall adequacy of the presentation of information in the company's annual report.'

Auditor's Responsibility

....We conducted our audit in accordance with Auditing Standards. Those standards require that we comply with ethical requirements and plan and perform the audit so that we can confirm the financial statements are free from material misstatement. The directors however are wholly responsible for the accuracy of the financial statements and no liability for errors can be accepted by the auditor.

An audit involves performing procedures to obtain as much audit evidence as possible in the time available about the amounts and disclosures in the financial statements.

An audit also includes evaluating the appropriateness of accounting policies used and the reasonableness of all accounting estimates made by management as well as evaluating the presentation of the financial statements......'

Required

Identify and explain the errors in the above extract.
Note. You are not required to redraft the report. **(10 marks)**

(c) The directors of Hood Enterprises have prepared a cash flow forecast for submission to the bank. They have asked you as the auditor to provide a negative assurance report on this forecast.

Required

Briefly explain the difference between positive and negative assurance, outlining the advantages to the directors of providing negative assurance on their cash flow forecast. **(4 marks)**

(Total = 20 marks)

84 MSV (AIR 6/07) (amended) 36 mins

(a) ISA 700 *Forming an opinion and reporting on financial statements* indicates the basic elements that will ordinarily be included in the audit report.

Required

List six basic elements of an auditor's report. Briefly explain why each element is included in the report. **(6 marks)**

(b) You are the audit manager in charge of the audit of MSV Co for the year ended 28 February 20X7. MSV Co is based in a seaside town and hires motor boats and yachts to individuals for amounts of time between one day and one week. The majority of receipts are in cash, with a few customers paying by debit card. Consequently, there are no trade receivables on the statement of financial position. The main non-current assets are the motor boats and yachts. The company is run by four directors who are also the major shareholders. Total income for the year was about $10 million.

The following issues have been identified during the audit.

Issue 1

Audit tests on sales indicate a deficiency in the internal control system, with a potential understatement of income in the region of $500,000. The deficiency occurred because sales invoices are not sequentially numbered, allowing one of the directors to remove cash sales prior to recording in the sales day book. This was identified during analytical procedures of sales, when the audit senior noted that on the days when this director was working, sales were always lower than on the days when the director was not working. **(8 marks)**

Issue 2

During testing of non-current assets, one yacht was found to be located at the property of one of the directors. This yacht has not been hired out during the year and enquiries indicate that the director makes personal use of it. The yacht is included in the non-current assets balance in the financial statements. **(6 marks)**

Required

For each of the issues above:

(i) List the audit procedures you should conduct to reach a conclusion on these issues;

(ii) Assuming that you have performed all the audit procedures that you can, but the issues are still unresolved, explain the potential effect (if any) on the audit report.

Note. The mark allocation is shown against each of the two issues.

(Total = 20 marks)

85 Galartha (12/07) **36 mins**

(a) You are the audit manager in JonArc & Co. One of your new clients this year is Galartha Co, a company having net assets of $15 million. The audit work has been completed, but there is one outstanding matter you are currently investigating; the directors have decided not to provide depreciation on buildings in the financial statements, although International Accounting Standards suggest that depreciation should be provided.

Required

State the additional audit procedures and actions you should now take in respect of the above matter. **(6 marks)**

(b) Unfortunately, you have been unable to resolve the matter regarding depreciation of buildings; the directors insist on not providing depreciation. You have therefore drafted the following extracts for your proposed audit report.

1. '...We conducted our audit in accordance with International Standards on Auditing. Those Standards require that we comply with ethical requirements and plan and perform the audit to obtain reasonable assurance about whether the financial statements are free from material misstatement (remaining words are the same as a normal unmodified report).
2. As discussed in Note 15 to the financial statements, no depreciation has been provided in the financial statements which practice, in our opinion, is not in accordance with International Accounting Standards.
3. The provision for the year ended 31 September 20X7, should be $420,000 based on the straight-line method of depreciation using an annual rate of 5% for the buildings.
4. Accordingly, the non-current assets should be reduced by accumulated depreciation of $1,200,000 and the profit for the year and accumulated reserve should be decreased by $420,000 and $1,200,000, respectively.
5. In our opinion, except for the effect on the financial statements of the matter referred to in the preceding paragraph, the financial statements present fairly, in all material respects ... (remaining words are the same as for an unmodified opinion paragraph).'

The extracts have been numbered to help you refer to them in your answer.

Required

Explain the meaning and purpose of each of the above extracts in your draft audit report. **(10 marks)**

(c) State the effect on your audit report of the following alternative situations:

(i) Depreciation had not been provided on any non-current asset for a number of years, the effect of which if corrected would be to turn an accumulated profit into a significant accumulated loss.

(ii) JonArc & Co were appointed auditors after the end of the financial year of Galartha Co. Consequently, the auditors could not attend the year end inventory count. Inventory is material to the financial statements.

(*Note.* You are not required to draft any audit reports.) **(4 marks)**

(Total = 20 marks)

Answers

ACCA examiner's answers

Remember that you can access the ACCA examiner's solutions to questions marked '**Pilot paper**', '**12/07**', '**6/08**' or '**12/08**' on the BPP website using the following link:

www.bpp.com/acca/examiner-solutions

Additional question guidance

Remember that you can find additional guidance to certain questions on the BPP website using the following link:

www.bpp.com/acca/extra-question-guidance

1 Audit regulation

Text reference. Chapter 2

Top tips. This question is a good test of your knowledge of audit regulation. There are two parts for five marks each so your answers need to be fairly detailed. The key is to make sure you stick to the correct time allocation – so don't spend longer than nine minutes on each part. Use short paragraphs in your answer.

Easy marks. This question should be straightforward to answer.

(a) **Development of ISAs**

ISAs are set by IAASB, the International Auditing and Assurance Standards Board, which is a technical standing committee of IFAC, the International Federation of Accountants.

ISAs are developed in consultation with interested parties within the profession and outside of it. They are also developed with due regard for national standards on auditing.

Subjects for detailed study are selected by a subcommittee established for that purpose. The IAASB delegates to the subcommittee the initial responsibility for the preparation and drafting of auditing standards and statements.

As a result of the study, an exposure draft is prepared for consideration. If approved, the exposure draft is distributed for comment by member bodies of IFAC and to other interested parties.

Comments received in response to the exposure draft are then considered and it may be revised as a result. If this revised exposure draft is approved, it is issued as a definitive International Standard on Auditing or as an International Auditing Practice Statement.

(b) **Role of professional bodies in the regulation of auditors**

One of the key professional bodies is the ACCA.

The role of the ACCA varies from country to country depending on the legal requirements for the regulation of auditors in those countries.

In some countries governments regulate auditors directly, in others, the profession is self-regulating or a mixture of the two. In Europe, there is a tradition of government being directly involved in the regulation of auditors.

However, in the UK, regulation of the profession is devolved to Recognised Supervisory Bodies (RSB) and ACCA is one such RSB.

Training and entry requirements

The ACCA imposes certain requirements which must be fulfilled before a person can become a member of ACCA, and student members have to qualify by passing exams and fulfilling training requirements. There is also a commitment to Continuing Professional Development (CPD).

Ethics

The ACCA issues an ethical code which all students and members must comply with.

Investigation and discipline

The ACCA monitors its members' work and conduct and may impose punitive measures such as fines or exclusion from membership.

2 Corporate governance

(a) Voluntary codes of corporate governance

Advantages of voluntary codes	Disadvantages of voluntary codes
Allow organisation to maintain flexibility	Risk of non-compliance with the code
Irrelevant areas can be left unapplied	Results in lack of comparability between companies
Potential saving of unnecessary implementation costs	Difficult for shareholders to make investment decisions

(b) Requirements of the board

- Every company should be headed by an effective board
- There should be clear division of responsibilities at the head of the company between running the board and executive responsibility for running the business
- A balance of executive and non-executive directors
- A formal, rigorous and transparent procedure for appointment of new directors
- Induction for all directors on joining the board
- Formal and rigorous annual evaluation of the board's own performance, its committees and individual directors
- Planned and progressive refreshing of the board with all directors to be submitted for re-election at regular intervals

(*Note.* Only four were required.)

(c) Audit committee

An audit committee is a sub-committee of the board of directors of a company and usually comprises a number of non-executive directors.

The objectives of such a committee include monitoring the integrity of the financial statements, reviewing the company's internal financial controls and risk management systems, monitoring the effectiveness of internal audit, monitoring the external auditor's independence and objectivity and making recommendations in respect of the appointment of the external auditor.

The Combined Code recommends that the board establishes an audit committee consisting of at least three (or, in the case of smaller companies, two) members who should all be independent non-executive directors.

3 Ethical issues

Text reference. Chapter 4

Top tips. As this is a 10 mark question, you must not run over time – don't spend more than nine minutes on each part. Part (a) is straightforward. Part (b) is trickier but if you are familiar with this area, you should find it no problem.

Easy marks. Part (a) is where you will find the easier marks in this question.

(a) Threats to independence and objectivity

Self-review

A self-review threat may occur when a previous judgement needs to be re-evaluated by members responsible for that judgement. Examples include providing internal audit and tax services to an external audit client.

Self-interest

A self-interest threat may occur as a result of the financial or other interests of members or of immediate or **close family** members. Examples include gifts and hospitality and overdue fees.

Advocacy

An advocacy threat arises when an audit firm promotes a position or opinion to the point that subsequent objectivity is compromised. An example would be acting as an advocate on behalf of an assurance client in litigation or disputes with third parties.

Familiarity

A familiarity threat arises when, because of a close relationship, members become too sympathetic to the interests of others. This can result in a substantial risk of loss of professional scepticism. An example would be long association with an audit client.

Intimidation

An intimidation threat arises when members of the assurance team may be deterred from acting objectively by threats, actual or perceived. Examples include family and personal relationships, litigation, and close business relationships.

(b) Confidentiality

The fundamental principle of confidentiality requires members of the ACCA to refrain from disclosing information acquired during the course of professional work. Information may only be disclosed where the client has given consent, there is a public duty to disclose, or there is a legal or professional right or duty to disclose. Information acquired in the course of professional work must not be used for personal advantage or for the advantage of a third party.

Obligatory disclosure

- Money laundering
- Treason
- Drug-trafficking
- Terrorism

Voluntary disclosure

- Necessary to protect the member's interests
- Disclosure is compelled by process of law
- Public duty to disclose
- Disclosure is to non-governmental bodies which have statutory powers to compel disclosure

4 External audit

Text references. Chapters 1 and 7

Top tips. Read the requirements carefully.

Part (a) asks for an explanation of the purpose and role of the audit in the context of a large company.

For 10 marks it is clearly not going to be enough to give a basic definition so you need to think about how to expand on the definition.

This requirement does not give you any help in structuring your answer so before you start to write decide on two or three headings to use and plan how you will arrange the points you want to make under these headings.

Part (b) is more clearly sub-divided. The requirement asks about the interim and final audit and the body of the question lists out the main procedures at each of these stages. You should be able to use this as a plan for your answer.

Notice that it is not **enough** to list procedures; the requirement asks you to '**explain**'. Re-read the points you have made to check that each is **explained**.

Easy marks. In part (a) there are few easy marks, but you should be able to explain in general terms the purpose and role of an audit.

In part (b) the easy marks were to be found by looking at each stage of the audit flagged in the question and explaining one or two basic procedures for each.

Examiner's comments. In part (a), most candidates made important statements regarding the purpose of the audit in terms of providing an opinion on the financial statements. However, following this, most answers tended to spend an excessive amount of time explaining issues of auditor independence and liability rather than focusing on other purposes of an audit.

Common errors included focusing the answers on too few points and not considering the effect of the audit on third parties.

Part (b) was answered well where candidates provided an overview of the procedures and processes, mentioning six to eight different points in their answers. The main area where comment was not expected in answers was on the initial process of client acceptance, as the implication was that the client had been accepted and the interim audit was commencing. A common error was spending too much time on one area, especially the determination of audit risk and explanation of the risk model.

Marking scheme

		Marks
(a)	Training material: purpose of external audit and its role Up to 2 marks per point to a maximum of	10
(b)	Main audit procedures and processes: interim and final audit Up to 1 mark per point to a maximum of	10
		20

(a) **Purpose and role of external audit**

Basic definition

(i) The objective of an audit of financial statements is to enable the auditor to express an opinion whether the financial statements are prepared, in all material respects, in accordance with an applicable accounting framework. The opinion is often worded as ...*give a true and fair view.*

(ii) The nature of the audit is to give reasonable (but not absolute) assurance that the financial statements are free from material misstatement. This should add to the credibility of the financial statements.

Regulatory framework

(i) In a large company, the owners of the business, the shareholders, are unlikely to be involved in the management of the business and therefore depend on the information provided to them by the directors to let them assess the performance of the business and to make decisions such as whether to stay invested in that business or how to cast their votes in respect of the directors' appointment.

(ii) The directors have a duty of stewardship of the company on behalf of the shareholders and the preparation of annual financial statements is part of their accountability towards the shareholders. An unmodified audit opinion should reassure the shareholders that the information is free from any significant misstatement or manipulation.

(iii) The role of the auditor is that of an independent expert who gathers evidence and issues an opinion that will indicate, to shareholders and other third parties who may use the financial statements, the degree of reliance that should be placed on the information. Third parties who may benefit from the assurance given in the auditor's report could include lenders, potential investors or potential suppliers.

(iv) Under the legal framework, and the rules of recognised professional bodies such as the ACCA, there are strict requirements as to who may carry out audits to ensure that only properly qualified people can perform this service. The ACCA also issues ethical rules to ensure that the auditor is genuinely independent. This regulatory framework should maintain the credibility of the role of the audit.

(b) (i) **Main audit procedures and practices during the interim audit**

(1) The auditor will obtain a thorough knowledge of the business by discussion with client management and reading relevant trade publications.

(2) Preliminary analytical procedures will be performed on interim accounts in order to identify any major changes in the business or unexpected trends.

(3) The client's accounting systems will be documented, or documentation prepared in prior year audits will be updated.

(4) An assessment will be made of **inherent risk** and **control risk**.

(5) An appropriate **materiality** level will be estimated.

(6) The information obtained during the planning stage will be **documented** along with an outline of the audit strategy to be followed.

(7) If control risk has been assessed as low in particular areas, then **controls testing** will need to be performed on the controls to confirm the initial assessment of the risk. These tests of controls will be started at the interim audit although they will generally need to be performed on a sample of items extending right over the accounting period so may need to be completed at the final audit.

(8) The **detailed audit approach** should be prepared. Programmes of audit procedures, both tests of controls and substantive procedures, will be designed to show the work that needs to be done and to enable subsequent review of audit completion.

(9) If substantive procedures are to be performed that involve checking a sample of transactions selected to cover the whole accounting period, it is likely that some of these procedures will also be started at the interim audit, but these will again be completed at the final audit.

(ii) **Main audit procedures and practices during the final audit**

(1) The tests that were started at the interim visit, both tests of controls and substantive procedures should be completed.

(2) Year-end balances may be verified through confirmations obtained from third parties such as:

- Receivables
- Payables
- Banks

(3) If the client has carried out a year-end inventory count, detailed procedures will be carried out to check the accuracy of the compilation of the year-end inventory listing and also to follow up any evidence gathered by the auditor when attending the inventory count.

(4) Detailed calculations will need to be obtained of any estimates the client has made at the year-end such as allowances for receivables, depreciation and provisions. Procedures will need to be performed to:

- Assess the reasonableness of the methods used to make the estimates
- Check the calculations; or
- Develop point estimates to evaluate management's point estimates.

(5) Analytical procedures will be performed on the draft accounts to consider whether the view given by the financial statements is in line with the auditor's understanding of the business.

(6) The auditor must review the directors' assessment of whether the business is a going concern. The auditor must consider whether the assumptions made by the directors are reasonable and whether it is appropriate to prepare the accounts on the going concern basis.

(7) A review of events after the reporting period must be performed in order to assess whether any appropriate adjustments or disclosures as required by IAS 10 have been dealt with correctly.

5 International Standards on Auditing

Text reference. Chapter 2

Top tips. Make sure you answer each requirement in turn, putting your answer in the required letter format, and using sub-headings based on the requirements to give your answer more structure.

Easy marks. As suggested above, easy marks are available if your knowledge in this area of the syllabus is sound.

Examiner's comments. This question was based on a short scenario, but otherwise was essentially factual, requiring knowledge of the ISA setting process.

Most candidates provided a letter to their friend, obtaining some presentation marks. Part (a) was almost always well answered, with many candidates obtaining full marks. Part (b) caused some confusion, although the key points regarding how different jurisdictions apply ISAs were normally made. In part (c), most candidates correctly stated that auditors should follow ISAs. In part (d), again, most candidates correctly noted that ISAs apply to any size of entity.

Weaknesses included explaining what happens when a company does not follow an ISA, rather than when an audit or does not follow an ISA, stating that small companies did not need an audit, without then going on to show that the principles of ISAs actually applied to any size of entity and in the UK, explaining the process of SAS setting rather than ISA setting.

Marking scheme

		Marks
One mark for each valid point		
(a)	Due process to produce an ISA	
	Subcommittee – areas for ISAs	1
	Exposure draft (ED) via IAASB and issued	1
	Comments on ED	1
	Amendment of ED and issue of ISA	1
	Other relevant points (each)	1
	Maximum marks	**4**
(b)	Authority of ISAs	
	Apply to audit of FS	1
	May apply to other statements	1
	Basic principles in bold type	1
	Explanatory text in normal type	1
	Must read all ISA to understand application	1
	ISA not override requirements of national countries	1
	Where relevant country use ISA and not issue own guidance	1
	National requirements differ – use national	1
	Adopt changes so that the ISA can be used	1
	Other relevant points (each)	1
	Maximum marks	**8**
(c)	Extent to which auditor follows ISAs	
	Should follow wherever possible	1
	Do not follow where audit more efficient	1
	Must justify departure	1
	Other relevant points (each)	1
	Maximum marks	**4**

		Marks
(d)	ISAs apply to small entities	
	Applicable to any entity	1
	Appropriate ISAs to be followed	1
	Letter format/why writing	1
	Other relevant points (each)	1
	Maximum marks	4
		20

1 Any Road
Any Town
NT1 1ZZ

Dear Carmen,

Thanks for your letter, it was really nice to hear from you.

I'm going to set out in my letter the queries you raised regarding the regulatory framework which applies to auditors.

(a) *The due process of the IAASB involved in producing an ISA*

ISAs are produced by the **International Auditing and Assurance Standards Board**, IAASB, which is a technical standing committee of the International Federation of Accountants, IFAC.

Initially an **exposure draft** is produced for consideration by the IAASB. If this is approved, it is circulated to the member bodies of the IFAC (such as ACCA) and any other interested parties. It is also published on the IAASB's website. These bodies make **comments** on the exposure draft which is then amended as necessary. The exposure draft is then re-issued as an ISA or an International Auditing Practice Statement, IAPS.

(b) *The overall authority of ISAs and how they are applied in individual countries*

ISAs must be applied in the audits of historical financial information.

ISAs contain **auditor's objectives, basic principles** and **requirements** (including essential procedures) together with related guidance in the form of explanatory and other material. The whole text must be considered in order to understand and apply the basic principles and essential procedures.

ISAs do not override the requirements for the audit of entities in individual countries. To the extent that ISAs conform with local regulations in regard to a particular subject, the audit in that country in accordance with local regulations will automatically comply with the ISA on that subject. Where local regulations differ from or conflict with ISAs, member bodies should comply with the obligations of members in the IFAC constitution, ie encourage changes in local regulations to comply with ISAs.

(c) *The extent to which an auditor must follow ISAs*

There may be **exceptional circumstances** under which the auditor may judge it necessary to depart from an ISA in order to achieve the objective of an audit more effectively. In this case, the auditor must be prepared to **justify** and document the reason for the departure. This situation is likely to be the exception rather than the rule.

(d) *The extent to which ISAs apply to small entities*

ISAs apply to the audit of financial information of any entity, regardless of its size. However, small entities possess distinct characteristics, such as a **lack of segregation of duties**, which mean that auditors must adapt their audit approach when auditing the financial statements of a small company. This is likely to include a substantive-based audit approach and more reliance on written representations, for example.

The IAASB published a 'questions and answers' document in August 2009 which highlights how the design of the clarity ISAs enables them to be applied in a manner proportionate with the size and complexity of an entity. This publication is helpful for those firms auditing small companies.

I hope this helps. Please let me know if I can be of any more assistance to you. Hope to hear from you soon.

Yours sincerely,

Amy Chan

6 Jumper

Text reference. Chapter 3

Top tips. Make sure you answer this question using a memo format as stated in the requirement (presentation marks are available). The best way to approach this question is to take each issue in turn from the scenario and deal with it separately. Your answer should include sub-headings for each issue as this will give it more structure. A detailed knowledge of the Combined Code is not required so don't panic. Use the clues in the scenario, for example, the company does not have an internal audit department, Mr Sheppard is both the Chief Executive and the Chairman of the company.

Easy marks. There aren't many easy marks as such in this question but use the question scenario to structure your answer and apply your knowledge of corporate governance.

Examiner's comments. The overall standard for this answer was quite good, with many international stream candidates obtaining very high marks. However, common errors included providing a history of corporate governance regulations (normally with a UK focus), not explaining the points made, providing detailed lists on the work of an audit committee, not providing the memo format required by the question and thus not gaining the mark for presentation.

Marking scheme

	Marks
1 mark for identifying the corporate governance problem, 1 for explaining why this is a problem and 1 for recommending a solution	
CEO and chairman	3
Composition of board	3
Director appointment	3
Review of board appointment	3
Board pay	3
Internal control	3
Internal audit	3
Financial statements	3
Audit committee	
Other relevant points (each – but limit to 1.5 marks if not mentioned in the scenario)	1.5
Memo format/why writing	2
	20

Memorandum

To: Jumper & Co
From: A Manager, Tela & Co
Date: Today
Subject: SGCC and Corporate Governance

SGCC does not appear to be following corporate governance codes for a number of reasons which are outlined below. Recommendations of changes to address these weaknesses are also suggested.

Chief Executive and Chairman Roles

Mr Sheppard is both the Chief Executive Officer and the board chairman of the company. Corporate governance codes indicate that there should be a **clear division of responsibilities** between running the board of directors and running the company's business, ie no single individual should have unfettered powers of decision.

In order to address this, the company should appoint a **separate chairman** who meets the independence criteria set out in the codes. This would ensure that Mr Sheppard does not have too much power within the company.

Board Composition

The board consists of five executive and two non-executive directors. To follow good corporate governance practice, the board should consist of a **balance of executive and non-executive** (preferably independent) directors such that no one individual or group of individuals can dominate the board's decision-making. Half the board (excluding the chairman) should preferably be independent non-executive directors (unless the company is small). In the case of SGCC, there are only two non-executive directors out of seven and it is not clear how independent they are.

The company should appoint more independent non-executive directors to the board to achieve a balance of half non-executive directors and half executive directors.

Board Appointments

Mr Sheppard makes appointments to the board himself. Good corporate governance suggests that any appointments to the board should be done through a **nomination committee**, the majority of the members of which should be independent non-executive directors and which should be chaired by the chairman or an independent non-executive director. This ensures transparency of appointment of board members.

The company should establish a nomination committee consisting of mainly non-executive directors. Formal job descriptions should also be published to make the appointment process as transparent as possible.

Monitoring of Targets

At present there are no formal targets or reviews of board policies carried out. The board should undertake a formal and rigorous **review** of its own performance, its committees and of individual directors annually. This should also be stated in the annual report. The performance evaluation of the chairman should be undertaken by the non-executive directors.

SGCC should address this by ensuring that **performance targets are** set for each director and that their performance is reviewed annually. Non-executive directors should review the performance of the Chairman.

Remuneration of Board Members

Currently Mr Sheppard decides the level of remuneration for himself and the board members without considering performance. A significant proportion of executive directors' remuneration should be structured so that rewards are linked to performance. For non-executive directors, remuneration should reflect the time commitment and responsibilities of the role.

A **remuneration committee** should be set up for determining the level of remuneration for directors and no director should be involved in deciding his own remuneration. This committee should consist of at least three non-executive directors to set the remuneration for executive directors and the chairman. The remuneration of non-executive directors should be determined by the board itself (or the shareholders if required by the articles of association of the company).

Review of Internal Controls

The internal controls of the company are monitored by the senior accountant and a detailed review assumed to be undertaken by the external auditors. It is not sufficient to rely on this to test the overall effectiveness of controls within the company.

The board should conduct a review of the company's internal controls at least annually and report to shareholders that this has been undertaken. This could be facilitated by establishing an **internal audit department**.

Audit Committee

It is not clear whether there is an audit committee. Good corporate governance would require an **audit committee**, comprising at least three members who are independent non-executive directors, which can monitor the external auditors.

The board should set up an audit committee to allow them to maintain an appropriate relationship with the external auditors.

Internal Audit Department

SGCC does not have an internal audit department. Listed companies, such as SGCC, should **review the need** for an internal audit department at least annually.

Given the lack of formal controls at SGCC, an internal audit department should be established as soon as possible. It should report its findings to the audit committee.

Financial Statements

The company produces annual financial statements with detailed information on past performance. However, the board of directors should also produce information in the **annual report** setting out their view of how the company will perform in the future for the benefit of shareholders and potential investors.

Kind regards,

A Manager

7 ZX

Text references. Chapters 3 and 5

Top tips. Firstly note the requirement for a memo format – make sure you do this as marks are available for presentation. Structure your answer by using sub-headings for each of the two requirements. For both the requirements you are asked to 'explain' so make sure that you don't simply produce a list of points. You need to explain each point in order to score the marks available.

Easy marks. There were no very obvious easy marks in this question but at the time it was set, the examiner had recently written an article about the regulatory framework and corporate governance. If you had read that article it would have provided a basic framework that would let you identify some of the key principles of corporate governance that would have got you started in planning an answer.

Examiner's comments. The standard of answers to part (a) was unsatisfactory. The majority of answers took a page or two of the answer book to explain the background to corporate governance. This approach showed one of the classic mistakes in writing exam answers – not reading the question. The question was actually about the role of internal audit in corporate governance, not about the history of corporate governance. Reasons for weaker answers included:

- Not providing a memo format (one mark was available for this)
- Stating areas where internal audit could assist with corporate governance but not how that would be provided. For example, stating that internal audit could assist with fraud, but not stating that their presence could act as a deterrent.
- Explaining the duties of directors – not internal audit

Answers to part (b) were of a higher standard than those for part (a) mainly because candidates started writing straightaway about the advantages and disadvantages of an audit committee. Some weaker answers tended to explain the composition of the audit committee, rather than moving straight into the advantages and disadvantages.

Marking scheme

		Marks
(a)	Board reports	2
	Internal control	2
	Application of ISAs	2
	Communication with external auditors	2
	Communication to the board	2
	Risk management	2
	Prevent/detect fraud	2
	Allow other relevant points	2
	Maximum marks	**10**

		Marks
(b)	One mark for explaining the area and one mark for applying to the situation in ZX	
	Advantages	
	Public confidence	2
	Financial reporting	2
	Communication	2
	Friend of the board	2
	Disadvantages	
	Lack of understanding of function	2
	Role of non-executive directors	2
	Cost	2
	Allow other relevant points	2
	Maximum marks	**10**
		20

From: Chief Internal Auditor
To: Board of ZX Ltd
Subject: Role of Internal Audit and Audit Committee
Date: Today

(a) Areas where the internal audit department can assist the directors with the implementation of good corporate governance include:

(i) **Internal controls**

The directors are responsible for assessing the risks faced by the company, implementing appropriate controls and monitoring the effectiveness of those controls.

The internal audit department could assist the board in a number of ways:

- They could review the directors' risk assessment and report on its adequacy
- In certain areas (perhaps in respect of the accounting system) they could actually carry out the risk assessment
- They could review and report on the adequacy of the controls that are to be implemented
- They could carry out annual audits of the effectiveness of controls (performing tests of the controls), identifying weaknesses and making recommendations for improvements

It would be inappropriate for them to be involved at every stage, ie assessing risks, designing controls and reviewing their effectiveness as this would mean that they are checking their own work. This would undermine the credibility of their reports.

In some sense the existence of an internal audit serves as a control procedure in its own right. An example would be that the existence of an internal audit department is likely to act as a deterrent against fraud, and so helps the directors meet their responsibilities to implement appropriate controls to prevent and detect fraud.

(ii) **Financial statements**

Good corporate governance requires the directors to prepare financial statements that give a balanced and understandable view. As the internal audit department has experience in accounting and auditing and is led by a qualified Chartered Certified Accountant it can assist the directors in applying accounting standards and meeting the expectations of readers of the accounts (particularly as these expectations will greatly increase if ZX proceeds with the possible listing).

(iii) **Board reports**

A principle of good corporate governance is that the board should be properly briefed. The internal audit department can review the reports that are presented to the board to ensure that they are properly prepared and presented in a way that can be easily understood.

(iv) **Communication with external auditors**

Although it is mainly the audit committee (if one has been established) that will act as a channel of communication between the external auditors and the board, it will often be the case that the external and internal auditors will work together on some areas. This could be the case if the external auditor found it appropriate to rely on internal audit reports on some areas (for example, on periodic inventory counting procedures) or where the external auditor wants to extend computer assisted testing over the whole year under the supervision of the internal auditors. This could add value to information available to the board where areas have been considered by both groups of auditors.

(v) **Knowledge of corporate governance and auditing standards**

As qualified professionals the internal audit department will have up to date knowledge of corporate governance requirements and of developments in auditing standards. They will be able to help the board keep up to date with what is expected of them under the codes of corporate governance and with what will be expected of them from the external auditors.

(b) **Advantages and disadvantages of an audit committee**

(i) *Advantages*

Proposed listing

If ZX is listed it will in all probability have to follow tighter requirements such as the Combined Code on corporate governance in the UK. The establishment of an audit committee is considered good practice under this code. If ZX did not establish one it would have to disclose the non-compliance with the code in that respect and this might affect shareholder confidence in respect of the accounting and auditing functions within the company.

'Critical friend' of the board

An effective audit committee will be made up of individuals with relevant knowledge and experience, who are independent of the day-to-day running of the company. This will give the shareholders confidence that there is some independent oversight of the board which should help ensure that the company is being run in the best interests of the shareholders. They should also be able to advise the executive directors on areas such as corporate governance where their own knowledge may be incomplete.

Communication

The existence of an audit committee gives an effective channel of communication for the external auditors. It means there is a quasi-independent body with whom the external auditor can discuss contentious audit issues such as disagreements over accounting treatments rather than going directly to the board who have made the decisions on those matters.

This may increase stakeholders' confidence in the financial statements and the audit process.

Financial reporting

The non-executive directors are expected to have a good knowledge of financial reporting. In the case of ZX this should prove a useful source of advice to the board. Also, externally, it should increase confidence in the financial reporting processes and reports of ZX.

Appointment of external auditors

The audit committee, rather than the board, would recommend which auditors should be appointed. They would also review annually any circumstances, such as provision of other services, which might threaten the perceived independence of the external auditor. This should again increase the confidence that readers of the financial statements have in the objectivity of the opinion given by the external auditors and hence the credibility of the financial statements,

(ii) *Disadvantages*

Cost

Although the non-executive directors will not require full time salaries, the level of fees that will be required to attract suitably experienced individuals may be significant but must be weighed against the benefits which will be derived especially in view of the planned listing.

Knowledge and experience

The board may question whether individuals from outside ZX will have adequate experience of the business to make a useful contribution to the board. As explained above, it is their very independence that adds value to their role as well as their particular experience in respect of financial accounting and corporate governance issues.

Responsibilities

The current board may be concerned that the establishment of an audit committee of non-executive directors may diminish their powers in running the company. It could be seen as another tier of management. They should be assured that the audit committee would act in support of the board, not as an alternative to it.

8 Conoy

Text references. Chapters 3 and 5

Top tips. Part (a) is purely knowledge based and you should be familiar with contrasting the roles of the internal and external audit from your studies. Using a tabular approach will help to improve the clarity of your answer.

It is important you take account of Conoy's specific circumstances in part (b). You are given specific problems which an audit committee may help to alleviate, so these should form the basis of the benefits. For example, there is a lack of financial reporting expertise, so this is where a proposed audit committee can add significant value, especially as both the auditors and the bank have expressed concerns in this area.

Easy marks. Knowing how the roles of internal and external audit differ is essential. You should be able to obtain full marks in part (a).

Examiner's comments. In part (a) candidates could obtain full marks by identifying four areas to contrast internal and external auditors against (for example, who they reported to) and explain that difference in their answer. Many candidates provided this type of answer, many using a columnar format, which made for clear presentation and clarity of marking. Inadequate answers tended not to provide a clear contrast between the two sets of auditors or be presented as a one long paragraph making individual points difficult and sometimes impossible to identify.

In part (b) some satisfactory answers showing how an audit committee could assist the company in the scenario were produced. Many answers, however, tended to list the benefits of an audit committee with little or no reference to the detail in the scenario. The main weakness in many answers was explaining the constitution of the audit committee or the work of other committees rather than the benefit of an audit committee.

ACCA examiner's answer. The ACCA examiner's answer to this question can be found at the back of this kit.

Marking scheme

		Marks
(a)	**Difference – internal and external audit** 2 marks for each point. 1 for point in relation to internal audit and 1 for explaining the point in relation to external audit. – Objectives – Reporting – Scope of work – Relationship with company – Other relevant points **Maximum marks**	**8**
(b)	**Benefits of audit committee** Up to 2 marks for each point. 1 for the benefit and 1 for applying that benefit to Conoy Co. 1 mark only where point stated in general terms – Assistance with financial reporting – Enhance internal control systems – Reliance on external auditors – Appointment of external auditors – Best practice – corporate governance – Independent advice to board – Advice on risk management – Other valid points eg may be cost benefits over time. **Maximum marks**	**12**
		20

(a) **Internal and external auditors' roles contrasted**

	Internal audit	External audit
Objective	To add value and improve an organisation's operations.	To express an opinion on the truth and fairness of financial statements.
Reporting	Reports to the board of directors, or other people charged with governance, such as the audit committee. Reports are confidential between the auditors and the directors and management of the organisation.	Reports to the shareholders or members of a company on the truth and fairness of the accounts. Audit report is publicly available to the shareholders and other interested parties.
Scope	Work relates to the operations of the organisation.	Work relates to the financial statements.
Relationship with the company	Often employees of the organisation, although sometimes outsourced.	Independent of the company and its management. Usually appointed by the shareholders.

Top tip. In 4 (a) you could have also contrasted the roles in respect of **planning and the collection of evidence**. However, only four areas needed to be contrasted to pick up all of the available marks.

(b) **Benefits to Conoy of forming an audit committee**

Improved financial reporting

Now that the finance director has left, the company appears to have no-one internal with appropriate financial reporting knowledge for a company which appears to be of a considerable size (employing 2500 staff).

The establishment of an audit committee should include recruiting personnel with financial reporting experience, therefore improving the quality of financial reporting and allowing the board more time to concentrate on running operations, which is particularly important given their 'hands on' approach.

Strengthening the internal audit position

Currently the internal audit position is poorly supported and reports directly to the board who do not understand the reports. As a result the control environment will be weak resulting in low motivation to monitor and maintain important internal controls.

The establishment of an audit committee will strengthen the position of the internal audit function, by providing a greater degree of independence from management. It should also promote the need for a strong control environment to the board, which should then lead to implementation of an appropriate internal control system.

Strengthening the position of the external auditor

If internal audit findings are not understood, it is likely the same is true of weaknesses reported by external auditors Anders & Co.

The audit committee, if established, will strengthen the external auditor's position by providing a channel of communication and forum for issues of concern.

Strengthening the independence of the external auditor

The external auditors are currently appointed by the Conoy board. This could result in a familiarity threat to the independence of the external auditors if they develop too close a relationship with the board over time.

An audit committee can recommend the appointment of the external auditors based on appropriate criteria only (quality of service, independence and competence for example). This will help prevent such an independence issue arising.

Non-executive director

There are currently no non-executive directors and therefore no independent advice given when making key decisions.

Ideally there would be equal numbers of executive and non-executive directors; however the non-executive director appointed as part of the proposed audit committee may at least contribute an independent view.

Increased credibility

The bank's concerns over financial reporting highlights the company's failure to follow best practice when it comes to corporate governance and it is already affecting relations with stakeholders.

Establishing the audit committee should increase public confidence in the credibility and objectivity of Conoy's financial statements. It will also demonstrate to the bank that although Conoy is not required to comply with specific corporate governance regulation, the company is prepared to take steps to move towards corporate governance best practice.

Top tip. You may think of other valid benefits not listed above. As long as you clearly explain these, marks will be awarded accordingly.

9 Ethical dilemma

Text reference. Chapter 4

Top tips. This question looked at the issue of an ethical dilemma faced by an internal auditor. The key here is to use a little common sense and to ensure that the comments which you make are as specific to the scenario as possible. Part (b) is a more typical type of question but you do need to think carefully about the impact which the situation has on the audit report.

Easy marks. Part (a) is the more straightforward section.

Examiner's comments. On the whole part (a) was well answered with most candidates being aware of the fact that a member of the ACCA should not falsify documents even if instructed to do so by his employer. A number of candidates said that they would inform the bank of the situation, therefore breaching confidentiality. This course of action would normally only be taken regarding issues of national security or public interest. Part (b) was not well answered with many candidates showing a lack of understanding of the effect of the issue on the auditors' report.

Marking scheme

		Marks
(a)	Request to alter accounts Up to 2 marks per point up to a maximum of	10
(b)	Implications for the audit, the auditor's report and the relationship between the firm and the client Up to 2 marks per point up to a maximum of	10
		20

(a) **Course of action**

(i) *Legitimate changes*

The action taken will depend on the **nature of the changes** made to the documents. Bad debt and depreciation charges are balances which are subject to a great deal of judgement. They are not absolutes and are often revised from one period to the next. Provided that any changes made to these are in order to present information more fairly, rather than to achieve specific results, the internal auditor would be able to accept these as **legitimate**. For example information about the recoverability of certain debts may have been received or perhaps the usage of certain assets may have been revised. Whilst these types of change do not constitute changes in policy and therefore do not need to be disclosed in the financial statements it would be important to bring them to the attention of the bank.

Before the internal auditor could sign off the documentation he would review the records to ensure that they do in fact show that the bank's targets have been met.

(ii) *Falsification of records*

It would be **unethical** for a member of the ACCA to falsify the internal control records and it would be in contravention of the ACCA's *Code of Ethics and Conduct*. Depending on the nature of the alterations they could constitute fraud which is a criminal offence.

As the internal auditor is being asked to do this by his employer it is obviously a difficult situation. Steps which he might take would include discussing the matter with the Board of Directors and the Audit Committee to ensure that they are aware of the legal implications. Concerns should also be made in writing.

The internal auditor may also wish to **seek legal advice** in order to protect himself and could also contact the ACCA for clarification of the ethical implications.

The internal auditor should not bring the issue to the attention of the bank as this would be a **breach of confidentiality**. Reporting to third parties is normally confined to matters of public interest and national security, neither of which seems to be relevant here.

Ultimately if the internal auditor is not satisfied with the response of the directors he needs to consider his position and whether he should **resign**.

(b) **Implications**

(i) *Audit of financial statements*

The fact that changes are being made, apparently to satisfy criteria set down by the bank **increases audit risk**. The auditor will need to be sensitive to the possibility of the existence of other areas where changes may have been made with the same objective in mind. Risk is also increased by the absence of two key members of staff, a situation in itself which appears highly unusual.

The external auditor needs to assess the materiality of the changes made to bad debts, depreciation and in respect of the leases. The criteria set down by the bank may be more sensitive than audit materiality, therefore whilst an issue for the bank it may not be as significant from the audit point of view.

The external auditor will need to establish **the reasons for the changes** in the treatment of bad debts, depreciation and leases to determine whether they can be justified. As the change in the treatment of leases constitutes a change in accounting policy the auditor needs to ensure that this is based on a truer and fairer view and that the impact has been **adequately disclosed**.

(ii) *Auditors' report*

Depending on the results of the audit work the auditors' report may be affected as follows:

Opinion qualified on the grounds that the financial statements are not free from material misstatement – if the auditor does not agree with the changes made to bad debts, depreciation and leases including the level of disclosure provided (assuming they are material).

Inclusion of an 'emphasis of matter' paragraph (but unqualified) – if the auditor believes there is doubt about the ability of the company to continue as a going concern this would be drawn to the attention of the readers in an emphasis of matter paragraph. If the situation was not properly disclosed this could result in a modified audit opinion.

(iii) *Continuing relationship*

If the external auditor is satisfied that changes made to treatments and accounting policies are legitimate there are no implications for the ongoing relationship.

If the external auditor has concerns over the integrity and honesty of the client in the way it has presented financial information the auditor should consider whether he wishes to continue with the relationship at all.

10 Confidentiality and independence

Text reference. Chapter 4

Top tips. This is a fairly straightforward question dealing with client confidentiality and the ethical issues around independence. In part (b), use the scenario to identify the risks to independence and take each issue in turn, using a separate sub-heading for each. There are plenty of clues in the scenario to help you, for example, the company has been an audit client of the firm for eight years, the finance director is the daughter of the audit partner. As well as identifying the risks to independence, make sure you suggest how to mitigate those risks – this is specifically asked for in the question requirement.

Easy marks. These are available in part (a). You should be familiar with the guidelines to auditors concerning client confidentiality and the situations where an auditor may disclose information as set out in the ACCA's *Code of ethics and conduct*.

Examiner's comments. Part (a) required candidates to explain situations where an auditor could disclose confidential information concerning a client. While this was a factual question, it did focus on an important ethical area with which candidates should be familiar. Most candidates obtained a pass standard in this section, with a minority obtaining full marks. However weaker candidates did not provide enough detail for some of the comments made or suggested that disclosure would be made to any government department for virtually any reason.

Part (b) was based on a scenario and asked candidates to identify and explain the risks to independence identified in the scenario. Many candidates provided a clear format to their answer, identifying individual points with a heading and clearly explaining the issues involved. The only major common error was that some candidates correctly identified and explained the independence risk, but then did not explain how that risk could be mitigated. However, many candidates used a three-column format (for the risk, why it was an independence issue, and how to mitigate the risk) which limited the extent to which this error occurred.

Marking scheme

		Marks
(a)	General rules	
	Statement don't normally disclose without good reason	1
	Simply stating rules	1
	Client consent	
	Public duty to disclose	1
	Legal or professional duty to disclose	1
	ACCA Code of ethics – obligatory disclosure	
	Implied agreement not to disclose	1
	Exemptions	1
	Disclose to proper authority	1
	Court demands disclosure	1
	ACCA Code of ethics – voluntary disclosure (0.5 area 0.5 example)	
	Protect member's interest	1
	Public duty	1
	Also allow other ethics where appropriate, eg person not considered fit and proper to carry out work	1
	Allow 1 bonus mark where specific information about a candidate's jurisdiction is given	1
	Maximum marks	**8**
(b)	1 for identifying and explaining area	
	1 for explaining why an ethical issue	
	1 for the resolution of the problem	
	Gives potential for 3 marks per section	
	Areas for discussion per the scenario	
	Audit partner – time in office	3
	Unpaid taxation fees	3
	Fee income	3
	Allyson Grace	3
	Meal	3
	Maximum marks	**12**
		20

(a) **Situations where an auditor may disclose confidential information about a client**

Auditors have a professional duty of confidentiality and this is an implied term of the agreement made between the auditor and the client. However there may be a legal right or duty to disclose confidential information or it may be in the public interest to disclose details of clients' affairs to third parties. Also the client may have given the auditor consent to disclose confidential information. These are general principles only and there is more specific guidance which is discussed below.

Obligatory Disclosure

If the auditor knows or suspects that his client has committed money-laundering, treason, drug-trafficking or terrorist offences then he is obliged to disclose all the information he has to a competent authority.

Under ISA 250 *Consideration of laws and regulations in an audit of financial statements* auditors must also consider whether non-compliance with laws and regulations may affect the accounts. They might have to include in the audit report a statement that non compliance with laws and regulations has led to significant uncertainties (in an emphasis of matter paragraph), or may consider modifying the audit opinion if there is a disagreement over the way specific items have been treated in the accounts.

Voluntary Disclosure

Voluntary disclosure includes where the auditor considers that disclosure is reasonably necessary to protect his interests, for example to allow him to sue for outstanding fees or to defend an action for negligence.

Other examples of voluntary disclosure include when disclosure is compelled by law such as when the auditor has to give evidence in court. There may be a public duty to disclose such as if an offence has been committed which is contrary to the public interest. Disclosure may be required to non-governmental bodies which have statutory powers to compel disclosure.

(b) **Risks to independence**

Audit Partner

Mr Grace has been the audit partner on the audit of Ancients for the last eight years. His independence and objectivity are likely to be impaired as a result of this close relationship with a key client and its senior management.

This threat could be addressed by appointing another audit partner to the audit of Ancients and rotating partners at suitable intervals thereafter.

Tax Fees Outstanding

There are taxation fees outstanding from Ancients for work that was done six months previously. In effect, McKay & Co are providing an interest-free loan to Ancients. This can threaten independence and objectivity of the audit firm as it may not want to qualify the accounts in case the outstanding fees are not paid.

This can be addressed by discussing the issue with the directors of Ancients and finding out why the fees have not been paid. If the fee is still not paid the firm should consider delaying the start of the audit work or even the possibility of resigning.

Fee Dependence

Ancients is one of McKay & Co's most important clients and the firm provides other services to this client as well as audit, including taxation services. Also the company is growing rapidly. Generally objectivity and independence are considered to be threatened if the fees for audit and recurring work exceed 10% of the firm's total fees for a listed client such as Ancients.

This threat could be mitigated by reviewing the total of the audit and recurring fee income from Ancients as a % of McKay & Co's total fee income on a regular basis and possibly limiting the provision of the other services if Ancients is providing 5-10% of the total fee income of the firm.

Relationship to Financial Director of Ancients plc

Allyson Grace, the daughter of Mr Grace, has recently been appointed the Financial Director of Ancients. The independence of Mr Grace could be threatened because of their close family relationship. The code of ethics does not define 'close family relationships' but lists factors that should be considered, such as the position the immediate family member holds with the client and the role of the professional on the assurance team. As Financial Director, Allyson has direct influence over the financial statements and as engagement partner, Mr Grace has ultimate responsibility for the audit opinion, so there is a clear threat to objectivity and independence.

This threat to independence could be mitigated by the appointment of another audit partner to this client.

Meal

The fact that Allyson Grace wants to take the audit team out for an expensive meal before the audit commences could be considered a threat to independence as it might influence the audit team's decisions once they start the audit of the financial statements. The ethics rules state that gifts or hospitality from the client should not be accepted if the benefit is significant.

This threat could be mitigated by declining the invitation.

11 NorthCee

Text references. Chapters 3 and 4

Top tips. This is a 20-mark question on ethical issues and corporate governance considerations for a listed company, both important areas of the syllabus.

Part (a) is worth 10 marks for identifying and explaining the independence issues, but make sure you also explain how each threat could be managed – this is specifically asked for in the requirement. The best way to approach this part of the question is to go through the scenario carefully and methodically, noting down the issues as you go on and then developing them further. You can give more structure to your answer and make it 'marker-friendly' by using a sub-heading for each factor.

In parts (b) and (c) you need to apply your knowledge of a recognised code of corporate governance, such as the Combined Code, to the scenario in the question. You must explain your answers fully, not merely produce a list of points. In part (b), each action is worth one mark so make sure that you provide a sufficiently detailed answer to this part of the question. Similarly, in part (c), you need to submit four well explained points to score maximum marks.

Easy marks. The more straightforward marks are available in part (b) of this question but make sure you explain the actions, rather than just list them, in order to achieve maximum marks.

Marking scheme

		Marks
(a)	Audit risks 10 marks. 0.5 for identifying risk area, 1 for explanation of risk and 1 for stating how to resolve. Maximum 2.5 for each area.	
	Rotation of audit partner	
	Preparation of financial statements	
	Attendance at social event	
	Unpaid taxation fee	
	Inheritance	
	Other relevant points (each)	
	Maximum marks	**10**
(b)	Meeting corporate governance requirements, 6 marks. 1 mark for each point.	
	Chief executive officer (CEO)/chairman split	1
	Appoint NED	1
	NED with financial experience	1
	NEDs to sub-committees of board	1
	Internal audit	1
	Internal control system	1
	Contact institutional shareholders	1
	Financial report information	1
	Other relevant points (each)	1
	Maximum marks	**6**

		Marks
(c)	Communication with audit committee, 4 marks. 1 each point.	
	Independence from board	1
	Time to review audit work	1
	Check auditor recommendations implemented	1
	Review work of internal auditor (efficiency, etc)	1
	Other relevant points (each)	1
	Maximum marks	4
		20

(a) **Threats to independence**

Same audit partner and long-standing audit client

NorthCee has been a client of Dark for five years, during which time the audit partner has remained the same. This gives rise to a **familiarity threat**.

The threat can be mitigated by **rotating** the audit partner. ACCA's *Code of ethics and conduct* states that for listed companies, the engagement partner should be rotated after no more than five years and should not return until a period of five years has passed. Therefore, although NorthCee is not yet listed, the firm could consider this. It could also ensure that an **independent internal quality review** of the audit work is undertaken.

Preparation of financial statements

The firm has been asked to continue to prepare the financial statements for the company, as well as carry out the audit. This gives rise to a **self-review threat**, as there could be a perception that the firm will not apply sufficient professional scepticism to its own work.

This threat can be mitigated by having **separate teams** for each engagement so that auditor independence is still retained. The other option would be for Dark to **decline the engagement** to prepare the financial statements.

Attendance at evening reception

The audit partner and audit manager have been asked to attend an evening reception where NorthCee will present its listing arrangements to banks and existing shareholders. This gives rise to a **familiarity threat**, as the acceptance of the hospitality could lead to a closer relationship with client management and a risk of placing too much trust in their representations.

This threat can be reduced by the firm **declining the invitation** to attend the reception.

Overdue taxation fees

Dark has provided taxation services to NorthCee which is generally considered not to pose a self-review threat. However, there are overdue fees which can be considered as a **loan** to the client and therefore poses a **self-interest threat**. There could be a perception that the firm would be reluctant to qualify its opinion in the face of the risk of not receiving the overdue fees.

This threat can be mitigated by firstly **discussing** the overdue fees with the senior management of NorthCee and, as a last resort, **considering resigning** if they are not paid.

Inheritance of share capital

The audit manager has inherited 5% of NorthCee's share capital as a result of a death in the family. This poses a **self-interest threat** and ACCA guidance states that a member of the assurance team should not hold a direct financial interest in a client.

This threat would therefore be mitigated by the audit manager **declaring the interest** to the firm and then **disposing** of the shares straightaway. An alternative would be to **move the audit manager** to another client.

(b) **Actions required to meet corporate governance requirements**

The company should appoint a **Chairman and Chief Executive** for its board of directors and these must be different people with clear divisions of responsibility so that no one individual has unfettered powers of decision.

The company should appoint a **mixture of executive and non-executive directors** for the board. The ratio of non-executive directors to executive directors should be the same so that no individual or small group of individuals can dominate the board's decision taking.

The company should set up an **internal audit department** which can review its internal controls and report findings to the audit committee.

The company should establish **remuneration and nomination committees**. The nomination committee should consist of a majority of non-executive directors and the remuneration committee should have at least three non-executive directors.

There should be a **terms of reference document** established to set out the scope of the audit committee.

The company should set up **procedures and policies** to establish a sound system of internal control.

(c) **Communication with audit committee**

Dark must communicate with NorthCee's audit committee for this and future audits so that the external auditors are reporting their findings and recommendations to a set of people which consists of an independent element (in the form of the non-executive directors).

The audit committee also provides a means for the external auditors to communicate with the company and raise issues of concern.

The audit committee will have more time to examine the external auditors' reports and recommendations and this provides comfort that recommendations and other matters are being considered and reviewed.

The audit committee provides a forum for Dark in the event of any disputes with the management of NorthCee.

12 Stark

Text references. Chapters 4 and 5.

Top tips. This question is scenario-based on ethics and internal audit. In part (a), use the information you've been given to help with your answer and remember the five types of threat identified in the ACCA's *Code of Ethics and Conduct.* You could present your answer to this part in a tabular format so you can link the threats and related safeguards together easily. In part (b), don't just state the general benefits of having an internal audit department – make sure you can relate them to Stark, the company in the question.

Easy marks. This question is relatively straightforward and there are many easy marks available here. You should be comfortable with the topic of professional ethics for part (a), and in part (b), as long as you can make your answer relevant to the company in the question, you ought to be able to score good marks.

Examiner's comments. The standard of answers to this question was satisfactory. In part (a), not providing sufficient points was the main reason for a candidate not achieving a pass standard. In part (b) most candidates obtained a pass standard by stating generic points about the benefits of internal audit.

Marking scheme

		Marks
(a)	1 for each ethical threat and 1 for explanation of how to mitigate that threat = 2 marks per linked points Part (i) therefore is 6 marks total and part (ii) is 6 marks total Engagement partner – time providing service Engagement partner's daughter takes part in audit Payment for investment advice Gift of balloon flight from client Contingent fee – taxation work Representing client in court	
	Maximum marks	12
(b)	2 marks per well-explained point Regulation Reports to the board Liaison with external auditors Monitor effectiveness of internal control Value for money audit Risk assessment Taxation services	
	Maximum marks	8
	Total marks	20

(a) **Threats and safeguards**

(i) *Ethical threats*	(ii) *Possible safeguards*
Familiarity	
Mr Son has been the engagement partner for Stark for the past nine years. This gives rise to a familiarity threat because of his long association with this one client which could impair his objectivity and independence.	Mr Son should be rotated off the audit. The ACCA's Code of Ethics and Conduct states that for listed companies, engagement partners should be rotated after no more than five years and not return to that client until a further period of five years has elapsed. Although Stark is not stated as listed, partner rotation should be made.
Mr Son's daughter Zoe will be part of the audit team of Stark. This also gives rise to a familiarity threat because her father is the engagement partner and this may impair objectivity.	Whilst Mr Son is still the engagement partner for this audit, his daughter should not be part of the audit team of Stark.
Intimidation	
There may be an intimidation threat from the Finance Director of Stark who has made a statement regarding the calculation of the fees for taxation services. The audit firm may feel that it has to accept this in order to keep Stark as a tax client.	The engagement partner should explain to the Finance Director that although his firm can provide taxation services to Stark, the fees charged must be based on the time spent on the work.
Advocacy	
An advocacy threat may arise as the Finance Director is expecting Ali & Co to represent his company in a dispute with the taxation authorities.	There are no safeguards which could be put in place to mitigate this threat and so the firm must decline to represent Stark in this dispute.

(i) *Ethical threats*	(ii) *Possible safeguards*
Self-review	
The firm also provides taxation services to Stark and this may give rise to a self-review threat as staff may end up reviewing their own work.	There is no real problem with the firm providing tax services to Stark as long as the firm uses separate engagement teams for the audit and tax work.
Self-interest	
Mr Far, the audit senior, received investment advice from the company and intends to do so in the future. A self-interest threat may arise as a result which could impair his objectivity.	If Mr Far paid for the services received from Stark as any other customer would, there is potentially no problem. However, this should be discussed with the engagement and ethics partners and he may be advised not to use the services of Stark in the future.
The client is expecting the tax fee to be based on a % of tax saved – this is a form of contingent fees. This gives rise to a self-interest threat because the firm will want to save as much tax as possible in order to charge as high a tax fee as possible.	There are no safeguards that can be put in place to mitigate this threat and so the firm should not agree to the proposed fee arrangement for taxation services.
The client has arranged a balloon flight for the audit team. This could give rise to a self-interest threat in the form of gifts and hospitality.	The Code of Ethics and Conduct states that gifts and hospitality should only be accepted where the value is modest. In this case, it would be appropriate to decline the balloon flight so as not to impair the firm's independence and objectivity.

(b) **Benefits of an internal audit department**

An internal audit department could look at existing procedures and systems in operation at Stark and make lots of useful recommendations to tighten up areas of weaknesses in controls.

An internal audit department could carry out value for money audits, looking at the economy, efficiency and effectiveness of processes and activities within the entity.

The internal auditors could examine the IT systems in place and make recommendations regarding these, including looking at the programmed controls.

The internal auditors could undertake financial audits to substantiate information in management and financial reporting.

The internal audit department could make recommendations in respect of good corporate governance, even though the company may not be required to comply with corporate governance guidelines.

The external auditors might be able to rely on work undertaken by the company's internal auditors and this in turn could result in a reduced audit fee.

The company has to comply with financial services regulations so an internal audit department could undertake work to ensure that it is complying with all required legislation and regulations.

The presence of an internal audit department within the company would present a positive image to clients of the company and to shareholders.

13 Internal audit function

(a) Internal audit activities

- Review of systems (internal control, management, operational, accounting)
- Monitoring of systems against targets and making recommendations
- Value for money, best value, information technology, financial audits
- Operational audits (procurement, treasury, human resources)

- Monitoring or risk management
- Special investigations (for example, fraud detection)

(b) Internal auditors versus external auditors

Objectives

The objective of internal auditors is to add value and improve an organisation's operations, whereas the objective of external auditors is to express an opinion as to whether the financial statements of an organisation are true and fair.

Scope of work

Internal auditor's undertake work on the operations of an organisation, whereas external auditor's focus on the financial statements.

Reporting responsibilities

Internal auditors report to the board of directors or audit committee and produce reports that are private and for the use of directors and management only. External auditors report to the shareholders or members of the company as to the truth and fairness of the financial statements. The audit report produced by external auditors is publicly available.

(c) Outsourcing

'Outsourcing' is subcontracting a process to a third party company, that is, purchasing the service externally. Services that are typically outsourced include internal audit, accountancy and payroll functions.

Advantages of outsourcing internal audit	Disadvantages of outsourcing internal audit
Service provider has expert knowledge and can provide skilled staff.	Independence and objectivity issues if internal audit department is provided by same firm as external auditors.
Cost-savings in terms of employee salaries, training costs, recruitment expenses.	Cost may be high enough to force entity to choose not to have an internal audit department at all.
Immediate internal audit department provided.	Frequent staff changes resulting in poor quality service being providing due to lack of understanding of client's systems and operations.

14 Internal audit

Text reference. Chapter 5

Top tips. This question covers the relatively straightforward topic of internal audit and the extent to which it can be relied on by the external auditor. The main problem is that the requirements cover the same aspects albeit from different angles. In this situation it is important to plan your answer to avoid repeating the same points. Also remember the importance of using the scenario. Three specific internal audit services are described. Think about their relevance to the external auditor. They may not all be equally useful.

Easy marks. These are available in part (a) and part (c). Notice that you can use your knowledge of the ISA 610 criteria for assessing the internal audit function as a framework for your answer (objectivity, technical competence due professional care, communication).

Examiner's comments. This was a very straightforward question for which many candidates were well prepared. More marks would have been scored if candidates had dealt separately with the three internal audit functions described. A large number of candidates incorrectly assumed that the same independence requirements applied to both internal and external auditors.

Marking scheme

		Marks
(a)	Reliance on work of internal auditors Up to 2 marks per point to a maximum of	6
(b)	Information required Up to 2 marks per point to a maximum of	6
(c)	Circumstances in which it would not be possible to rely on the work of internal audit Up to 2 marks per point to a maximum of	4
(d)	External auditor work Up to 1.5 marks per point to a maximum of	4
		20

(a) **Extent of reliance on internal audit**

In general terms the extent to which the external auditor relies on the work performed by the internal auditor depends on:

- Their **objectivity**
- The extent they are free to **communicate** openly
- Their **technical competence**
- Whether the work is performed with **due professional care**

This applies to the three situations noted as follows:

Cyclical audit of internal controls

The extent of reliance will depend on whether the work is **properly planned, supervised, reviewed and documented**. It will also depend on the **scope** of the work performed. Work on controls relating to finance and information services will be of more relevance to the external auditor as they are likely to have a greater impact on the financial statements than operations or customer support.

The external auditors will wish to rely on the work done by the internal auditors regarding the information services' restructure. The amount of independent work which will need to be performed will depend on the results of the post-implementation review as this will provide evidence as to the success of the restructuring.

Structure review every four years

This information will be useful to the external auditor in his assessment of the overall **control environment**. The extent of reliance will depend largely on when the last review was performed. A review performed this year will be of more relevance than one carried out four years ago.

Review of risk management

ISA 315 requires the external auditor to obtain an understanding of the business risks faced by the company in order to assess their potential implications for the financial statements. The internal auditor's review of the **effectiveness of risk management** measures would be invaluable in obtaining this understanding. The extent to which this could be relied upon however would be affected by any constraints placed on the internal auditor in his ability to perform this work and express his conclusions. The external auditor would also need to consider whether management have acted on the recommendations and the way in which these actions have been evidenced.

(b) **Information required**

- Records detailing the qualifications and experience of internal audit staff.
- Procedure manuals setting out the organisation's quality control standards for internal audit and evidence that this is monitored and reviewed.

- For the cyclical audit of the operation of internal controls working papers showing:
  - That the work is adequately planned, executed and reviewed
  - The results of tests of controls particularly in respect of finance and information systems
- For the restructuring of the information services function:
  - Documentation showing the way in which the restructure was planned and the basis on which decisions were made
  - The results of the post-implementation review
  - Any documents relating to this function prior to the change (as part of the year would have been based on the old system)
- For the review of the structure of internal controls:
  - The most recent report produced to determine how up to date the information is.
- For the annual review of risk management measures working papers showing:
  - Planning of this work
  - Results of key tests performed (controls, substantive)
  - Key conclusions
  - Management responses

(c) **It may not be possible to rely on the work of internal audit in the following situations:**

- If severe restrictions are placed on internal audit by management such that they cannot act independently.
- If the scope of the work is such that it covers aspects of the business which are of little relevance to the external auditor.
- If internal audit does not have access to senior management and/or no action is taken as a result of internal audit recommendations.
- If the team members lack the technical competence to perform the work. This might include the lack of an appropriate qualification, lack of experience and training.
- If internal audit work is not conducted with due professional care ie it is not properly planned, reviewed and documented.

(d) **It will be necessary for the external auditor to perform his own work in the following circumstances:**

- Where balances are **material** to the financial statements. This is because the external auditor cannot delegate responsibility for the audit opinion. The external auditor needs sufficient appropriate evidence on which to form his opinion and auditor generated evidence is the most reliable.
- In areas of **increased risk**. This will include areas where complex accounting treatments are involved or where judgement is required. In this instance inventory is likely to be a risk area, as well as being material. Leasing transactions may also be complex and will therefore require independent appraisal by the external auditor.
- Where the **objectives of the internal audit work differ** from those of the external auditor. The roles of the internal and external auditor are very different. In some instances whilst the internal auditor may have done some work on a particular area the approach taken may not be adequate for the purposes of expressing an opinion on truth and fairness. This is particularly the case where the internal audit department concentrates on operational aspects rather than matters which affect the financial statements.

15 Value for money audit

Text references. Chapters 5 and 10

Top tips. This is a question on deficiencies in the purchases system of a company, but from an internal audit point of view. Don't be put off by this – stay focussed and use the information in the scenario to generate your answer in part (b). A good way to set out your answer to part (b) (i) is by using a columnar format – this ensures that you link deficiencies to recommendations and gives more structure to your answer. Part (a) should be very straightforward for four marks. Part (c) is trickier because you need to think of other deficiencies that would be generated by a value for money audit so you need to apply your knowledge to this particular company.

Easy marks. In part (a), easy marks are available for explaining the purpose of the three Es in relation to a value for money audit.

Note. The marking scheme has been revised to reflect any necessary amendments made to the question and/or answer.

Marking scheme

			Marks
(a)	One mark per point		
	Explanation of		
	Value for money		1
	Economy		1
	Efficiency		1
	Effectiveness		1
	Maximum marks		**4**
(b)	Deficiencies two marks each. One for identifying the deficiency and one for recommendation to overcome that deficiency.		
	(i)	Transfer info – purchase requisition to order form	2
		Purchase requisition destroyed	2
		Order form no copy in ordering department	2
		No copy order form in goods inwards department	2
		GRNs filed in part number order	2
		Other relevant points (each)	2
		Maximum marks	**10**
	(ii)	Chief buyer authorising all orders	2
		Individual items ordered	2
		Routing of GRN	2
		GRNs filed in part number order	2
		Lack of appropriate computer system	2
		Other relevant points (each)	2
		Maximum marks	**6**
			20

(a) The three 'Es' relate to economy, efficiency and effectiveness in value for money audits.

Economy relates to the attainment of the appropriate quantity and quality of physical, human and financial resources (inputs) at the lowest cost.

Efficiency is the relationship between goods or services produced (outputs) and the resources used to produce them. An efficient process would produce the maximum output for any given set of resource inputs, or would have minimum inputs for any given quantity and quality of product or service provided.

Effectiveness is concerned with how well an activity is achieving its policy objectives or other intended effects.

(b) (i)

Internal control deficiency	Recommendation
A clerk transfers information from the order requisition to an order form. This could result in errors in orders being made after the buyer has authorised the requisition.	The order form should be signed off as authorised to confirm that the details on the requisition match those on the order form.
The order requisition is thrown away once the chief buyer has authorised it. Any subsequent queries on orders cannot be checked back to the original requisition.	The order requisition form should be retained with the order form in case of query or dispute regarding items ordered.
No copy of the order form is retained by the ordering department. This means that goods could be ordered twice in error or deliberately. It also means that queries on deliveries cannot be chased up.	A three-part pre-numbered order form should be used and one copy should be retained by the ordering department with the requisition form.
The Goods Inward Department does not retain a copy of the Damaged Goods note. If the note is lost on the way to the ordering department, or there is a query, the Goods Inward Department has no record of goods returned.	Four copies of the Damaged Goods note should be retained. One copy could be retained by the Goods Inward Department, one sent to the ordering department, one to the department who requested the goods, so they are aware that there will be a delay and one to the supplier.
The Ordering Department does not keep a record of goods received, so is unable to check which orders are closed or to chase up suppliers.	The Ordering Department should match orders to GRNs and mark orders as closed once all goods have been received.
The Goods Inwards Department files GRNs in order of the supplier's goods reference. This could make it difficult to find a GRN at a later date if the department is not aware of the supplier's reference.	GRNs should be filed in date order, or by PO number.

(ii)

Additional deficiency	Recommendations
There is no delegated level of authority for authorising order requisitions – the chief buyer has to authorise all requisitions.	A delegated level of authority should be introduced for the authorisation of order requisitions.
The ordering department receives many orders in the day and some of these are for duplicate items. Any volume discounts for ordering bulk items would therefore not be obtained.	Orders should be reviewed on a daily or weekly basis so that orders for the same item from different departments can be aggregated to take account of volume discounts.
The structure of the department could be improved; there is just one buyer and five purchasing clerks. This could cause problems when the buyer is on holiday, sick or leaves permanently. It may indicate inefficiency.	The department's staffing structure should be reviewed with a view to training one of the purchasing clerks to fill the buyer's role in instances of holiday or sickness.
There is insufficient communication to the department that created the purchase requisition of how the order is progressing. They do not know that their order has been made and would not find out if the goods are delivered but have to be returned due to damages.	A tracking system should be developed for orders so that the department that made the requisition can check when their goods have been ordered, the expected delivery date and then find out about any problems with the delivery.

16 MonteHodge

Text reference. Chapter 5

Top tips. This question relates to internal audit so you need to remember what the internal audit function does within an organisation before you attempt to tackle it.

Part (a) is on the advantages and disadvantages of outsourcing the internal audit function – this seems straightforward enough but look at the mark allocation - there are eight marks on offer, so you need to ensure your answer is sufficiently detailed to score well.

In part (b) which is for 12 marks, you must make sure your answer is relevant to the client, MonteHodge – don't launch into an answer that only discusses the advantages and disadvantages of internal audit departments in general. The question specifically asks you to consider the advantages and disadvantages for the company in the question scenario, therefore make sure that you do use the information provided – planning your answer first is therefore vital.

Easy marks. Part (a) is on the advantages and disadvantages of outsourcing the internal audit function so should not be difficult, however do note that the requirement states 'discuss' – a list of advantages and disadvantages won't be sufficient for the eight marks potentially available here.

Examiner's comments. In part (a), although the overall standard of answers was high, some answers were not detailed enough to score well or did not focus on outsourcing as required by the question. In part (b), candidates were expected to relate their answers to the scenario provided but some answers did not and so failed to score well. Another weakness in this part of the question was a lack of sufficient explanation for the points made.

Marking scheme

		Marks
(a)	1 mark for each well-explained point	
	For outsourcing internal audit	
	– Staff recruitment	
	– Skills	
	– Set up time	
	– Costs	
	– Flexibility of staffing arrangements	
	– Independence of external firm	
	– Other valid points	
	Against outsourcing internal audit	
	– Staff turnover	
	– External auditors	
	– Cost	
	– Confidentiality	
	– Control	
	– Independence (where services provided by same firm)	
	– Other valid points	
	Maximum marks	8
	(Note to markers – there is no split of marks between advantages and disadvantages.)	

		Marks
(b)	Up to 2 marks for each well-explained point	
	For internal audit	
	– VFM audits	
	– Accounting system	
	– Computer systems	
	– Internal control systems	
	– Effect on audit fee	
	– Image to clients	
	– Corporate governance	
	– Lack of control	
	– Law change	
	– Assistance to financial accountant	
	– Nature of industry (financial services)	
	– Other relevant points	
	Against internal audit	
	– No statutory requirement	
	– Family business	
	– Potential cost	
	– Review threat	
	– Other relevant points	
	Maximum marks	**12**
		20

(a) Outsourcing the internal audit department

Advantages

Staff do not need to be recruited externally as the service provider should be able to provide good quality audit staff.

The service provider has different specialist skills and can assess what management's requirements are, and the company will have access to a broad range of skills.

Outsourcing can provide an immediate internal audit department.

Associated costs such as recruitment and training can be eliminated if the function is outsourced.

The contract can be for a specific time period, depending on the needs of the company.

Outsourcing can be used on a short-term basis.

Disadvantages

There will be independence and objectivity issues if the firm providing the internal audit function is also the same as that providing the external audit service.

The cost of outsourcing the internal audit function may be high enough to force the directors to choose not to have such a function in place at all.

Outsourced internal audit staff may change frequently resulting in a poor service being provided due to lack of understanding of the client's systems and operations.

(b) MonteHodge

Reasons for an internal audit department

There is a lack of internal control systems in place but an internal audit department could look at existing procedures and systems and make lots of useful recommendations to tighten up controls.

The internal audit department could make lots of useful recommendations in respect of good corporate governance, even though the company is not required to comply with corporate governance guidelines. If the directors did decide to float the company in the future, it would have to comply with such guidelines.

The external auditors might be able to rely on internal audit work undertaken by the company's internal auditors and this in turn could result in a reduced audit fee.

The company will have to comply with financial services regulations in the future so an internal audit department could undertake work to ensure that it is complying with all required legislation and regulations.

The presence of an internal audit department within the company would present a positive image to clients of the company.

The internal audit department could review the systems in place such as the stock market monitoring system and assess whether upgrades are required.

The internal audit department could provide benefit to the financial accountant, who is not qualified, in the areas of accounting regulations and the internal control system, for example.

Reasons against an internal audit department

Setting up an internal audit department from scratch could prove expensive in terms of both time and money. The company will incur recruitment costs and the cost of additional staff salaries.

The company does not have to have an internal audit department in place as it is not listed and therefore under no obligation to comply with recommended codes of corporate governance such as the Combined Code.

The company's shareholders consist of six members of the same family. There is therefore not the same requirement to provide assurance on systems and internal controls as there would be to shareholders in a public company.

The directors and senior management may feel threatened by the presence of internal auditors looking at systems and controls.

17 Audit risk and planning

(a) *Audit risk*

Audit risk is the risk that the auditor expresses an inappropriate audit opinion when the financial statements are materially misstated.

Audit risk has two major components: one is dependent on the entity being audited and is the risk of material misstatement arising in the financial statements (made up of inherent risk and control risk).

Inherent risk is the susceptibility of an assertion to a misstatement that could be material individually or when aggregated with other misstatements, assuming there were no related internal controls.

Control risk is the risk that a misstatement that could occur in an assertion and that could be material, either individually or when aggregated with other misstatements, will not be prevented or detected and corrected on a timely basis by the entity's internal control.

The other component of audit risk is dependent on the auditor and is the risk that the auditor will not detect material misstatements in the financial statements – this is known as detection risk.

Audit risk can be summarised by the following equation:

Audit risk = inherent risk × control risk × detection risk

(b) *Matters to be documented during audit planning*

- Discussion amongst the audit team about the susceptibility of the financial statements to material misstatements
- Key elements of the understanding gained of the entity
- Identified and assessed risks of material misstatement
- Significant risks identified and related controls evaluated

- Overall responses to address the risks of material misstatement
- Nature, extent and timing of further audit procedures linked to the assessed risks at the assertion level
- Where reliance is to be placed on the effectiveness of controls from previous audits, conclusions on how this is appropriate

(*Note.* Only six were required.)

(c) *Factors affecting the form and content of audit working papers*

- The size and complexity of the entity
- The nature of the audit procedures to be performed
- The identified risks of material misstatement
- The significance of the audit evidence obtained
- The nature and extent of exceptions identified
- The need to document a conclusion or basis for a conclusion not readily determinable from documentation of work performed or audit evidence obtained
- The audit methodology and tools used

(*Note.* Only six were required.)

18 Twinkletoes

Text references. Chapters 6, 7 and 9

Top tips. This question looks at the familiar topic of risk but rather than being asked to identify risks you are asked to consider risk classification. The key here is not to panic but to try to think through the issues. Notice for example that you are the internal not the external auditor. This means that you need to think about risk from management's perspective. This is particularly important in part (a) and (b). Also notice that the examiner tries to give you a clue in part (b) in the note. The examiner is trying to get you to think about the fact that not all the receivables within the same category will be as risky as others. Even in a generally high risk category those balances that have no history of non-payment will be less risky. What makes this category risky or not? What is the impact of this category on receivables overall? Are all the balances within a category the same or do some have characteristics which either increase or decrease the risk? These are the types of question which you should be asking.

Easy marks. These are available in part (c) of the question where you are asked to recommend internal controls. You should be familiar with the basic examples eg credit checks, credit limits etc but make sure that you try to adapt these according to the nature of the balance. For example major accounts are likely to be managed in a different way to smaller accounts.

Examiner's comments. Most candidates demonstrated appropriate knowledge although a minority focused on the audit of receivables.

In part (a) errors included discussing audit risk and the risk model. This was not required as the question was focusing on risks within the business. No marks were awarded for these points.

In part (b) common errors included not explaining the choice of risk category and inappropriate classification. This was particularly apparent in relation to overseas receivables. In spite of the fact that they were paying in advance many candidates still classified them as high risk purely based on the fact that they were overseas.

In part (c) most candidates appreciated the need to split their answer into sections. However in spite of this, there was a lack of discrimination between the controls which would be applied to each of the different categories with the same controls being repeated several times over. Higher marks were scored where candidates thought about the nature of the different debts, suggested appropriate controls and described why these controls were necessary.

Common errors in part (c) included confusing control risk with internal controls and therefore documenting audit tests and listing controls over the whole of the sales system rather than confining their answer to the receivables ledger.

Marking scheme

		Marks
(a)	Risk classification Up to 1 mark per point to a maximum of	4
(b)	Classification of risks for receivables Up to 2 marks per point for each category to a maximum of	8
(c)	Internal controls Up to 1 mark per point to a maximum of	8
		20

(a) **Risk classification**

- Risk classification helps management run the business because it is part of the overall process of identifying and assessing risks. Risk can exist on an individual department level or on a strategic level and will potentially affect all aspects of the business. As such it is an essential part of business management.
- Risk must be managed by the company. The company will aim to identify risk, determine a policy and implement a strategy. The classification of risk will be a key factor in deciding the best policy and how to implement the strategy.
- Risk classification enables effective use of resources. Resources can be directed towards dealing with high and medium risk problems so that the benefits are maximised.
- Risk classification assists management in adopting the right response to risk. For example a low risk might be accepted. A high or medium risk should be reduced (eg by instituting a system of internal control as protection) or transferred (eg by taking out insurance).

(b) **Risks relating to trade receivables**

(i) *Small retail shops*

This group of balances collectively is significant as it represents one third of the total value of receivables. Risk is also affected by the increase in the insolvency rate of small shoe shops. However accounts that are overdue are medium risk (as opposed to high risk) as individual balances will not have a material impact on receivables overall as the amounts involved are comparatively small. Balances which are not overdue are low risk.

(ii) *Large retail shoe shops*

The overseas accounts are low risk as they pay for goods in advance although the fact that this business is being lost may represent a different type of risk to the business in future. Large overdue accounts are likely to be assessed as high to medium risk depending on the proportion which are overdue. This category in total accounts for approximately 22% of receivables. If the majority of these were overdue the risk would be high. If, as is more likely, fewer of these are overdue the risk is medium. The accounts which are not overdue are low risk.

(iii) *Chains of discount shoe shops*

The large overdue accounts will be medium/low risk. The risk is reduced from high/medium to medium/low in spite of the size of the accounts due to the fact that the shops are well established high street chains. Whilst they may take a little 'unofficial' credit it is unlikely that they will be unable to pay.

(iv) *Mail order companies*

Existing accounts will be low risk as there has been no history of bad debts in this category. The new accounts will be assessed as medium risk. New accounts would normally be assessed as high risk particularly where there are a large number of them as there are in this case. However as this category has not experienced any problems in the past the overall risk can be reduced to medium.

(c) **Internal controls**

All customers

- Credit checks and references should be obtained for all new customers before credit is given.
- Where new customers place large orders before a credit history has been established payment should be in advance or on delivery.
- Credit limits should be set for all customers. These should be regularly reviewed to ensure that sales are not being made to customers who have already exceeded their credit limit.
- Standard credit terms should be applied eg 30 days for local customers and 45 days for overseas customers. Any extension to these standard terms should be authorised in advance.

Slow paying customers

- Credit controllers should be specifically assigned the task of chasing these debts on a regular basis.
- Where customers consistently fail to pay and balances are significantly overdue no further credit sales should be made to the account in question.

Larger accounts

- These should be allocated an account manager who would not only be responsible for securing the sale but also for ensuring that payment is received on a reasonable basis.

Overseas customers

- Controls will be required as the company is due to offer overseas customers credit terms. (Currently they pay up front.)
- Payment terms should reflect the practical difficulties of transferring funds eg terms could be extended.
- Controls should be in place to minimise the exposure of Twinkletoes to exchange rate differences eg payment in the local currency of Twinkletoes.

19 Specs4You

Text reference. Chapter 7

Top tips. This is a question on audit working papers. Part (a) was a straightforward test of knowledge of the purposes of audit working papers. You may have thought of purposes other than those in the answer below and any three valid purposes would gain full marks. In part (b), you could present your answer in a tabular format – eight marks are available here so make sure you describe the information you expect from each document. In part (c), there are nine marks available so try to generate at least six well-explained points and you will be well on your way to passing this part of the question.

Easy marks. Easy marks are available in part (a) of this question – you should be able to achieve the maximum three marks available without any problems. Part (b) should also be straightforward as long as you think about the client you are auditing and the types of documentation that a company would hold that would be useful to an auditor at the planning stage of an audit.

Examiner's comments. The overall standard of answers to part (a) was satisfactory, but some candidates misinterpreted the question and wrote about types of test, such as analytical procedures or listed the types of working papers.

In part (b) the requirement left candidates with a wide range of points to make, from the previous year's audit file to company brochures. Many provided good lists of documents but common errors included:

- Not explaining the information to be obtained from each document
- Listing non-documentary sources of evidence
- Not providing sufficient points. The full eight marks could not be obtained with only three or four points
- Focusing on the current audit file in too much detail

In part (c) candidates who took the approach of mentioning anything that appeared to be 'strange' such as the lack of initial of a preparer correctly identified the problems with the working paper. Again errors included the failure to explain the points made. For example, stating that the working paper did not have a page number, but then not explaining that this meant that it could not be filed or retrieved easily from the audit file.

Marking scheme

		Marks
(a)	1 mark per point	
	Assist planning	1
	Assist supervision	1
	Record of audit evidence	1
	Other relevant points	1
	Maximum marks	**3**
(b)	0.5 for document, 0.5 for information obtained	
	Memo and articles	1
	Financial statements	1
	Management accounts	1
	Organisation chart	1
	Industry data	1
	Financial statements similar companies	1
	Prior year audit file	1
	Internet news sites	1
	Permanent audit file	1
	Board minutes	1
	Other relevant points	1
	Maximum marks	**8**
(c)	1 mark per relevant point (0.5 for area, 0.5 for explaining why working paper poor quality)	
	Page reference	1
	Year end	1
	No preparer signature	1
	Poor job from reviewer	1
	Vague test objective	1
	Not an audit assertion	1
	Sufficient audit evidence obtained?	1
	Lack of appropriate referencing	1
	Test results unclear	1
	Conclusion not consistent with results found	1
	Other relevant points (each)	1
	Maximum marks	**9**
		20

(a) **Purposes of working papers**

- To assist the audit team to plan and perform the audit
- To assist relevant team members to direct, supervise and review audit work
- To provide a tangible record of the audit evidence obtained to support the auditor's opinion as to the truth and fairness of the financial statements

(b) **Specs4You documentation**

Prior year audit file

This will provide useful information on the audit approach used, results of testing, areas of concern etc which were encountered in the previous year.

Prior year financial statements

These will provide valuable information on the income statement and statement of financial position and allow the auditor to undertake an analytical review at the planning stage to identify potential areas of risk. They will also provide information on the accounting policies used by the company.

Current year budgetary information and latest management accounts

These will allow the auditor to see how the company is progressing in the current year and also provide budgetary information that can be used to carry out analytical review.

Organisation chart

This will allow the auditor to see how the company is structured and will highlight key personnel that will be useful for the audit.

Details of store locations

The auditor can see where the stores of Specs4You are located which will be useful for the year-end inventory count and other visits.

Staff listing

The staff listing will be useful as it will provide contact details for key staff that the audit team may need to speak to during the course of the audit.

Internet site of Specs4You

If the company has an internet site, this can provide valuable background information and also highlight current news.

Memorandum and articles of association

These will provide information on the objectives of the company and how it is structured.

(c) **Working paper**

The working paper does not identify who prepared it so it makes it difficult for the reviewer to follow-up any queries arising during the review.

The working paper has not been dated by the person who prepared it.

The working paper does not completely state the year-end that the audit relates to. This means that the working paper could be filed in an incorrect audit file.

The audit assertion has not correctly been identified so does not tell the reviewer what the work is trying to achieve.

The audit assertion has been confused with the objective of the audit work.

The working paper does not tell the reviewer where the details of the items tested can be found – there should be adequate cross-referencing so that the reviewer does not have to go through all the working papers to find these.

The method of sample selection and number to test have not been clearly explained in the working paper. It simply states that 15 purchase orders were selected, but not the basis for the selection of this number nor how the sample was selected.

The conclusion reached contradicts the results of the audit work, since errors were found in the testing but the conclusion states that purchase orders are completely recorded in the purchase day book.

The working paper does not appear to have been referenced in accordance with the firm's agreed referencing system which means it may be incorrectly filed.

20 Tempest

Text references. Chapters 6 and 7

Top tips. When a case study question includes both narrative and numerical information, you must take time to read all of the information several times to identify all the points that you can develop in your answer. While you should not get too bogged down in number crunching, a little bit of basic ratio analysis here, eg profit margins and days sales in receivables will give you some more practical points to raise in your audit strategy.

If you need to do detailed calculations, such as the ones for materiality in this answer, it is a good idea to put them into an appendix.

Easy marks. The only genuinely easy marks here were in part (a) where sound knowledge of ISA 300 could give you full marks.

Examiner's comments. Part (a) was answered well although there was a tendency for some students to provide answers that were far too detailed for the marks available. In part (b), where a risk was identified, not all students succeeded in explaining why the risk was important. Some answers to part (b) did not take into account the scenario, ie the type of company and its business.

Marking scheme

		Marks
(a)	**ISA 300 – Planning**	1
	Audit work performed in an effective manner	1
	General approach and strategy for audit	1
	Attention to critical areas	1
	Amount of work	1
	Discussion with audit committee	1
	Basis to produce audit program	1
	Other relevant points	1
	Maximum marks	**5**
(b)	**List of tests at 1 mark per relevant point**	
	Audit strategy	
	Type of audit	1
	ISAs to be used	1
	Overview of Tempest	1
	Key dates for audit	1
	Overview of approach	
	Industry details	1
	Fall in GP%	1
	Materiality	
	How determine	1
	Risk areas (state with reason for risk)	
	COS	1
	Inventory	1
	Trade receivables	1
	Non-current assets	1
	Long term liabilities	1
	Audit approach	
	Compliance testing	1
	New inventory system – transfer of balances	1
	New inventory system – test end of year balances	1
	New inventory system – test during year	1

	Marks
Other risk areas	
Information on going concern	1
Related party transactions	1
Inventory count assistance	1
Any other general points 0.5 mark	
Maximum marks	15
	20

(a) Audit planning is important for the following reasons:

- It ensures that **appropriate attention** is devoted to important areas of the audit. For example, overall materiality and performance materiality will be assessed at the planning stage and this will mean that when the detailed audit plan is drawn up, more procedures will be directed towards the most significant figures in the financial statements.
- Planning should mean that **potential problems are identified and resolved** on a timely basis. This could be in the sense of identifying financial statement risks at an early stage, so allowing plenty of time to gather sufficient relevant evidence. It could also relate to identifying practical problems relating to the gathering of evidence and resolving those through actions such as involving other experts being built into the detailed audit plan.
- Planning helps ensure that the audit is **organised and managed in an effective and efficient manner**. This could relate to, for example, ascertaining from the client when particular pieces of information will be available so that the timings of the audit are organised so as to minimise waste of staff time and costs.
- Planning assists in the **proper assignment of work** to engagement team members. Once the main risk areas have been identified at the planning stage, the engagement partner can then make sure that staff with suitable experience and knowledge are allocated to the engagement team.
- Planning **facilitates direction, supervision and review** of the work done by team members. Once procedures have been designed and allocated to members of the team, it is easier for the manager and partner to decide when work should be completed and ready for review. It will also make it easier for them to assess during the audit whether work is going according to the original plan and budget.

(b) **Audit Strategy**

Client: Tempest
Year-end: 31 December 20X7
Prepared by: A. Manager

Scope of audit

Tempest is subject to a normal statutory audit. It cannot take advantage of any reporting or audit exemptions.

The financial statements are prepared under IFRS.

The audit will be carried out under International Standards on Auditing.

Tempest trades in fittings for ships and stores its inventory at ten different locations. As in previous years, we have carried out year-end procedures at the three locations with the most significant inventory balances plus three others on a rotational basis, using staff from our most conveniently located offices. This year, due to the change in accounting systems we will carry out year-end procedures at all of the locations.

Timings

- Interim audit
- Final audit
- Audit staff planning/briefing meetings
- Meeting with directors (or audit committee, if one exists)
- Approval of financial statements by the board
- Issue of audit report

Materiality for the financial statements as a whole

Preliminary calculations of materiality for the financial statements as a whole are based on the forecast financial statements and are set out in Appendix 1. These materiality levels will need to be reassessed when the actual financial statements for the year ended 31 December 20X7 are available and performance materiality levels will also need to be determined.

Materiality for income statement items should be set in the region of $40,000 (being at the upper end of the range based on profit before tax).

Materiality for statement of financial position items should be set in the region of $200,000, based on total assets.

Materiality levels for the financial statements as a whole are generally lower than those for the prior year, suggesting performance materiality levels will also be lower. This is likely to increase sample sizes for procedures; this is appropriate in light of the indications that there may an increased risk of error this year.

Higher risk areas

(i) **Inventory**

The forecast year end inventory figure is significantly lower than in the prior year. Coupled with the mid-year change in the accounting system for inventory there is a risk of material error in inventory quantities or valuation.

(ii) **Sales**

Sales are forecast to have increased by 12% over the prior year. Compared to the average year on year growth of only 7% for the industry in general there is a risk that sales may be overstated.

(iii) **Profit**

Gross profit margin has fallen to 17.3% (20X6 21.9%) and net profit margin has fallen to 0.9% (20X6 4.1%). This could indicate errors in cut off or allocation or that the company has been cutting prices in order to win market share and has let profitability suffer. Although there is no specific indication of immediate going concern difficulties, this strategy may not be sustainable in the longer term.

(iv) **Receivables**

Days' sales in receivables are forecast to have increased to 47 days (36 days in 20X6). This may indicate problems with the recoverability of the receivables and a risk that impairments in value of the receivables' balances are not recognised.

(v) **Non-current assets**

There is a decrease in this balance of $900,000. This is far in excess of what could be explained by depreciation of assets that comprise mainly properties. It may be that there have been disposals in the year. This raises the possibility of incorrect accounting or inadequate disclosures.

Also in relation to the non-current assets, if the inventory balance has genuinely decreased to approximately 15% of its previous level, some of the storage locations may be redundant. It could be that the reduction relates to impairment write-downs and it could be the case that further write-downs are needed.

(vi) **Related party transactions**

Given the information that one of the directors purchased a yacht during the year it may be that he has purchased fittings from Tempest Ltd. There is a risk that any related party transactions have not been fully disclosed.

Audit approach

Where possible evidence should be obtained from tests of control so that detailed substantive procedures can be reduced.

Special emphasis will be needed in respect of inventory accounting. Procedures will include:

- Obtaining an understanding of how the transfer of balances to the new system was carried out. Direct testing of balances from the old to new systems may be needed as well as reviewing evidence of control procedures carried out by the client at the point of changeover.
- A sample of sales and purchase transactions should be traced through the new system to check whether additions to and deletions from inventory are being made correctly.
- Test counts of inventory at the various locations should be performed at the year-end and agreed to the inventory records as at that date.

Testing of items in the income statement will need to include:

- Consideration of the revenue recognition policies being used
- Cut-off testing on sales and costs of sales
- Comparison of expense classifications from year to year

The review of events after the reporting period should focus on:

- Any substantial adjustments to the inventory figure
- Evidence of recoverability of receivable balances
- Any information suggesting further reductions in profitability of the business
- Management accounts and cash flow projections for the post year end period

Appendix 1

Materiality ($'000)

½ –1% of revenue (½% × 45,928 – 1% × 45,928)	230	to	459
5-10% of profit before tax (5% × 436 – 10% × 436)	22	to	44
1-2% of total assets (1% × 10,300 – 2% × 10,300)	103	to	206

21 Bridgford Products

Text references. Chapters 6, 7 and 9

Top tips. You need to read part (b) of this question carefully as the examiner wants you to focus on the problems highlighted in the question; a general essay on planning procedures is not required. If you were unsure, you should have realised when planning your answer that there was sufficient information given for you only to have time to discuss the points mentioned.

Easy marks. These are available in part (a). You must be able to explain the basic importance of planning an audit.

(a) Auditors should plan their work for the following reasons.

(i) The **objectives** of the audit are **set**. For a company this is producing an audit report in accordance with legislation and ISA 700, but there may be other regulatory requirements involved, for example if the client is a financial services company.

(ii) Attention is **devoted** towards the **key audit areas**. These will be areas which are **large** in **materiality** terms, where there is significant risk of material misstatement, or which have had **significant problems** in previous years.

(iii) **Staff** are **briefed**. The audit strategy should provide enough detail about the client to enable staff to carry out the detailed work effectively. Budgets should ensure that appropriate time is spent on each audit area.

(iv) The **efficiency** of the **audit process** should be **enhanced**. Good planning should ensure that the **right staff** are **selected**, that **information technology** is used **appropriately,** and that maximum use is made of schedules prepared by the client and of the work of **internal audit**.

(v) The **timing** of the audit is **appropriate**. Staff will need to be available to carry out an inventory count and circularisation of receivables at the year-end. If use is to be made of work done by the client or internal audit, then this work will need to have been completed in time for the final audit. The timing should also allow sufficient time for the audit to be completed so that the financial statements can be signed on the date desired by the client.

(vi) **Review** is **facilitated**. Setting out an audit plan and budgets at the planning stage means that the reviewer has measures against which the work can be examined at the end of the assignment.

(b) (i) *Management accounts revenue and profit*

Assuming the level of sales is maintained until January, revenue for the year will be $156 million, which is a 42% increase on last year. However, on the same assumptions profit will be $4.8 million, a decrease of 40%. The auditors will need to determine the reasons for the differences, in particular:

(1) **Erosion** of the **gross profit margin** because of decreased selling prices or problems with purchases (discussed below).

(2) **Increased bad debt allowance** or **contingency provision** (discussed below).

(ii) *Computerised inventory control system*

(1) The **reliability** of the new computerised inventory system will have to be **tested**. The auditors will have to check whether the system is in accordance with the **needs** of the **client**, the **staff** properly **trained, proper documentation provided** and **inventory quantities transferred correctly**. The auditors, using **computer-assisted audit techniques,** will need to check that the system adequately identifies and ages inventory.

(2) The auditors will also need to assess the **reliability** of the **inventory count procedures**. This will mean ascertaining **how often inventory** is **counted** and the procedures for **correcting differences** found between actual counted inventory and inventory recorded on the computer. The auditors would need to arrange to **attend** one or more of the **inventory counts** to check whether the laid-down procedures are being followed. They should check the **reasons** for the **differences** found on other inventory counts, because if the differences are large, this will indicate the computer records and/or inventory count procedures are inadequate.

(3) Ideally the work on the computer system and perpetual inventories procedures should be carried out before the year-end, in case problems with the system warrant the auditors asking for a **full inventory count** to be done at the year-end.

(iii) *Reliability problems*

(1) The auditors would need to check that **appropriate allowance** had been made against the balances outstanding on these customers' accounts by reviewing correspondence and any payments made since the year-end.

(2) There may be **claims** over and above the amounts owed. The auditors would need to check the likelihood of the claims being successful by examining correspondence with the customers and the company's lawyers, and discussions with the directors and lawyers. The company may also be in difficulties with the trading standards authorities.

(3) The problems with reliability may mean that some **existing inventories** has to be **written down.** The auditors will need to check what the company has done about the reliability problems, and the allowance that need to be made against year-end inventories to reduce it to net realisable value, and for credit notes.

(4) The problems over reliability may lead to **further bad debts** and **claims** of which the client and auditors are not yet aware. The auditors should also consider whether the legal consequences and bad publicity might impact so seriously as to call into question the company's ability to continue as a **going concern.**

(iv) *Sales increase*

(1) The concern here is that the new customers to whom credit has been granted are **poor credit risks.** The client does not have the assurance of previous settlement records that it has with existing customers. The more attractive terms may attract new customers who are having difficulty paying their current suppliers within the agreed credit period.

(2) The volume of new customers may mean that **credit granting** and **credit control procedures** have been **less strict** than in previous years. This may be evidenced by the increase in the age of receivables from 1.6 to 4.1 (and the increase in actual period over allowed period from 0.6 to 1.1 months).

(3) The increased age may mean that the client and auditors have **difficulty** in **identifying doubtful debts** until some months after the debt arises.

(4) The failure to receive cash may mean that the client is suffering **cash flow problems.** The auditors will need to check that the increases in settlement times have been incorporated into cash flow forecasts.

(v) *Management changes*

(1) The auditors need to **ascertain** the **reasons** for the dismissal. They need to confirm whether the dismissal was for **fraud**. If it was, the auditors will need to assess whether the company has identified the true **extent** of the fraud, what the **monetary loss** was and whether **other staff** were involved. Extensive substantive work will be needed on the areas affected.

(2) The financial director and purchases manager may be pursuing a claim for **unfair dismissal**; if so, disclosure or a provision may be required.

(3) The absence of the finance director may mean that certain **controls**, for example that all significant transactions have to be approved, have **lapsed**. The auditors would also need to assess the **qualifications** and **reliability** of the chief accountant, because these factors will impact upon whether the accounts will be prepared in time, and the likelihood of problems with them. The auditors may have to allow for spending significant time on checking the adequacy of accounting records. They may also have to spend more time overall on the audit than in previous years, as the client may be less able to assist because of its staff problems.

(4) The effect of the **absence** of the **purchasing manager** needs to be considered. Again controls may have lapsed, and this may have increased the risks of **other frauds** in the areas of inventory or purchases. Also there may be problems of **over-valuation of inventory**, caused by purchase of the wrong inventory or purchase of inventory at excessive prices. The auditors would also need to assess whether the **new** purchasing **manager** appears to be **operating effectively**.

22 Parker

Text references. Chapters 6 and 7

Top tips. Read the scenario carefully. Think carefully about the context. Going concern involves auditing future projections, not past transactions.

Easy marks. Part (a) is fairly straightforward and the mark allocation gives a clue as to the level of detail required – a basic definition of *'audit risk'* cannot be worth four marks on its own. You need to add an explanation of the three component parts of audit risk.

In part (b)(i) a careful reading of the scenario should give you some ideas about issues to mention in your answer. It is not enough simply to restate phrases from the question; you need to clarify *why* you think they will give rise to risks.

You should have learned about the main procedures an auditor would follow to review the directors' assessment of the going concern status of a company. This would give a good foundation to your answer to part (b) (ii) but you should try to make it detailed and relevant to the question.

Examiner's comments. Part (a) was answered very well.

In part (b) most candidates showed appropriate application of knowledge to the scenario, identifying the risks and explaining the effect of those risks. Some candidates split the answer into three sections of *inherent, control* and *detection* risks but marks were awarded for relevant points whether or not this split was made. A minority of candidates simply identified the risk areas but did not explain the relevance of the point being made.

Part (b) (ii) allowed candidates to show their knowledge of going concern reviews but the focus of answers should be on Parker so issues such as possible lack of forecasts, (lack of director control) could be mentioned. Some answers emphasised the audit of the statement of financial position but not the audit work going forward into the future; these answers were not adequate.

Marking scheme

			Marks
(a)	**One mark each explaining the following. Allow 0.5 where explanation incomplete**		
	Audit risk		1
	Inherent risk		1
	Control risk		1
	Detection risk		1
	Maximum marks		**4**
(b)	(i)	**1 mark per point**	
		Overtrading (expanding rapidly turnover, new product lines, cash reserves, credits/liquidation)	
		Internet trading (different products, naïve directors, new systems, higher returns, inventory obsolescence)	
		Control environment (overall weak, extent of errors not known, directors attitude, lack of skill Fin accountant, material error FS)	
		Bank loan (additional finance, audit disclaimer, liquidation)	
		First year of audit (audit report expectations, unreliable accounting systems, time needed – resist director pressure)	
		Maximum marks	**10**
	(ii)	**Key points 1 for each point**	
		Financial position of company – budgets etc	2
		Bank letter	1
		Bank correspondence	1
		Enquiries with directors	2
		Management accounts	1
		Letter of representation	1
		Final decision going concern	1
		Board minutes – review after year enc	1
		Other good relevant points	1
		Maximum marks	**6**
			20

(a) The term 'audit risk' literally means the risk that the auditor will give an incorrect opinion. The concern for the auditor is that he/she may issue an unmodified opinion in circumstances where there are material misstatements in the financial statements.

It can be analysed into three separate components:

(i) **Inherent risk**

This arises from factors specific to the business or its operating environment and which make errors more likely to occur. It could result from complex transactions, such as leases, or from pressures on management to achieve particular targets.

(ii) **Control risk**

This is the risk that the audit client's internal control does not prevent errors occurring or detect them after the event so that they may be corrected. This could be due to failures in the control environment, such as management allowing a culture of carelessness towards control procedures to develop or to failures of specific control procedures, for example, a lack of proper reconciliation of payables ledger balances to supplier statements could allow misstatements in trade payables to go undetected.

(iii) **Detection risk**

This is the risk that the auditor's substantive procedures do not detect material errors that exist. One component of this is sampling risk. Many audit procedures are performed using samples so introducing the possibility that whilst the sample may have been free from errors, there could be material misstatements elsewhere in the population.

There are a variety of other reasons why the auditor may fail to detect errors. These include lack of experience and time pressure.

(b) (i)

Matters	Audit risks associated with Parker Ltd
(1) The company sells books, CDs, DVDs and similar items	These goods are subject to fashions and trends, and this is a very competitive business where undercutting of sales prices is common. As a result, inventory values could be overstated if some lines cannot be sold or have to be sold at substantially discounted prices.
(2) Parker is a new audit client	This increases the detection risk for the auditor, as the firm has no previous experience of the company. This makes it harder to establish which areas of Parker's accounting systems are most susceptible to errors and also means that less reliance can be placed on analytical procedures.
(3) Online ordering over the internet	This may increase the control risk as the ordering and sales system is reliant on the security and procedures of not only Parker itself but also its counter parties and service provider etc.
(4) Expanding the range of goods	The proposed new products are also subject to fashions and trends so may increase the risk of incorrect inventory valuation. It may also be the case that the directors are moving into areas of business where they have less experience so the problems may be increased by poor buying decisions. If the expansion is unsuccessful, the company's going concern status may be threatened.
(5) Mail order accounting system	The high level of manual input appears to introduce many errors into the records. This could lead to errors in sales and receivables in the financial statements. The related invoicing errors may destroy customer goodwill and in the longer term may add to the threats to the company's going concern status.
(6) Directors' attitude to internal control	The directors appear to disregard the importance of internal control, meaning that no efforts are being made to detect and correct the errors mentioned above.

Matters	Audit risks associated with Parker Ltd
(7) Unqualified company accountant	The accountant seems to have been appointed solely because he is a friend of the directors rather than for his skill and experience. Also, as he is not a member of a reputable professional body, he is under no ethical obligations if he does have any doubts about the integrity of management.
(8) Requirement for high level of borrowing	There must be doubts over whether a business which is suffering so much pressure on its margins and is moving into new areas of activity is going to be able to generate sufficient profit to repay its loans. This will also raise the question of whether the company can continue as a going concern.
(9) Meeting with bank after the year end	The directors will want to present a healthy set of financial statements to the bank manager so there will be a risk that figures may have been manipulated. There will be an increased risk of error throughout the financial statements, particularly in areas that are at all subjective.
(10) Directors expect an audit report with an unmodified audit opinion to be signed before the meeting with the bank	This increases detection risk as the auditor is under time pressure and also will lack evidence of events after the reporting period. If the new loan is essential to the company's going concern status it may be difficult for the auditor to reach an opinion before the completion of the loan negotiations.

(ii) **Enquiries**

(1) Enquire about management's views on the prospects for profitability of the planned new lines of business.

(2) Enquire into any planned cost cutting to improve the company's profit margins.

(3) Enquire into whether there have been any problems with the operation of the online ordering system.

Procedures

(1) Obtain management's forecasts and projections and:

- Assess reasonableness of assumptions (for example, compare projected margins with those achieved by similar businesses)
- Review projections to verify that they have been based on these assumptions
- Review projections to check that all the information is consistent. For example, as the directors are planning to increase the inventory levels, check that allowance has been made for related increases in inventory holding costs.
- Calculate ratios, eg receivables days, to check reasonableness

(2) Review loan agreements for terms and conditions of existing borrowings and consider whether it appears likely that interest and capital payments can be met.

(3) Review minutes of board and committee meetings to assess management's views of the proposed new lines of business.

(4) Review correspondence with bank for any indications of the current relationship between Parker and its bankers and the likelihood of the bank providing more finance

(5) These reviews should all be continued in the period after the year end date right up to the date of the auditor's report.

(6) Obtain written representations from management acknowledging their responsibility for:

- Assessing the going concern status of the company
- Making reasonable assumptions in preparing forecasts and projections
- Deciding on the appropriate basis of preparation of the financial statements

23 EuKaRe

Text references. Chapters 6, 9 and 17.

Top tips. This question is about audit risk in the context of a charitable organisation so when you come to part (b) on the areas of inherent risk, you must bear in mind the type of organisation you are dealing with. Part (b) is on inherent risk areas and is worth 12 marks so you should be able to come up with six risk areas. Make sure you explain the effect of each risk on the audit approach, if you want to score well. Part (c) should be straightforward on the control environment as long as you keep in your mind the fact that the client is a charity and bear in mind the particular issues relevant to not-for-profit organisations.

Easy marks. Part (a) is straightforward knowledge and you should be very familiar with the audit risk model. There is no reason why you shouldn't be able to score the four marks available here. You should also be able to score well in part (c) on the control environment at the charity.

Examiner's comments. In part (a) common errors included explaining audit risk in terms of errors in the financial statements rather than inappropriate audit reports and omitting to explain that inherent risk is linked to the nature of the entity. In (b) the standard of the answer varied considerably. It appeared that the use of a charity was marginally concerning, although this was within the bounds of study. In part (c) the standard of answers was inadequate. Common errors included restating points from part (b) as also relevant to part (c) and omitting the question completely from the candidate's answer.

Marking scheme

		Marks
(a)	1 mark for explanation of each term	
	Audit risk	
	Inherent risk	
	Control risk	
	Detection risk	
	Maximum marks	4
(b)	1 mark for each area of inherent risk and 1 mark for explaining the effect on the audit = 2 marks per linked points	
	Income voluntary only	
	Completeness of income	
	Funds spent in accordance with charity objectives	
	Taxation rules	
	Reporting of expenditure	
	Donation for specific activities	
	Maximum marks	12
(c)	1 mark for each point on weak control environment	
	Lack of segregation of duties	
	Volunteer staff	
	Lack of qualified staff	
	No internal audit	
	Attitude of trustees	
	Maximum marks	4
	Total marks	20

(a) **Audit risk**

Audit risk is the risk that the auditor expresses an inappropriate audit opinion when the financial statements are materially misstated. Audit risk is a function of the risk of material misstatement and the risk that the auditor will not detect such misstatement (detection risk). The risk of material misstatement has two components: inherent risk and control risk. Audit risk can be summarised by the following equation:

Audit risk = Inherent risk × Control risk × Detection risk

Inherent risk is the susceptibility of an assertion to a misstatement that could be material, individually or when aggregated with other misstatements assuming that there were no related internal controls.

Control risk is the risk that a misstatement that could occur in an assertion and that could be material, individually or when aggregated with other misstatements, will not be prevented or detected and corrected on a timely basis by the entity's internal control.

Detection risk is the risk that the auditor's procedures will not detect a misstatement that exists in an assertion that could be material, individually or when aggregated with other misstatements.

(b) **Inherent risk areas**

Detailed constitution

The charity has a detailed constitution which sets out how money may be spent. This increases the inherent risk of the audit.

The auditors will need to spend time examining and becoming familiar with the constitution and design their audit procedures with this in mind.

Limit on administration expenditure

The constitution states that administration expenditure cannot exceed 10% of income in any year. This increases inherent risk as management may be tempted to misstate income or administration expenditure so this limit is not breached.

Special attention will need to be devoted to income and expenditure to ensure that the 10% limit is not breached legitimately.

Uncertainty of future income

The charity relies wholly on voluntary donations for its income which means that it cannot be assured of receiving a minimum level of income from one year to the next. This increases the risk of it not being able to continue.

The auditors must bear in mind whether the charity can continue as a going concern when carrying out their final review procedures. This will involve discussion with management and examination of budgetary information.

Cash donations

Some of the donations received will be in the form of cash collected from the public. There is a risk of misappropriation of cash as a result.

Controls over cash should be examined as this is an area open to misappropriation and theft.

Donations from individuals

Some donations have clauses about how the money can be spent. This again increases inherent risk because money may be misspent without regard for the conditions in place.

Where donations have been received with clauses attached, the auditors will need to do detailed work to ensure the conditions have not been breached.

Taxation legislation

There are complex rules in place regarding the taxation of charities.

The audit team will need to familiarise itself with the taxation rules for charities to ensure that this area is correctly dealt with.

(c) **Control environment**

The control environment at EuKaRe may be weak for a number of reasons.

The staff working at the charity may be volunteers who may not have accounts experience and who may also not work there full-time. There may also be a high staff turnover because of the nature of the work.

There may be a lack of segregation of duties in place due to the number of staff working at the charity. This means that trustees may play a role in the day to day running of the charity and there is therefore a risk of override of any controls that are in place.

The charity may not have an internal audit department in place due to its size or the equivalent of an audit committee to monitor its effectiveness.

There may also be a lack of budgetary information being produced on a timely basis which increases the control risk from the auditor's point of view.

24 BearsWorld

Text reference. Chapter 11

Top tips. Part (a) should be reasonably straightforward for 10 marks. Each procedure is worth two marks, one for explaining it and one for an example. This should give you an idea of how much to write for each one. Part (b) is trickier but again you can split the question up as you are asked to consider each procedure in turn. Use the clues in the scenario to help you with your answer.

Easy marks. Part (a) contained the easiest marks. ISA 500 *Audit evidence* is a key standard so you should be able to explain the main techniques of gathering audit evidence. As long as you took care to avoid the traps, eg talking about procedures relating to receivables when the question states there are none, it should have been reasonably easy to think of relevant examples for most of them.

Examiner's comments. Part (a) required an explanation of five different types of evidence and then applied this knowledge to a scenario where controls were weak – by implication the auditor would be looking for substantive evidence and this should be shown in the examples provided.

Answers were generally of a high standard. The main weaknesses were:

- Provision of examples without actually explaining what the collection method was. For example forgetting to mention that inspection actually meant looking at assets or documents to check existence or other assertions
- Some confusion between observation and inspection
- Some confusion relating to the use of analytical procedures

Answers to part (b) varied. Weaker answers tended to repeat information from part (a) or provide inappropriate examples. A significant minority did not attempt part (b), possibly due to time pressure at the end of the exam.

Marking scheme

			Marks
Types of evidence			
(a)	(i)	Types of audit evidence Award one mark for each well explained point. Allow 0.5 for simply stating the appropriate area.	
		Analytical procedures	1
		Inquiry	1
		Inspection	1
		Observation	1
		Computation	1

	Marks
(ii) Examples of evidence	
Award one mark for each well explained point. Allow 0.5 for simply mentioning the appropriate test	
Analytical procedures	1
Inquiry	1
Inspection	1
Observation	1
Computation	1
Maximum marks	**10**

Suitability of methods of gathering evidence

(b) Part (a) required candidates to state tests that could be carried out in BearsWorld. (b) takes this forward to actually considering whether each type of testing would be used in BearsWorld. Candidates should be able to identify that some methods of gathering evidence such as enquiry are of more use than others. Note – also allow procedures as if used in BearsWorld by director – question could be read this way.

Types of audit evidence

Award one mark for explaining whether each technique is suitable for BearsWorld and one mark for explaining limitations in that technique to a maximum of	**10**
	20

(a) **Analytical procedures**

(i) Analytical procedures mean the study of **trends and ratios** in financial and non-financial information. It is used within **audit planning** to identify risk areas and also as a means of gathering **substantive evidence**, for example by calculating an estimate of a particular figure based on knowledge of the business and comparing this to the actual figure.

(ii) A comparison of gross profit percentages month by month for BearsWorld could be performed and any unusual fluctuations investigated as these could indicate errors such as omission of sales, loss of inventory or other errors.

Inquiry

(i) Inquiry means requesting information. This could be from individuals within the company, either orally or in written representations, or in formal written requests to third parties.

(ii) In BearsWorld a relevant example would be to send a standard confirmation letter to the company's bank (could be illustrated with an example of enquiry to client staff).

Inspection

(i) Inspection means looking at documentation, books and records or assets. This could be done to confirm existence of an asset, to verify values or to provide evidence that a control has taken place.

(ii) The inventory of cuddly toys at the year-end could be inspected as part of the evidence relating to its value. The inspection would give evidence as to whether the inventory was in good saleable condition (could be illustrated with an example of inspection of documentation).

Observation

(i) Observation means watching a procedure being carried out. It is usually used as a means of gathering evidence about the internal controls in a company.

(ii) In BearsWorld it night be appropriate to observe the procedures that are carried out when the post is opened to assess whether controls exist to prevent the misappropriation of cash.

Recalculation

(i) Recalculation means the reperformance of an arithmetical process within the accounting system. This could involve re-checking a manual calculation or using a computer-assisted audit technique to reperform casts within the accounting records.

(ii) Depreciation is likely to be a significant expense within a manufacturing company such as BearsWorld. The auditor should recalculate this expense.

(b) The usefulness of **analytical procedures** depends on a number of factors including the reliability of the underlying information. It seems that, as a small business, BearsWorld has little segregation of duties and formal controls. This casts doubt on the reliability of the information and hence the conclusions that might be drawn from the analytical procedures.

Inquiry evidence from third parties will be essential in the audit of BearsWorld. As well as the bank confirmation it may be necessary to send confirmation letters to suppliers to obtain third party evidence of the liabilities at the year-end. Inquiry evidence from sources within BearsWorld will be obtained mainly from Mr Kyto and its reliability will be very dependent on how the auditors assess his integrity.

Inspection of documents will be a major part of the evidence gathered in the audit of BearsWorld. Supplier invoices will be inspected to verify values and to confirm that purchases and expenses are genuinely business items. There may be limits to the reliance that can be put on this as in a poor control environment it may be difficult to confirm whether documentation is complete.

Observation may be the only way to gather evidence about controls such as any that may exist over the opening of post. This type of evidence is limited in its usefulness for two reasons:

- It only provides evidence that the control operated at the point in time that the auditor carried out the test
- Client staff are likely to perform their duties exactly according to the company's procedures manual when they are aware that the external auditor is observing them whereas this may not be the case on any other day of the year

To place reliance on controls and reduce substantive testing the auditor needs evidence that controls operated effectively over the whole of the accounting period so the observation would be of limited usefulness. Observation of controls in operation over the year-end inventory count might be more useful as this is a one-off, rather than daily, procedure. If the auditor could see that the inventory count was being carried out in a well-controlled way then it may be possible to reduce substantive testing on the inventory sheets.

Re-calculation is a good check of the **accuracy** of invoices and control accounts. However it only covers figures that that have been recorded in the accounts, and will not identify omitted figures.

25 Porthos

Text reference. Chapter 11

Top tips. The important thing here is to read the question and apply your knowledge to the requirements. Key words to notice were *'advantages'* in part (a), *'difficulties'* in part (c) (i) and *'explaining the reasons'* in both parts (b) and (c)(ii).

The other thing to remember here is that you can get a long way with common sense. You may not have much audit experience but the chances are that you have ordered goods (not necessarily tennis racquets!) over the Internet. In part (b) you should think about what you'd expect to happen when you do that. Once you have thought about it in this way it should be much easier to think what sort of test data the auditor could use to test the system.

Take care not to confuse test data and audit software, a common mistake which could lead to a score of zero in either (a) or (c) (ii).

Easy marks. This was a fairly tough question but basic, rote-learned knowledge of CAATs would help you get started on parts (a) and (c).

Examiner's comments. The standard of answers to this question varied considerably. Part (a) was answered very well. In part (b), areas of weakness included confusing test data and audit software and relating answers to the scenario.

Part (c)(i) was answered well but part (c)(ii) was not, with weaknesses including repeating examples of test data or explaining systems testing but without using audit software. In summary, this is an area to revisit in a future examination.

Marking scheme

			Marks
(a)		**Advantages of CAATS – 1 mark each**	
		Test program controls	1
		Test more items quickly	1
		Test actual records	1
		Cost effective after initial setup	1
		Supplement traditional testing	1
		Other relevant points	1
		Maximum marks	**4**
(b)		**Examples of test data 0.5 for test and 0.5 for explanation**	
		Negative quantities	1
		High quantities	1
		Lack of payment details	1
		Invalid inventory code	1
		Invalid credit card details	1
		Invalid address	1
		Other relevant points	1
		Maximum marks	**6**
(c)	(i)	**Difficulties of using audit software – 1 mark each**	
		Setup costs	1
		Not available for bespoke systems	1
		Too much output/program errors	1
		Dangers of live testing	1
		Other relevant points	1
		Maximum marks	**4**
	(ii)	**Tests using audit software – 1 mark each**	
		Cast SDB	1
		Inventory ageing	1
		Sample inventory year end	1
		Sales invoices sample	1
		Completeness of recording – numeric sequence check	1
		Invoices paid for – should be no receivables	1
		Large credit notes	1
		Other relevant points	1
		Maximum marks	**6**
			20

(a) **Advantages of Computer-Assisted Audit Techniques (CAATs)**

Time savings

Potentially time-consuming procedures such as checking casts of ledgers can be carried out much more quickly using CAATs.

Reduction in risk

Larger samples can be tested, giving greater confidence that material errors have not been missed

Testing programmed controls

Without CAATs many controls within computerised systems cannot be tested, as they may not produce any documentary evidence. This gives greater flexibility of approach.

Cost effective

Many CAATs have low set-up costs, such as where information is downloaded from the client's system onto the auditor's copy of the same system. Even where CAATs have had to be written specially for a particular audit, the on-going costs will be minimal as they can be reused until the client changes its systems.

(b)

Test data	Reason
Order for unusually high quantities, eg 20 racquets	This would identify whether any reject controls requiring special authorisation for large orders are effective. This control would also prompt the customer to recheck the quantity if they had accidentally keyed in the wrong quantity.
Orders with fields left blank	This would give evidence as to whether orders could be accepted that prove impossible to deliver because, for example, the name of the town has been omitted from the delivery address.
Orders with invalid credit card details	This will identify whether the controls over the ordering system will protect the company from losses arising from credit card frauds.
Orders with details of customers on retailers' 'blacklists' or of cards that have been reported as stolen	This will identify whether the company has effective procedures to ensure that their system is regularly updated for security. This should reduce the risk of bad debts.
Order with invalid inventory code	This will show whether the system will alert the customer to the code error and prompt them to check it. This should ensure that the correct goods are dispatched.
Order with complete and valid details	This order should be accepted by the system so will allow the auditor to inspect the order confirmation to determine whether the order details are transferred accurately into the dispatch system.

(c) (i) **Difficulties of using audit software**

- The **costs** of designing tests using audit software can be substantial as a great deal of planning time will be needed in order to gain an in-depth understanding of the client's systems so that appropriate software can be produced.
- The **audit costs in general may increase** because experienced and specially trained staff will be required to design the software, perform the testing and review the results of the testing.
- If errors are made in the design of the audit software, audit time, and hence costs, can be **wasted** in investigating anomalies that have arisen because of flaws in how the software was put together rather than by errors in the client's processing.
- If audit software has been designed to carry out procedures during live running of the client's system, there is a risk that this **disrupts** the client's systems. If the procedures are to be run when the system is not live, extra costs will be incurred by carrying out procedures to verify that the version of the system being tested is identical to that used by the client in live situations.

(ii) **Audit tests using audit software**

Test	Reason
Test casts and extensions of inventory listing	To verify the accuracy of the calculation of the final inventory figure.
Reperformance of the ageing of inventory in the inventory listing	To ensure that the ageing is accurate before using an aged listing to identify items that might be obsolete and hence need to be written down.
Selecting a sample of inventory lines to count at the year-end inventory count	This will be a quicker and more objective method of selecting a sample rather than doing this manually.
Performing a sequence check on the sales invoice numbers issued over the year.	This will give assurance in respect of the completeness of recording of sales.
Select a sample of credit notes, perhaps including all those over a certain value	This will be an effective means of selecting a sample so that the auditor can trace supporting documentation to check that credit notes have only been issued for valid reasons eg returns of racquets, and with appropriate authorisation.
Cast the sales day books for the year	This will give evidence that the sale figure has been calculated accurately.
Match dates of sales invoices/date posted to ledgers with date on related despatch data	This will give evidence that sales cut-off has been performed accurately.

26 Tirrol

Text references. Chapters 6 and 11

Top tips. The study text contains a list of benefits of using Computer Assisted Audit Techniques (or CAATs), but in part (a) (i) you should link these to the scenario by using those most relevant to the situation given. For example being able to test more inventory items quickly is especially relevant as you are told there is only a short time in which to complete the audit.

The second part of (a) is relatively straightforward because the facts in the scenario should help you to highlight a range of problems. Because there are a number of problems you could state (including some not listed in the answer below), and potential ways to overcome them, just be careful not to exceed your time allocation. You will need your full allotted time in the more difficult part (b).

In part (b) you must maintain a focus on evaluating the systems documentation. Although internal audit has prepared the documentation and their ability must be evaluated, your answer must include the steps you would take to evaluate the accuracy of the documentation itself.

Easy marks. With 10 marks available in part (a) (ii), you should be able to pick up on problems relatively easily as you read through the scenario. For example you know the work needs to take place in July and the scenario specifically states July is major holiday period for your firm. There is then usually more than one way to overcome each problem and any valid suggestions will gain a mark.

Examiner's comments. In (a) part (i), most candidates demonstrated basic knowledge of the use of audit software explaining the 'standard' benefits of time, cost, use of actual data in the computer etc. A few candidates made some good links to the scenario, for example, explaining how data could be amalgamated to avoid having to visit the 25 branches in the company.

In (a) part (ii), again most candidates provided a range of valid points and obtained decent marks.

In part (b) the main area of weakness related to candidates spending too much time explaining the appointment and general work of internal audit rather than placing reliance on this function.

ACCA examiner's answer. The ACCA examiner's answer to this question can be found at the back of this kit.

Marking scheme

			Marks
(a)	(i)	Benefits of audit software 1 mark per benefit – 0.5 for identifying the benefit and 0.5 for explaining the benefit. – Standard systems – Use actual computer files – Test more items – Cost – Other relevant points	
		Maximum marks	**4**
	(ii)	Problems in the audit of Tirrol 2 marks for each problem. 1 for explaining the problem and 1 for explaining how to alleviate the problem. – Six week reporting deadline – Timescale – software issues – First year audit costs – Staff holidays – Non-standard systems – Live testing – Usefulness of audit software – Other relevant points	
		Maximum marks	**10**
(b)		Reliance on internal audit documentation 1 mark per point – Appropriate qualifications – Produced according to plan – Problems with use noted – Documentation logical – Compare to live system – Use documentation to amend audit software – Other relevant points	
		Maximum marks	**6**
			20

(a) **Tirrol**

(i) **Benefits of using audit software**

(1) **Ability to test all locations**

The software in each of the 25 different locations is the same; therefore the audit software will not need to be adapted for each location resulting in time (and therefore cost) savings.

(2) **Ability to gain more evidence**

It will be possible to test more transactions using the audit software than simply manually scanning print outs. For example the audit software can search all items for exceptions, such as negative or very high quantities. The additional information will give the auditor increased comfort that the stock figure is reasonably stated.

(3) **Source files tested**

The actual computer files will be tested from the originating programme, rather than print outs from spool or previewed files which are dependent on other software (and therefore could contain errors or could have been tampered with following export).

(4) **Long term cost-effectiveness**

Using audit software is likely to be cost-effective in the long-term if the client does not change its systems.

(ii) **The audit of Tirrol – problems and potential solutions**

Problem	How the problem can be overcome
There is a tight reporting deadline. The firm has only one and a half months following the year end to complete the audit but needs to ensure it obtains sufficient appropriate audit evidence.	Careful planning of the audit engagement is needed including special consideration of using more experienced audit team members to ensure standards are upheld despite the tight deadline.
Tirrol is a new client and this is the first time the firm will have audited this company. Extra time will be needed to document the understanding of the entity, its environment and its systems, and there will be additional work involved to verify material opening balances. This will result in extra costs which will need to be budgeted for.	The additional time should be identified at the planning stage and budgeted for. The audit manager will need to monitor the work as it is carried out and be able to provide evidence of any instance where overruns are caused by the client (eg for failing to make files available on a timely basis). The client may then be more likely to accept separate bills for the additional work.
Rewriting of audit software is required before testing, which then needs to be carried out on a live basis, but this must be completed before 15 August 20X9.	The audit will need to be carefully planned to ensure the team includes an expert on the audit software. A clear timetable must be agreed with the client setting out availability of access to the system, files and personnel required to complete testing.
It is likely there will be limited staff available in July due to anticipated holidays and the fact the Tirrol audit is probably being planned after other assignments having just gained the assignment through a competitive tender.	Planning and timetabling should be commenced as soon as possible, but it may be necessary to request staff be seconded from other offices if necessary (if Cal & Co. has other offices). Another option may be to reschedule other audit assignments to free up staff (where the clients may not be as time sensitive).
Testing on a live basis is potentially risky as the audit testing could potentially corrupt client data and leave Cal & Co. susceptible to legal action.	Cal & Co should make sure the client runs back ups of data before each audit test is commenced while the system is live.

(b) **Evaluation of internal audit documentation**

ISA 610 *Using the work of internal auditors* sets out the general rules an auditor must follow when evaluating work of the internal auditors. Application of these rules results in the following procedures.

Evaluating the competence and ability of the internal auditors will include:

- Obtaining details of relevant IT or accountancy qualifications held by the internal auditors
- Establishing how this and other projects to produce systems documents is planned and tested (for example are testers independent of those producing the documents)
- Establishing how the documentation is used in internal audit work, obtaining evidence of its use and finding out if it has been updated where problems have been found.

Evaluating the accuracy of the documentation itself will involve:

- Comparing the document with the actual system (by following a transaction through the system using the diagram) to ensure it is an accurate record.
- Ensuring the diagram includes clear and consistent symbols and keys throughout
- Ensuring the documents contain evidence of proper review and authorisation by senior internal audit personnel.

27 Serenity

Text references. Chapters 6 and 19

Top tips. Part (a) of this question should be straightforward as you are asked to explain the purpose of risk assessment procedures and outline sources of audit evidence that can be used for this part of the audit. In part (b), you have to identify issues to be considered during the planning stage of an audit. There are lots of clues in the question scenario so the best way to approach this part of the question is to go through the scenario line-by-line, jotting down issues as you go. This will give more structure to your answer, as will the use of sub-headings for each issue you identify.

Easy marks. These are available for basic technical knowledge in part (a) for six marks on risk assessment procedures and sources of evidence and part (c) for four marks on explaining what negative assurance means.

Marking scheme

			Marks
(a)	One mark per point		
	(i)	Purpose of risk assessment – understand client	1
		Material misstatements	1
		Knowledge of classes of transactions	1
		Association risk	1
	(ii)	Evidence from inquiry (with example)	1
		Analytical review (with example)	1
		Observation (with example)	1
		Maximum marks	**6**
(b)	One mark per point		
	Skills necessary?		1
	Self-review threat		1
	Acceptance non-audit work		1
	Fee income		1
	Internal audit – fee pressure		1
	Client growth		1
	Association threat		1
	Advocacy threat		1
	Report on cash flow		1
	Possible going concern		1
	Other relevant points (each)		1
	Maximum marks		**10**
(c)	Key points one for each point = knowledge outside scenario		
	Accuracy of cash flow not confirmed		1
	'Reasonable' – not T&F		1
	Nothing to indicate cash flow is incorrect		1
	Forecast relates to future – uncertainty		1
	Conditions may not turn out as expected		1
	Other relevant points (each)		1
	Maximum marks		**4**
			20

(a) (i) Risk assessment procedures are performed at the planning stage of an audit to obtain an understanding of the entity being audited and to identify any areas of concern which could result in material misstatements in the financial statements. They allow the auditor to assess the nature, timing and extent of audit procedures to be performed.

(ii) Sources of audit evidence that can be used as part of risk assessment procedures.

- Inquiries of management
- Prior year financial statements
- Current year management accounts and budgets
- Analytical procedures
- Observation and inspection

(b) *Poor internal controls and rapid growth*

The accounting systems of Serenity Co are changing rapidly and the control systems are difficult to maintain as the company continues to grow. This indicates that the **internal controls are likely to be poor** so control risk and the risk of material misstatements in the accounts will be high. Therefore a **fully substantive audit** is likely and Mal & Co must ensure it has enough time and resources to obtain sufficient audit evidence to support the figures in the financial statements.

Reliance on internal audit department

Serenity Co has only **recently established** its internal audit department so Mal & Co needs to be very careful in deciding whether it can place reliance on the work performed by internal audit and ultimately in a reduced external audit fee, as desired by the financial controller. Additional time and work would be required to assess internal audit so an immediate reduction in the fee is very unlikely.

Additional services required

Serenity Co requires additional services of review and implementation of control systems but Mal & Co must consider whether it has sufficiently skilled **resources** to carry out this additional work as it is a small firm with a number of clients in different sectors.

Fee income

The additional work required by Serenity Co will result in increased fee income to Mal & Co. The audit firm must ensure that its **fee income** from this one client does not breach the guidelines set by the ACCA's Code of Ethics. These state that the fee income from an unlisted client should not exceed 15% of the firm's total fees.

Self-review threat

The additional work required on the review and implementation of control systems at Serenity Co could result in the risk of **self-review**. Mal & Co must ensure it implements appropriate safeguards to mitigate this risk, such as separate teams to carry out the review work and the external audit. This may be difficult in a small audit firm. It would also be essential to ensure that the client makes all the management decisions in relation to the systems.

Legal status of new mobile

The legal status of the new mobile product is not known – it may be illegal. Any **adverse publicity** generated as a result will impact on Mal & Co as the auditors of the company. The audit firm needs to consider carefully whether it wants to be associated with Serenity Co. The fact that the company is planning to make a product of dubious legality raises questions about the **integrity of the directors**, and the audit team should be cautious in relying on any written representations provided by the directors.

Reliance on cash flow statement for licence

The granting of the licence to market the mobile is dependent on the financial stability of the company. Mal & Co may be asked to provide a report on the company's cash flow statement for the following financial year. This needs to be considered carefully – Mal & Co must ensure it has sufficient experienced **resources** for this work and determine what kind of **assurance** is required.

Going concern assumption

The company is **growing rapidly** and is relying on the granting of a licence for the new mobile, whose legal status is not known. These factors may indicate a possible **going concern risk** which should be monitored carefully.

(c) 'Negative assurance' refers to when an auditor gives an assurance that nothing has come to his or her attention which indicates that the financial statements have not been prepared according to the identified financial reporting framework, ie the auditor gives his or her assurance in the absence of any evidence to the contrary.

Negative assurance is given on **review assignments** such as the review of a company's cash flow statement. Such a statement relates to the future so is based upon **assumptions** that cannot be confirmed as accurate. The auditor cannot therefore confirm positively that the statement is materially true and fair.

28 Tam

Text references. Chapters 6, 7 and 11

Top tips. This is a question on audit sampling and includes both knowledge-based and scenario-based aspects. In parts (a) and (c), don't just simply produce one line definitions for the terms in the question – you need to explain them fully in order to score well. In part (b), break the question down into three parts for each of the comments made by each of the audit team – this means you need to aim to write sufficiently to score three marks for each comment. Breaking the question down like this into smaller parts makes it more manageable and less daunting.

Easy marks. These are available in parts (a) and (c) of the question, provided you are comfortable with audit sampling and the concept of materiality.

Marking scheme

			Marks
(a)	One mark per point		
	(i)	Sampling risk	
		Explanation	1
		Example	1
		Non-sampling risk	
		Explanation	1
		Example	1
	(ii)	Sampling risk	
		Controlled by	1
		Non-sampling risk	
		Controlled by	1
		Allow other relevant points	1
		Maximum marks	**6**
(b)	One mark per point		
	Audit manager comments		
	Explanation of sampling method		1
	Small population		1
	Transactions material		1
	Audit senior points		
	Explanation of sampling method		1
	Population homogenous – therefore use statistical sampling		1
	Time to produce sample		1
	Audit junior points		
	Explanation of sampling method		1
	Sample selection not random		1
	Can't draw valid statistical conclusion		1
	Allow other relevant points		1
	Maximum marks		**9**

		Marks
(c)	One mark per point	
	Definition	
	Materiality – omission or misstatement	1
	Materiality – size of the item	1
	Important because:	
	Financial statements incorrect	1
	Directors/owners know of errors; auditor reporting to	1
	Third parties rely on financial statements	1
	Other relevant points	1
	Maximum marks	5
		20

(a) (i) '**Sampling risk**' is the risk that the auditor's conclusion, based on a sample, may be different from the conclusion reached if the entire population were subject to the same audit procedure. There are two types of sampling risk. In the first type, the auditor concludes in a test of controls, that controls are more effective than they actually are, or in a test of details, that a material error does not exist when it actually does. In the second type, the auditor concludes in a test of controls, that controls are less effective than they actually are, or in a test of details, that a material error exists when it actually does not.

'**Non-sampling risk**' arises from factors that cause the auditor to reach an incorrect conclusion for any reason not related to the size of the sample. For example, the auditor may rely on audit evidence that is persuasive rather than conclusive, the auditor may use inappropriate audit procedures, or the auditor misinterprets audit evidence and fails to recognise an error.

(ii) Sampling risk can be controlled by the audit firm by **increasing sample size** for both tests of control and tests of detail.

Non-sampling risk can be controlled by the audit firm by **proper engagement planning**, **supervision and review**.

(b) The audit manager wants to check all the invoices in the year. This would involve checking around 500 invoices. This would be impractical in terms of time and cost for the directors of Tam Co. Although 500 is not a huge population, it is unlikely that the firm would test 100% in practice.

The audit senior wants to select a sample using statistical sampling techniques. This would involve calculating a sample size appropriate to the auditor's assessment of factors such as risk, required confidence level, tolerable misstatement and expected error. Such a sample can still produce valid conclusions and in this case, the population consists of items showing similar characteristics. Where statistical sampling is used all the items in the population must have an equal chance of being selected, so the sample should be picked using a method such as random number tables or a systematic basis. Provided that the sales invoices are sequentially numbered, this should be easy to apply in the example.

The audit junior's suggestion is to use a 'random' method of selecting samples manually and choosing a few important ones. This approach would not be appropriate because the auditor is not choosing the sample randomly as there would be bias involved and implies that 'haphazard' selection would be used. Valid conclusions would not be able to be drawn because statistical sampling had not been used to select the sample.

(c) Information is material if its omission or misstatement could **influence** the economic decisions of users taken on the basis of the financial statements. Materiality depends on the size of the item or error judged in the particular circumstances of its omission or misstatement. Materiality also has **qualitative**, as well as **quantitative**, aspects which must be considered. The auditor will determine materiality levels for the financial statements as a whole, but will also set lower levels of **performance materiality**:

- To reduce to an appropriately low level the risk that undetected or uncorrected aggregate misstatements exceed materiality for the financial statements as a whole.
- For particular classes of transactions, account balances or disclosures.

Materiality for the financial statements as a whole is often calculated as a percentage of different items in the financial statements, such as revenue, profit before tax or net assets. In the case of Tam Co, materiality is likely to be based on 0.5 – 1% of revenue, ie $350-700k.

The auditors of Tam Co must form an **opinion** on whether the financial statements are free from material misstatement because there is a requirement for an audit under local legislation for this company. Other users of the accounts may also be relying on the outcome of the audit, such as the bank since the company has recently taken out a five year bank loan to finance an expansion. The bank would be very interested in the accounts of Tam Co as a basis for assessing whether the company will be able to repay the loan. Users of the financial statements expect to receive reasonable assurance that the information is 'presented fairly in all material respects' or is 'true and fair'. This implies that there are no material misstatements or omissions.

29 Ajio

Text references. Chapters 6 and 7

Top tips. The key to part (a) of the question is to ensure that you explain the risk rather than simply identifying the risk factor. For example you may decide that the fact that the organisation is a charity as opposed to a company is a risk in itself but to score well you need to expand and explain why eg volunteers lack expertise. Also notice that you are asked to consider the implications for overall audit risk. Here you need to think about the relationship between the different components of risk.

In part (b) you do need to think sensibly about the practicalities of the fund raising events. How is the cash collected? What happens to it when it is returned to Ajio? How is the income recorded? Once you have thought about the sequence of events it will be much easier to devise audit tests for each stage.

Easy marks. In part (a) although you should ideally explain the risks make sure that you at least identify the risk factors. Remember these can normally be taken from the scenario itself. In part (b) audit tests relating to expenditure should be relatively straightforward. In this case the fact that the entity is a charity does not make a significant difference.

Examiner's comments. Generally the answers were good however many candidates did not read the information carefully and answered the question as if Ajio was a company. In part (b) candidates were asked for audit tests relating to fund raising events. Many candidates gave answers based on the charity as a whole. Some answers did not take into account the fact that the charity was a small one. These went into great detail about segregation of duties and other control procedures which would not have been appropriate in these circumstances.

Marking scheme

		Marks
(a)	Risks and implication for audit risk Up to 2 marks per point to a maximum of	10
(b)	Audit tests – fund raising events Up to 2 marks per point to a maximum of	10
		20

(a) **Risks**

Inherent and control risks (risk of material misstatement)

The complexity and extent of regulations

There is a risk that the charity will **fail to comply** with new and existing regulations. It may also be involved in activities which are not compatible with its charitable status. This is particularly the case where small charities like Ajio are involved as they may not be run by individuals with the required expertise. The fact that the accounts are prepared by a recently retired accountant should reduce the auditor's assessment of this risk however.

Completeness of income

There is a risk that **income may be misstated**. This risk is increased by the high levels of cash donations made as these are not supported by any documentary evidence. Cash may be misappropriated or errors could be made in counting and recording. Completeness of income from bequests would also be difficult to confirm as there is no predictable pattern in terms of their receipt. This risk is likely to be increased by the fact the Ajio is unlikely to have sophisticated controls in place.

Uncertainty of future income

Due to the **unpredictable nature of income** there is a risk that the charity will undertake projects which it subsequently finds it is unable to finance. This factor will also make it more difficult for the auditor to assess whether the charity is viable on an ongoing basis.

Skills and qualifications of trustees

Control risk is increased if the trustees do not have the skills required to manage the affairs of the charity. It will also be affected by the extent to which they are involved and the amount of time which they are able to devote to its affairs.

Use of volunteers

Control risk is increased by the use of volunteers. The charity is dependent upon their integrity and commitment. Shortcomings may arise from a lack of training and from their attitude in that they may resent formal procedures. Bogus volunteers may commit fraud.

Quality of paid staff

Lack of resources may result in staff being employed who are not sufficiently qualified. In the case of Ajio a part-time bookkeeper has been employed instead of a full time accountant. If this individual is under constant time pressure the **risk of errors** in the accounts is increased.

Lack of formal procedures

There is a risk that the charity may be run in an informal manner which will result in a **poor control environment**. This problem is likely to be accentuated by a lack of segregation of duties due to the small number of staff involved.

Detection risk

Recent appointment

Detection risk is increased by the fact that the firm has only recently been appointed. The audit team will not be able to rely on their experience of this audit from previous years. In addition the regulations are new. There is a risk that the auditors will fail to perform specific procedures required by the regulations due to a lack of familiarity with them. Adequate planning will reduce this risk.

Reduced reliance on analytical procedures

Due to the unpredictable nature of income it may be more difficult to rely on the results of analytical procedures to assess the **completeness of income**. This increases detection risk as analytical procedures are one of the key tests in this area. The results of alternative procedures will reduce this risk.

Implications for overall audit risk

The aim of the auditor is to reduce overall audit risk (the risk of issuing an inappropriate opinion) to a reasonable level. Audit risk is a function of the risk of material misstatement (inherent risk and control risk) and detection risk. As inherent risk and control risk in Ajio appear to be high/medium **detection risk will need to be low**. This will be achieved by increasing audit work eg increasing sample sizes. Risk areas will also be targeted, in this case income and cash being key balances.

(b) **Audit tests**

Income

- Attend a fund raising event and observe procedures to confirm that they are in accordance with the guidance set down by the charity eg use of sealed collection boxes.

- Count cash at the end of the day and agree to returns submitted by volunteers.
- Match returns submitted with amounts on the bank paying-in slips.
- Trace entry of cash received to cash book and bank statements.
- Review the preparation of monthly bank reconciliations.
- Compare amounts received by cash collections with previous years balances and forecasts. Discuss major fluctuations with trustees.
- Obtain representations from the trustees regarding the completeness of income.

Expenditure

- Obtain a breakdown of expenditure relating to fund raising events and check that the nature of the cost is reasonable.
- For a sample of expenses trace the cost to a supporting invoice or other documentation.
- Compare the overall level of expenditure with previous years and with budgets. Discuss any major fluctuations with management.
- For a sample of major expenses confirm that the expenditure has been authorised by the trustees.

30 B-Star

Text references. Chapters 7, 10, 11 and 14

Top tips. Part (a) requires a list of the main sections of an audit strategy document, an explanation of the purpose of each section and an example relevant to the company in the scenario. A tabular approach using the three mini requirements as headers will help you structure your answer and make sure you answer the question fully. Don't worry if the examples you came up with are not the same as those listed, as long as they are relevant you will be awarded marks.

Part (b) involves identifying risks in part (i) and then in part (ii) requires a **discussion** of the extent two different approaches can be used to confirm completeness of income. Note the requirement does not ask you to simply list procedures. Using facts specific to B-Star will give you the discussion points you need. For example, the controls stated in the scenario are not documented so this limits the usefulness of tests of controls.

Part (c) asks for a list of specific **analytical** procedures – do not confuse these with other substantive procedures. Your procedures need to be specific in order to gain full marks. Think about the industry in which B-Star operates and remember that estimates and expectations should be formed using information outside of the accounting system when testing completeness.

When answering questions like part (d) don't be tempted to write all the procedures you know for testing receivables balances. Just include those most relevant to the scenario. There are only a limited number of marks available here, so spend the allotted time and then move on.

Easy marks. Part (c) and (d) both involve listing procedures so there is no ambiguity here. As long as your procedures are specific to the scenario you should be able to pick up most of the marks available.

Examiner's comments. In part (a) a significant number of candidates did not appear to be aware of what an audit strategy is. Many candidates did not even attempt the question. Of those candidates attempting the question, answers tended to fall into two main categories:

Firstly, setting out sections of the strategy, and providing clear examples. Answers in this category included candidates who were not clear of the actual headings of the strategy, but even so attempted to think 'big picture' about the audit and make comments accordingly. These answers were usually satisfactory.

Secondly, focusing on the detail of the audit. Answers in this category listed income, expenditure, asset and liability headings and then attempted to show the detailed testing required for each section. The lack of focus on the overall audit approach limited the marks that could be awarded. This type of answer was unsatisfactory.

(b) Part (i) was generally answered well with many candidates being quite realistic and/or inventive regarding how either cash could be stolen or visitors to the park obtain entry without paying. A minority of answers tended to focus on control weaknesses without actually stating how this affected completeness of income. Part (ii) was almost always answered inadequately. Almost all candidates appeared to see the words '*tests of controls and substantive procedures*' and therefore provided a long list of possible tests of control and substantive procedures on the sale system. Unfortunately, the question requirement was '*discuss the extent to which tests of control and substantive procedures could be used to confirm the assertion of completeness of income...*', a completely different question.

In part (c) The main weakness in many answers was the lack of discrimination between substantive procedures and substantive *analytical* procedures. Almost all answers included one or more pure substantive procedure with a minority focusing on this type of procedure to the exclusion of analytical procedures.

In part (d) Most candidates appeared to understand the question and provided an appropriate range of procedures. The main weakness in many answers was the confusion between the audit of sales and the audit of receivables. A minority of candidates explained how the total sales figure could be audited, for example, testing receipts through the sales day book to recording in the sales ledger.

ACCA examiner's answer. The ACCA examiner's answer to this question can be found at the back of this kit.

Marking scheme

			Marks
(a)	Audit strategy document 0.5 for each section of audit strategy document, 0.5 for explaining the purpose of that section, 1 for the relevant example from B-Star scenario. Procedure – Understand the entity's environment – Understand the accounting and control systems – Risk and materiality – Timing and extent of audit procedures – Co-ordination, supervision and review of work – Other relevant points **Maximum marks**		8
(b)	(i)	Risks re completeness of sales and cash receipts 1 for each risk Procedures – The computer system does not record sales accurately – Cash not recorded – Tickets are issued but no payment is received – that is the sale is not recorded – Cash is removed by the ticket office personnel, etc – The account clerks miscount the amount of cash received from a ticket office – Other relevant points. **Maximum marks**	4
	(ii)	Use of tests of controls and substantive procedures Up to 1 for each valid response and up to 2 for showing whether the procedure is valid for B-Star case. Weaknesses – Tests of controls – Substantive procedures **Maximum marks**	6

Marks

(c) Analytical procedures

1 mark each for each valid procedure

(i) Ticket sales for one day
- Proof in total
- Compare sales day-by-day
- Compare sales to souvenirs sales
- Compare ticket offices day-by-day and staff rotation
- Compare cash receipts to ticket sales
- Other relevant points

Maximum marks 4

(ii) Ticket sales for year
- Prior year income * 15%
- Adjust for rainy days
- Compare actual and budget
- Industry trends
- Other relevant points

Maximum marks 4

(d) Year end receivables
- Individual balances to list of receivables
- Cast list
- Cut-off
- Direct confirmation
- Alternative procedures to direct confirmation
- After date sales – debit notes
- Presentation in financial statements
- Other relevant points

Maximum marks 4

30

(a) **Audit strategy document**

Section	Purpose	Example relevant to B-Star
Characteristics of the engagement	Provides details of the industry and regulatory environment the client operates in. Describes the entity's activities.	B-Star is a theme park and as a result will need to comply with significant health and safety regulation.
Reporting objectives, timing of the audit engagement and nature of communications	Provides details of the client's reporting dates, the proposed timetable and dates for proposed meetings with management.	B-Star is starting to plan less than a month before the year end to be audited. It may be necessary to schedule an initial meeting with management pre year end to ensure any necessary year end testing can be carried out (eg non-current asset verification, spares inventory count.)
Significant factors, preliminary engagement activities, and knowledge gained on other engagements	Identifies areas where there is a greater risk of material misstatement and a greater susceptibility to fraud. Details management's commitment to design, implementation and maintenance of a sound internal control environment. Details the basis for setting materiality.	B-Star makes cash sales. This increases the susceptibility to fraud. An approach which can appropriately test the completeness of income is needed.

Section	Purpose	Example relevant to B-Star
Nature, timing and extent of resources	Details the audit team members and their responsibilities. States the budget for the audit engagement.	The client is experiencing relatively rapid growth in terms of customer numbers. An assessment should be made as to whether additional staff or more experienced staff are required to carry out the proposed testing.

(b) (i) **Risks affecting completeness of sales and cash receipts**

1 Sales are incorrectly recorded on the computer, or information is not properly transferred to the accounts office

2 Cash is lost or stolen by the security guards before passing on to the accounts clerks.

3 The accounts clerks miscount the cash, or remove it and do not record it in the cash book

4 There is an error when recording the cash book totals in the nominal ledger

(ii) **Completeness of sales and cash receipts**

Use of tests of control

Tests of control are designed to obtain audit evidence of the design of the accounting and internal control systems and the operation of the internal controls throughout the period. If the controls over the completeness of sales and cash receipts are expected to be operating effectively, the auditor may seek to rely on these and will test these controls.

In B-Star's case, there are relevant internal controls (such as the agreement of the sales information transferred from each office to the cash totals), but there is no evidence that these controls are documented (such as signatures on the documents checked or signatures on a related checklist).

In the absence of documented controls the auditor could use observations (for example observing the clerks carrying out their checks) and inquiry to obtain some evidence over the completeness of income. However, given that planning is taking place so close to the year end, the chance to observe the controls occurring during the financial year to be audited is limited and the auditor is unlikely to gain sufficient appropriate audit evidence over completeness of income using only tests of controls.

Use of substantive procedures

Substantive procedures include analytical procedures and tests of detail of transactions, account balances and disclosure.

Analytical procedures include comparing figures in the accounts with expectations and investigating variances from these expectations. For B-Star there is data available to form an estimate of the expected level of income without using the accounting records. The actual results can be compared with this estimate and differences can be investigated and corroborated where necessary.

Tests of detail could be used to follow transactions through the sales system (from ticket issue to nominal ledger) to ensure each ticket tested has been recorded. This will be time consuming so sampling techniques will be applied, with the sample sizes dependent on the extent of evidence gained from analytical procedures and tests of control.

(c) **Substantive analytical procedures**

(i) **Ticket sales for one day**

1 Compare daily sales against budgeted sales and investigate there is a valid reason for large variances (for example bad weather resulting in low attendance).

2 Perform proof in total by multiplying ticket price by number of tickets sold.

3 Compare sales across the different categories with previous days. For example if ticket sales have gone up from previous days, have souvenir sales increased also?

4 For daily credit card sales, investigate whether the commission total represents a reasonable percentage of credit card sales made.

(ii) **Ticket sales for the year**

1 Perform proof in total for income from ticket sales:

- Obtain sales for the previous year
- Multiply by 115% to reflect increasing customer numbers
- Adjust for the number of rainy days by adding (or deducting) 50% of the new daily average for each rainy day below (or above) the average 30 days of rain.

2 Compare annual sales against budgeted sales and discuss variations with management, requesting corroborative evidence where necessary.

3 Compare B-Star's performance with other theme parks and in light of industry reports on, for example, customer numbers. Ask the management for explanations where there are apparent anomalies.

(d) **Audit procedures on credit card receivables balance**

1 Agree each individual credit card company's ledger account balance to the list of credit card receivables.

2 Cast the list of credit card receivables and agree the total to that shown on the receivables control account.

3 For the final day of the financial year being audited and the first day of the next financial year, agree sales income totals from the ticket office records to the cash book and receivables ledger to ensure they were recorded in the proper period.

For an appropriate sample (for example a sample including material items and other items selected randomly from the residual population):

4 Circularise the credit card companies and obtain direct confirmation of year end balances where possible. Where circularisation is not possible or confirmations are not received, obtain evidence of existence by ensuring cash was received post year end in respect of year end balances.

31 Rhapsody

Text references. Chapters 3 and 10

Top tips. Part (a) of this question is on deficiencies in the sales system and you should find it reasonably straightforward. You've been asked to set out four deficiencies so work on the basis that there are three marks available for each deficiency, implication and recommendation, plus a further two marks overall for your presentation. Setting out your answer to this part in a tabular format would be sensible since this enables you to link deficiencies, implications and recommendations easily. When making recommendations, bear in mind your knowledge of the client from the question scenario so that your recommendations are pertinent and sensible – think about what you would recommend if you were working in the internal audit department of this company for real.

Easy marks. Easy marks are available in part (b) of this question on the advantages of audit committees. However, you should also be able to score two easy marks in part (a) as you are told in the requirement that two marks are available for presentation – don't throw these away by preparing a poorly presented answer.

Examiner's comments. The overall standard of answers to part (a) was satisfactory. Common errors included:

- Not obtaining the format marks
- Including deficiencies not included in the scenario
- Not linking the deficiency, its effect and a recommendation
- Writing too much. A sentence or two for each deficiency, effect and recommendation was sufficient

In part (b) many candidates provided between four and six points with appropriate explanation. Common errors included:

- Not explaining the point made. For example, stating 'better communication' without explaining why this was an advantage
- Providing a lengthy introduction explaining the role of non-executive directors and audit committees

Note. The marking scheme has been revised to reflect any necessary amendments made to the question and/or answer.

Marking scheme

		Marks
(a)	Content of report – 1 mark each for	
	Identifying deficiency	
	Effect of deficiency	
	Recommendation to remove deficiency	
	Recording of orders	3
	Control over orders and packing lists	3
	Obtaining payment	3
	Completeness of orders	3
	No check on goods in inventory when ordered	3
	Two part packing slip insufficient	3
	Sales invoice not sent to customer	3
	Inventory only updated on despatch	3
	Other relevant points	3
	Maximum marks	**12**
	Format of answer – appropriate headings	1
	Format of answer – report format	1
		2
	Maximum marks this section	**14**
(b)	1 mark per relevant point	
	Independent reporting	1
	Help internal audit implement changes	1
	Shareholder/public confidence	1
	Directors' obligations	1
	Communication external auditors	1
	Independence external auditor	1
	Other relevant points (each)	1
	Maximum marks this section	**6**
		20

(a) **Report**

To: Audit committee, Rhapsody
From: Internal audit department
Subject: Deficiencies in the sales system, Seeds Division
Date: Today

The deficiencies we found from our work on the sales system, the implications of those deficiencies and possible recommendations to mitigate them are set out below.

Deficiency	Implication	Recommendation
Orders placed on the internet are manually transferred onto the inventory control and sales system.	Errors could be made when this transfer is made, resulting in incorrect inventory figures and the wrong orders being sent to customers, resulting ultimately in loss of customers and goodwill.	The systems should be integrated so that once the order is placed, it automatically updates the inventory and sales systems.
A random code is generated for each order, which is based on the name of the employee inputting the details, the date and the products ordered.	There is no easy way to track orders because the coding system is random so any queries may take a long time to resolve and orders not yet despatched will be difficult to monitor.	If the systems are automated, the computer should generate a numerical code automatically once the order is placed and this will mean orders can be monitored more easily.
Customers' credit cards are charged after despatch of the order has taken place, rather than when they place the order.	If payments are rejected, then the company will lose out on sales income, resulting in increased levels of bad debts and falling profit margins.	The credit card should be charged as soon as the customer has placed the order over the internet. This will reduce the level of bad debt and ensure payment is received before the goods are sent out.
There is no control in place to monitor orders that have not been despatched or those that remain uninvoiced.	Outstanding orders will result in queries from customers and ultimately result in loss of these customers and a loss in income.	Orders should be monitored on a regular, weekly basis to identify any that have not been despatched so that queries can be dealt with on a timely basis.

(b) **Advantages of an audit committee**

- They can improve the **quality** of financial reporting by reviewing the financial statements on behalf of the Board of Directors.
- They have the potential to create a **climate of discipline and control** which may reduce the opportunity for fraud occurring within the company.
- They allow non-executive directors to contribute an **independent judgement** and play a positive role in the organisation.
- They assist the Finance Director by providing a **forum** in which he can raise issues of concern.
- They strengthen the position of the external auditor by providing a **channel of communication** and a forum for issues of concern.
- They strengthen the position of internal audit by providing a greater degree of **independence** from management.
- They may **increase public confidence** in the credibility and objectivity of the financial statements.

32 Risk assessment and internal control

Text references. Chapters 9, 10 and 11

Top tips. This question tests your knowledge in two different ways. Part (a) requires an explanation of five key procedures which are fundamental to the audit process. You should have a sound understanding of these. Part (b) is more demanding as it examines internal controls in the context of a scenario. The key here is to ensure you consider the elements of the cycle mentioned in the question (ie receipts, processing and recording of orders and collection of cash) and that you both **describe** and **explain the purpose** of the controls you would expect to see.

Easy marks. Part (a) represents 10 relatively straightforward marks as you should be able to explain the five procedures listed.

Examiner's comments. Overall part (a) of the question was reasonably well answered. Those who lost marks did so because their answers were too general. Some candidates also seemed confused about the difference between the various types of test. In part (b) candidates lost marks for failing to address all aspects of the requirement. For example, (b) (i) asked for controls regarding the receipt, processing **and** recording of orders. Other problems included the out-dated approach taken to segregation of duties with many candidates failing to take account of modern computerised systems.

Marking scheme

		Marks
(a)	Key procedures Up to 1 mark per point up to a maximum of subject to maximum of 2 for each of the five categories	10
(b)	Internal controls	
	(i) Receipt, processing and recording Up to 1 mark per point to a maximum of	6
	(ii) Collection of cash Up to 1 mark per point to a maximum of	4
		20

(a) **Explanation of procedures**

(i) *Documentation of accounting systems and internal control*

Auditors are required to obtain an understanding of the business they are to audit. As part of that process they record the accounting and internal control systems to enable them to plan the audit and develop an effective audit approach. This allows the auditor to determine the adequacy of the system for producing the financial statements and to perform an initial risk assessment.

There are a number of different techniques which may be used to record the system. These include **narrative notes, flowcharts and questionnaires**. The extent of the work will depend on the **nature of the organisation and the practical circumstances**. For example in a smaller company where a substantive rather than controls based approach is to be taken, a detailed record of internal control would not be necessary. For a new client with a large and complex system a much more detailed review would be required.

(ii) *Walk-through tests*

Walk through tests are performed by the auditors to confirm that their **recording and understanding of the system is correct**. They are often performed as the recording of the system takes place or in conjunction with the tests of controls.

The process involves the tracing of a sample of transactions from the start of the operating cycle to the end and *vice versa*. For example a sales transaction could be traced from the initial order through to the entry in the nominal ledger accounts.

(iii) *Audit sampling*

Audit sampling involves the **application of audit procedures to a selection of transactions** within a population (ie rather than applying the procedures to 100%). The auditor then obtains and evaluates the evidence in order to form a conclusion about the population as a whole.

Sampling is normally adopted for practical reasons as in most cases it would be too time consuming to audit the whole population. A number of different techniques can be used in order to select the sample including random, systematic or haphazard selection. When designing the size and the structure of the audit sample the auditor will need to consider **sampling risk** – the risk that the sample is not representative of the population as a whole, meaning that results cannot be extrapolated.

(iv) *Testing internal controls*

Tests of controls are used to **confirm the auditor's assessment of the operation of the control system**. They are tests to obtain audit evidence which confirm that controls have been carried out correctly and consistently.

For example a control activity over the payment of supplier invoices could be that all invoices are authorised by the purchases manager's signature. The auditor would test this control by looking for evidence of this on a sample of paid purchase invoices. As this is a test of controls rather than a substantive procedure the size of the balance on the invoice is irrelevant and any exceptions potentially show a failure in the system.

The results of this work will then determine **the extent to which further substantive procedures are required**. If controls have proved to be effective less additional work is required. If controls are not in place or are not effective more additional evidence will be required.

(v) *Deviations*

If deviations from the application of control activities are found the auditor will need to determine whether this is an isolated incident or evidence of a more comprehensive breakdown in procedures. This will normally be confirmed by extending the sample size and testing more transactions.

If the problem is an anomalous error arising from an isolated incident, no further formal action is required (although the auditor may wish to mention it to management informally).

If the breakdown is more comprehensive the auditor needs to consider the impact this will have on this particular aspect of the audit and the **audit approach as a whole**. An unexpectedly high deviation rate, which is in excess of the tolerable rate of deviation set by the auditor, will mean the auditor will need to re-assess audit risk.

If a compensating control cannot be identified and tested satisfactorily, a substantive approach will need to be adopted.

(b) **Internal control activities**

(i) *Receipts, processing and recording of orders*

All orders should be recorded on **pre-printed sequentially numbered documentation**. This could be a four part document, one copy being the order, one copy being the despatch note, one copy being sent to the customer as evidence of the order and the last copy retained by the accounts receivable clerk.

To ensure completeness of orders a **sequence check** should be performed on the documents either manually or by computer. Any missing documents should be traced.

As the clerk inputs the order the system should automatically check whether the customer remains within its **credit limit**. Any orders which exceed the credit limit should be rejected.

In exceptional circumstances where credit limits are to be exceeded this should be authorised by the department manager. Orders should also be rejected if the customer has a significantly overdue balance.

As the order is being input the system should check whether the item required is **in inventory**. This is possible as the ordering and inventories systems are integrated. If items are unavailable the order should be rejected. This will enable the clerk to inform the customer which will enhance customer service.

Periodically an **independent review should be performed of the standing data on the system**. A sample of credit limits should be checked to ensure that they have been calculated in accordance with the standard formula. Any breaches should be investigated. Similarly the price of flowers should be matched against an up to date price list.

Sales invoices should be posted automatically to the sales daybook and accounts receivable ledger. An accounts receivable control account reconciliation should be performed on a monthly basis and any discrepancies should be investigated and dealt with.

Customer statements should be generated by the system automatically. Any queries raised by the customer on receipt of these should be investigated promptly. Any resulting credit notes should be authorised.

(ii) *Collection of cash*

Details of all **bank transfers** received should be input into the cash book/bank control account and the accounts receivable ledger and accounts receivable control account.

Entries in the accounts receivable ledger should be **matched** against specific invoices. Any unallocated cash should be investigated via an exception report.

On a monthly basis a **bank reconciliation** should be performed. Together with the accounts receivable control account reconciliation and the following up of queries on customer statements this will help to ensure that the cash is correctly recorded and allocated.

On a monthly basis an **aged receivables** listing should be generated. The company should have procedures in place for the chasing of debts which the credit controller would follow ranging from a telephone reminder to the threat of legal action.

33 Atlantis Standard Goods

Text reference. Chapter 10

Top tips. Part (a) of this question should be straightforward as you should be very familiar with the sales cycle and the control objectives over sales. In part (b), note that the requirement is asking you to tabulate the audit tests and explain why you are carrying them out. A structured approach would take each point in turn from the scenario. Think about the assertions you are testing against and make sure that your audit tests are specific to the company and not vague. The reason for the test should explain clearly why you are doing it, for example, 'To verify that order details are accurately recorded on the website'.

Easy marks. These are available in part (a). It is important that you are familiar with the control objectives for both sales and purchases.

Examiner's comments. In part (a), many candidates obtained full marks by providing five clear objectives, however, many candidates spent far too much time writing about systems which scored few marks and wasted time. Common errors included writing too much for the five marks available and poor explanation of objectives.

In part (b) the scenario was built around an internet trading company (such as Amazon). The issue being addressed was that the control objectives within a computerised system would be the same as in a manual system, although the methods of implementation and testing would be different. The standard of answers here was very variable. The main weaknesses were writing in general terms about sales systems or providing tests that were not relevant to the scenario. Given that this type of question is focused on basic audit work, candidates are strongly advised to revise how systems are tested.

Marking scheme

		Marks
(a)	One mark for each valid control objective	
	Supply of goods – good credit card rating	1
	Orders correctly recorded	1
	Orders despatched to correct customer	1
	Despatches correctly recorded	1
	Despatches relate to orders	1
	Invoices relate to goods supplied	1
	Other similar correct points (each)	1
	Maximum marks	5

		Marks
(b)	Key points 1 for each test and 0.5 for explanation of why the test is required	
	Input of order details	1.5
	Orders pending to despatch file	1.5
	Completeness of receivables – credit card company	1.5
	Orders pending to receivables file – sales complete	1.5
	Review orders pending – old items	1.5
	Cast receivables ledger – completeness	1.5
	Goods awaiting despatch file to despatch department	1.5
	Despatch department – agree back to orders awaiting despatch	1.5
	Update of inventory records	1.5
	Customer signature for receipt of goods	1.5
	Incomplete information despatch department computer	1.5
	Items not flagged 'order complete' despatch department computer	1.5
	Other good relevant points (each)	1.5
	Maximum marks	**15**
		20

(a) Control objectives for the ordering, despatch and invoicing of goods:

- To ensure that orders are **correctly recorded**
- To ensure that orders are **fulfilled correctly**
- To ensure that goods are supplied to **authorised customers** only
- To ensure that all goods sold are **invoiced correctly**
- To ensure that goods are sent to the **correct customer**
- To ensure that all goods despatched are **recorded**
- To ensure that all invoices raised relate to **goods and services supplied** by the business

(b) Audit tests on the sales and despatch system:

Audit tests	Reason for test
For a sample of days, cast the sales day book and agree the total to the nominal ledger accounts for that day.	To check the numerical accuracy and to ensure that the amount updated to the ledger is complete and accurately posted.
Access the website and input order details for selected goods. Then trace these details to the orders pending file.	To ensure that order details are accurately recorded on the website.
Take a sample of orders from the orders pending file and perform the following: • Agree the details to the orders awaiting despatch file • Agree the sales details and amount to the monthly reimbursement from the credit card company and to the sales ledger file	To ensure that the details of the order on the website have been completely and accurately transferred to the orders awaiting despatch file. To confirm that amounts received from customers are complete and accurate and that the ledger and accounts are not misstated.
Review the goods awaiting despatch file for old items and inquire why these are still on file.	To ensure that reasons for orders not being processed are being obtained. Overdue items could indicate delays in obtaining credit and authorisation.
Take a sample of orders from the goods awaiting despatch file and agree the details to the information on the despatch department computer.	To ensure that orders are transferred to the despatch department correctly.
Take a sample of items on the despatch department computer: • Agree to inventory records for correct updating • Confirm that the customer signature is on file agreeing receipt of the goods	To ensure that the inventory system records the item and that inventory records are accurate. To confirm that evidence of receipt of goods is present to confirm that goods ordered have been delivered.

Audit tests	Reason for test
Take a sample of goods from the computer in the despatch department and check for evidence of delivery. Where no evidence is available, investigate further.	To ensure that goods have been received and that processes for following up non-delivery/receipt are operating.
Take a sample of items from the despatch department computer that are not flagged 'order complete' and investigate further.	To confirm that the despatch of goods process is operating correctly and that incomplete items are investigated fully.

34 Cosmo

Text reference. Chapter 10

Top tips. Read through the examiner's comments about the real answers to this question (below). Notice that again, a point is raised that candidates should answer the question set. Always read the requirement carefully once or twice to make sure that you are not suffering from a case of wishful thinking. It sometimes helps if you read a requirement before reading through a scenario attached to a question – although you have to beware answering the question without reference to the scenario. You should be capable of identifying control problems and setting them out in a 'deficiencies, consequences, recommendations' format. You might find that using a columnar format is useful in such questions. The answer below has not used that format, but has been set out more as it is likely such a letter would be in practice. It would have been acceptable to use the columnar presentation in your answer, however.

Easy marks. These are available in part (a) of the question. In addition in part (b), having identified the deficiency, the consequence and recommendation should follow, so you should feel confident of scoring a substantial number of the 15 marks available.

Examiner's comments. This was a question in a recognised format, that could have been answered very well but, surprisingly, was not. In part (a), many candidates properly identified the wide variety of errors and misappropriations that could occur if purchases and capital expenditure were not properly controlled, but a number of candidates did not read the question properly and instead suggested internal controls that should be in place in such systems. In part (b), almost all candidates included a 'covering note', which was not asked for and for which no marks were awarded. The question asked for deficiencies, potential consequences and recommendations in a form suitable for inclusion in a report to management. There was also a great deal of repetition in answers to this question. The overall impression was that answers were sloppy.

Note. The marking scheme has been revised to reflect any necessary amendments made to the question and/or answer.

Marking scheme

		Marks
(a)	Error and misappropriations 1 mark per point to maximum of	5
(b)	Report to management 3 marks per point to maximum of	15
	Note: To obtain full marks in this section, the deficiencies, consequences and recommendations must be identified.	20

(a) **Errors and misappropriations – purchases system**

- Goods could be bought which are not genuinely for the company
- Goods/materials could be bought at inappropriately high prices
- Goods which have not been ordered could be accepted/paid for
- Genuine liabilities might be unrecognised, resulting in loss of supply
- Liabilities which are not genuine might be created as part of a fraud

(b) **Report to management – Cosmo**

Complex purchasing system

Deficiency

The purchasing system is complex. This can be seen in the distinction between capital and revenue purchases and also the use of two systems to purchase goods running in parallel.

Consequence

The complexity of the system wastes management time and at worst, could in itself result in errors being made in classification or which could result in business interruption or problems in relationships with suppliers.

Recommendation

The purchases system should be revisited and simplified. This could be done by the internal audit department. Alternatively, we would be happy to be engaged separately to provide advice on the simplification of your system.

Consortium system

Deficiency

The new system of purchasing is not used comprehensively for all purchases.

Consequences

This is likely to lead to confusion and could lead to the company making necessary purchases twice or not at all.

Recommendation

Steps should be taken to integrate the entire purchasing function with the consortium system to avoid confusion.

Deficiency

The consortium system can only be operated by two of the production controller's junior staff.

Consequences

This has two significant consequences:

- There are insufficient people trained to operate the major purchasing system and the company may find that they could be unable to operate their systems if those capable are absent.
- The people who can use the system are employed in the production department, meaning that there is a lack of segregation of duties in the purchasing function, which could lead to error and/or purchasing fraud.

Recommendation

The purchasing department staff should be trained to use the new Consortium system and they should be the only people who use the system, so that they operate as an authorisation function to purchases.

Circumvention

Deficiency

The automatic re-ordering system and the capital expenditure system both operate inefficiently and staff members are required to circumvent the system in order to be able to get on with their jobs.

Consequence

Staff may become accustomed to habitually overriding the systems, which will cause systems to be inefficient and fail to achieve company objectives.

Recommendation

The system should be improved and staff reminded that circumvention of the system is not acceptable. This is likely to have to be an initiative led by senior staff, who may have permitted/encouraged circumvention of systems in the past.

Information Technology Systems

Deficiency

The new purchasing system appears to take up a significant amount of disk space and cause problems to other programmes.

Consequence

This may result in a significant 'jam' in the company's overall system, or even cause errors in related systems.

Recommendation

Technical advisers should be engaged to review the system and discover whether there is an error with the new system, or whether the capacity of the company's infrastructure is sufficient. It may be that the company's IT policy needs to be reviewed. Again, we could provide such a service for the company, if required.

35 SouthLea

Text references. Chapters 9, 10 and 11

Top tips. In part (a), there are eight marks available for identifying the control deficiencies and suggesting controls to overcome them. The best way to present your answer is in a columnar format because this allows you to link each deficiency with a recommendation. Make sure you explain the deficiencies you have identified fully, as required by the question. Go through the scenario carefully, noting down potential deficiencies as you do so. Part (b) is a straightforward question on the respective responsibilities of external and internal auditors for the detection of fraud. Part (c) is also a straightforward question on the use of an external consultant. First identify the factors to consider – these can form the sub-headings for your answer – and then explain those factors in more detail.

Easy marks. Easy marks can be achieved in parts (b) and (c) of this question on fraud responsibilities and the factors to consider when appointing an external consultant.

Note. The marking scheme has been revised to reflect any necessary amendments made to the question and/or answer.

Marking scheme

		Marks
(a)	Control deficiencies and recommendations. 8 marks. 1 for explanation of deficiency and 1 for internal control recommendation. Maximum 2 per deficiency/recommendation.	
	Maximum marks	8
(b)	Fraud and External/Internal audit. 6 marks. 1 for internal audit work and 1 for external audit. Maximum 2 per point.	
	Main reason for audit work	
	Materiality	
	Identification of fraud	
	Other relevant points	
	Maximum marks	6

		Marks
(c)	Use of expert. 1 mark per valid point.	
	Qualification	1
	Experience	1
	References	1
	Project management skills	1
	Access to information	1
	Acceptance by other staff	1
	Other relevant points (each)	1
	Maximum marks	6
		20

(a) **Wages system – deficiencies and recommended controls**

(i) Deficiency	(ii) Internal control recommendation
The foreman is in a position to set up fictitious employees onto the wages system as he has authority to issue temporary employee numbers. This would allow him to collect cash wages for such bogus employees.	The issue of new employee numbers should be authorised by a manager and supported by employee contract letters etc.
The two wages clerks are responsible for the set up and maintenance of all employee records. They could therefore, in collusion, set up bogus employees and collect cash wages from them.	The list of personnel should be matched with the payroll by a manager and all new employee records should be authorised before being set up on the system.
The wages clerks are responsible for making amendments to holidays and illness etc. They could make unauthorised amendments which affect individual staff members' pay.	Any amendments to standing data on the wages system should be done by an authorised manager so that unauthorised amendments are not made. A log of amendments should be regularly reviewed.
The computer system calculates gross pay and any deductions but these are hand-written by the wages clerks for the staff pay packets, so errors could be made and incorrect wages issued.	A payslip should be generated by the computer system and including in the wage packet to reduce the chance of errors in deductions and gross pay being made.
The computer automatically calculates gross pay and deductions, however there is no check to ensure the calculations are accurate.	One of the wages clerks should check the gross pay and deductions for a sample of employees to gain assurance that the computer is calculating amounts correctly.
The foreman distributes cash wages to the employees. He could therefore misappropriate any wages not claimed.	The distribution of wages should be overseen by another manager. Any unclaimed wages should be noted on a form and returned to the wages department.

(b) **Responsibilities for the detection of fraud**

External auditors

It is not the responsibility of the external auditors to detect fraud within a client. This responsibility lies with the management and those charged with governance.

ISA 240 *The auditor's responsibilities relating to fraud in an audit of financial statements* sets out guidance in this area. It states that the auditor shall maintain an attitude of professional scepticism throughout the audit, recognising the possibility that a material misstatement due to fraud could exist, notwithstanding the auditor's past experience of the honesty and integrity of the entity's management and those charged with governance.

The auditor is required to consider the potential for management override of controls and recognise that audit procedures that are effective in detecting error may not be appropriate in detecting fraud due to the nature of fraud.

As part of the audit planning process, the audit team must discuss the susceptibility of the client's financial statements to material misstatement by fraud.

Internal auditors

Responsibility for the prevention and detection of fraud lies with the management and those charged with governance at the client. To this end, management should place a strong emphasis on fraud prevention and fraud deterrence.

Internal audit can help in this regard because its aim is to review the internal control systems of the company to ensure they are effective and efficient. Part of this review could involve detailed work to ensure that fraud was not occurring. The internal audit department could also be required to undertake special projects to investigate suspected instances of fraud.

(c) **Factors to consider when appointing an external consultant:**

Qualifications

The professional qualifications of the consultant should be considered. He should be appropriately qualified to carry out the work required.

Experience

The technical experience of the consultant should be considered as he should be sufficiently experienced to undertake the assignment. He should also be familiar with the system being implemented.

Cost and service

The company should consider the cost to be incurred for replacing the wages system. It should also consider what the cost includes, for example, whether it includes a servicing agreement.

Availability

The company should consider whether the consultant will be available post-implementation to assist with any teething problems and other issues that might arise.

Training

The company should consider whether staff who will be using the new system will require training in order to be able to use the new package.

References and background

The company should consider who the consultant works for or whether he works alone and details of his previous clients and work.

36 Burton Housing

Text references. Chapters 10 and 17

Top tips. Don't forget what you are auditing here – it is useless to suggest controls or audit tests which are suitable for a large manufacturing organisation. Questions on organisations other than commercial companies are often based on their income and expenditure.

Easy marks. This question is made more difficult by the fact that it is based on a small charity rather than a company. The requirements themselves however are familiar. Provided you are prepared to think about the nature of the organisation and tailor your comments you should be able to pick up good marks.

(a) (i) **Rental income**

Internal control over the system for recording rents are weak because there are no real checks on the work of the bookkeeper who could therefore easily commit a fraud or make undiscovered errors.

The main control problems here are as follows.

(1) **Lack of segregation of duties** between recording invoices, recording cash, receiving cash and banking cash.

(2) **Authorisation of bad debt write offs** should rest with the chief executive not the housing manager.

(3) An **independent check** is required to compare amounts received to expected rent based on occupancy levels.

My audit procedures will be greater in the areas of where there are deficiencies in internal control and I will perform the following procedures:

(1) **Compare rental income to previous levels and to budget**. Analytical review can be used to check occupancy, the level of empty flat/weeks and the level of bad debts. The theoretical rental income is 30 × weekly rent (ie on full occupancy).

$$\therefore \text{Occupancy (\%)} = \frac{\text{Actual rental income}}{\text{Theoretical rental income}} \%\text{, so:}$$

Empty flat rate (%) = 100 – Occupancy (%)

The level of occupancy can be checked to the housing manager's reports and compared to prior years. Investigate discrepancies between calculated occupancy and reported occupancy.

(2) Select a sample of weeks from the year and **check** the **posting** of all **invoices** for rent for all flats to the sales ledger. Where there is no invoice I will check to the occupancy report that the flat was empty. This will check that the invoices have been posted to the correct sales ledger account.

(ii) **Control over receipt and recording of rent**

Control activities which should be in operation here include the following.

(1) **Reception** staff should **issue receipts** for rent, reconciling cash to copy receipts before handing over the money to the bookkeeper. **Differences** between cash and receipts should be **investigated** and a note kept of the cash handed over.

(2) A **check** should be made by a senior (independent) official, eg the chief executive, between the **cash received** by the reception staff and the **cash** banked and **posted** to the sales ledger.

(3) **Complaints** from residents about rent payments should be **investigated** by an independent member of the management committee, particularly where residents claim to have paid rent, but it has not been received. (The use of rent books for residents might avoid the loss of individual receipts.)

Main audit checks to be carried out

(1) Select a sample of days from during the year and **check** from the **reception staff's receipts** and record of cash to the **banked cash** and the postings to the sales ledger. Check that the money is banked promptly.

(2) **Check** that **disputes** about rent are **investigated** independently and a written report made to the management committee.

(3) **Investigate** any **problems** found. Any weaknesses in the system should be reported to the management committee.

(iii) **Postings of credit notes/bad debts/adjustments**

There should not be too many adjustments of this type, but they should be reviewed as any fraud could be 'lost' in such adjustments.

I will select a sample of all these items (probably based on size) and carry out the following procedures.

(1) **Agree to supporting documentation** (explaining why rents returned, or steps to recover rent before writing it off).

(2) **Check authorisation** has been given by the chief executive (for all these items).

(3) **Adjustments** to correct errors will be **checked** to the original entry and the calculations redone.

(4) Where a **credit note** has been issued, I will **check** that the **resident was originally charged** for that period and that amount.

(5) For **bad debts**, I will check that the **debt was old** and that the **resident had left**; also check that the Association tried to chase the customer and collect the money.

At the year end, any credit balances which exist may indicate overpayment by residents. I will also **look** for any **old balances** which may need to be written off. These bad debts should be checked by the chief executive to ensure that they are not a result of misappropriation by staff.

(b) **Income and expenditure of restaurant**

(i) Select a sample of days during the year. For each day obtain the till roll and **compare** the **amount of money** taken in sales with the **amount banked**. (The till rolls should be retained for each year at least until the audit is over.) Small discrepancies can be ignored, but substantial differences must be investigated in full.

(ii) Use the above sample to check that any **credits given** by the till (ie after the total button has been pressed) have been **authorised** by the restaurant manager.

(iii) **Observe the cashier(s)** at **work**, as unobtrusively as possible, in order to ascertain whether they are using the till correctly and whether they have few opportunities to misappropriate cash (ie by not recording sales). Relevant controls will include frequent and regular supervision by the restaurant manager, use of video cameras etc (these should also help to prevent shoplifting of chocolate bars and other small objects).

(iv) **Calculate an average actual gross profit** for the restaurant by comparing selling price to the cost of ingredients for a range of meals/snacks. Amounts used can be assessed by sampling meals and the restaurant manager's calculations of amounts to be purchased can be assessed. I will compare the average gross profit I have assessed to the gross profit in the draft accounts. Any difference will represent **wastage** and should be reasonable compared to previous years (and perhaps the level of wastage seen at other restaurants etc audited by the firm).

(v) The **gross profit** in the draft accounts should be **compared to the previous year's accounts** and any differences investigated.

(vi) The **ratio of wages to sales** should be **calculated and compared** to previous periods. Any discrepancies or differences should be investigated. The weekly/monthly wages bill should be reviewed and any significant variations investigated (including variations in tax paid). Any variations caused by staff leaving/joining should be checked to the relevant tax forms.

(vii) Select a sample of purchase invoices as listed in the purchase ledger and **trace the authorised purchase invoice** (ie the food was received) and **the purchase order**. I will check that all purchases are appropriate to the sales made in the restaurant. To overcome the weakness in control where the restaurant manager orders the food and authorises the invoice, the chief executive should authorise the invoice instead.

(viii) The **closing inventories** of food should be **checked**. Most inventory should not be very old and its age and value should be comparable with previous years (frequency of delivery will indicate the inventory age).

(ix) **Discover** whether there are any **fictitious staff** being paid by **meeting** each member of staff. The **documentation for leavers and joiners** can be **checked** and that no payments were made to them after leaving or before joining. **Rates of pay** should be **agreed to personnel files** or management committee minutes. **Overtime** should be **authorised** by the restaurant manager (on the timesheet) and by the chief executive (on payment). Employees should sign for their pay packets and I might attempt to witness this in operation.

(x) **Consider** whether, overall, the **figures** in the restaurant accounts are **reasonable**, based on the above audit work. If any **large costs** have been found I will **vouch** these to **authorised documentation**. In particular, I will look carefully for possible understatement of sales or overstatement of costs (both of which might indicate a fraud).

Criticisms of the system should be reported to the chief executive and the management committee. Any material unexplained differences might cause me to qualify my report ('material' amounts may not be very large in this situation).

37 Delphic

Text references. Chapters 11 and 14.

Top tips. This question tests your understanding of the implications of a computerised accounting system and in particular the use of audit software. In practice almost all accounting systems will be computerized to some degree so it is highly likely that computer issues will be examined regularly.

Part (a) asks you to explain the audit procedures that should be carried out using audit software on the receivables balance. The best approach to adopt is to try to think of the basic audit work that would be performed on receivables and then consider how audit software can used to assist. You are then asked to explain why that procedure is being performed. Make sure you understand this requirement. You are being asked to justify why you would perform the test eg to confirm the recoverability of receivables, not why you are using audit software.

Part (b) then asks you to explain the problems of using audit software and how they can be resolved. In general terms you should be familiar with the problems, however try to make your answer as specific to the scenario as you can.

Part (c) asks you to explain the concept of 'auditing around the computer' and to discuss why this approach increases audit risk. You may find this part of the question tricky but it is only worth 3 marks so don't panic.

Easy marks. This is the toughest question on the paper so there are no easy marks as such. However, if you adopt a methodical approach and try to use the information in the scenario it is still possible to achieve a good mark.

Examiner's comments. In part (a), candidates had to explain audit procedures using audit software for receivables' balances and also explain the reason for each procedure. Weaknesses included focusing answers on test data rather than audit software, explaining points on the audit of sales, explaining procedures to test program controls, explaining tests using manual systems, and structuring answers around the different types of audit evidence. Overall, the standard of answers for this part was inadequate.

Part (b) was on problems of using audit software at a specific client and how to overcome those problems. The overall standard was again inadequate, with weaknesses being to state general issues rather than client-specific ones and not including methods to overcome issues identified.

In part (c), candidates had to explain the concept of auditing 'around the computer'. Most candidates did not appear to understand this term. Common errors included explaining the audit risk model, explaining how CAATs could be used to audit computer systems, and suggesting that the term meant looking at computer controls only. Again, the standard of answers was very poor.

Marking scheme

		Marks
(a)	Up to 2 marks for each procedure and explanation. 1 for the procedure and 1 for the explanation. Limit procedure to 0.5 if cannot be sustained from Delphic's systems.	
	– Cast sales ledger	
	– Compare ledger balance to credit limit	
	– Review balances, ensure not excessive	
	– Calculation of receivables days	
	– Stratification of balances/audit sample selection	
	– Verify items in ledger	
	– Aged receivables analysis	
	– Other valid tests	
	Maximum marks	9

Marks

Note to markers – no distinction is made between test of control and substantive procedures for this question. Marks can be obtained from either type of test or other relevant uses of audit software eg sample selection.

(b) 2 marks for each point. 1 for explaining the problem and 1 for showing how it can be resolved.
Tests ideally must be related to the scenario; allow half marks if not related.

- Cost
- Lack of software documentation
- Change in client's system
- Outputs obtained
- Use of copy files
- Other relevant points

Maximum marks 8

(c) Explanation of auditing around computer = 1 mark
1 mark for max two problems 1

- Actual computer files not tested
- Difficult to track errors
- Other relevant points

Maximum marks 3

20

(a)

Procedure	Reason for procedure
Test casting of the sales ledger and comparison with the total on the sales ledger control account.	To verify the accuracy of the final receivables figure.
Stratification of receivables balances and selection of a sample for direct confirmation based on this stratification.	To ensure that the sample selected includes all material items and a sample of smaller balances.
Calculation of receivables days at each month end.	To monitor control over cash collection during the year. In addition a substantial increase in receivables days may indicate recoverability problems.
Checking of the ageing of receivables (or production of an aged receivables analysis if not produced by Delphic Co).	To ensure that the ageing is accurate before using the information to identify irrecoverable receivables as part of valuation testing.
Tracing a sample of sales invoices to the sales day book and cash receipts to the cash receipts book.	To ensure that sales invoices and cash receipts have been accurately recorded in the accounting records.

Top tips. The following additional points would also be valid:

Comparison of the balance in a sample of individual receivables accounts with their credit limits.	To ensure that controls over credit limits are being applied effectively.
Review of sales ledger balances for unusual items, for example: – Journal entries – Accounts with significant adjustments or credit notes	To identify unusual transactions on the sales ledger so that they can be investigated.
Selection of a sample of credit notes over a certain value issued after the year end.	To determine the need to make adjustments against current period balances.

(b) Use of audit software

Potential problem	How it can be solved
(i) Cost As this is the first year that the auditor has used audit software there will be substantial set-up costs.	The auditor should reconsider whether the use of audit software is a cost-effective approach. A cost-benefit analysis should be performed to assist in this decision making process, to decide how much audit software can be effectively used this year.
(ii) Incomplete documentation The lack of software documentation makes the use of audit software more complex and time-consuming. The result may be an inefficient audit with disruption and added cost to the client.	The incompleteness of documentation should be a significant factor in the auditor's cost-benefit analysis.
(iii) Changes to the system The computer system is to be changed next year. This means that the set-up costs incurred this year will not be recouped in future.	Again this should be a factor in the auditor's cost-benefit analysis.
(iv) Reason for the change in audit approach The change in approach has been made to enable the auditor to fully understand the computer systems. There is the possibility that without careful planning the audit software will not produce the information which the auditor requires. Audit software generally produces very specific and detailed information which may not be suitable for obtaining knowledge of the system.	The audit manager should set clear objectives as to the purpose of tests performed using audit software and the output which he is expecting.
(v) Use of copy files As the audit software is to be applied to copy files there is no guarantee that they are genuine or that they will operate in the same way as the actual files.	The auditor should supervise and observe the copying of the files to ensure that they are genuine. Alternatively he could request the use of live files.

(c) Auditing around the computer

Auditing around the computer means that the auditor identifies the input into the computer system and then compares the expected output with the actual output. The processing performed 'in between' by the computer software is not directly audited by the auditor.

This increases audit risk because:

- Evidence regarding the accuracy of processing is obtained indirectly – the software itself is not audited
- Manual audit procedures may result in smaller samples being selected as compared to the use of audit software
- The audit opinion may need to be modified if the auditor is unable to obtain sufficient appropriate audit evidence regarding the processing of transactions.

38 Matalas

Text references. Chapters 5, 10 and 15

Top tips. This question deals with internal audit and controls in the petty cash system. The emphasis in this question is on your ability to apply your knowledge so you must read the scenario very carefully. Make sure that your answer is tailored specifically to the circumstances which are described.

Part (a) asks you to consider the issues which limit the independence of the internal audit department of Matalas Co. The easiest approach to take is to look carefully at each piece of information given about the internal audit department and then ask yourself whether it gives rise to an independence issue. Also notice that you need to recommend ways of overcoming these problems so make sure you address both aspects of the requirement. For 8 marks you will need to identify 4-5 limitations with solutions.

Part (b) asks you to identify deficiencies in the petty cash system and to make recommendations to overcome each deficiency. A two-column format here would be useful. There are a number of different methods you can use to help you to identify deficiencies. As you read through the information try to think of the controls you would ideally want to see in a petty cash system. Do these controls exist in Matalas' system? Alternatively you might want to think of the different categories of control (eg authorisation, physical controls). Does the current system include these? Having identified the deficiency you should then be able to recommend a control to overcome the problem.

Easy marks. There are no easy marks as such in this question although you should be very familiar with requirement in part (b). You should be able to score well on this section.

Examiner's comments. Part (a) was generally answered well. However weaknesses included stating points in the answer that were not mentioned in the question scenario, including points that were not necessarily best practice, putting in points on petty cash weaknesses which were relevant to part (b) of the answer, and not explaining the reason for the weakness.

In part (b), candidates had to explain the deficiencies in the petty cash system and recommend a control to mitigate that deficiency. Some candidates failed to provide an adequate explanation of the points made. Others suggested deficiencies that were not mentioned in the scenario. Where recommendations were required, some candidates made suggestions that were completely impractical. It is therefore important for candidates to consider the type of client when thinking about ways to overcome deficiencies in systems.

Note. The marking scheme has been revised to reflect any necessary amendments made to the question and/or answer.

Marking scheme

		Marks
(a)	2 marks for each independence factor. 1 for explaining the issue and 1 for mitigating that factor. – Reporting system – Scope of work – Actual audit work – Length of service of internal audit staff – Appointment of chief internal auditor – External auditor assistance with internal audit? (additional to answer) – Other relevant points	
	Maximum marks	8

Marks

(b) 2 marks for each control deficiency. 1 for explaining the deficiency and 1 for control over that deficiency.

- Size of petty cash balance
- Security of petty cash box
- High value petty cash expenditure – individual items
- Authorisation of petty cash expenditure
- Counting of petty cash
- No review of petty cash vouchers – signing of imprest cheque
- Vouchers not pre-numbered
- Other relevant points

Maximum marks 12

20

(a) Limitations and recommendations

(i) *Limitation*

The internal audit department implements controls within the accounting systems. This impairs independence as the internal audit department is effectively responsible for auditing control systems which it has implemented. It is unlikely that the internal audit department will be able to be fully objective in assessing these.

Recommendation

The internal audit department should not establish controls within the accounting systems. Where this has already occurred a different member of the internal audit staff should audit the controls.

(ii) *Limitation*

All internal audit staff have been employed by Matalas for between 5-15 years. This long length of service may lead to over-familiarity with the systems and controls being reviewed, making it more difficult for the internal auditors to identify errors or areas where improvements could be made.

Recommendation

There should be a system of staff rotation into the accounting departments, with other staff being brought into the internal audit department.

(iii) *Limitation*

The CEO appoints the chief internal auditor. This limits the independence of the internal audit department as it is possible that the CEO will choose someone who he believes will be less critical of his work and the way in which the company operates.

Recommendation

The chief internal auditor should be appointed by the audit committee. If there is no audit committee the appointment should be approved by the board of directors.

(iv) *Limitation*

The chief internal auditor reports to the finance director. This limits independence because the chief internal auditor is reporting to the individual responsible for many of the systems and processes which the internal audit department audits. The chief internal auditor may be intimidated by the fact that he is effectively reporting on his direct superior and may not feel that he is able to highlight all of his concerns.

Recommendation

The chief internal auditor should report to an audit committee or the board collectively.

(v) *Limitation*

The finance director is involved in deciding the scope of the work of the internal audit department. This limits independence as the finance director can influence the areas which the internal auditors will work on. The finance director could use this influence to ensure that attention is not directed towards issues which are contentious and which he does not want to be audited.

Recommendation

The chief internal auditor should decide the scope of the internal audit work. If there is an audit committee it could advise the internal audit department's work.

(b)

Deficiency	Control
The amount of cash held in the petty cash box is high ($5,000) in comparison to the average monthly expenditure of ($1,538). This increases the risk that the cash will be stolen or that errors will be made in counting.	The amount of the petty cash balance at each branch should be reviewed. Based on an average monthly expense of $1,538, a balance of $2,000 would seem reasonable.
The petty cash box is not physically secure as it is kept on a bookcase in the accounts office. This increases the risk of theft.	The petty cash box should be kept in the branch safe or in a locked drawer in the accountant's desk.
Reimbursement for petty cash expenditure takes place without evidence of the expenditure being incurred eg receipt. This may result in false claims being made.	All petty cash claims should be supported by a receipt.
The petty cash vouchers are not authorised – they are only signed by the individual claiming reimbursement.	All petty cash vouchers should be authorised by the accounts clerk.
In some instances significant items are purchased through petty cash (up to $500). These are not authorised prior to the purchase being made. This could result in unnecessary expense being incurred by the business.	Expenditure over a certain limit (eg $50) should be authorised in advance.
There is no indication that the vouchers are pre-numbered, meaning that the branch cannot confirm completeness of the vouchers. Unauthorised claims could be made and then blamed on missing vouchers.	Petty cash vouchers should be pre-numbered. On entry into the petty cash book the sequential numbering should be checked to ensure that all expenditure has been completely recorded.
There is a lack of segregation of duties. The petty cash is counted by the accounts clerk who is also responsible for the cash balance. There is no additional independent check on the petty cash balance.	The accountant should check the petty cash count to confirm the accuracy of the balance and ensure that the asset is safeguarded.
Whilst the accountant confirms that the cheque to reimburse petty cash agrees to the journal entry to the general ledger, the petty cash vouchers are not reviewed to support the amounts involved.	The petty cash vouchers should be reviewed by the accountant to confirm that the monthly petty cash expenditure agrees to the reimbursement cheque and journal entries.

39 Cliff

Text reference. Chapter 10

Top tips. When you read the requirements you should spot that this is a very practical question based on a scenario. You need to identify the tasks you are being given in the requirements then read the scenario carefully, several times, to find practical points to make.

For part (a), highlight relevant points in the scenario and make a brief note in the margin to remind you of what the related 'problem' is.

For each point you should write one or two sentences only. To score well on this sort of requirement, you need to make enough (here the 'target' is 8) separate points rather than elaborate at great length on any one point.

In (b) you should spot that the requirement effectively gives you an answer plan. You need to make FOUR recommendations, along with advantages and disadvantages of each. This makes it easy to guess how the 12 marks are being allocated.

Spend some time thinking up recommendations – if you think of more than four, select the four you have most to say about and use only those.

Keep yourself on track and help the marker by using subheadings of **'Recommendation'**, **'Advantages'** and **'Disadvantages'** for each of your points.

Easy marks. Some people may well feel that there are no 'easy marks' in a question of this type! There are certainly no marks available here for simply repeating facts that you have memorised from your studies. The best advice on tackling this sort of scenario is to use your common sense and imagination and make some practical points about the business being discussed. The easiest way to improve your mark would be to re-read your answer and check if all your points are obviously addressing a supermarket – if not, it's worth using a couple of minutes to sharpen up the commonsense detail.

Examiner's comments. Many candidates correctly used the information provided in the scenario to include relevant comments in their answers. Good answers to part (a) contained about five or six problems with some explanation to show their relevance to the scenario. Poorer answers to part (a) tended to be repetitive or to cover insufficient relevant points.

Common errors included:

- Stating a potential problem but not showing exactly why it was a problem. For example, making the point '*management accounts produced twice a year*' was a repeat of part of the scenario. Additional explanation was needed to show why this is a problem.
- Spending time on less relevant areas. For example, explaining detailed problems with the receivables' ledger which was not mentioned in the scenario.

Part (b) was normally very well answered with candidates providing four recommendation/advantages/ disadvantages sections in their answers.

Common errors included:

- Including less relevant recommendations in the answer.
- Not explaining the points being made. Some answers were in bullet point format with limited explanation.

Marking scheme

		Marks
(a)	Problems expected at Cliff: poor internal control Up to 1-$1\frac{1}{2}$ marks per point to a maximum of	10
(b)	Four recommendations, explanation of advantages and disadvantages: improvements to internal control Up to 3 marks per issue to a maximum of	12
(c)	Impact on audit approach 1 mark per point to a maximum of	5
(d)	Interim report to management 1 mark per point to a maximum of	3
		30

(a) **Problems at Cliff resulting from poor internal control**

(i) The local decision-making in respect of purchasing may lead to Cliff missing out on discounts that would be available if goods were bought in greater quantities.

(ii) As the nature of the inventory is foodstuff, and as such, perishable, the lack of control over inventory could mean that Cliff has to write off significant amounts of unsaleable food that is past its sell by date.

(iii) If no controls exist to identify when fresh food is past its sell by date the business could be at risk of prosecution under Food Safety legislation.

(iv) If the local managers are not making good decisions regarding purchasing there could be stock outs of certain lines of goods, losing potential sales and perhaps losing future business if customers decide to shop at other, better-stocked supermarkets.

(v) There is a lack of centralised control over the accounting system. Errors arising on the stand-alone computers in each supermarket may go undetected and senior management will not have good quality information for decision-making.

(vi) Misappropriations of inventory may go undetected, as there is no regular system of inventory counting. Supermarket products are at high risk of being stolen either by staff or others.

(vii) The fact that management accounts are only produced twice a year reduces their usefulness. Pilfering or other fraudulent activity could be going on for several months before there is any chance of it being identified through review of management accounts.

(viii) All of the above problems are likely to be exacerbated by the declining quality of staff employed by Cliff.

(b) **Recommendations to the senior management of Cliff**

(i) **Recommendation 1**

A new computerised accounting system should be implemented, integrating the sales, purchases and inventory accounting systems.

Advantages

This would give the head office management up to date information about inventory levels so that purchase orders can be placed in time to avoid stock outs. More information about sales patterns would assist in better purchasing planning in the medium to longer term.

Disadvantages

The cost of implementing this system would be substantial. Also, there would be further costs of training the staff who will operate the system. It is also likely that there will be 'teething problems' when the system is first used. Information may be flawed and the problems that the new system is supposed to solve may in fact be made worse temporarily.

(ii) **Recommendation 2**

Management accounts should be produced monthly and reviewed by senior management. Ideally these accounts should be prepared for each individual supermarket and also analysed by different product lines.

Advantages

This should allow senior management to identify any poorly performing supermarkets promptly allowing action to be taken to rectify problems. Unprofitable product lines could also be identified and dropped from the supermarkets' range.

Disadvantages

If these accounts are used as part of a more centralised decision-making process it could be that decisions are made that are not in the best interest of a particular supermarket as demand for various types of food is likely to vary between different geographical areas of the country.

(iii) **Recommendation 3**

Sales pricing decisions should be taken centrally.

Advantages

This should help the business maximise its profits by charging appropriate prices for products. Management could also implement policies of discounting on certain lines designated as 'loss-leaders' which may have the effect of attracting new customers into the supermarkets.

Disadvantages

Again the centralised decisions may not be optimal for each individual supermarket. In addition, this would imply a significant change in the culture of the business and established supermarket managers, used to having a great deal of autonomy, may become de-motivated or leave.

(iv) **Recommendation 4**

There should be regular inventory counts at the supermarkets.

Advantages

For efficiency in inventory management and ordering in the food business it is essential to have reliable inventory records. The inventory counts, if properly followed up with amendments being made to book inventory figures, will ensure the quality of the inventory records. This should also act as a deterrent against any staff pilferage of goods.

Disadvantages

Significant staff time will be needed to plan and carry out these inventory counts. This will result in extra costs to the business. It may also cause some disruption to the business if supermarkets have to be closed while the inventory counting is done.

(c) **Internal control environment at Cliff**

The internal control systems at Cliff appear to be very poor. This is demonstrated by the lack of adequate monitoring (management accounts are produced only twice a year), lack of procedures to count inventory regularly, lack of integration of systems and poor quality staff.

This will result in the auditors being unable to place reliance on the controls in place because control risk will be high. Tests of controls would not be undertaken and the audit will most likely have to take a fully **substantive-based approach**, using both analytical procedures and tests of detail on all the key account areas (inventory, sales, purchases and cash).

The impact of this is that the audit will be **less efficient** than it would be if controls could be relied upon and therefore it is more likely to be **more expensive** to the client as it will require more time to be spent on audit work. A detailed report to management will also have to be prepared, setting out the deficiencies in the various systems and recommendations to mitigate those deficiencies.

(d) **Report to management**

The report to management can be a very useful tool for the management of an entity, even though it is just a by-product of the external audit. It sets out deficiencies in the control system, the implications of those deficiencies and recommended controls to overcome them.

At the interim stage of the audit, the report to management can be issued to highlight any such deficiencies that have come to the attention of the auditors during this visit and allows management time to start implementing the recommendations.

It is also preferable to report deficiencies identified at this stage of the audit on a timely basis, rather than waiting for the end of the audit process, as the issues will be fresh in the minds of the auditors and client. It also shows the auditor's continuing interest in the future of the company and demonstrates the added value of the external audit, which can sometimes be perceived negatively by organisations and their staff.

In summary, sending the letter out on a timely basis gives a favourable impression to the client and could encourage an early and positive response to the recommendations being made.

40 Blake

Text references. Chapters 8, 9, 10, and 11.

Top tips. This question is worth 30 marks and there is a lot of information to take in so it's easy to feel bogged down and start panicking when you come to answer it. However, take a step back and tackle each part in turn, treating it as a mini question. Using this approach makes the question seem less daunting and more manageable.

Part (a) should be straightforward on the control objectives of a wages system. This is worth two marks so assume that it is ½ mark per objective so you need to state four objectives. Don't confuse control objectives with controls or tests of controls – this is a common area of misunderstanding for F8 students.

Part (b) is for 14 marks and note that there are two marks going for presentation. Therefore assume the remaining 12 marks are for the content of your answer so make sure you state four deficiencies, consequences and recommendations as required by the question. You could use a tabular format for your answer so that each deficiency is correctly linked to its consequence and recommendation.

Part (c) is on substantive analytical procedures you could perform on the salary system – think about this before you start writing. There are six marks available here so you need to plan your answer to this part first.

Easy marks. There are easy marks available in part (a) for the control objectives of a wages system. Part (d) should also be straightforward as long as you don't just provide a list of types of procedure – you need to explain each procedure and how they can benefit the auditor.

Examiner's comments. The majority of candidates answered part (a) well. Overall, the standard of answers for part (b) was high. A minority of candidates did not obtain a pass standard either due to a lack of knowledge of wages systems or because this question was answered last and insufficient time was allocated to produce a full answer. The standard of answer for part (c) was inadequate. Many candidates did not distinguish between substantive *analytical* procedures, or simply provided vague points. In part (d) most candidates appeared to understand the question and provided an appropriate range of procedures. Inadequate answers tended only to list procedures and then provide little or no detail on the procedure itself.

Note. The marking scheme has been revised to reflect any necessary amendments made to the question and/or answer.

Marking scheme

		Marks
(a)	0.5 mark for each valid objective	
	Maximum marks	2
(b)	Management letter – 1 mark for each deficiency, 1 for each possible effect and 1 for each recommendation = 3 marks* 4 sets of points = 12 marks	
	Logging in process not monitored	
	Overtime not authorised	
	Poor password control (cat's name)	
	Transfer total wages not checked	
	Employees leaving details sent on e-mail	
	Other valid points	
	4 points *3 marks each =	12
	Letter format	1
	Introduction and conclusion to letter	1
	Maximum marks	14
(c)	1 mark for each valid procedure and 1 for expectation of result of procedure = 2 marks for each procedure	
	Total salary cost	
	Average salary	
	List of payments each month	
	Other valid points	
	Maximum marks	6
(d)	0.5 marks for stating each procedure, 0.5 for explaining each procedure and 1 mark for discussing the use of that procedure = 2 marks for each	
	Procedure	
	Confirmation	
	Observation	
	Inquiry	
	Recalculation	
	Reperformance	
	Analytical procedures	
	Note inspection procedure not valid as stated in question	
	Maximum marks	8
	Total marks	30

(a) **Objectives of a wages system**

- To ensure that employees are only paid for work they have done
- To ensure that pay and deductions have been calculated correctly and authorised
- To ensure that recorded payroll expenses include all expenses incurred
- To ensure that the correct employees are paid
- To ensure that transactions are recorded in the correct period
- To ensure that wages are correctly recorded in the ledger
- To ensure that the correct amounts have been paid over to the taxation authorities

(*Note*: Only four were required.)

(b) **Wages system management letter**

Management

Blake Co

Please find in the attached appendix to this letter our report on the deficiencies discovered in the wages system as a result of our audit work. We also set out our suggested recommendations to mitigate these deficiencies.

Yours sincerely,

A Partner

ABC Accountants

Appendix

Deficiency	Consequence of deficiency	Recommendation
Shift workers can log in and out just by using their electronic identification cards.	Workers can be paid even if they are not working because the time recording system logs them in and out when their cards are scanned and they are paid from and to this time.	The shift manager should agree the number of workers with the computer records at the start and end of the shift.
Overtime is not authorised appropriately or monitored.	Workers could be paid at overtime rates when they are not actually working and could collude with the shift foreman for extra overtime without actually working it.	All requests for overtime must be authorised by the shift manager. Overtime costs should also be monitored regularly.
The code word for the time recording system is generally known within the department.	Unauthorised individuals could log onto the system and enter extra hours so that they are paid more than they should be. Fictitious employees could also be set up on the system.	The code word should be changed immediately to one containing random letters and numbers. The system should be set up so that the code word has to be changed on a regular basis, such as every six weeks.
Payments into workers' bank accounts are made by one member of accounts staff, without any authorisation	Unauthorised payments into workers' and fictitious bank accounts could be made.	The payroll should be authorised by the Finance Director or another senior manager prior to payments being made.
Review of wages payments is done every few weeks by the financial accountant, seemingly on an ad hoc basis.	There is no regular monitoring of wages by senior management.	The Finance Director should review payroll costs on a weekly basis so that he can assess whether they are reasonable and any unusual amounts can be investigated.

(*Note*: Only four were required.)

(c) **Substantive analytical procedures**

(i) Perform a proof in total of the salaries charge for the year using the prior year charge and increasing it for the pay increase and taking account of any starters or leavers in the period.

The figures should be comparable with the exception of the salary increase and any starters or leavers in the year.

(ii) Perform a comparison of the annual charge to the prior year and to the budgeted figure. Where the variance is significant, investigate further to ascertain why.

The figures should be comparable with the exception of the salary increase of 3%.

(iii) Review monthly salaries month by month.

The figures should be about the same each month, except for July and November when the pay rise and annual bonus were paid respectively. Any starters or leavers would also be reflected in the relevant month.

(d) **Audit procedures**

Observation

Observation consists of looking at a process or procedure being performed by others. It could be used here to observe employees scanning their cards when they start and finish a particular shift. However, its use is limited because it only provides evidence that the process happened at the time of observation. It should be used in conjunction with other audit procedures.

Inquiry

Inquiry consists of seeking information of knowledgeable individuals, both financial and non-financial, throughout the entity or outside the entity. This can be used to find out how the time recording system works by interviewing relevant staff so would be a good procedure to use.

Recalculation

Recalculation consists of checking the mathematical accuracy of documents or records. It could be used to calculate the hours worked according to the information on the time recording system.

Reperformance

Reperformance is the auditor's independent execution of procedures or controls that were originally performed as part of the entity's internal control, either manually or using computer-assisted audit techniques. The auditor could test the controls in place within the time recording system using CAATs.

Analytical procedures

Analytical procedures consist of evaluations of financial information by studying plausible relationships among both financial and non-financial data. They can be used in this case to compare the time recorded per the system to the standard hours per employee plus any overtime worked.

(Note: Only four were required.)

Tutorial note: Confirmation would not be a valid procedure in this question because confirmation is a type of inquiry where a representation of information or of an existing condition is obtained directly from a third party.

41 Using the work of others

(a) Criteria to be considered when assessing whether to place reliance on internal audit work include the following:

Objectivity of function

The external auditor should consider whom the internal auditors report to and whether they are subject to any conflicting responsibilities, constraints or restrictions. This will affect the capability of the internal auditors to communicate significant matters openly.

Scope of function

The external auditors should consider the extent and nature of assignments performed by the internal auditors and the action taken by management as a result of internal audit reports.

Technical competence

The external auditors should consider whether the internal auditors have adequate technical training and proficiency.

Due professional care

The external auditors should consider whether the work of internal audit is properly planned, supervised, reviewed and documented.

(b) Audit evidence that could be obtained from an expert

- Valuations of assets such as land and buildings, plant and machinery, works of art, precious stones
- Determination of quantities or physical condition of assets
- Determination of amounts using specialised techniques or methods, such as an actuarial valuation
- Measurement of work completed and to be completed on contracts in progress
- Legal opinions concerning interpretations of agreements, statutes and regulations

(*Note*: Only four were required.)

(c) Factors to consider when evaluating the work carried out by an auditor's expert:

- Relevance and reasonableness of the work and consistency with other audit evidence
- Relevance and reasonableness of any assumptions and methods used
- Relevance, completeness and accuracy of any source data used

If the results of the expert's work do not provide sufficient, appropriate audit evidence or are inconsistent with other audit evidence, the auditor needs to resolve the matter. This could be done through discussions with the entity and the expert, applying additional audit procedures, including engaging another expert, or modifying the auditor's opinion in the auditor's report (this is a last resort if the issues are still unresolved after all the other avenues have been explored).

42 Expert

Text references. Chapters 2, 11 and 12.

Top tips. On the 10 mark question of the F8 paper, the key thing to remember is to stick to your time allocation for this relatively straightforward knowledge-based question. Resist the temptation to write down all you know about the subject matters in question.

Easy marks. This question on the F8 paper will allow you to pick up many easy marks as the questions are all knowledge-based.

Examiner's comments. Parts (a) and (b) were well answered. In part (c) a majority of candidates provided 4 valid assertions, with an appropriate audit procedure. However, a significant number of incorrect points were made such as not linking the audit procedure with the assertion and defining the assertion rather than providing an audit procedure for that assertion.

Marking scheme

		Marks
(a)	1 mark for each factor	
	Professional qualification	
	Experience and reputation	
	Objectivity	
	Other valid points	
	Maximum marks	3
(b)	1 mark for each right of the author	
	Access to company books	
	Obtain information/explanation company officers	
	Receive notice of/attend certain meetings	
	Speak at certain meetings	
	Receive copies certain resolutions	
	Other valid points	
	Maximum marks	3

		Marks
(c)	0.5 for each assertion and 0.5 for each procedure	
	Completeness	
	Existence	
	Valuation	
	Rights and obligations	
	Disclosure	
	Maximum marks	4
	Total marks	10

(a) **Factors to consider when assessing competence and objectivity of an auditor's expert**

The auditor should consider whether the expert is certified or licensed by an appropriate professional body or has membership of such a professional body.

The auditor should also consider the expert's experience and reputation in the field in which he is seeking audit evidence.

Finally the auditor should consider whether the expert is employed by the audited entity or is related in some other way such as by being financially dependent on the entity or having investments in it. Such relationships would impair the expert's objectivity.

(b) **Rights of auditors**

Auditors have a right of access at all times to the books and accounts of the audited entity.

They have a right to require from the company's officers such information and explanations that they think necessary for the performance of their duties as auditors.

They have a right to attend any general meetings of the company and to receive all notices of and communications relating to such meetings which any member of the company is entitled to receive.

They have a right to be heard at general meetings which they attend on any part of the business that concerns them as auditors.

They have a right to give notice in writing requiring a general meeting to be held for the purpose of laying the accounts and reports before the company.

They have a right to receive a copy of any written resolution proposed.

(*Note*: Only three were required.)

(c) **Assertions relating to non-current assets**

Existence

Physically inspect a sample of non-current assets stated on the assets register to confirm whether they exist or not.

Completeness

For a sample of assets selected by physical inspection, agree that they are listed on the assets register to confirm completeness of information.

Valuation and allocation

For a sample of assets on the assets register, recalculate net book values in accordance with the entity's accounting policies to ensure that year-end values are correctly stated.

Rights and obligations

For a sample of assets on the assets register, inspect relevant third party documentation such as purchase invoices, deeds for land and buildings etc to confirm that the entity owns them.

43 Audit techniques and sampling

(a) Factors to consider when using analytical procedures as substantive audit procedures

- The objectives of the analytical procedures and the extent to which their results are reliable
- The degree to which information can be analysed
- The availability of information
- The reliability of the information available
- The relevance of the information available
- The source of the information available
- The comparability of the information available
- Knowledge gained from previous audits

(*Note*: Only six were required.)

(b) An accounting estimate is an approximation of the amount of an item in the absence of a precise means of measurement. Examples where accounting estimates are used in the financial statements include:

- Allowances to reduce inventory and accounts receivable to their estimated realisable value
- Depreciation and amortisation
- Accrued revenue
- Deferred tax
- Provision for a loss from a lawsuit
- Losses on construction contracts in progress
- Provision to meet warranty claims

(*Note*: Only four examples were required.)

(c) Statistical sampling is any approach to sampling that involves random selection of a sample, and the use of probability theory to evaluate sample results, including measurement of sampling risk. Non-statistical sampling is where the auditor does not use statistical methods and draws a judgemental opinion about the population. Sample selection methods include:

- Random selection
- Systematic selection
- Haphazard selection
- Sequence or block selection
- Monetary unit sampling

(*Note*: Only three examples were required.)

44 Sampling methods

Text references. Chapters 8, 11 and 19

Top tips. This question is purely a knowledge based question. Read the questions carefully. You are only required to list four methods in (a) and four assertions in (b) so don't waste time listing more than that.

Easy marks. Accurately recalling your knowledge from the appropriate sections of the study text will gain you maximum marks.

Examiner's comments. Part (a) was relatively well answered.

In part (b) most candidates provided four valid points; however, there was significant confusion regarding which assertions related to classes of transactions even though study material clearly makes that distinction.

In part (c) one concern was the minority of candidates who provided a page or more of answer for what was only 2 marks. Those marks were normally obtained within the first paragraph meaning the rest of the answer was not required. In this situation, poor examination technique led to time pressure later in the examination.

ACCA examiner's answer. The ACCA examiner's answer to this question can be found at the back of this kit.

Marking scheme

		Marks
(a)	1 mark for each method. 0.5 for stating the method and 0.5 for brief explanation. – Random – Systematic – Haphazard – Sequence – MUS – Judgemental	
	Maximum marks	4
(b)	1 mark per assertion. 0.5 for stating the assertion and 0.5 for explaining the assertion. – Occurrence – Completeness – Accuracy – Cut-off – Classification	
	Maximum marks	4
(c)	Up to 2 marks for valid explanation of – Modified	
	Maximum marks	2
		10

(a) **Sampling methods**

Methods of selecting a sample acceptable according to ISA 530 *Audit Sampling*:

Random selection ensures that all items in the population have an equal chance of selection, eg by use of random number tables or random number generators.

Systematic selection involves selecting items using a constant interval between selections, the first interval having a random start.

Haphazard selection is selection of a sample without following any particular structured technique. It may be an alternative to random selection provided auditors are satisfied that the sample is representative of the entire population.

Block selection may be used to check whether certain items have particular characteristics. For example an auditor may use a sample of 50 consecutive cheques to test whether cheques are signed by authorised signatories rather than picking 50 single cheques throughout the year.

> **Top tip**. **Monetary unit sampling** is the other principal method listed in ISA 530.

(b) **Assertions**

Assertions from ISA 315 *Identifying and assessing the risks of material misstatement through understanding the entity and its environment* relating to classes of transactions and events include:

Occurrence: transactions and events that have been recorded have actually occurred and pertain to the entity.

Completeness: all transactions and events that should have been recorded have been recorded.

Accuracy: amounts and other data relating to recorded transactions and events have been recorded appropriately.

Cut-off: transactions and events have been recorded in the correct accounting period.

> **Top tip. Classification** is another assertion that could have been listed and explained relating the recording of transactions.

(c) **Audit report term**

The auditor will modify the audit opinion within the audit report as required by ISA 705 *Modifications to the opinion in the independent auditor's report,* where there is evidence of material misstatement or there is insufficient appropriate audit evidence to conclude on a material area or matter.

The three types of modified opinion are:

1 A qualified opinion (where the effect is, or could be, material but not pervasive)

2 An adverse opinion (where the effect is pervasive), and;

3 A disclaimer of opinion (where the effect of possible misstatements could be pervasive).

45 External confirmations

(a) Positive circularisations require a response, whatever the response may be whereas negative circularisations only require a response from the customer if he disagrees with the balance stated as outstanding on the circularisation letter. The negative method is used less frequently and only when internal controls within the audited entity are considered to be strong.

There are two types of positive circularisation. The first is where the amount is stated on the letter and the customer is asked whether he agrees or disagrees with this amount. If he disagrees, he is asked to give reasons. This has the disadvantage that the customer might just agree to the balance without checking or agree because it is less than what is actually owed. The advantage is that disagreements might bring other matters to the auditor's attention such as faulty inventory or pricing issues.

The second method is where the customer is asked to confirm the amount owed. This method is likely to result in fewer responses because more effort is required to obtain the balance.

(b) External confirmations can be used for the following:

- Bank balances and other information from bankers
- Inventory held by third parties
- Property title deeds held by lawyers for safe custody or as security
- Investments purchased from stockbrokers but not delivered at the year-end date
- Loans from lenders
- Accounts payable balances

(c) The bank confirmation letter could ask for the following information:

- Balances due to or from the client on current, deposit, loan and other accounts
- Any nil balances on accounts
- Accounts closed during the period
- Maturity and interest terms on loans and overdrafts
- Unused facilities
- Lines of credit/standby facilities
- Any offset or other rights or encumbrances
- Details of any collateral given or received
- Contingent liabilities
- Confirmation of securities and other items in safe custody

(*Note*: Only six were required.)

46 Analytical procedures, sampling and CAATs

(a) Factors to consider when assessing the reliance that can be placed on the results of analytical procedures

Materiality of the items involved

If inventory balances are material, then auditors should not rely solely on analytical procedures.

Other audit procedures

In the audit of receivables, other audit procedures such as the review of subsequent cash receipts may confirm or dispel questions arising from the application of analytical procedures to an aged profile of customers' accounts.

Accuracy of predictions

Auditors would expect greater consistency in comparing the relationship between gross profit and sales from one period to the next than in comparing discretionary expenses such as research costs or advertising expenditure.

Frequency with which relationship is observed

A pattern repeated monthly as opposed to annually (for example, payroll costs).

Assessment of inherent and control risks

If internal controls over sales order processing are weak, and control risk is assessed as high, the auditors may rely more on tests of individual transactions or balances than on analytical procedures.

(Note: Only three were required.)

(b) 'Sampling risk' is the risk that the auditor's conclusion, based on a sample of a certain size, may be different from the conclusion that would be reached if the entire population was subjected to the same audit procedure. It can be reduced by increasing the sample size for both tests of controls and substantive procedures.

'Non-sampling risk' is the risk that the auditor reaches the wrong conclusion for any reason unrelated to the size of the sample, such as using inappropriate procedures or misinterpreting evidence and failing to recognise a misstatement or deviation. It can be reduced by proper engagement planning, supervision and review.

(c) 'Audit software' consists of computer programs used by auditors to process data of audit significance from the client's accounting system. It may comprise generalised audit software or custom audit software. It is used for substantive procedures.

'Test data' involves entering data such as a sample of transactions into the client's accounting system and comparing the results obtained with pre-determined results. Test data is used for tests of controls.

Advantages of CAATs

- Auditors can test program controls as well as general computer controls
- A greater number of items can be tested more quickly and accurately
- Transactions can be tested, rather than paper records that could be incorrect
- CAATs are cost-effective in the long-term if the client does not change its systems
- Results can be compared to results from traditional testing and if correlation exists, overall confidence is increased

47 Wear Wraith

Text reference. Chapter 12

Top tips. This is a fairly straightforward question on non-current assets. In part (a), think about the objectives when testing non-current assets, ie ownership, existence, valuation, completeness. You are asked to 'list' the audit work so make sure you are specific and succinct in your answers. In part (b), the best approach is to take each category of non-current assets in turn and deal with each separately. Note that the requirement specifically tells you to ignore the railway trucks. The motor vehicles are a bit more complicated than the land and buildings and plant and machinery categories but you should, from the scenario, spot that the disposals in the year relate to vehicles that were five years old whereas the policy is to depreciate these over three years.

Easy marks. In part (b), easy marks are available for considering the land and buildings and plant and machinery categories first. You should remember from your financial reporting studies that land is normally not depreciated. From the plant and machinery figures, you should be able to identify fairly quickly from a quick scan of the figures that the depreciation on the disposals exceeds their cost value.

Examiner's comments. In part (a), many candidates obtained a good pass by stating six or seven clear audit tests on non-current assets. The tests were clearly related to the scenario. Some candidates, however, simply stated every possible test on non-current assets with no regard at all for the scenario. Spending a little time planning and thinking about the scenario is advisable prior to writing the answer. Overall, the standard was disappointing, with the average standard being a very marginal pass.

In part (b), candidates were required to identify any issues concerning the note that should be raised with management. The implication was that such issues would be unusual, not basic issues such as obtaining evidence of existence of the assets. It was therefore disappointing to see some candidates simply repeating all the audit tests again, having already done this in part (a). Weaknesses included a lack of knowledge of the information provided in a non-current asset note and suggesting that the note had arithmetical errors when the question explicitly stated that this was not the case.

The overall standard for this question was disappointing. The content of many answers showed that candidates are not always familiar with the use of scenarios in auditing questions. Question practice on how to apply scenario information to specific question requirements is needed.

Marking scheme

		Marks
(a)	One mark for each valid test	
	Board minutes	1
	Non-current asset ledger	1
	Non current asset note	1
	Inspect trucks	1
	Purchase invoices	1
	Depreciation policy OK?	1
	Depreciation disclosure amount	1
	Depreciation accurate calculation	1
	Treatment of any sales tax	1
	Confirm NBV using specialist or trade journal	1
	Other relevant points (each)	1
	Maximum marks	**10**

		Marks
(b)	Key points up to 2 marks for explaining the problem and 1 mark for stating the solution	
	Land and buildings – depreciation of land	3
	Plant and machinery – depreciation eliminated > cost	3
	Motor vehicles – depreciation calculated not = disclosure note	3
	Motor vehicles – may be depreciating too quickly	3
	Maximum marks	**10**
		20

(a) **Audit work to perform on railway trucks**

- Reconcile the draft note figures for railway trucks to the non-current asset register and general ledger to ensure that the amount stated in the accounts is accurate.
- Cast the non-current assets note and check that it agrees to the amount disclosed in the statement of financial position.
- Vouch a sample of additions in the year to supporting third party documentation such as invoices from suppliers to ensure that the amounts stated are correct and to confirm ownership.
- Review board minutes authorising purchase of the trucks in the year to confirm authorisation.
- Recalculate the depreciation charge for the year based on the total cost of the trucks and the stated depreciation policy and check that this has been charged in the income statement and stated correctly in the non-current assets note.
- Vouch the existence of a sample of railway trucks in the accounting records to the physical asset.
- Verify completeness of railway trucks by taking a sample of trucks by physical inspection and checking that they have been recorded in the accounting records and the non-current asset register.
- Check that the depreciation policy for railway trucks is appropriate by reference to industry standards and the accounts of other similar companies to Wear Wraith.
- Check the treatment of sales tax for a sample of assets to ensure it is correct, eg capitalised where it is non-recoverable.

(b) **Non-current asset issues to discuss with management**

Land and Buildings

The depreciation rate of 2% has been correctly applied however the charge for the year has been based on the total balance ie land and buildings. Per IAS 16, land is not generally depreciated as it is considered to have an unlimited life. Therefore the building element of the total should be separated out in order to calculate the charge for the year on the buildings element only.

Plant and Machinery

The depreciation charge for additions and existing plant and machinery has been correctly calculated by applying 20% to the year-end balances (ie charging a full year's depreciation in the year of acquisition for new additions). Disposals costing $100,000 occurred in the year but the depreciation eliminated on these is $120,000, which is greater than the total cost, has been adjusted for which is incorrect. This must be discussed with management and any identified errors should be adjusted for accordingly.

Motor Vehicles

The depreciation charge on the motor vehicles sold has correctly been adjusted for at $325,000 as they were fully depreciated assets at the time of disposal. However, the motor vehicles were 5 years old, whereas the policy for motor vehicles is to depreciate them over 3 years. This indicates that management should review the useful economic life of motor vehicles in order to assess whether the current policy is still appropriate.

The charge for the year appears to have been incorrectly calculated, as it seems to have been charged over 4 years rather than over 3 years. The charge for the year of $425,000 is less than it should be according to the rate per the depreciation policy for motor vehicles. Therefore either the policy has changed or the calculation has been performed incorrectly. This issue should be discussed with management to ascertain the reason and the appropriate amendment made, ie either to the policy note or to the charge for the year. This would not constitute a change in accounting policy (as it is a change in an accounting estimate, per IAS 18) so there would be no need to amend prior year figures.

48 Tracey Transporters

Text references. Chapters 12 and 14

Top tips. In part (a), a good way of setting your answer out and giving it more structure would be to use a tabular format, ie 'Audit test' in one column and 'Reason for test' in the other column. Make sure that you do explain the reasons why you are carrying out each test – this is specifically requested in the question requirement. In part (b), think about the audit assertions first and make sure your audit work adequately covers them in your answer.

Easy marks. The marks in this question should be achievable fairly easily. Use the information in the scenario and give your answers as much structure as possible.

Examiner's comments. Answers to part (a) varied considerably. Well-prepared candidates provided excellent lists of tests, with appropriate explanations, which were relevant to the scenario. However the majority of candidates had difficulty explaining the tests.

Specific reasons for weak answers included:

- Including tests on the non-current assets register. Given that this was a sales audit, it was not clear why these tests were included here, and again in part (b)
- Providing comments such as 'check casting' without specifying which documents are to be cast, or why
- Explaining the audit of receivables without linking this to the objectives of completeness and accuracy of sales
- Explaining the systems and controls that should be in place rather than auditing the system. This did not meet the requirement of explaining audit tests.

The overall standard of answers to part (b) was much higher than for part (a). The majority of candidates managed to provide a sufficiently broad list of tests. Specific reasons for weaker answers included:

- Not fully explaining the points, eg saying, 'Obtain company records for ownership' but not actually stating which records needed to be obtained.
- Stating unclear or incorrect audit procedures, eg 'obtain non-current asset register, take sample of vehicles and see vehicle to check completeness of the register'. This is actually checking the accuracy of the register. Checking for completeness would normally involve seeing an asset then checking that it was included.
- A small minority of candidates mentioned tests on other areas of the statement of financial position. It was not clear whether the need to audit non-current assets had been identified. More focused answers are needed to obtain a pass standard.

Many candidates would benefit from taking a minute to jot down the assertions and then ensure that their answer covered all of them.

Marking scheme

		Marks
(a)	Sales testing Audit tests on completeness and accuracy of sales income Watch for tests being combined – be generous where two tests are given in the same point Normally award 1 mark per point to a maximum of	10
(b)	Non-current asset testing List of tests at 1 mark per relevant test to a maximum of	10
		20

(a)

Audit test	Reason
Enquire about and observe the procedures used when bookings are received over the telephone.	The biggest risk of incomplete recording of orders relates to those received by telephone. Evidence is needed that checking and supervision occurs at this point.
With the client's permission, enter a sample of test data into the VMS booking system and review the details logged on the system.	This will confirm that there are no flaws in the system causing omission or error at the input stage.
For a sample of e-mail orders, agree details to the VMS booking system.	This will identify errors arising when the e-mail details are input to the VMS system.
For a sample of booking records within the VMS system, agree the details to the corresponding invoice produced by the receivables ledger programme.	This will identify whether information is transferred completely and accurately between the two modules of the system.
For a sample of invoices, agree the hire prices charged to the master file record of approved prices.	This will identify whether the full approved prices are being charged to customers.
For a sample of credit notes issued in the year, agree to supporting documentation and check for evidence of authorisation by the appropriate level of management.	This will check that credit notes are only issued and sales entries reversed when there is a valid reason.
Cast the list of invoices issued in one month (or other appropriate period) and agree the total to the entry made to the nominal ledger.	This will identify whether the journals posted to the nominal ledger are complete and accurate.
Cast the sales account in the nominal ledger and agree the total to the sales figure in the draft income statement.	This will identify whether any arithmetical errors have arisen in the accounting system and whether any errors have arisen in the transfer of information from the accounting system to the financial statements.
Perform analytical procedures, comparing the following ratios to prior years (or month by month if the information is available): – Turnover per vehicle – Gross profit margin Obtain explanations and corroborate evidence for any unexpected variations.	If material amounts have been omitted from sales it would be likely to have a significant effect on these ratios.
Review the results of audit procedures on receivables, such as the results of any direct confirmation of balances, and consider whether any errors identified also have an effect on the sales figure.	The double entry effect of errors needs to be considered and if, say, a confirmation reply from a customer reveals that an amount has been incorrectly posted to the receivables account, this will have a corresponding effect on sales.

(b) **Audit work on vehicles**

(i) Obtain a schedule reconciling the movement on the vehicles cost account and vehicles depreciation account over the year and agree:

- Opening balances to prior year audit files
- Closing balances to non-current asset register and nominal ledger

(ii) Cast the columns for costs, depreciation and net book value in the non-current asset register.

(iii) Select a sample of additions in the year from the non-current asset register and:

- Agree to the purchase invoice to confirm ownership *(rights and obligations assertion)* and that the correct amount has been capitalised, excluding any revenue items such as petrol or road tax *(valuation and allocation assertion).*
- From the date on the purchase invoice confirm that the purchase has been recorded in the correct accounting period *(occurrence assertion).*
- Physically inspect the vehicle to confirm existence (or alternatively, if the vehicle is out on hire at the time inspect the hire documentation, insurance policy and vehicle registration document) *(existence assertion).*

(iv) From the company's insurance policy, agree a sample of vehicles currently owned (and hence insured by TT) to the non-current asset register *(completeness assertion).*

(v) Review the repairs and maintenance expense account and agree any unusually large amounts to invoices to check that no purchases of a capital nature have been misclassified *(completeness assertion).*

(vi) Obtain a list of disposals in the year and:

- Inspect to confirm that the vehicle has been removed from the non-current assets register
- Agree sales proceeds to the cash book

(vii) Perform a proof in total of the depreciation charge for the year, applying the depreciation rate as disclosed in the financial statements to the opening balance *(valuation assertion).*

(viii) For a sample of individual vehicles from the non-current asset register, reperform the depreciation calculation *(valuation assertion).*

(ix) Review the depreciation policy for reasonableness *(valuation assertion)* by:

- Reviewing for consistency with prior years
- Comparing it with that used by other companies in the industry
- Considering whether significant gains or losses have arisen on disposals during the year
- Comparing the useful life applied in the depreciation calculation to the age of the lorries that were sold during the year

(x) Review the notes to the accounts to check that:

- The depreciation policy has been disclosed, and
- The movements on the vehicles cost and depreciation have been appropriately disclosed in the non-current assets note *(disclosure assertion).*

(Note. The audit testing assertions are included in the answer as candidates are likely to structure their answer around these headings but there are no specific marks for mentioning them.)

49 MistiRead

Text references. Chapters 4 and 13

Top tips. This is a question on inventory and ethics. Part (a) should be straightforward on the advantages of a perpetual inventory system. In part (b), make sure that as well as listing the audit procedures to perform, you also explain why you are doing them – use the clues in the scenario to help you generate specific audit procedures – for example, you are told that internal audit carries out continuous inventory checking so make sure you address this in your answer. There are four short requirements in this question and you should be able to score reasonably well by sticking to the time allocation for each and also by using the information provided to you in the question scenario where relevant.

Easy marks. Easy marks are available in part (c) of this question on explaining the fundamental principles of professional ethics as set out in ACCA's *Code of Ethics and Conduct.* You should also be able to score well on part (a) on the advantages of a perpetual inventory system.

Examiner's comments. Answers to part (a) were sometimes more in a list format than providing an explanation of the advantages of a perpetual inventory system, stating advantages rather than explaining them. For example, stating an advantage as ' increased control over inventory' without mentioning the advantage of decrease in theft. In part (b) the key point to note was that the procedures could place at any time in the year, not simply at the year end. The point became the main weakness in many answers as candidates wrote all they knew about inventory checking – at the year end. In part (c) most answers mentioned the areas of integrity, objectivity and independence, although briefly. A typical answer provided a single sentence explanation. Some provided incorrect or limited explanations of the principles. For example mentioning ' an accountant must be independent' without actually providing and explanation of the term. In part (d) candidates had to suggest what to do when a client will not sign the letter of engagement. Most candidates managed to suggest that resignation might be appropriate but few suggested other actions such as talking to the directors or reminding the directors of their duties to provide information to the auditor.

Marking scheme

		Marks
(a)	1 mark each advantage	
	No disruption	1
	Identify slow moving damaged inventory quicker	1
	Always have actual inventory details available	1
	Increased control storekeepers	1
	Limit audit tests	1
	Other relevant points	1
	Maximum marks	**4**
(b)	0.5 for procedure, 0.5 for explaining purpose	
	Meeting with internal audit	1
	Continuous inventory > book inventory	1
	Book inventory > continuous inventory	1
	Condition of books	1
	Opinion on accuracy continuous inventory system	1
	All lines counted once per year	1
	Computer record amendment to actual inventory levels	1
	Acceptable procedures on return of inventory	1
	Other relevant points	1
	Maximum marks	**6**
(c)	1 mark for explaining concept and 1 for applying to accountants	
	Integrity	2
	Objectivity	2
	Independence	2
	Maximum marks	**6**
(d)	1 mark each	
	Discuss with directors	1
	Requirement to make information available to auditor	1
	Limitation in scope of audit work	1
	Modification of audit report	1
	Possibly not work for client	1
	Other relevant points	1
	Maximum marks	**4**
		20

(a) **Advantages of a perpetual inventory system**

- Allows a year-end count to be avoided as inventory is counted throughout the year, thereby minimising disruption at the year-end
- Enables the company to maintain greater control over inventory because inventory balances are known at any time
- Errors can be investigated quickly and corrected and slow-moving or obsolete inventory can be identified more quickly
- External auditors can rely on the system, thus reducing the level of substantive work required on inventory at the year-end

(b) **Audit procedures to confirm accuracy of continuous inventory checking at MistiRead**

Audit procedure	Reason
Review the results of continuous inventory checking carried out by internal audit, including a review of working papers	To confirm that the work has been carried out appropriately and that external auditors can rely on the results of that work
Examine the procedures in place for carrying out continuous inventory checking	To ensure that policies and procedures regarding continuous inventory checking are adequate
Observe continuous inventory checking being carried out during the year	To confirm that inventory checking is being carried out properly and in accordance with documented procedures
Follow-up inventory counts observed	To ensure that all discrepancies are fully investigated and resolved
For a sample of inventory items on the system, agree it to book inventory and for a sample of items in inventory, agree to inventory records	To ensure that the company maintains adequate inventory records
Discuss program of inventory counting with internal audit staff and review the year's inventory counts	To provide assurance that all inventory lines are counted at least once a year

(c) **Fundamental principles of professional ethics**

The ACCA's *Code of Ethics and Conduct* sets out five fundamental principles of professional ethics: integrity, objectivity, professional competence and due care, confidentiality and professional behaviour.

Integrity

The code states that members should be straightforward and honest in all business and professional relationships. Integrity also implies fair dealing and truthfulness. Members should not be associated with reports, returns, communications or other information where they believe that the information contains materially false or misleading statements, contains statements or information furnished recklessly or omits or obscures information required to be included where its omission or obscurity would be misleading.

Objectivity

The code states that members should not allow bias, conflicts of interest or the undue influence of others to override professional or business judgements. They may be exposed to situations which may impair their objectivity. Relationships that bias or unduly influence professional judgement should be avoided.

Independence

Independence is not one of the fundamental principles of professional ethics. However, it is related to the fundamental principle of objectivity because maintenance of independence demonstrates adherence to objectivity. Members have to be both independent and seen to be independent – independence requires independence of mind and independence in appearance.

(d) **Actions to take regarding unsigned audit engagement letter**

- Meet with the directors of MistiRead in person to discuss the issue further and to establish what their concerns are
- Explain that auditors have a right to all information and records that they might require for their audit
- Explain that one of the fundamental principles of professional ethics is that of confidentiality, which means that the auditors cannot disclose any information to third parties without the proper and specific authority of the client
- Explain the possible impact on the audit report – if the auditors are unable to perform work on research and development expenditure as a result, and the possible effects could be material, this will lead to a qualified audit opinion due to an inability to gain sufficient appropriate audit evidence

50 Coogee

Text reference. Chapter 14

Top tips. To answer this question you need a good knowledge of ISA 540 *Audit of accounting estimates, including fair value accounting estimates, and related disclosures.* Try to establish which assertions you are trying to test, as this will help you to focus testing in the right area. In part (c), for example, you will need to verify the completeness of the allowance, amongst other things.

Easy marks. To score well in this type of question you need to identify the key issues. In this case you are dealing with balances which are estimates made by management. The focus of your audit work will therefore be to establish how management estimated the figure, and then to determine how reasonable this is.

(a) **Approaches to gaining audit evidence re estimates**

- Review and perform procedures on the process used by management to arrive at the estimate
- Develop an auditor's point estimate for comparison with management's point estimate
- Review subsequent events which confirm the estimate made

(b) **General allowance: procedures**

Two approaches can be taken.

(i) *Review and perform procedures on the process*

(1) Obtain details of the general allowance and the aged receivables analysis which supports it.

(2) Review the results of sales transactions tests to ensure that the system for ageing receivables works effectively.

(3) Find out from management the method of calculation of the allowance.

(4) Check whether it is the same method as in previous years and if not whether the amendment is reasonable. Consider management's explanation for the method and ensure that the method has been correctly applied.

(5) Recalculate the allowance.

(6) Compare to the receivables ledger to ensure that all relevant balances have been included.

(7) Check that none of the balances in the specific allowance have been included in the calculation, by review.

(8) Consider whether last year's allowance was reasonable in the light of events since last year's audit.

(9) Consider the results of any customer's circularisation undertaken. Customers may recognise the debt which will imply that they intend to make payment. If they acknowledge the debt it may be worth asking the client to contact them to agree on a payment timetable.

(10) Calculate ratios concerning receivables and allowance as a percentage of debt. They should be comparable to the previous year.

(11) Enquire whether the allowance has been considered and approved by the directors.

(ii) *Consider subsequent events*

(1) Test a sample of the balances in the receivables ledger to see if any cash has been received since the year end.

(2) Enquire of the credit controller as to whether any cash has been received on these accounts since the year end.

(c) **Specific allowance**

(i) Obtain a list of the bad debts.

(ii) Check that the list has been correctly totalled by recasting it.

(iii) Discuss the debt with the credit controller to ascertain why these are considered bad.

(iv) Review the correspondence with the customer to ascertain whether the customer intends to pay or not.

(v) If there is no correspondence, consider why. If the client has not chased the debt, it suggests that they expect to receive the money.

(vi) Check cash receipts after date to ensure that the amount is still outstanding by inspecting bank statements and remittance advices.

(vii) Scrutinise lists of companies going into receivership up to the date of signing to ensure none of them are customers of the company.

(viii) Ask the company solicitors whether they have started legal proceedings against any receivables against which allowances have been made.

(ix) If they have, review correspondence with solicitor or inquire of solicitor the likelihood of the debt being recovered.

(x) Ascertain whether the customer is 'on stop'. If not, enquire why the company is still trading with the customer. It may be because the debt is not really bad.

(xi) Scrutinise board minutes since the end of the reporting period to ascertain whether any subsequent events require the provision to be changed.

(xii) Review credit notes issued since the end of the reporting period and consider if any of them mean that the provision should be changed.

(xiii) Ensure that the allowance has been scrutinised and authorised by the directors by inspecting the relevant documentation.

51 Duckworth Computers

Text reference. Chapter 15

Top tips. The question specifically tells you to assume the recipient has no knowledge in part (a). You should ensure that you write your answer so that someone who knows nothing about auditing could audit the bank reconciliation.

Easy marks. Parts (b) and (c) should represent reasonably straightforward marks.

(a) (i) Audit procedures to verify bank reconciliation

Tests of details of balances

(1) Confirm the bank balances per the client's working papers and general ledger to the bank letter on the file and the bank statements.

(2) Check the receipts on the list of receipts to the bank statement for October, to ascertain if the outstanding deposits on the bank reconciliation are the only ones that are outstanding. Check that any deposits on the bank statement which are not on the list of receipts for October were listed as reconciling items on the September bank reconciliation.

(3) Check the payments on the list of payments to the bank statement for October, to ascertain if the unpresented cheques on the bank reconciliation are the only ones that are outstanding.

Check that any cheques on the bank statement which are not on the list of payments for October were listed as reconciling items on the September bank reconciliation.

(4) Check that any reconciling item on the September bank reconciliation that is still outstanding is included on the October bank reconciliation.

(5) Verify reconciling items on the October bank reconciliation.

- Trace the outstanding deposits and cheques on the reconciliation to November bank statements to ensure that they clear the bank in reasonable time.
- Agree the returned cheque to the entries on the bank statement for correctness.
- Agree that the bank charges on the reconciliation statement agree to the bank statement and that they are the only such charge that has not been included in the cashbook.

(6) List all the items that are still outstanding from the bank reconciliation at the end of the audit and put the list on the report to partner section of the file, for his attention.

(ii) **Audit objectives**

(Numbers in this answer refer to the number of the points in part (i).)

(1) This is to agree the accuracy of the bank balance.
(2) This is to test the completeness of the bank reconciliation.
(3) This is to test the completeness of the bank reconciliation.
(4) This is to test the completeness of the bank reconciliation.
(5) This is to verify the existence of the reconciling items on the bank reconciliation.
(6) This is to highlight items where there may be doubt as to their existence.

(b) **Reliability of bank statements**

Bank statements are **third party evidence** as they are issued by the bank

However, the bank sends them to the client so they are **not third party evidence received directly from the third party.** This means that there is scope for the client to adjust them in some way if the client wants to deceive the auditor.

It is rare for such a fraud to occur but the auditor should be **aware of the possibility of such evidence tampering** and treat the evidence accordingly.

Should the auditor have grounds to fear that the evidence will be tampered with, the auditor **could request bank statements directly from the bank**. The auditor would have to obtain the client's permission for this.

(c) (i) **Auditing around the computer**

This is where the auditor audits the information input to a computer and audits the output of the computer but does not audit the computer processing of the information.

Auditing through the computer

This is where as well as auditing input and output, the auditor checks the processing routines and program controls of the computer as well.

(ii) **Situations where it is inappropriate to audit around the computer**

In general terms the inappropriateness of auditing around the computer increases with the **complexity of the computer program.**

Specifically, it is inappropriate to audit around the computer when the **computer generates totals for which no detailed analysis can be obtained.** It is also inappropriate in the absence of control totals and audit trails.

It is also inappropriate to audit around the computer where the **use of CAATs could reduce control risk and the level of substantive procedures significantly,** or substantive procedures could be done more efficiently by the use of CAATs. This is likely to be the case where a significant amount of use is made of the computer by the business and valuable information is contained within it.

52 Cash audit

Text reference. Chapter 15

Top tips. This question has a number of small parts, each of which is straightforward. You should be able to put together an answer to this question that gains you a high mark. Probably the worst thing that can happen on this question is that you allocate your time badly, and don't give yourself an opportunity to finish collecting the easy marks available for this question, or fail to answer other questions properly because you overran on the straightforward one. Don't fall into this trap. Allocate your time to each part of this question and be strict with yourself if you start to run over. Remember to state your points simply, and in a fashion that makes the marker's life easier. For example, in part (a), it would be appropriate to use bullet points to set out your points.

Easy marks. These are available for part (c) which is based on knowledge.

Examiner's comments. Generally reasonably well answered. Common mistakes included confusing audit objectives and control objectives, stating that the auditor would only need to count cash at shops near the office and confusion regarding the matters that would be confirmed in a bank letter.

Marking scheme

			Marks
(a)	Errors and misappropriations – cash		
	(i)	Receipts Up to 1 mark per point to maximum of	2
	(ii)	Payments Up to 1.5 marks per point to maximum of	3
	(iii)	Interest and charges Up to 2 marks	2
(b)	Principal audit objectives Up to 2 marks per point to max of		8
(c)	Why auditors seek bank confirmations – matters confirmed Up to 1 mark per point to a maximum of		5
			20

(a) **Errors and misappropriations**

(i) *Receipts paid into bank accounts*

- The money could be **stolen** before it is banked. This will be easier if it is cash, but even cheques could be fraudulently diverted to personal accounts.
- If the bank records are not reconciled to the company's records, receipts could be **incorrectly entered** into the company's records.

(ii) *Payments made out of bank accounts*

- Payments could be **misappropriated** if cheques are signed with no backing documentation, as they could be fraudulently made out to members of staff or other third parties.
- Similarly, if there is no backing documentation reviewed when cheques are made out, non-business expenses could be paid for by the company.
- If payments are not recorded properly in the company records, suppliers may be paid more than once for an invoice, as the company will have no control over what payments have been made. Alternatively, suppliers may not be paid at all, and this could lead to **operational problems**.

(iii) *Interest and charges debited and credited to bank accounts*

- If the company does not record items debited or credited directly to their bank account, the amounts in their own records will be incorrect.
- Also, banks sometimes make mistakes in the amount of interest they credit to your account or the charges they take out. If the company does not check these, it could lose money.

(b) **Audit of cash**

The key audit objectives in the audit of cash are to verify the assertions of **existence**, **completeness/valuation**, **rights and obligations**, and **occurrence**.

Existence

The auditors will verify existence by carrying out cash counts. They will not necessarily need to carry out counts in every store. However, they should rotate the stores which they visit on an annual basis, and should not simply visit certain stores close to their offices because it is easy to do so.

This will involve checking that the cash in the tills equates with the cash records. Any items such as 'IOUs' should be investigated thoroughly. Unless staff have made purchases, it is extremely unlikely that the auditors should find IOUs in a shop.

Completeness and valuation

It will be important to ascertain that there is no unrecorded cash. Cash records at head office and at the stores must be reconciled. There should also be attention paid to the cut-off between cash at stores and head office at the year end, so that no cash is missed 'in transit'.

Rights

The auditors must ensure that the company has rights in the cash. This will be particularly relevant to cheques (are they made out to the company?) and the credit card vouchers (none are to third parties).

Occurrence

Lastly, the auditors must check that the cash transactions relate to the relevant year. The auditors should carry out a review of cheques in the till and ensure that they are dated prior to the year end. They should also check credit card vouchers.

(c) **Bank letters**

The auditors request confirmations from the bank to provide **third party evidence** about the **existence** and **valuation** of bank balances.

Details requested usually include:

- Details of all accounts held at the year end date
- The balance on each of the accounts at that date
- Details of any guarantees or security from the client
- Details of any facilities the bank extends to the client (eg overdraft)
- Whether the bank is aware the client has any other banking relationships

The bank may also confirm that it holds title deeds on behalf of the client. The auditor might want access to these as part of his non-current asset testing.

53 Metcalf

Text references. Chapters 8 and 16

Top tips. This is a question on audit evidence. The majority of the marks are available in part (b) for 16 marks but don't be daunted by this – this part of the question is then split down into three separate parts so deal with each one in turn and it won't seem so overwhelming. To score well in this part of the question, you need to be specific in your description of the substantive procedures you would carry out, as well as explain why you are doing them. Remember to consider the mark allocation against each of the areas in part (b) – the part on trade payables is worth nine marks whereas accruals is worth three marks so make sure the depth of your answers reflect this.

Easy marks. Easy marks are available in part (a) of this question on the factors to consider when evaluating the sufficiency of audit evidence. However, you should also be able to score reasonably in part (b) on substantive audit procedures provided that you explain why you are carrying out those procedures.

Examiner's comments. In part (a) many candidates simply omitted answering this question, indicating a lack of knowledge, or possibly not being able to think of general factors affecting sufficiency of evidence. The overall average standard of answer in part (b), especially in part (i), was unsatisfactory. Common errors in this part included:

- Focusing answers on the audit of purchases, rather than creditors/payables
- Omitting standard procedures on payables such as cut-off testing or casting and agreeing the list of payables to the financial statements
- Not explaining the purpose of procedures
- Too much 'checking'; in other words, not stating the audit procedure. For example, 'check the supplier statement' is not an audit procedure because it is unclear what the statement is being checked for. The actual procedure must be stated, for example ' obtain supplier statements and reconcile to the purchase ledger account to identify invoices omitted from the ledger'. If there is one word that could be banned from an auditing answer, the examiner would choose 'check'.

The standard for parts (b) (ii) and (iii) was better overall, showing that the audit of accruals and provisions was normally understood.

Marking scheme

		Marks
(a)	1 mark per point (0.5 for point and 0.5 for explanation)	
	Assessment of inherent risk	
	Materiality of the item	
	Nature of the accounting and control systems	
	Control risk	
	Experience from previous audits	
	Result of audit procedures	
	Source and reliability of information available	
	Other relevant points	
	Maximum marks	4

		Marks
(b) (i)	Trade payables (0.5 for test and 0.5 for explanation)	
	List of payables – cast and agree to general ledger	
	Agree list to payables ledger and ledger to list	
	Analytical procedures	
	Select sample for testing – rationale for sample	
	Supplier statement reconciliation – agree balances	
	Treatment of non-reconciling items	
	Cut-off – prior year end – invoice to GRN	
	GRN to invoice prior year end	
	Cut-off – post year end	
	Debit balances treatment	
	Maximum marks	9
(ii)	Accruals (0.5 for test and 0.5 for explanation)	
	Obtain list cast and agree general ledger	
	Analytical procedures	
	Payments made post year end	
	Supporting documentation	
	Maximum marks	3
(iii)	Legal provision (0.5 for test and 0.5 for explanation)	
	Discuss with directors	
	Lawyer letter	
	Correspondence with customer	
	Letter of representation	
	Post year end payment (if possible)	
	Maximum marks	4
		20

(a) **Factors concerning the sufficiency of audit evidence**

Source of evidence

The auditor will be concerned about the **source** of the evidence, that is, whether it is generated by the entity being audited or by a third party or if it is auditor-generated evidence.

Materiality of the amount

More audit evidence would be required when examining more **material balances**, and the lower the level of materiality set.

Inherent and control risks

The **higher** these risks are, the more audit evidence will be required in order to provide assurance over figures in the financial statements.

Accounting and control systems

Depending on whether the systems in place are **reliable** or not, this will influence the amount of audit evidence required to support various audit assertions.

(b) **Substantive procedures in the audit of current liabilities**

Substantive procedure	Reason for test
(i) Trade payables	
Undertake an analytical review on a breakdown of the trade payables figure, comparing this year's closing balance to the previous year's closing balance. Investigate further if the difference is significant.	To confirm the reasonableness of the figure in the current year's financial statements.
Select a sample of trade payables for further testing, agreeing the amounts to supporting documentation such as invoices and purchase orders and post year-end payments. Focus the sample on material balances, but include other smaller items too.	To confirm the accuracy of amounts recognised in the financial statements and their correct inclusion as liabilities in the year-end accounts.
Match a sample of items on the trade payables listing to the ledger and vice versa.	To confirm the completeness and existence of trade payables.
Cast the trade payables listing and agree the total figure to the figures recorded in the accounting system.	To confirm the completeness of the amount.
Obtain the supplier statements for a sample of suppliers and reconcile the year-end balances stated on these to the amounts recorded in the ledger.	To confirm the accuracy, completeness and existence of amounts outstanding at the year-end.
For a sample of purchase invoices recorded just before the year-end, match these to the relevant goods received notes to confirm that the goods were received prior to the year-end.	To confirm accurate application of cut-off.
For a sample of goods received notes received just after the year-end, trace these to the appropriate purchase invoice.	To confirm accurate application of cut-off.
For a sample of debits on the payables listing, seek explanations from appropriate client staff to establish why these have arisen and whether they have been correctly recorded.	To confirm correct disclosure of amounts within payables.
(ii) Accruals	
Undertake an analytical review on the accruals figure, comparing this year's closing balance to the previous year's and to the current year's budget. Investigate further if the difference is significant.	To confirm the reasonableness of the figure in the current year's financial statements.
Perform cut-off tests for a sample of invoices received just before and just after the year-end.	To ensure that invoices received before the year-end but unpaid at the year-end and relating to goods and services received in the year are included as trade payables and that invoices received after the year-end that relate to goods and services received in the year are included within the accruals balance.

Substantive procedure	Reason for test
(ii) Accruals	
Review a sample of payments made after the year-end.	To verify the completeness of accruals by identifying any amounts that relate to goods and services received in the year and which should therefore be included within the accruals listing.
For a sample of accruals from the accruals listing, match back to supporting documentation such as invoices and purchase orders.	To confirm the accuracy of amounts recognised as accruals in the year-end figure.
(iii) Provision for legal action	
Inspect correspondence relating to the provision for legal action.	To obtain further information and evidence to support the recognition of the provision in the financial statements.
Inspect calculations to support the $60,000 provision figure.	To confirm the accuracy of the amount recognised in the financial statements.
Discuss with directors how the figure has been arrived at.	To confirm that the amount recognised in the statement of financial position and income statement of $60,000 is reasonable.
Discuss with legal advisers of Metcalf what their assessment of the case is and the likely costs involved.	To confirm that the conditions for recognising a provision have been met.
Review board minutes and other correspondence relating to this incident to ascertain when it happened.	To confirm that the conditions for recognising a provision in accordance with IAS 37 have been achieved.

54 Liabilities

Text reference. Chapter 16

Top tips. This question looks at audit evidence in relation to a number of liabilities and provisions. As with all evidence questions it is important that you try to think about the key risks associated with the balance for example, completeness or valuation, and then ensure that the audit work which you suggest tackles those aspects. Also think about how you phrase each point. Vague descriptions of audit evidence will not score many marks.

Easy marks. Although there are no easy marks as such in this question it is still a question which you should be confident of passing. Avoid overcomplicating matters and make sure you get the basic point down. For example the overdraft can be agreed to the bank statement, the loan can be agreed to a bank letter.

Examiner's comments. Students should avoid repetition by considering making a single reference to parts of the answer that are relevant to more than one section. Credit is only given once where the same point is mentioned a number of times. To score marks, evidence had to be specific. Disclosure issues were highlighted by the question and credit was given for specific reference to the relevant accounting standard. If a tabular format of answer is adopted repetition should be avoided.

Marking scheme

		Marks
(a)	Company A	
	(i) 10 year bank loan and bank overdraft Up to 1 mark per point to a maximum of	5
	(ii) Expense accruals Up to 1 mark per point to a maximum of	4
	(iii) Trade payables and purchase accruals Up to 1 mark per point to a maximum of	6
(b)	Company B Up to 1.5 marks per point to a maximum of	5
		20

(a) **Audit procedures** (assuming all balances are material to the accounts)

(i) *10 year bank loan and overdraft.*

- The reply to the year end bank letter should be reviewed. This should provide confirmation of the **existence** of the loan. It will also confirm details of any interest paid and any capital repayments.
- The bank letter should also be reviewed to determine whether the loan is **secured**, and if so, which assets provide security. Correspondence with the bank should be reviewed to determine the extent to which any covenants restrict the use of these assets.
- Minutes of board meetings should be reviewed to confirm that the loan has been **authorised**.
- Analytical review should be performed on the **loan interest charge** in the income statement. This could be performed on a reasonableness test basis.
- A check should be performed on the **split of the loan liability between current and long term liabilities**. This should comply with the relevant legislation. Disclosure of liabilities due after more than five years is required in the notes to the accounts together with details of any security.
- The **overdraft balance** should be confirmed to the year end bank letter and bank statement. A **bank reconciliation** should be prepared/reviewed to establish the validity of any reconciling items.
- An analysis of current liabilities should be obtained to confirm that the **overdraft is disclosed** as part of the current liabilities total.

(ii) *Expense accruals*

- A **breakdown of the accruals total** should be obtained and the casting checked. A comparison should be made between those expenses accrued for in the current period and the previous period in order to establish completeness. Any variations should be investigated.
- Further analytical review procedures would involve comparing the amounts accrued for individual expenses in comparison to previous years and budgets. Again any discrepancies would be investigated.
- The **basis of the calculation** of a sample of accruals should be reviewed. This may involve checking to documentation eg previous utility bills, as well as assessing any assumptions made.
- Where possible a sample of accruals should be agreed to subsequent invoices/bills received after the year end and/or payments made.
- A check should be made that the accruals balance is disclosed as part of current liabilities (unless any are due after more than one year).

(iii) *Trade payables and purchase accruals*

The nature and extent of the work to be performed in this area would depend on the initial assessment of risk at the planning stage and the evidence based on the tests of controls. However, the following types of procedures would normally be performed:

- Select a sample of payables from the payables ledger and obtain **direct confirmation** from the supplier, having sought the authorisation of the client.
- Any **differences** between the balance recorded by the client and those recorded by the supplier should be **reconciled and investigated**. Follow up procedures should be performed where there is no response.

  (Although this technique can provide useful audit evidence it is not always possible to carry it out. It may be that the client does not wish to co-operate or perhaps previous experience has shown that few suppliers respond. If this is the case alternative procedures should be performed.)
- Obtain any month end statements from key suppliers and perform a **reconciliation** of the balance. Where there are any disputes review any legal correspondence to assess the likely outcome.
- An **aged payables listing** should be obtained and any old outstanding balances should be investigated. Analytical review should be performed by comparing the current level of payables with prior periods and fluctuations investigated.
- For a sample of payables confirm their accuracy by tracing the balances back through the system from their entry in the nominal ledger to the initial supporting documentation.
- Obtain a schedule of purchase accruals and cast. Agree to supplier invoices received after the year end.
- Perform **cut-off procedures**. Check from goods received notes with serial numbers before the year-end to ensure that invoices are either posted to the payables ledger prior to the year-end or are included on the schedule of accruals. Review the schedule of accruals to the movements in inventories to determine that none relate to items received after the year-end.

(b) **Provisions for warranty claims**

Matters to consider:

- This is a high risk aspect of the audit as it is dependent upon the **judgement of the directors**.
- If the directors' judgement has proved reliable in the past the risk of error decreases.
- Whether the item meets the definition of a provision as defined in IAS 37.
- In particular there must be a present obligation leading to a probable outflow of resources. This will depend on the specific terms although it is likely that a claim under warranty would meet the definition.
- Whether the basis for the calculation of the provision is **reasonable** in the light of prior experience and consistent with previous years.
- The extent to which any provisions created in previous years have been under or overprovided. Any subsequent adjustment can be used as a means of manipulating the recognition of profits.
- Whether the company has any **insurance** which would mitigate the effects of any claims under warranty.
- The existence and reasons behind any current claims.
- This would help to establish whether the current provision is adequate and depending on the reason for any claims may indicate a need to consider the valuation of inventories held.

Evidence

- Review the **terms of the warranty** to establish that the company does have an obligation to compensate and under which circumstances.
- Obtain a **calculation of the provision**. Check for mathematical accuracy and discuss the basis with the directors to assess whether it is a reasonable and consistently applied method.

- Compare the level of provision with **previous years** and assess the accuracy of previous provisions by contrast to actual claims made.
- Obtain copies of any **insurance policies** to establish the possibility of any losses being covered.
- Review any **legal correspondence** to determine the reasons for and the status of any ongoing claims.
- Review the **level of claims** being made after the year-end.

55 Boulder

Text reference. Chapter 16

Top tips. Part (a) of this question basically involves straight rote learning. The financial statement assertions from ISA 315 are core knowledge. It is important to write a sentence for each point – as the requirement asks you to 'List and describe'. If you just list out the terms, you are unlikely to pass this part.

Part (b) was more difficult. 14 marks is a high allocation for audit procedures on payroll, but if you read the scenario and question requirement carefully, there are quite a few clues on how to break down 'payroll' and generate enough distinct points.

- Avoid getting the two parts confused. Part (i) is looking at payroll balances in the statement of financial position and part (ii) at payroll transactions in the income statement.
- Use the scenario to identify the different elements of payroll in this company – factory, both directly employed and agency staff, sales and admin staff as well as directors. There are also two different types of bonuses mentioned.
- Finally, take care over how you write the answer. Make sure that you given enough detail about each procedure that you are describing.

Easy marks. In part (a) there were some easy marks for knowing the financial statement assertions. This emphasises how important it is to have a good knowledge of the key ISAs.

In part (b) the easiest marks were probably those to be gained from good use of the clues in the question, for example the use of the clock cards should have given ideas for detailed substantive procedures and the information about the calculation of the bonuses should have suggested some specific analytical review procedures.

Examiner's comments. Part (a) was relatively easy. Common errors included:

- Stating an assertion without stating what the assertion meant
- Listing comments that were not assertions eg '*the balances must be materially correct*'.

In part (b) some candidates were confused between the statement of financial position and income statement split in this question. Many candidates provided an appropriate list of substantive tests using the scenario to give detail within the answer. There are two main areas of weakness: firstly the use of the term '*check*' as in '*check the list of employees*'. This was simply not precise enough to show what substantive test was being explained. The second weakness was lack of planning. Common errors included:

- Including **tests of controls** although the requirement clearly asked for **substantive procedures**.
- Lack of breadth in answers.

Marking scheme

		Marks
(a)	Six financial statement assertions Up to 1 mark per point to a maximum of	6
(b)	Substantive audit procedures	
	(i) Payroll balances in position statement, Boulder Up to 1 mark per point to a maximum of	10
	(ii) Payroll transactions in the income statement, Boulder Up to 1 mark per point to a maximum of	4

Marks

Note. Some flexibility can be used in marking for the allocation of marks between (b)(i) and (ii). There is some crossover.

20

(a) **Financial statement assertions**

(i) **Occurrence** – the transactions or events that have been recorded genuinely occurred during the accounting period.

(ii) **Valuation** – assets and liabilities have been included in the financial statements at appropriate amounts.

(iii) **Rights and obligations** – the entity holds or controls the right to assets and liabilities are obligations of the entity.

(iv) **Existence** – assets and liabilities recognised on the statement of financial position genuinely exist as at the reporting date.

(v) **Classification** – transactions and events have been recorded in the correct accounts.

(vi) **Accuracy** – amounts and other data relating to recorded transactions and events have been recorded appropriately.

(Cut-off is another assertion mentioned in the ISA but only SIX were required by the question.)

(b) **Substantive audit procedures on payroll balances**

(i) The balances relating to payroll in Boulder are likely to be:

- Unpaid wages and salaries
- Accrued bonuses for sales staff and directors
- Liabilities for tax and national insurance
- Unpaid amounts due to the agency relating to the temporary factory staff

All of these amounts included in the statement of financial position should be tested as follows:

- Agree the position statement figures to supporting schedules and check the schedules for arithmetical accuracy
- The individual amounts on the supporting schedules should be agreed to the trial balance
- Agree the position statement figures to payments after the reporting date

(ii) Agree the unpaid wages and salaries to the latest payroll calculations before the year-end

(iii) Agree the totals due in respect of tax and national insurance to the latest payroll summary prior to the year end and review the amounts for reasonableness as a proportion of the total gross wages and salaries. This should be compared with previous months and explanations obtained for any unexpected variations.

(iv) A sample of the tax and national insurance calculations should be reperformed.

(v) Correspondence with the tax authority should be inspected for any evidence of further amounts due to them.

(vi) The terms of the sales staff bonus should be agreed to their contract of employment and the calculation reperformed. The figure used for the final quarter's sales should be agreed to audit work performed on sales.

(vii) The terms of the directors' bonus should be agreed to their contract of employment and the calculation reperformed. If the payment of this bonus requires special approval by the board or shareholders, inspect documentary evidence of this approval to verify that a liability exists at the year-end.

(viii) The amount due to the agency should be agreed to:

- The documents signed by factory supervisors confirming the amount of work done
- The agreement with the agency

(ix) If the amount is material a confirmation request could be sent to the agency to confirm the amount due to them.

Substantive audit procedures on payroll transactions

(i) Analytical procedures should be performed as follows:

- Total factory wage cost (including agency staff) should be measured as a proportion of sales each month
- Total sales salaries and bonuses should be measured as a proportion of sales each month
- Administrative salaries per employee should be calculated for each month

Any unexpected variation should be investigated by enquiries of management and corroborative evidence obtained for their explanations.

(ii) For a sample of payroll expense entries, test as follows:

- Agree total expense to weekly/monthly payroll summaries
- For a sample of individual pay records the calculation of basic pay should be checked verifying the number of hours worked to the clock card and the hourly rate to that approved by management for factory workers and to contracts for administrative and sales staff.

(iii) The disclosure of directors' emoluments should be checked against statutory requirements.

(iv) The classification of payroll expenses between the income statement headings should be compared to the prior year's audited financial statements to check consistency.

56 Newthorpe

Text references. Chapters 12 and 13

Top tips. In (a)(i) and (iii) note that you should have checked the completeness of the client's schedules, a test that would not be necessary here for inventory in (a)(ii) because of the satisfactory results of the inventory counting. You should have considered separately in (a)(i) and (ii) inventory and non-current assets that had been sold, and inventory and non-current assets that had not been sold.

It is important whether the company has acknowledged any liability, and also whether any reimbursement may be obtained. Our answer draws a distinction between the costs of the legal action and potential damages. It may well be that the costs need to be accrued, as they are virtually certain to be incurred. By contrast liability for damages needs to be disclosed but not accrued, since it is possible but not virtually certain that the company will incur the liability.

You needed to indicate giving an example or two how the auditors could check the likely sales value of non-current assets to be sold, but you would not have needed to go into the level of detail we have about each category of non-current asset.

Easy marks. There are relatively few easy marks in this question, part (b)(i) being the most straightforward but only worth three marks. To pass the question you need to take a step by step approach to avoid getting bogged down in the information. Break the question down so for example in part (a)(i) think about the NRV of plant and equipment and inventories separately. Also remember that you are looking at estimates. Think about how these figures have been calculated by management.

(a) (i) **Procedures (should be weighted towards high-value items)**

Plant and equipment

(1) **Check** that the **non-current assets register** can be **reconciled** with the **accounting records** to ensure it is complete.

(2) **Check** a sample of **non-current assets** in the non-current asset register to the **client's schedule** to ensure that the client's schedule is **complete.**

(3) For items that are shown as sold, **check** the **value** of the **sales proceeds** to **supporting documentation,** checking that title has been transferred, the sales price and date of completion. Confirm payment to cash book.

(4) For items that have yet to be sold **obtain evidence** of likely **sales prices** and **review correspondence** with possible buyers to assess likelihood of items being sold. Sales/scrap values are likely to be low. Any expensive, specialised machinery may be hard to sell. **Use trade press** to **check sales/scrap values** considering age, condition etc.

(5) **Check** whether any **costs of disposal** will be **significant** (will the assets have to be moved piece-by-piece, or are transportation costs significant).

Inventories

(1) **Check** the **selling prices** of **inventories sold since the year-end** to **sales invoices** and **cash book.** If a number of different items have been sold at the same time, check whether the basis of allocation of sales proceeds appears to be reasonable.

(2) **Assess** the **reasonableness** of **management's point estimates** of realisable value of inventories that has not yet been sold by **reviewing sales before** the **year-end, comparing** the **values** with **inventories** that has been **sold since** the year-end and considering **offers** made which have not yet been finalised.

(3) For unsold inventories, **assess** reasonableness of **provisions for selling expenses** by comparison of selling expenses with inventories sold.

(4) **Review** the **records of inventory counting** for any items noted as **damaged, obsolete** or **slow-moving** and confirm that the realisable value of these items is appropriate (in most cases it is likely to be zero).

(5) **Discuss** with management any **significant disagreements** in estimates of net realisable value, and how inventory where there is little recent evidence of sales value was valued.

(ii) **Procedures**

(1) **Check** that **employees** who appear on the **payroll** when the factory was shut either **appear** on the **schedule** of **redundancy payments** or on the **payroll** of **another factory**.

(2) **Check** that **employees** who appear on the **schedule of redundancy payments** were **employed** by the **factory** that has **shut** by **examining pre-closure payrolls**.

(3) **Check** that **redundancy pay** has been **calculated correctly** by checking whether employees have received their **statutory** or **contractual** entitlement.

(4) **Check** that the **figures used** in the **calculation** of **redundancy pay** are **correct**. For employees whose redundancy package is based on service and salary, **check** details of **service** to **personnel records** and **final salary** to the **last payroll.** For employees whose redundancy payment is based on their service contract, confirm details to service contract.

(5) **Check schedule of redundancy payments** to **cash book** to confirm that payments have been made as indicated on the schedule.

(6) For **redundancy payments** that are **in dispute**, **review correspondence** and **obtain legal advice** about the likely outcome.

(b) (i) IAS 37 states that a provision should be recognised in the accounts if:

(1) An entity has a **present obligation** (legal or constructive) as a result of a past event
(2) A **transfer** of **economic benefits** will **probably** be **required** to settle the obligation
(3) A **reliable estimate** can be made of the amount of the obligation.

Under IAS 37 contingent losses should not be recognised. They should however be disclosed unless the prospect of settlement is remote. The entity should disclose:

(1) The **nature** of the liability
(2) An estimate of its **financial effect**
(3) The **uncertainties** relating to any possible payments
(4) The likelihood of any **re-imbursement**.

(ii) **Tests to determine likelihood and amount of damages**

(1) **Review** the director's **service contract** and **ascertain** the **maximum amount** to which he would be entitled and the **provisions** in the service contract that would **prevent** him making a **claim**, in particular those relating to grounds for justifiable dismissal.

(2) **Review** the results of the **disciplinary hearing. Consider** whether the company has acted in accordance with **employment legislation** and its **internal rules,** the **evidence** presented by the **company** and the defence made by the **director.**

(3) **Review correspondence** relating to the case and **determine** whether the **company** has **acknowledged** any **liability** to the director that would mean that an amount for compensation should be accrued in accordance with IAS 37.

(4) **Review correspondence** with the company's **solicitors** and **obtain legal advice**, either from the company's solicitors or another firm, about the likelihood of the claim succeeding.

(5) **Review** correspondence and contact the company's solicitors about the likely **costs** of the case.

(6) **Consider** the **likelihood** of **costs** and **compensation** being **reimbursed** by **reviewing** the company's **insurance arrangements** and contacting the insurance company.

(7) **Consider** the **amounts** that should be **accrued** and the **disclosures** that should be made in the accounts. Legal costs should be accrued, but compensation payments should only be accrued if the company has admitted liability or legal advice indicates that the company's chances of success are very poor. However the claim should be disclosed unless legal advice indicates that the director's chance of success appears to be remote.

57 Crighton-Ward

Text reference. Chapter 18

Top tips. Make sure you read each of the requirements carefully in this question. In part (b), you can break the question down further into two parts for five marks each – take each of the issues in turn and deal with them separately. Note that the requirements in parts (a), (b) and (c) are either to 'discuss' or 'explain', so make sure you do this and that your answers aren't simply a list of bullet points.

Easy marks. In this question the easiest marks were in the factual parts (a) and (c). In these parts a reasonable knowledge of the basic principles of ISA 580 *Written representations* would have brought you close to full marks, taking the pressure off in the significantly harder 'application' requirement.

Examiner's comments. In part (a) most candidates took the correct approach, explaining purposes such as provision of audit evidence and confirmation of responsibilities. A significant number of incorrect approaches were taken, such as:

- Explaining a letter of weakness
- Explaining the process of obtaining a representation letter
- Providing a list of contents of the letter

Part (b) allowed candidates to apply their knowledge of representation letters. Many candidates were confused as to when a representation letter point was needed. Well-prepared candidates recognised the need for a representation letter point regarding the legal liability due to the lack of other evidence and included a convincing paragraph to include in the letter. The issue of depreciation was dismissed because of the evidence provided in the scenario.

Part (c) allowed candidates to demonstrate their knowledge of procedures for obtaining a representation letter and the actions necessary if the procedure breaks down. Some candidates explained the process of discussion with directors through to qualification, and even resignation. Other focused on the auditor modifying the audit report. While modification was an option, emphasising this area above others severely limited the marks that could be awarded. A minority assumed that the letter was not required and detailed other audit procedures that could be used. Given that audit work was complete, obtaining sufficient evidence from other sources appeared to be unlikely.

Note. The marking scheme has been revised to reflect any necessary amendments made to the question and/or answer.

Marking scheme

		Marks
(a)	Representations – one mark per relevant point to a maximum of	5
(b)	One mark per relevant point	
	Lion's Roar	
	Lack of supporting evidence	1
	Amount material	1
	Claim not justified and reason	1
	Treatment in financial statements (alternative provide allow)	1
	Draft paragraph for representation letter – maximum of	2
	Depreciation	
	Have sufficient evidence	1
	Examples of evidence and effect on depreciation charge (1 mark each)	1
	Example of evidence 2	1
	Matter not therefore crucial	1
	Auditor must provide audit evidence to support 'feelings'	1
	Maximum marks	**10**
(c)	Key points 1 for each point	
	Meet with directors	1
	Possible amendments to letter	1
	Issue – potential modification (qualified opinion)	1
	Reason for modification	1
	Issue – reliance on subsequent representation letter	1
	Could resign if situation serious enough	1
	Maximum marks	**5**
		20

(a) The purpose of a representation letter is to improve the **reliability** of audit evidence when the auditor wants to place some reliance on oral representations from management. This is appropriate when it relates to a matter that is material to the financial statements and:

(i) The matter is **subjective**
(ii) Knowledge of the facts is **confined** to management
(iii) The auditor cannot reasonably expect to obtain **sufficient evidence** from other sources

The representation letter is **not a substitute** for other evidence and any contradictions between the representations and other evidence must be investigated.

The representation letter also serves the purpose of obtaining **written representations** from management about certain responsibilities. Management will be requested to provide written representations that:

(i) Management has fulfilled its responsibility for the preparation and presentation of the financial statements as set out in the terms of the engagement and in accordance with the applicable financial reporting framework
(ii) Management has provided the auditor with all relevant information and all transactions have been recorded and are reflected in the financial statements.

Written representations required by ISAs (other than those stated above) may also be included on the representation letter.

(b) **Lion's Roar**

The amount of the claim being made against Crighton-Ward is **material** being 53% of profit before tax.

None of the other evidence that auditors might expect to help them assess the likelihood of the company having to pay out in respect of the claim is available here. The solicitors cannot determine the liability and there appears to have been no settlement or any further negotiations after the end of the reporting period.

In the circumstances the auditors will have to place some **reliance** on the directors' viewpoint as they have the best understanding of the circumstances relating to the normal expectations of the vehicles in their very specialised line of business.

For these reasons this matter should be included in the management representation letter.

A suitable paragraph would be:

'A customer has lodged a claim for $4m against the company. The directors are of the opinion that the claim is not justified and it is not likely that the company will have to make a payment. For this reason no provision has been made for the amount but it has been disclosed as a contingent liability. No similar claims have been received or are expected to be received.'

Depreciation

It appears that sufficient evidence has been obtained in respect of the depreciation charge. The method is consistent with prior years and with other companies in the sector. In addition there are no significant gains or losses on disposals, which also indicates that there is no material over or under depreciation. It appears that the matter is not critical to the financial instruments.

As the only worry over the depreciation is the 'feeling' of an apparently inexperienced audit senior, and no suggestion of a lack of the evidence that would normally be expected, it would not be necessary or appropriate to include this matter in the representation letter.

(c) In response to the directors' refusal to sign the letter of representation the auditor should:

(i) Discuss with the directors the reasons for their refusal and remind them that the need for a letter of representation was notified to them in the engagement letter

(ii) Discuss whether there is any alternative form of words that the directors would be prepared to sign and that would still meet the needs of the auditor

(iii) If the directors continue to refuse to sign the letter, the auditor should request this decision to be formally minuted by the board

(iv) The failure to provide the representations is likely to result in the auditor being unable to obtain enough audit evidence in this area and the auditor will have to consider the implications for the auditor's report. It appears that a qualified opinion due to an inability to obtain sufficient appropriate audit evidence will be appropriate using the words 'Except for the possible effects of..'

(v) Discuss the matter with the audit committee

(vi) Question the directors' integrity and review audit conclusions

(vii) Consider whether the position is untenable and resignation is the only option

58 Jayne

Text reference. Chapter 15

Top tips. This is a fairly straightforward question on audit evidence in relation to bank balances. In part (a) (ii), note the requirement to explain the audit assertions that are and are not supported by the examples of external confirmations provided in part (a) (i). In part (b) (i), again note the requirement to explain the procedures for obtaining a bank report for audit purposes – it isn't enough to simply produce a list of bullet points.

Easy marks. These are available in part (a) of the question for listing examples of external confirmations and in part (b) for explaining the procedures for obtaining a bank report for audit.

Marking scheme

			Marks
(a)	(i)	0.5 for each relevant source of evidence	
		Accounts receivable letter	0.5
		Solicitor letter	0.5
		Bank confirmation letter	0.5
		Inventory held at third party	0.5
		Accounts payable letter	0.5
		Other relevant letters	0.5
		Maximum marks	**2**
	(ii)	Two marks for each type of audit evidence One mark for stating assertion supported and one for stating assertion not supported 0.5 for valid assertion and 0.5 for explanation	
		Accounts receivable letter	2
		Solicitor letter	2
		Bank confirmation letter	2
		Inventory held at third party	2
		Accounts payable letter	2
		Other relevant letters	2
		Maximum marks	**8**
(b)	(i)	Award one mark for each well explained point. Allow 0.5 for simply stating the appropriate area	
		Ensure bank letter required	1
		Produce letter in accordance local regulations	1
		Client authorises disclosure	1
		Send to bank – before end of accounting period	1
		Bank complete and send to auditor	1
		Audit procedures	1
		Bank balances to accounts	1
		Loans disclosure	1
		Maximum marks	**5**
	(ii)	Substantive procedures – 0.5 per procedure	
		Trial balance	0.5
		Agree bank balance to computer system	0.5
		Agree bank balance to financial statements	0.5
		Bank reconciliation	0.5
		Obtain copy	0.5
		Cast	0.5
		Agree to TB	0.5
		Agree to bank statement	0.5
		Lodgements	0.5
		Unpresented credits	0.5
		Other relevant procedures (each)	0.5
		Maximum marks	**5**
			20

(a) (i) External confirmations

- Bank letter for bank balances
- Accounts receivable confirmation
- Accounts payable confirmation
- Solicitor's letter for opinion on legal case outcome

- Inventory held by third parties

(*Note.* Only four are required.)

(ii) *Bank letter*

This provides audit evidence on the **existence** of bank accounts held by the company as confirmation is received directly from the bank.

It may not provide audit evidence of **completeness** because it will not provide evidence of bank accounts held at other banks.

Accounts receivable confirmation

This provides audit evidence of the **existence** of a receivable at the year-end because a reply is received from each customer who has been circularised.

It does not provide audit evidence of the **valuation** of the receivable at the year-end – confirmation of the debt by the customer does not guarantee that it will be paid.

Accounts payable confirmation

This provides audit evidence of the **existence** of a payable at the year-end because a reply is received from each supplier who has been contacted.

It does not provide audit evidence of the **completeness** of accounts payables at the year-end, since there may be liabilities in existence that have not been recorded by the client and could not have been selected in the sample.

Solicitor's letter

This provides audit evidence of the **existence** of legal claims at the year-end.

It does not provide audit evidence of the **valuation** of claims at the year-end because of the uncertainty involved and the level of judgement required to make an assessment of the likely outcome.

Inventory held by third parties

This provides audit evidence of the **existence** of inventory held because a confirmation is received from the third party.

It does not provide evidence of the **valuation** of the inventory at the year-end, as it will not indicate the condition and saleability of the inventory.

(b) (i) **Procedures for bank reports**

- The bank requires explicit written authority from the client to disclose the information requested.
- The auditor's request must refer to the client's letter of authority and the date of this. Alternatively it may be countersigned by the client or accompanied by a specific letter of authority. For joint accounts, letters of authority signed by all parties are required.
- The request is sent by the auditor and should aim to reach the branch manager at least one month in advance of the client's year-end and should state both the year-end and the previous year-end.
- The bank will complete the letter and send it back directly to the auditor.

Audit procedures to be carried out on a bank report

- Agree the balances per the bank letter to the client's bank reconciliations and the balance per the financial statements.
- Agree the interest charges to the interest amount in the financial statements and ledger.
- Agree any outstanding loan amounts to the liabilities figure in the accounts and check that all required disclosures have been made.

(ii) **Substantive procedures on bank balances**

- Check arithmetic of bank reconciliations.

- Agree the balance per the bank accounts to the bank reconciliation and to the financial statements and the ledger.
- Trace outstanding cheques per the bank reconciliation to the cash book and to after-date bank statements.
- Agree any uncleared lodgements to after-date bank statements.
- Obtain explanations for any large or unusual items not cleared at the time of the audit.
- Compare cash book and bank statements in detail for the last month of the year and check items outstanding at the reconciliation date to bank statements after the year-end.
- Confirm that uncleared bankings have been paid in prior to the year-end date by examination of paying-in slips.

59 FireFly Tennis Club

Text references. Chapters 12, 14 and 17

Top tips. This is a fairly straightforward question on audit work to undertake on income and expenditure, however you need to bear in mind that the entity being audited is a not-for-profit organisation so remember the particular issues associated with such bodies. Use the information in the scenario to help you generate ideas for your answers. Part (c) should be fairly straightforward if you can apply your knowledge of the audits of not-for-profit organisations but remember that the question is asking you to discuss the issues so you need to produce a logical, coherent answer to score well in this part.

Easy marks. You should be able to score reasonably well in parts (a) and (b) of this question on the audit work to perform on income and expenditure, provided that you make good use of the information in the scenario and that the audit work you describe is as specific as possible.

Marking scheme

		Marks
(a)	Income – one mark per relevant point	
	All income	
	Paying-in slips to bank statements	1
	Paying-in slips to cash book confirm amounts agree	1
	Analysis correct in cash book	1
	Cast cash book	1
	Agree totals per cash book to the financial statements	1
	Membership fees	
	Compare list of members to determine how many members 20X5	1
	Analytical review of subscriptions – overall process	1
	AR – calculating approximate fee income	1
	Agree subscriptions to FS accounting for differences	1
	Court hire fees	
	Obtain list of court hire fees/calculate for week hire fee	1
	Confirm hire fee to paying-in slip – account for differences	1
	Other relevant tests	1
	Maximum marks	**10**
(b)	Key points one for each point	
	Expenditure analysis back to cash book	1
	Cast cash book	1
	Cash book to purchase invoice – amounts and analysis in CB	1
	Expenditure *bona fide* the club	1
	Investigate any other expenditure	1
	Other relevant points	1
	Maximum marks	**5**

		Marks
(c)	Key points one for each point	
	Lack of segregation of duties	1
	Lack of authorisation controls	1
	Cost	1
	Management override	1
	Use of volunteers – lack of training	1
	Lack of profit motivation	1
	Other relevant points (each)	1
	Maximum marks	5
		20

(a) **Audit work on completeness of income**

- **Compare** current year income for both membership fees and court hire to the prior year figures to confirm the reasonableness of the amounts. Investigate any large variances (eg greater than 10%) by enquiry of the treasurer.
- Carry out a **proof in total** on membership fees by taking the annual membership fees and the number of members in the year. Membership fees are $200 per year. New members joining during the year pay 50% of the total fees. There were 50 new members and 430 at the start of the year. Therefore, membership fee income should be $(430 \times 90\% \times 200) + (50 \times 50\% \times 200) = \$82,400$.
- **Agree membership fee income** to the financial statements to ensure it has been disclosed correctly.
- **Agree court hire fee** income to the financial statements to ensure it has been disclosed correctly.
- Review the list of court hire in the club house for court hire during the year and calculate the expected income from court hire by multiplying this by $5. Compare this to the income from court hire in the cash book, bank paying-in slips and financial statements and seek explanations for any differences by enquiry of the treasurer.
- **Compare** the list of bankings for membership fees prepared by the secretary to the cash book and to the paying-in slips to ensure amounts reconcile.
- **Review** paying-in slips for the analysis between court hire fees and membership fees and agree these to the analysis in the financial statements.
- **Agree** amounts on paying-in slips to the amounts in the cash book to ensure accuracy and completeness of recording. Also check these to the amounts on the bank statements.

(b) **Audit procedures on completeness and accuracy of expenditure**

- For a sample of expenditure invoices during the year, check the details to confirm that the expenditure is *bona fide* for the club, ie that it relates to court maintenance, power costs for floodlights, or tennis balls for championships.
- Reconcile the debit card statements to the cash book and receipts and to the financial statements. Investigate any discrepancies and seek explanations for them from the treasurer.
- Review the analysis in the accounts for each expenditure type, selecting a sample of payments from the cash book and tracing back to the invoice and to the financial statements to check that the analysis is correct.
- Perform an analytical procedure on expenditure by comparing the amounts for the current year to the prior year for each of the three types of expenditure to confirm whether it appears reasonable. For any large variances (say, greater than 10%), investigate further to obtain satisfactory explanations.

(c) Internal control testing has limited value when auditing not-for-profit entities such as the Firefly Tennis Club because of the **lack of segregation of duties** due to the small number of staff, who may or may not be qualified. In the case of the tennis club, there appear to be two members of staff responsible for running the club and preparing the accounts – the treasurer and the club secretary.

Another issue is that the majority of the income may be in the form of **cash**. At Firefly Tennis Club, all income is cash-based and the controls over this appear to be weak, for example, non-members leave court hire fees in a cash box. This is open to theft and misappropriation by users or by staff.

There is also a **lack of authorisation controls** in place. For example, the treasurer pays for all expenditure items using the club's debit card but there is no system in place for another person to review and authorise the purpose of the expenditure.

In such a small organisation, it may not be possible to implement a **system of internal control** because of the very small number of staff and also because of the cost involved in setting up such a system.

60 Walsh

Text references. Chapters 10 and 11

Top tips. In part (a), don't just explain what CAATs are – read the question requirement carefully – you have to provide examples from the company in the question scenario to demonstrate the advantages of using CAATs in an audit. Part (b) should be very straightforward as the requirement is to list examples of audit tests to perform on the wages system. In part (c) again, you need to explain the benefits and drawbacks of using test data but applying your knowledge to the company in the question scenario.

Easy marks. Easy marks are available in part (b) of this question where you are asked to list audit tests to perform on the wages system.

Marking scheme

		Marks
(a)	Award one mark for explaining the use of CAAT and one mark for application to Walsh	
	Testing programmed controls	2
	Test larger number of items	2
	Test actual accounting records	2
	Cost	2
	Other relevant points	2
	Maximum marks	**8**
(b)	Audit tests – one mark per test	
	Recalculation of net pay	1
	Usual items – zero wages payments	1
	Unreasonable items – large payments	1
	Violation system rules – amendment of data	1
	New analysis – analytical review of wages	1
	Completeness checks – all employees clocked in and out	1
	Other relevant tests	1
	Maximum marks	**6**
(c)	Use of audit test data – one mark per point	
	Data submitted by auditor	1
	Live and dead testing	1
	Create dummy employee in Walsh	1
	Check accuracy of processing of wages	1
	Problem – damage client computer	1
	Problem – remove auditor data	1
	Problem – cost	1
	Other relevant tests	1
	Maximum marks	**6**
		20

(a) There are two main types of computer assisted audit technique (CAAT) – **audit software** and **test data**. Audit software involves the use of computer programs by the auditor to process data of audit significance from the entity's accounting system. Test data is entering data into an entity's computer system and comparing the results with predetermined results.

The benefits of CAATs include the ability to **test program controls** as well as general internal controls associated with the system. For example, in the case of Walsh Co's wages system, one of the controls in the system is the generation of a report if overtime over 10% of standard hours is done.

CAATs allow auditors to test a **greater number of items** more quickly and accurately. In the case of Walsh Co, CAATs can be used to test a sample of wage and deduction calculations to provide evidence that these are being correctly calculated by the system.

CAATs enable the auditor to **test transactions electronically** rather than paper records of transactions.

CAATs can be **cost-effective** in the long-term, provided the client does not change its systems. In the case of Walsh Co, the wages system has just been implemented so this is likely to remain in place for a few years.

(b) Examples of audit tests to perform on Walsh Co's wages system using audit software.

- Analytical review of wages by carrying out a proof in total test of wages cost for the year.
- Looking for unusual amounts such as large payments or negative amounts by analysing the transaction data for wages in the year.
- Recalculation of pay and deductions for a sample of employees to confirm that the system is calculating amounts correctly.
- Selecting a sample from the data file for wages to perform detailed substantive testing.
- Checking access to the system to ensure that only authorised personnel, such as the financial accountant, have access.
- Testing for completeness to confirm that an electronic record exists for all employees who have clocked in and out.

(c) Test data is a type of CAAT which involves entering data into the entity's computer system and comparing the results obtained with predetermined results.

Using test data should help in the audit of Walsh Co's wages system because it could be used to test specific controls in the system, such as password access to the system, which should be controlled so that only authorised personnel have access to it. It can also be used to test the control in place for the report produced when overtime greater than 10% of standard hours is done.

One of the main problems with the use of test data as an audit technique is that any resulting corruption of data files has to be corrected. This can be difficult with real-time systems which often have built-in controls to ensure that data entered cannot be easily removed without leaving a mark.

Another problem is that test data only tests the operation of the system at a single point of time and auditors are only testing controls in the programs being run and controls they know about.

61 ZPM

Text references. Chapters 5 and 11

Top tips. In this question, you need to think about the scope of work from both internal and external audit points of view. Also use the information in the scenario to help you, for example, it states that the company has 103 stores in eight different countries so it would be impossible for the external auditors to visit each one so this is an area where they could potentially place reliance on the work of internal audit.

Easy marks. These are available in part (a) of the question. Even if you aren't familiar with the detail of ISA 610, you should be able to score well on this part of the question.

Examiner's comments. In part (a), for five marks, candidates were asked to explain the factors that the external auditor will consider when evaluating and testing the work of the internal auditor but many candidates found this difficult. The main problem was in distinguishing between factors for reliance on internal audit and factors for reliance on the work of the internal auditor. ISA 610 provides lists for both of these activities (paragraphs 13 and 17), although there is potentially some overlap. Some candidates provided long lists of points, leaving the examiner to determine which were relevant whereas some simply did not attempt the question at all.

Part (b) produced a wide standard of answers ranging from very good to very poor. Weaknesses included providing generic lists of the objectives of internal and external audit, repeating information from part (a) in part (b) (iii) and stating that internal audit or was responsible for the inventory count in part (b) (i). Few candidates actually mentioned key areas such as checking the efficiency of the procurement department, or the legal issues affecting the marketing department.

The overall standard for this question was quite poor, with only a minority of candidates obtaining a clear pass standard. As many candidates answered this question last, answers often became quite lengthy with candidates finding it extremely difficult to remain focused on the question requirement. Spending some time planning, identifying the points to make, and then making those points clearly and concisely would significantly improve the standard of the answers submitted.

Marking scheme

			Marks
(a)	One mark for each valid point		
	Training and proficiency		1
	Work supervised and reviewed		1
	Evidence available to support opinion		1
	Conclusions reached are appropriate		1
	Unusual matters correctly resolved		1
	Maximum marks		**5**
(b)	Inventory count		
	(i)	Check of control system over counting inventory	1
		Examples of control system eg counting in teams	1
		Carrying out test counts	1
		Not relevant – carrying out counts by internal audit	0
	(ii)	Ensure inventory materially correct in FS	1
		Attend inventory count to check control system/quantities	1
		Note ZPM focus on quantities + reason	1
	(iii)	Rely on IA to test control systems – lack of staff and 103 stores	1
		Does not mean not carry out any work	1
		Review differences between IA and external auditor results	1
	Procurement system		
	(i)	Company policies followed	1
		Example of policy – no specific ones required	1
	(ii)	Purchases and payables figures correct in FS	1
		Control system for procurement working effectively	1
	(iii)	External auditor rely on IA where work relevant for FS audit	1
		Work reduced only – still carry out some testing	1
	Marketing		
	(i)	Aims such as ensuring information available	1
	(ii)	External auditor not interested – not impact FS	1
	(iii)	No reliance needed	1
	Maximum marks		**15**
			20

(a) **Factors to consider when evaluating the work of the internal auditor**

- The work should be performed by internal audit staff who have adequate technical training and proficiency as internal auditors. This can be confirmed by checking that training programmes are in place and the qualifications of staff are adequate.
- The work of assistants should be properly supervised, reviewed and documented. This can be confirmed by reviewing internal audit working papers and procedure manuals.

- Sufficient and appropriate audit evidence should be obtained to be able to draw reasonable conclusions. This can be checked by reviewing internal audit working papers and reports.
- Conclusions reached should be appropriate and any reports prepared should be consistent with the results of work performed. Again this can be confirmed by reviewing working papers and reports.
- Any exceptions or unusual matters disclosed by the internal audit team should be properly resolved.

(b) (i) **Objectives of the internal auditor**

Year-End Inventory Count

The objective of the year-end inventory count is to ensure that the figure for inventories in the financial statements is materially correct. The internal auditors will review the control system over inventory counting and ensure that all inventory is counted as well as performing test counts themselves to check the accuracy of the counting.

Procurement System

The objective of the internal auditor is to ensure that the procurement system is operating in accordance with company guidelines. For example, they will undertake work to ensure that all purchases are authorised, quantity discounts are received and goods received are documented and recorded appropriately.

Marketing Department

The objective of the internal auditor is to review the work of the marketing department to ensure that the operations of this department are managed effectively and efficiently. The internal auditor may also review the effectiveness of the information systems in the marketing department.

(ii) **Objectives of the external auditor**

Year-End Inventory Count

The objective of the external auditor is to determine whether inventory is materially correct in the year-end financial statements. Inventory should be valued appropriately at the lower of cost and net realisable value in accordance with accounting standards and legislation. In the case of ZPM the main risk appears to be inaccurate counting of inventory as some of it consists of lots of small items. The external auditor will attend the inventory count to check whether the quantities and condition of inventory are correctly recorded.

Procurement System

The objective of the external auditor is to determine whether payables and purchases in the financial statements are materially correct. If the testing allows the external auditor to conclude that the controls over procurement are operating effectively, this will form part of the evidence that purchases and payables are recorded completely and accurately, eg in the correct year of account.

Marketing Department

This may not be reviewed by the external auditor as it does not impact on the financial statements and its costs are unlikely to be material to the accounts.

(iii) **Extent of reliance**

Year-End Inventory Count

The company has over a hundred stores in various countries, making it impossible for the external auditors to attend the inventory count in every one of these. The external auditors can place reliance on the work of the internal auditors, in addition to their own attendance at a small sample of inventory counts. The external auditors will still have to review the work of internal audit to ensure that they can rely on the work undertaken. They should also compare their own results with those obtained by internal audit.

Procurement System

The external auditors may be able to rely on the work performed by internal audit on the controls over the procurement system as these are relevant to financial statement assertions such as completeness of liabilities. The external auditors will still have to carry out their own work on the system, although it will be reduced if they can place reliance on any of the work done by the internal auditors.

Marketing Department

It is unlikely that the work done by internal audit will be relied upon as the operations of the marketing department will not impact on the financial statements. However, external audit should review the internal audit report for any aspects that may impact on the financial statements such as advertising spend.

62 Zak

Text references. Chapters 11 and 15

Top tips. As with question 2 of the F8 paper, resist the temptation to write down everything you know about analytical procedures in part (a) of this question – consider the mark allocations and the specific requirements.

In part (b), it is not enough to simply calculate a few numbers without explaining them – there are nine marks available here so make sure that where you identify significant fluctuations, you can provide reasonable explanations for them.

Easy marks. This question is relatively straightforward and there are many easy marks available here. You should be very comfortable with the topic of analytical procedures and their application to different parts of the audit process so part (a) for eight marks should prove no problem.

Part (c) for three marks on the procedures for obtaining a bank confirmation letter should similarly be straightforward.

In part (b) you ought to be able to perform a few relevant calculations to gain some marks but remember to try and support them with some pertinent explanations.

Examiner's comments. Part (a) on analytical procedures was answered satisfactorily by the majority of candidates, however some answers did not provide the necessary breadth or simply omitted sections altogether, presumably due to lack of knowledge. Part (b) was not answered well due to lack of well-explained points and some basic calculations, as well as answers lacking structure and providing too much detail on the cash and bank balances which was not required. The overall standard of answers to part (c) of the question was adequate. The main weakness was from answers describing how to perform a bank reconciliation, which was not required.

Marking scheme

		Marks
(a)	Analytical procedures 1 mark for each valid, well explained, point	
	(i) – Obtain information, on client situation – Evaluation financial information	
	(ii) – Comparison prior periods – Comparison actual/anticipated results – Comparison industry information – Specific procedures for individual account balances (eg receivables) – Ratio analysis eg GP% year on year – Proof in total eg total wages = employee *average wage	
	Maximum marks	8

Marks

(b) Risks – income statement

0.5 mark, for identifying unusual changes in income statement. Award up to 1 more mark. Total 1.5 marks per point.

- Net profit
- Revenue
- Cost of sales
- Gross profit
- Administration
- Selling and distribution
- Interest payable
- Interest receivable (must be linked to the change in bank balance – not enough cash for interest received)

Maximum marks 9

(c) Bank letter

1 mark for each audit procedure

- evaluate need for letter
- Prepare bank letter – standard form
- Client permission
- Refer to standing authority at bank
- Letter direct to bank

Maximum marks 3

20

(a) Analytical procedures

(i) Analytical procedures consist of the analysis of significant ratios and trends including the resulting investigations of fluctuations and relationships that are inconsistent with other relevant information or which deviate from predictable amounts.

(ii) Types of analytical procedures

- The consideration of comparisons with similar information for prior periods, anticipated results of the client from budgets or forecasts, predictions prepared by the auditor, and industry information
- Analytical procedures between elements of financial information that are expected to conform to a predicted pattern based on the client's experience, such as the relationship of gross profit to sales
- Analytical procedures between financial information and relevant non-financial information, such as the relationship of payroll costs to the number of employees

(iii) Use of analytical procedures

Analytical procedures can be used at all stages of the audit, and must be used at:

- The planning stage in accordance with ISA 315 *Identifying and assessing the risks of material misstatement through understanding the entity and its environment* and;
- The final review stage in accordance with ISA 520 *Analytical procedures.*

During the audit planning stage, analytical procedures are used as a risk assessment procedure to obtain an understanding of the entity and its environment and to help determine the nature, timing and extent of audit procedures.

Analytical procedures can be used as substantive audit procedures during audit fieldwork when their use can be more effective or efficient than tests of details in reducing the risk of material misstatement at the assertion level to an acceptably low level.

Analytical procedures must be used at the final review stage of the audit where they assist the auditor in forming an overall conclusion as to whether the accounts are consistent with his understanding of the entity.

(b) Zak Co

Revenue

Although the directors have indicated that the company has had a difficult year, revenue has increased from the previous year by 18%. The auditors need to establish the reason for this increase as it does not correlate with the directors' comments.

Cost of sales

Cost of sales has fallen by 17% in comparison to the previous year – this is strange given that revenue has increased, as one would expect cost of sales to similarly increase. The reason for this decrease needs to be ascertained. It could be as a result of closing inventory being undervalued.

Gross profit

Gross profit has increased dramatically by 88% in comparison to the previous year. The reason for this needs to be examined, given that revenue has increased but cost of sales has decreased.

Administration costs

Administration costs have fallen slightly by 6%. This appears unusual given that revenue has increased from the previous year, as one would expect the increased revenue to lead to increased administration costs. Expenditure in this area may be understated perhaps as a result of incorrect cut-off being applied.

Selling and distribution costs

Selling and distribution costs have increased significantly by 42%. An increase is expected given that revenue has also increased, however the increase is not comparable. There may have been a misallocation between administration and selling and distribution costs – again this will need to be investigated thoroughly.

(c) Bank confirmation letter

- The client must give the bank explicit written authority to disclose the information requested to the auditor.
- The request letter should be written on the audit firm's headed paper.
- The auditor's request must refer to the client's letter of authority and the date of that authority.
- The request letter should reach the branch manager of the bank at least two weeks in advance of the client's year-end and should state that year-end and the previous year-end.
- The letter should state that the information should be sent directly to the auditor.

63 Springfield Nurseries

Text reference. Chapter 12

Top tips. You shouldn't find this question on the audit of non-current assets too tricky. Part (c) is probably the most difficult part. This question is typical of the sort of question you should expect on any main class of asset or liability on your exam paper. You need to be able to explain issues and identify audit tests to gain sufficient evidence about them. You might also have to comment on the implications of a situation for your audit conclusion and report.

Easy marks. Parts (a) and (b) are the more straightforward parts of the question. For part (a) a sensible approach would be to consider the relevant assertions first and then consider the associated risks.

For part (b) ensure that you deal with ownership and cost separately. You should also consider the reliability of the evidence you suggest.

(a) **Financial statement assertions for non-current assets**

Completeness

The amounts stated in the statement of financial position for non-current assets must represent all non-current assets used in the operations of the entity. Significant omissions could have a material effect on the financial statements. Where an entity has lots of small capital items, recording and tracking these can be an issue so good controls are important.

Existence

Recorded assets must represent productive assets that are in use at the reporting date. Where assets have been disposed, they must not be included in the statement of financial position. Items that are susceptible to misappropriation can also present issues.

Valuation

Non-current assets must be stated at cost or valuation less accumulated depreciation. Whether an entity has a policy or not of revaluing certain categories of its non-current assets can have a material effect on its financial statements. The depreciation policy in place must be suitable as this can also have a significant bearing on asset values on buildings and larges items of plant and equipment.

Rights and obligations

This is a key assertion for non-current assets because the entity must own or have rights to all the recorded non-current assets at the reporting date. For example, where an asset is leased by the entity, it may not have substantially all the risks and rewards associated with ownership and therefore should not recognise the asset on its statement of financial position.

Classification and understandability

Non-current assets must be disclosed correctly in the financial statements. This applies to cost or valuation, depreciation policies and assets held under finance leases.

(b) **Risks associated with non-current assets**

(i) *Existence*

There is a risk that the assets held in the books and reported in the financial statements are not represented by the assets actually in use in the garden centres. Alternatively, items may have been wrongly capitalised, when in actual fact they should have been charged to the income statement in the year in which they occurred.

(ii) *Rights*

There is a risk that assets are not actually owned by the company, but are hired or leased.

(iii) *Valuation*

There is a risk that assets are overstated. Depreciation may not have been charged correctly, to represent the use that has been gained from the asset.

(c) **Evidence available**

Asset	Ownership	Cost
Land and Buildings	Title deeds. These may be held at the bank or the client's solicitors. It may be possible to obtain confirmation of ownership from the central land registry office. The insurance policy should be checked to see whom the cover is in favour of.	The cost of the land and building can be traced to original invoices. The company may also have retained the original completion documents from the solicitor on the purchase of the land.

Asset	Ownership	Cost
Computers	The software licence will reveal who owns the software on the computer. There may also be a contract with a computer company.	The cost can be obtained from the original invoice.
Motor Vehicles	Ownership can be verified by obtaining the registration documents for the motor vehicles.	Again, invoices will reveal the cost. If the original invoice is not available, the list price might be available from a publication such as Glasses Guide.

(d) **Procedures re depreciation**

The purpose of depreciation is to write off the cost of the asset over the period of its useful economic life.

(i) *Buildings*

The buildings are being depreciated over 20 years.

To check the appropriateness of the depreciation rate of 5%, the auditor should:

- Consider the physical condition of the building and whether the remaining useful life assumption is reasonable
- Review the minutes of board meetings to ensure there are no relocation plans
- Consider the budgets and ensure that they account for the appropriate amount of depreciation. If they do not, they may give an indication of management's future plans.

(ii) *Computers and Motor vehicles*

The computers are depreciated at 20% reducing balance. This reflects the fact that the computers will wear out more of their value in the earlier years.

The reducing balance basis seems reasonable, given that computers and their software are updated frequently and therefore do wear faster early on in life.

The auditor should consider whether the assets are still in use.

He should review the board minutes to ascertain whether there are any plans to upgrade the system. He should also discuss the replacement policy with the directors.

The auditor should estimate the average age of the motor vehicles according to their registration plates and consider whether the life is reasonable in light of average age and recent purchases.

He should ask management what the replacement policy of the assets is.

(iii) *Equipment*

The motor vehicles are depreciated at 15% per year, or over 6-7 years.

The auditor should consider whether this is reasonable for all the categories of equipment, or whether there are some assets for which the technology advances more quickly than others.

He should consider the replacement policy.

(e) **Disagreement**

(i) *Action*

The auditor should discuss the reason why he disagrees with the depreciation policy with management. They may agree to amend the accounts.

He should then consider the materiality of the item in question. If it is depreciation it will impact on the statement of financial position and the income statement.

It is unlikely to be material to the statement of financial position. The net book value of assets other than buildings is likely to be small in relation to other assets such as inventory, and the impact of a change in rate not material. However, depreciation could be material to the income statement, particularly if the result was marginal and amendment would change the result from a profit to a loss.

(ii) *Impact on the audit report*

If the auditor concludes the depreciation rates used result in a material misstatement of the financial statements, the audit opinion will be modified. However, despite its materiality, the effect of using an inappropriate depreciation rate is unlikely to be pervasive, so the opinion issued will be a qualified 'except for' opinion, rather than an adverse opinion.

64 Snu

Text reference. Chapter 13

Top tips. This is a relatively straightforward question dealing with inventory count procedures. The main trap to avoid however is confusing the year-end count with the perpetual inventory system in part (a). Remember the perpetual inventory system involves maintaining book inventory records with continuous inventory counting to ensure that the records are accurate and up to date. Also note the need to read the question carefully and to reflect the information in the answer. For example, part (b) asks for the audit procedures which would be performed, not the continuous inventory count procedures themselves. In part (c) notice that you are not being asked to describe **how** to overcome the deficiencies but to describe **why** the deficiencies are difficult to overcome.

Easy marks. There are plenty of easy marks in this question. Parts (a) and part (b) are essentially knowledge based requirements so you should be looking to pick up good marks here. In part (a) think about why the auditor attends the year end inventory count. What is important about this balance (materiality?), what evidence is obtained (existence, value?).

Part (b) mentions a large, dispersed organisation. You need to think about the effect of this on the audit procedures (use of other offices, other firms, role of internal audit?).

Examiner's comments. Part (a) of the question was generally well answered.

In part (b) many described the continuous inventory counting procedures rather than the audit procedures.

Part (c) was well answered but too many candidates offered solutions to the weaknesses (deficiencies) rather than explaining why they were difficult to overcome.

Note. The marking scheme has been revised to reflect any necessary amendments made to the question and/or answer.

Marking scheme

		Marks
(a)	Importance of inventory counting Up to 2 marks per point to a maximum of	5
(b)	Perpetual inventory system Up to 1 mark per point to a maximum of	6
(c)	Risks associated with inventory Up to 1 mark per point to a maximum of	4
(d)	Deficiencies in counting instructions – why they are difficult to overcome Up to 2 marks per point to a maximum of	15
		30

(a) **Importance of year-end inventory counts**

Auditors are required to obtain **sufficient appropriate** evidence to support the inventory figure stated in the accounts. This is particularly relevant where inventories are material to the financial statements. Where perpetual inventory systems are not maintained the year-end count is the most reliable means by which the auditor can obtain the following audit evidence:

- **Quantity and existence** of inventory
- An indication of the **value** of inventory and the means by which management identify slow and obsolete items
- **Cut-off** details
- The overall **control environment** in which the inventory system operates
- Evidence of **fraud or misappropriation**

(b) **Audit procedures**

The following procedures would be performed in order to rely on a perpetual inventory system:

- **Check management procedures** to ensure that all inventory lines are counted at least once a year.
- Confirm that **adequate inventory records** are maintained and that they are kept up-to-date. Tests would include a comparison of sales and purchase transactions with inventory movements. Inventory records would also be checked for correct casting and classification of inventory.
- For a sample of counts at a number of locations the inventory count **instructions should be reviewed**.
- **Attend and observe** the counts at a sample of locations. (As the organisation is dispersed this may involve the use of staff from other offices.) Those visited should be chosen on the basis of the materiality of the inventory balance and whether the site is identified as high risk eg where controls have been weak historically. The remainder could then be visited on a rotational basis.
- Assess the extent to which the results of **internal audit work** can be relied on. As the organisation is large it is likely to have an internal audit function. Results of test counts performed by internal audit may reduce the extent of external audit test counts.
- Check that procedures are in place to **correct book inventories** for discrepancies identified at the inventory counts. Changes should be **authorised** and made accurately and on a timely basis.

(c) **Principal risks associated with the financial statement assertions for inventory**

One of the risks associated with inventory is its appropriate valuation. Inventory should be valued at the lower of cost and net realisable value per IAS 2 *Inventories*. Inventory can be a material figure in the financial statements of many entities, particularly manufacturing companies, and therefore appropriate valuation of inventory is very important, particularly for obsolete and slow-moving items. The valuation can also be a matter of judgement and this increases the risk associated with inventory.

Inventory in the statement of financial position must **exist** – this is another key assertion. Inventory can be subject to theft and misappropriation, and is often held at more than one location, and so controls to safeguard it are very important.

Cut-off is another key issue for inventory. All purchases, transfers and sales of inventory must be recorded in the correct accounting period as again inventory can be a material figure for many companies. Incorrect cut-off can result in misstatements in the financial statements at the year-end and this can be of particular concern where inventory is material. Auditors therefore need to consider whether the management of the entity being audited have implemented adequate cut-off procedures to ensure that movements into and out of inventory are properly identified and reflected in the accounting records and ultimately in the financial statements.

(d)

Deficiency	Explanation
Timing of the inventory count The count is due to take place on New Year's Day. This is unlikely to be popular with staff. Resentment and a desire to get the job done as quickly as possible may mean that the counts are not done thoroughly. There is also little time given to preparation before the count, a problem exacerbated by the fact that both the shops and warehouse are very busy in the period leading up to the count.	As the company operates seven days a week it would be difficult to find an alternative date for the inventory count. In addition it is at this time of year to coincide with the company's December year end. It would be expensive and difficult to find alternative staff to perform the task and it is unlikely that the business will change its year end simply because the inventory count is inconvenient. It may be possible to perform the count a week before or a week after the year end and roll forward/back the inventory calculation. This would involve closing the business for an extra day and would also involve a degree of reliance on inventory records.
There is a **lack of segregation of duties**. Mr Sneg is the inventory controller as well as being the count supervisor and count checker. This means that he is responsible for the physical assets as well as maintaining the book records. It would be possible therefore for Mr Sneg to cover up theft of inventory or mistakes made by himself. This situation affects the control environment of the overall performance of the inventory count.	In some respects this situation could be resolved if an alternative senior member of staff were made the inventory supervisor. However in family businesses it is common for a small number of loyal and trusted staff to bear the majority of the responsibility. There is likely to be strong resistance from Mr Sneg himself who would feel that his good character was being questioned. Other senior members of staff are also likely to be reluctant to take on a role for which they may feel they have little experience and understanding.
Counters will work on their **own**. Normally counts should be performed by pairs of counters as this reduces the risk of error.	Where there is a limited number of staff it may be difficult to work in pairs and get the count completed in the available time scale. Due to the timing of the count it will not be easy to get staff from other areas of the business to volunteer to take part.
This is of particular concern in this case as the company has a high turnover of staff. Counters are likely to be inexperienced and may not be motivated to do a good job.	Where staff turnover is high it is difficult to resolve the problem of inexperience in the short term. Management could consider the factors which contribute to staff leaving eg poor pay to determine whether these can be addressed in the medium term. However warehouse work is often unskilled and therefore an element of staff turnover is inevitable.
The treatment of inventory delivered to customers that has not yet been paid for is **incorrect.** The inventory should not be added back and the unpaid balances should be included as receivables.	There is no reason why this matter cannot be dealt with. The treatment of inventory not paid for should be corrected.

65 Textile Wholesalers

Text reference. Chapter 13

Top tips. This question deals with the year-end inventory count and cut-off procedures. This is a popular exam topic. When considering the inventory count procedures try to think through the practical steps involved. This will help you to generate ideas and will provide a sensible structure for your answer. Cut-off is an important area of your studies. Management should ensure they have proper cut-off procedures to cover all stages of the movement of inventories (ie receipt of goods, internal transfers and final sales).

Easy marks. These are available in part (a). Notice how (ii) follows on from (i). Once you have identified the procedures that the company's staff should be carrying out you can then use these points as a basis for the audit procedures. For example if the company procedure is to have full inventory count instructions the audit procedure would be to review these.

(a) (i) The procedures that the company's staff should carry out to ensure that inventories is counted accurately and cut-off details are recorded are as follows.

(1) Staff carrying out the inventory count should be issued with **full instructions** and so know how to proceed.

(2) Staff **counting inventories** should be **independent** of warehouse staff. They should count in **pairs**.

(3) A **senior member of staff** should **supervise the count**, carry out test counts and check at the end all inventories have been counted.

(4) All **inventory movements** should **stop** whilst the inventory counting is in progress.

(5) **Pre-numbered inventory sheets** should be used to record the counts and should be completed in ink signed by the counter. All sheets should be accounted for at the end of the inventory counting.

(6) The number of the **last Goods Received Note** and **Goods Dispatched Note** to be issued before the inventory counting should be recorded.

(7) Staff should **note the condition of inventories** where it is old or in poor condition.

(8) Staff should be designated **clearly defined areas** for counting to avoid double counting or inventory being missed. It may be possible to mark items in some way once they have been counted.

(ii) As auditor I would carry out the following checks.

(1) **Review** the company's **inventory counting instructions** to ensure they were comprehensive and complete.

(2) **Observe** the client's **staff** during the count to ensure they were complying with issued instructions.

(3) **Carry out some test counts** and note the results in my working papers. My test counts will be in both directions (from the inventory sheets to the inventories, thus checking the inventories exists, and *vice versa* to ensure inventories has been completely recorded).

(4) **Note any items** considered to be **old** or in **poor condition**.

(5) **Note** the **sequence** of inventory sheets issued.

(6) **Note down the last Goods Received Note and Goods Despatched Note** numbers, also details of last returns to suppliers and from customers.

(7) **Take copies of inventory sheets** and check during final audit to ensure client's staff have not subsequently changed them.

(b) **Importance of cut-off in the audit of inventory**

Cut-off is a key issue in the audit of inventory. All purchases, transfers and sales of inventory must be recorded in the correct accounting period as inventory can be a material figure for many companies, particularly manufacturing ones.

The points of purchase and receipt of goods and services are particularly important in order to ensure that cut-off has been correctly applied. The transfer of completed work-in-progress to finished goods is also important as is the sale and despatch of such goods.

Incorrect cut-off can result in misstatements in the financial statements at the year-end and this can be of particular concern where inventory is material. Auditors therefore need to consider whether the management of the entity being audited have implemented adequate cut-off procedures to ensure that movements into and out of inventory are properly identified and reflected in the accounting records and ultimately in the financial statements.

(c) Errors have been made in cut-off for items 2, 4, 5 and 6

(i)

GRN No	*Goods received in June 20X6*	*Adjustment* $
2	Invoice included in the purchase ledger and in accruals	5,164
4	Invoice not included in the purchase ledger and in accruals	(9,624)
	Goods received in July 20X6	
5	Receipt included in purchase ledger	8,243
6	Receipt included in accruals	6,389
	Increase in profit	10,172

Both purchases and payables will be decreased by this amount.

(ii) The incidence of error in this test is very high – four out of the seven items tested had been incorrectly treated. I would therefore **extend my test** to cover a larger number of GRNs over a longer period, both before and after the year end.

I would also ensure purchases that were treated as accruals had been **accrued correctly**.

I would check the treatment of goods on **invoices posted** early on the **following year** and check that invoices relating to following year deliveries had not been posted for this year.

I would also consider the results of the audit reconciliation of suppliers' statements to purchase ledger balances. This may highlight items which have been posted incorrectly (eg pre year-end invoices for goods received pre-year-end but not posted).

(d) **Perpetual inventory counting systems**

Perpetual inventory counting systems are where an entity uses a system of inventory counting throughout the year and are commonly used by larger organisations.

Where such a system is in place, the auditors used carry out the following work:

- Talk to management to establish whether all inventory lines are counted at least once a year.
- Inspect inventory records to confirm that adequate inventory records are kept up-to-date.
- Review procedures and instructions for inventory counting and test counts to ensure they are as rigorous as those for a year-end inventory count.
- Observe inventory counts being carried out during the year to ensure they are carried out properly and that instructions are followed.
- Where differences are found between inventory records and physical inventory, review procedures for investigating them to ensure all discrepancies are followed-up and resolved and that corrections are authorised by a manager not taking part in the count.
- Review the year's inventory counts to confirm the extent of counting, the treatment of differences and the overall accuracy of records, and to decide whether a full year-end count will be necessary.
- Perform cut-off testing and analytical review to gain further comfort over the accuracy of the year-end figure for inventory in the financial statements.

66 Rocks Forever

Text reference. Chapter 13

Top tips. Part (a) asks you to list and explain the reasons for the audit procedures used in obtaining evidence at an inventory count. Here a sensible structure would be to produce your answer in two columns but remember to answer fully and not to use a note form style. Think through the various aspects of the auditor's work. The role of the auditor is to assess the overall performance of the count to determine its reliability, not just to perform test counts. Also remember the importance of collecting information regarding cut-off. For 10 marks you are looking for about 10 points with 0.5 marks for the procedure and 0.5 for the explanation.

Part (b) asks for factors to consider when placing reliance on the work of the expert. For five marks you need about five points so you will need to generate a few ideas. If you are not familiar with ISA 620 don't panic. You should be able to produce a reasonable answer with a bit of common sense.

For part (c) the key is your accounting knowledge. Inventory should be valued at the lower of cost and net realisable value. Approach this part by thinking about the ways in which the cost of inventory can be confirmed. Then think about the way in which net realisable value can be established.

Easy marks. Overall this is a reasonably straightforward question looking at an aspect of the audit with which you should be familiar. All the marks are reasonably achievable, which is good news although you do need to apply your knowledge to the scenario. Part (b) is probably the most straightforward as you can use your knowledge of ISA 620 *Using the work of an auditor's expert* to structure your answer.

Examiner's comments. Part (a) was not answered well. The standard of answers indicated that students were unclear about procedures for inventory counting. Two common errors were providing detailed work on inventory valuation and explaining how to audit the control systems over the receipt and despatch of goods. Marks were lost for not providing a reason for the procedure.

Part (b) was answered satisfactorily on the whole, although some answers were too brief to obtain the five marks available.

Part (c) was not answered well at all, with students focusing on assertions other than valuation or on the inventory count.

Marking scheme

		Marks
(a)	Risks associated with inventory Upto 1 mark per point to a maximum of	3
(b)	Risks associated with inventory in Rocks Forever Upto 1 mark per point to a maximum of	4
(c)	One mark each for explaining each procedure. 0.5 for the audit procedure and 0.5 for explaining the relevance of the procedure up to a maximum of	12
(d)	Key points 1 for each point	
	Confirm need for expert – auditor not have appropriate skill	1
	Scope of work – relevant experience	1
	Scope of work – professional body	1
	No conflict with client	1
	Obtained appropriate evidence – appears reasonable	1
	Other good relevant points	1
	Maximum marks	6

		Marks
(e)	Key points 1 for each point	
	Statement of accounting standard	1
	Determination of cost	1
	Determination of NRV	1
	Professional values report – NRV evidence	1
	Other obsolete inventory	1
	Other good relevant points	1
		1
	Maximum marks	5
		30

(a) **Principal risks associated with the financial statement assertions for inventory**

One of the risks associated with inventory is its appropriate valuation. Inventory should be valued at the lower of cost and net realisable value per IAS 2 *Inventories*. Inventory can be a material figure in the financial statements of many entities, particularly manufacturing companies, and therefore appropriate valuation of inventory is very important, particularly for obsolete and slow-moving items. The valuation can also be a matter of judgement and this increases the risk associated with inventory.

Inventory in the statement of financial position must **exist** at the year end date – this is another key assertion. Inventory can be subject to theft and misappropriation, and is often held at more than one location, and so controls to safeguard it are very important.

Cut-off is another key issue for inventory. All purchases, transfers and sales of inventory must be recorded in the correct accounting period as again inventory can be a material figure for many companies.

(b) **Risks associated with inventory in Rocks Forever**

Rocks Forever is a company specialising in the sale of diamond jewellery. Inventory is therefore a material figure in the accounts of Rocks Forever.

Specific risks associated with inventory in Rocks Forever include existence – the nature of the inventory means that it is highly susceptible to theft and loss as it is a very attractive and valuable commodity.

Valuation is another key risk. The amount in the financial statements is material and the valuation of the jewellery is subjective as it is reliant on the judgement of expert valuers. The inventory should be valued at the lower of cost and net realisable value in accordance with accounting standards. However, given the nature of the inventory and the fact that sales are subject to changing trends and fashions, this is a key risk area.

(c) **Inventory count: procedures and reasons**

Audit procedures	Reason
Observe whether the client staff are following the inventory count instructions. This would include the following:	If proper procedures are not followed the auditor will not be able to rely on the count as relevant reliable audit evidence.
• Confirming that prenumbered count sheets are being used and that there are controls over the issue of count sheets.	Prenumbering of count sheets means that a completeness check can be performed and any missing sheets can be chased.
• Observing that counters are working in pairs of two.	This helps to prevent fraud and error.
• Confirming that inventory is marked once it has been counted.	Marking of inventory helps to prevent double counting of items.

Audit procedures	Reason
• Confirming procedures to ensure that inventory is not moved during the count.	If inventory is moved eg sold during the count the counters may become confused as to which inventory has been counted and which has not. Movements of inventory would also make it more difficult to establish whether proper cut-off procedures have been followed.
• Confirming that inventory held for third parties is separately identified.	Customer jewellery held eg for repair should not be included in the inventory figure.
• Confirming that the counters are aware of the need to note down any items which they identify as damaged.	Damaged items may need to be written down to their recoverable amount. This will affect the overall value of inventory.
Gain an overall impression of the levels and values of inventory held.	This will assist the auditor in the follow up procedures to judge whether the figure for inventory in the financial statements is reasonable.
Check that all inventory sheets issued have been accounted for at the end of the count.	This provides evidence that a complete record of the results of the inventory count has been obtained. If missing count sheets were undetected inventory would be understated.
Take copies of the count sheets at the end of the inventory count and retain on file.	This prevents management from being able to adjust the figures subsequently. It also enables the auditor, in his follow up procedures to trace inventory counted to the final inventory calculation.
Obtain cut-off details ie record details of the last sales invoice issued before the count and the last goods in record before the count.	This information will allow the auditor to determine whether cut-off is correct. Items sold before the count should be included as sales and not recorded in inventory. Items received from suppliers before the count should be recorded as liabilities and in inventory. Sales and purchases after the inventory count should not be accounted for in this year's financial statements.
Discuss with the valuer the results of his findings (eg that the diamonds are genuine and any obsolete/damaged goods which have been identified).	This evidence will support the subsequent valuation of inventory.
Make an assessment as to whether the inventory count has been properly carried out.	This will help the auditor to determine whether the procedure is sufficiently reliable as a basis for determining the existence of inventory.

(d) **Factors to consider**

- The need for an auditor's expert

  The auditor must consider the risk of material misstatement and whether there is the required expertise within the audit firm. In this case as inventory is material and this is the only client in the diamond industry which the firm has it would seem appropriate to use an expert. This need is increased by the specialised nature of the client's business.

- The competence of the expert

  The expert should be a member of a relevant professional body. The auditor should also consider the individual's experience and reputation in his field.

- The objectivity of the expert

  The opinion of UJ could be clouded if for example, if they were related in some manner to Rocks Forever. This could be a personal relationship or one of financial dependence.

- The scope of the expert's work

  If the auditor is to rely on this evidence it must be relevant to the audit of inventory. In this case UJ is considering issues which will impact on the valuation of inventory. This is of great importance to the auditor and is therefore relevant.

- Evaluation of the work performed

  The auditor will need to assess the quality of the work performed by the expert. The auditor will consider the following:

  – Source data used
  – Assumptions and methods used and their consistency with previous years
  – The consistency of the results of UJ's work with other audit evidence taking into account DeCe's overall knowledge of the business.

  In spite of the fact that the auditor's expertise is limited in this field DeCe may test the data used by UJ. For example comparative price information may be available from other shops or industry sources.

(e) **Inventory valuation: audit procedures**

The key principle is that inventory should be valued at the lower of cost and net realisable value.

Cost

For a sample of items agree the cost price to the original purchase invoice. Care should be taken to ensure that the invoice relates specifically to the item in question.

Net realisable value

Review the report produced by UJ for any indication that items are fake. (This is unlikely to be the case but should be confirmed.)

For a sample of items sold after the year end check that the sales price exceeds cost. Where this is not the case the item should be written down to its net realisable value.

Check that items valued by the valuer have been included in the inventory total at this valuation. If there are discrepancies the inventory balance should be revised to include UJ's valuation.

Obtain a schedule of the ageing of inventory. For items identified as slow moving discuss with management the need to make an allowance.

67 Westra

Text references. Chapters 10, 11 and 16

Top tips. This 30 mark question is split into four parts so it is very important that you spend the appropriate amount of time on each part – do not get bogged down in one part and then find out that you do not have enough time to answer the other parts of the question.

In parts (a) and (b), you can score one mark for each audit procedure and one mark for explaining the purpose of that audit procedure, therefore half the marks available are for your explanations. Make sure that you do explain the reasons fully. An appropriate way of setting out your answer for those two parts would be in a table format. Such a format ensures that you link each audit procedure to an explanation.

In part (c), you are asked to 'describe' control procedures over the trade payables master file. This means that, again, you need to explain the control procedure fully – you will not score the full marks available if you do not do this.

In part (d), you are asked to discuss how CAATs can be used in the audit of payables at this client. Although you need to understand what CAATs are and how they can be used, it is very important that you apply your knowledge to this particular scenario. A general answer on CAATs will not score well unless it is relevant to the circumstances in this question.

Easy marks. This is a challenging question and there are no easy marks as such. However by using the information in the scenario, you should be able to score relatively well in parts (a) and (c), provided you explain your answers as required by the requirements.

Marking scheme

Marks

(a) Audit procedures – purchases 12 marks. 1 for procedure and 1 for the reason. Limit to 5 marks in each category where stated briefly without full detail.

Audit procedure	Reason for procedure	Marks
Parts to GRN	Check completeness	
Parts no GRN number	System error or cut-off error	
GRN to computer	Parts received were ordered – occurrence	
GRN agree to invoice	Completeness of recording	
Review unmatched GRN file	Completeness of recording of liabilities	
Paid invoice – GRN attached	Confirms invoice in PDB	
Invoice details to payables ledger	Completeness and accuracy of recording	
Review unmatched invoices file	Indicate understatement of liability (lack of completeness)	
Payables ledger to purchase invoice	Liability belongs to Westra	
Payables ledger to payments list	Liability properly discharged – payments complete	
Payment list entries to invoice	Payment made for bona fide liability	
Payments list to bank statement	Confirms payment to supplier	
Bank statement entry to payments list	Confirms payment relates to Westra	
GRN cut-off testing	Accuracy of cut-off	
Maximum marks		12

(b) **Audit procedures – payables**, 8 marks. 1 for procedure and 1 for reason. Limit to 0.5 mark in each category where stated briefly without full detail.

Audit procedure	Reason for procedure	Marks
Obtain and cast list of payables	Ensure that the list is accurate	
Total of payables to the general ledger and financial statements	Confirm that the total has been accurately recorded	
Analytical procedures	Indicates problems with the accuracy and completeness of payables	
Agree payables to supplier statements	Confirm balance due from Westra	
Supplier statement reconciliation	Liabilities exist and belong to Westra	
Reconcile invoices	Confirms completeness and cut-off assertions	
Reconcile payments	Payment to correct supplier	
Review ledger old unpaid invoices	Credits O/S or going concern indicator	
After date credit notes	Payables not overstated	
FS categorisation payables	Classification objective	
Maximum marks		8

(c) **Controls over standing data**, 5 marks. 1 mark for explaining each control. 0.5 for poor/limited explanation.

Amendments authorised
How authorised (form or access control)
Reject deletion where outstanding balance
Keep record of amendments
Review list of suppliers – unauthorised amendments
Update supplier list on computer regularly

	Marks
Review computer control log	
Review list of suppliers – unauthorised additions	
Other relevant points (each)	
Maximum marks	5

(d) **Use of CAATs**

Review computer control log	
Identify old / obsolete – computer may already do this	
Test data – online payments system	
Use of CAATs – limited – lack of computer system integration	
Need to assess computer controls prior to use of CAATs	
Not cost effective – bespoke systems	
Limited use of CAATs in suppliers ledger	
Other relevant points (each)	
Maximum marks	5
	30

(a) **Substantive procedures**

Completeness

Audit procedure	Purpose
Perform analytical procedures on purchases, eg comparison to the prior year on a month-by-month basis, ratio of purchases to payables, gross profit % etc and investigate any significant fluctuations	To provide assurance on the completeness of amounts recorded in the accounts and to highlight any areas of concern for further investigation
For a sample of supplier invoices, trace amounts to the GRN, order and payables ledger	To confirm completeness of recording of purchases
Inspect the unmatched GRNs file and seek explanations for any old unmatched items and trace these to the year-end accruals listing	To provide assurance on completeness as these should be included in the year-end accrual
For a sample of amounts on the ledger, agree to the computerised payments list to verify the amount and supplier	To provide assurance that the payment list is complete and accurate

Occurrence

Audit procedure	Purpose
For a sample of amounts in the payables ledger, trace these to the invoice and other supporting documentation such as GRNs	To provide assurance on the occurrence assertion
For a sample of GRNs, agree back to the original order details	To provide assurance on occurrence
For a sample of payees on the computerised payments list, agree amounts back to the supporting documentation such as invoices and GRNs	To provide assurance that payment has been made for a *bona fide* liability of the company
For a sample of payments made after the year-end, trace back to the computerised payments list	To provide assurance that payment relates to the company
For a sample of payees on the computerised payments list, trace payment to post year-end bank statements	To confirm that payment was made to authorised suppliers of the company

Cut-off

Audit procedure	Purpose
For a sample of GRNs dated shortly before and after the year-end, agree that the amounts on invoices are posted to the correct financial year	To ensure that amounts are included in the correct financial period
Review the schedule of accruals and agree to GRNs, checking the date of receipt of goods to ensure that goods received after the year-end are not included	To ensure that amounts are included in the correct financial period
Inspect outstanding orders on the 'orders placed' file for any orders completed but not yet invoiced	To ensure that amounts are included in the correct financial period

(b) **Audit procedures on trade payables**

Audit procedure	Purpose
Cast the list of payables balances from the ledger at the year-end	To provide assurance that the list is complete and accurate
Reconcile the payables list from the payables ledger to the general ledger and accounts	To provide assurance that the figures are complete and accurate and correctly reflected in the financial statements
Perform analytical procedures on trade payables, comparing balance to prior year and investigating any significant fluctuations	To provide assurance on completeness and accuracy and to highlight areas of concern
For a sample of balances, trace amount to supporting supplier statements	To confirm the existence and accuracy of the amount outstanding at the year-end
Test cut-off by taking a sample of GRNs either side of the year-end and checking that amounts are included on the payables ledger for goods received before the year-end	To ensure that amounts are included in the correct financial period
Review disclosure of payables in the draft financial statements	To ensure that payables have been disclosed appropriately in the statement of financial position and notes as either current or long-term liabilities

(c) Control procedures over standing data on trade payables master file

- Access to the trade payables master file is limited only to authorised staff
- Amendments to standing data can only be made by authorised staff and all amendments must be authorised prior to input
- Access to the file is controlled by logins and passwords and passwords must be prompted to be changed regularly (say, every 90 days)
- Computer log is reviewed regularly by IT department to check for any unauthorised access or attempts to access the trade payables master file
- The list of suppliers should be reviewed regularly by a senior manager and those no longer used should be removed from the system

(d) Use of CAATs in audit of Westra

CAATs could be used in the audit of purchases and payables at Westra in a number of ways.

For example, audit software could be used to generate a **sample of ledger balances** to be agreed to supplier statements. CAATs could also be used to **reperform** the cost of the total on the file to ensure the file is a complete record of transactions. CAATs can also be used to perform **ratio calculations** for analytical procedures on the purchases and payables data. **Test data** could be used to undertake some controls testing on the trade payables master file, such as on data access and payments to suppliers.

However, generally for this audit, the use of CAATs is somewhat **limited** as the company uses a mixture of manual and computerised systems, and where computerised systems are used, they are not fully integrated with each other.

68 Strathfield

Text references. Chapters 11 and 14

Top tips. Part (a) should be reasonably straightforward, book learning. In part (b), there are nearly as many marks as there are categories of error. This implies a mark for each and means that if you do find the question difficult, you should try and state a simple reason for each part, rather than spending all the time on one error and not others. You should attempt a calculation in part (c), even if you have struggled with part (b), as doing a calculation based on your reasoning will gain you some marks, even if your reasoning is not exactly right.

Easy marks. These are available in parts (a)(ii) and (iii). You need to be familiar with the different methods of sample selection and should be familiar with the characteristics of each one.

(a) **Risks associated with the financial statement assertions for receivables**

One of the main risks associated with receivables is in respect of **valuation**. There is a risk of receivables and hence sales being overstated in the financial statements if they are over-valued. For example, if a customer has gone into liquidation before his debt has been settled, it may be very unlikely that the company will recover the debt and unless it is written-off, the accounts will be overstated. Any provision for bad and doubtful amounts should therefore represent a reliable estimate of the difference between gross receivables and their realisable value.

Incorrect **cut-off** is another issue with respect to sales and receivables because the entity may record the following year's sales in the current period or goods returned in the current period are not recorded as such, for example.

Classification is another important assertion for receivables, that is, that receivables are properly identified and disclosed in the statement of financial position. This could be a risk area where amounts have been factored, for example.

(b) **Sample selection**

(i) *Aspects of Sarah's approach which are inconsistent with sampling*

A key criterion of sampling is that all items in the population could have been picked. In **not selecting accounts <$100 or government accounts**, Sarah has not taken the right approach.

Her choosing the **ten highest accounts** is not really sampling either. The choice of those accounts was not random, haphazard or statistical.

(ii) *Alternative means of sampling material balances*

Sarah could **stratify the sample**. This would involve splitting the sample into sub-populations. She could do this on the basis of size, or alphabetically, for example. In this instance, size would be logical because it is a relevant factor as a high proportion of the value of receivables is likely to be in a small proportion of receivables.

If she did this on the basis of size, then she would be able to 100% test the material balances and then sample (by one of the methods above – random, haphazard or statistical) in the other populations.

Sarah could use **monetary unit sampling.** This identifies individual $s as the units, giving $s within higher value balances a greater chance of selection. Each $ is regarded as being in error proportionately to the error in the account balance of which it forms a part.

(iii) *Comparison of methods of sample selection*

- **Random**. This is where a sample is chosen on standard basis, such as mathematical tables.

- **Systematic**. This is where a sample is chosen by selecting the nth one when reading through the list of receivables or the ledger in order.
- **Haphazard**. This is where there is no method of any kind to the sample selection.

While haphazard to the layman appears to be random selection, this is not the case. The first two forms of sample selection are more mathematical than the last one. Haphazard is far more prone to bias than the other two as it can be influenced by such factors as ease of selection.

(c) **Qualitative aspects of differences**

Debts where confirmations have not been received are potentially uncollectable, if the client has moved without giving a forwarding address. They could be included in a projection of population error. However, given that such situations are unlikely to be representative of the sample, rather they are likely to be unique (in a similar way to disputes, below), they could be referred into a test for old or doubtful debts and an allowance probably made.

Cut –off differences. These errors only occur by their nature in a specific region of the trade payables balance, ie invoices received adjacent to the year end. It would not be appropriate to include them in a projection of total sample error. They should be referred into a cut off test and adjusted for as appropriate.

Invoicing errors. These are errors which could occur in any part of the sample. It is therefore justifiable to include them in an estimation of population error. As the amount of error in each item would increase with the size of the item, the ratio method of projecting the error should be used.

Invoices posted to the wrong customer accounts. This is a control error, rather than a substantive one. The value of the sample/balance is not affected by such an error. It should not be included in a projection of total error.

Disputed invoices. These are not necessarily errors and disputes are likely to be unique. The company may have issued credit notes against disputed amounts in the subsequent period. The auditor should assess the impact of any after date credit note on the year end balance. Any matter so dealt with should not be included in a projection of total error. However, disputed matters not settled in this way, are isolated but may be symptomatic, therefore they should be included in a projection of error.

In conclusion, the invoicing errors and any of the latter category of disputed invoices should be included in a projection of total population error. The other differences should all point to further audit tests and should be dealt with separately.

(d) **Projected error**

The projected error would be based on the invoicing errors using the ratio method.

The ratio method uses the formula:

$$\text{Most likely error in population} = \text{Error found in sample} \times \frac{\text{Population value}}{\text{Sample value}}$$

The material amounts selected for sampling should be excluded from the population value when the error is calculated.

The total value of the error is: invoicing, $600, disputed invoices, $1,500, total, $2,100.

Thus:

	$
Error in sample	2,100
Population value (2,350,000 – 205,000)	2,145,000
Sample value	265,450
Projected error	16,969

(e) **Computer-assisted audit techniques**

Sarah could use computer-assisted audit techniques (CAATs) in her work on receivables to some extent. For example, she could use CAATs to help her in her sample selection for balances to confirm by circularisation because the population and sample size required are both large. She could also use CAATs to select receivables over a certain age and therefore test them to make an assessment of their recoverability. Sarah could use CAATs to select customer accounts where the total balance is negative or zero so that these are not neglected in her sample.

She could also use CAATs to perform calculations and comparisons for analytical procedures, such as comparisons to prior year and budget and aged analysis to look at the pattern from year-to-year. She could use CAATs to reperform calculations such as totalling the sales ledger.

All these uses would assist in increasing the efficiency of the audit of receivables but the extent of their use will depend on the entity's systems.

69 Seeley

Text references. Chapters 9, 10, 11, and 14

Top tips. This question is worth 30 marks and there is a lot of information to take in so it's easy to feel bogged down and start panicking when you come to answer it. However, take a step back and tackle each part in turn, treating it as a mini question. Using this approach makes the question seem less daunting and more manageable. Note also the mark allocations against each part – these should help ensure you do not run over the time allocation for each question and force you to consider carefully before you start to write your answer.

In part (b), do as the requirement says and use the scenario – there will be lots of clues there and it will help you plan your answer. There are 12 marks available here for six tests of controls so each test of control is worth two marks, one for the actual test and one for explaining the reason for doing it. A tabular format for your answer would therefore be good here – it gives your answer structure and is a good way of presenting it coherently.

In part (d) (i), think about the process and use this to help plan your answer so it is well structured and thought out.

Easy marks. There are easy marks available in part (c) for audit assertions relating to the direct confirmation of receivables, providing you don't just list the assertions without also explaining them. Part (d) (ii) should also be straightforward as long as you don't just provide a list of types of balance to test but support your answer with some good explanations.

Examiner's comments. Part (a) was not answered well. Weaknesses included explaining how to audit the whole despatch and sales system and assuming the client would produce and audit the questionnaires. In part (b), it was evident that some candidates did not understand the difference between a test of control and a substantive procedure. Other criticisms included stating weaknesses in the control systems without mentioning any tests of control, including comments on the receivables system and providing detailed examples of substantive audit procedures. Answers to part (c) were relatively satisfactory although the main weakness was just stating four assertions without explaining them. Most answers for part (d) (i) were clear and to the point. A minority of answers either mentioned other parts of the receivables' circularisation or testing of the sales system, which was not relevant for this specific question. Part (d) (ii) was worth five marks. There was no limit to the number of categories that could be mentioned in the answer, although most candidates included up to five, showing an appreciation of the requirement and mark allocation. A significant minority of candidates spent the whole of the answer explaining one or two categories at the most, thus limiting the number of marks which could be awarded.

Marking scheme

		Marks
(a)	Accuracy of internal control questionnaires 1 for each well-explained step – Prior year audit file – System weakness identified not actioned by client – Review system documentation – Interview client staff – Walk-through check – Identify controls in above – Other relevant procedures **Maximum marks**	 4
(b)	Tests of control despatch and sales system 1 for stating procedure for 1 for the reason for that procedure. Limit marks to 0.5 where the reason is not fully explained. Maximum 2 marks per point. Procedure – GDN signature – despatch staff – GDN signature – accounts staff – Observe despatch system – Error report GDN numeric sequence – Credit limit control – Invoices – signed – Credit checking – either account setup or prior to despatch of goods – GDN signed by customer – shows receipt of goods – Observe the despatch system – Other relevant procedures **Maximum marks**	 12
(c)	Assertions – direct confirmation of receivables 1 for each good explanation. (Note any assertion is allowed if shoed linked to receivables circularisation) Assertions – Existence – Rights and obligations – Valuation and allocation (normally needs links to liquidator) – Completeness (where linked to invoices not recorded by client co) – Other relevant points **Maximum marks**	 4
(d)	Receivables circularisation procedures 1 mark per procedure (i) Procedure – List of receivables – Sampling method – Select balances for testing – Extract details from ledger – Prepare letters – client sign – Post letters – Choose date if not year end – Confirm with management can circularise receivables – Other relevant points	 5

Marks

(ii) Specific receivables for selection – 1 mark each explained point (must include reason for selection for full mark)

- Negative balances
- Material balances
- $0 to $20,000 balances
- Old balances
- Random sample remaining balances
- Other relevant points 5

Maximum marks **10**

30

(a) Internal control questionnaires

- Review the audit file from the previous year for any issues that arose that may need to be investigated further this year
- Discuss with appropriate staff at Seeley's the control system in place to ascertain whether there have been any changes during the year
- Obtain documentation and procedures from sales staff at Seeley's and review it and compare it to the questionnaires to confirm that there are no changes from the previous year
- Perform walk-through tests to confirm that the system has not changed from last year

(b)

Test of controls	Reason for test
For a sample of customers, review documentation regarding credit checking and issuing of identification cards for appropriate authorisation.	To ensure that only creditworthy customers have been authorised by an appropriate level of management.
For a sample of GDNs, inspect for signature of Seeley's warehouse staff and for customer signature.	To ensure that removal of goods recorded on the GDN has been authorised by appropriate warehouse staff.
For a sample of GDNs, inspect for signature of accounts department staff and match information to the accounting system.	To ensure that accounts staff have entered the information on the GDN onto the system.
For a sample of invoices, match product prices to the inventory master file.	To ensure that the information on the invoice is correct and in accordance with the inventory master file.
For a sample of invoices, inspect them for accounts staff signatures and match to information on their respective GDNs.	To ensure that information on invoices mirrors that on the GDNs and this check is performed by accounts staff.
Inspect error reports produced by the computer system and discuss with relevant staff the action taken to resolve discrepancies.	To ensure that any breaks in GDN sequence are properly followed up and resolved on a timely basis.

(c) Assertions relating to the direct confirmation of receivables

Existence

Recorded receivables actually exist. This is confirmed by the customer replying to the confirmation letter.

Valuation and allocation

Receivables are included in the accounts at the correct amounts. This is confirmed by the customer either agreeing or disputing the amount outstanding.

Rights and obligations

The client controls the rights to receivables and related accounts. This is confirmed by the customer responding to the letter from the client.

Cut-off

All transactions are recorded in the correct period. The receivables' circularisation will pick up cash-in-transit and other reconciling items that could be included in the wrong period.

(d) (i) Direct confirmation of receivables

- Obtain a receivables listing from the client and cast it and agree it to the balance per the ledger
- If possible, obtain an aged receivables analysis of the year-end receivables balance or perform one yourself
- Calculate the sample size based on materiality and tolerable error
- Extract the sample using an appropriate sampling technique
- Prepare confirmation letters on the client's headed notepaper and arrange for them to be signed by an appropriate member of the client's management such as the Chief Accountant or Finance Director
- Enclose a customer statement with the letter and a pre-paid envelope addressed to the auditors so that all replies are received by the auditors and not the client
- Post the letters off

(ii) Categories of receivables to circularise

Negative balances

There are 15 accounts with negative balances and a sample of these should be examined as it could be that payments have been posted to the wrong customer codes.

Material items

A sample of material balances should be circularised as the auditors need to obtain evidence that the receivables balance is not materially misstated in the accounts.

Old balances

A sample of old balances should be tested. Amounts outstanding that are older than two months comprise 20% of the total receivables balance. It may be that some of these should be written-off or provided against if recoverability of the amount appears unlikely.

Round-sum payments

A sample of round-sum amounts should also be circularised to ensure that balances are stated correctly.

Random sample

The remaining receivables required for testing should be selected on a random basis to ensure that amounts across the population are selected for testing.

70 DinZee

Text references. Chapters 10 and 13

Top tips. This 30 mark question is split into four parts so it is very important that you spend the appropriate amount of time on each part – don't get bogged down in one part and then find out that you do not have enough time to answer the other parts of the question.

Part (a) and (b) are very structured as you are told specifically the number of points which you are required to make. Ensure you do follow these instructions. Part (a) asks for procedures and explanation – 6 of the 12 marks available will be awarded for the explanation so make sure you do not miss out this step. Read the scenario carefully and tailor your answer specifically to the system described. The examiner wants to see that you have understood the information that you have been given and that you can design procedures accordingly.

In part (b) you must read the requirement carefully. Notice you are asked to specify the procedures you would perform **prior to** attending the inventory count, **not during** the count.

Part (c) asks you to identify deficiencies in the control system for counting inventory, to explain the deficiency and to recommend improvements. Make sure that your answer addresses all three requirements. A tabular format is a particularly useful way of presenting your answer.

Part (d) tests you knowledge of the difference between a test of control and a substantive procedure and then requires you to apply this knowledge. You should find this relatively straightforward.

Easy marks. Overall you should feel that you can tackle this question with confidence. Easy marks can be found in part (b) and part (c) provided you have a good understanding of the inventory count. You should also feel that you can score good marks in part (d).

Examiner's comments. Part (a) of this question was generally not well answered. Common errors included writing about testing general controls instead of controls over the purchases system, including procedures for the payments system rather than the purchases system, insufficiently detailed answers, and stating what the purchase system should do without stating any audit procedures. Students must be comfortable with the sales and purchases systems and the need to be able to provide clear audit procedures and explanations for those procedures – this will remain a key element of the audit and assurance paper.

Part (b) was an audit procedures prior to attending an inventory count. The key issue here was the requirement for procedures to undertake **prior** to the count – no marks were awarded for listing procedures relevant to actually attending the inventory count. Other weaknesses included not stating the procedure in sufficient detail or writing too much when the requirement was to 'list'.

Part (c) was generally well answered, although the main issues were not linking weaknesses (deficiencies) to explanations/recommendations and providing impractical solutions.

Part (d) was answered very poorly by a significant number of candidates, demonstrating a worrying lack of knowledge about substantive procedures and tests of controls. This is an important area which needs to be addressed.

Note. The marking scheme has been revised to reflect any necessary amendments made to the question and/or answer.

Marking scheme

		Marks
(a)	Audit procedures procurement and purchases system 1 for stating procedure and 1 for the reason for that procedure. Limit marks to 0.5 where the reason is not fully explained. Maximum 2 marks per point. Procedure – E-mails to order database – Order database to delivery note – Orders to inventory database – Paper goods receipt notes to inventory database – Orders database to payables ledger database – Computerised purchase invoice details to record of purchase invoice – Details of purchase invoice database to EDI purchase invoice received – Purchase invoice record to payables database – CAATs – cast PDB, trace to nominal ledger – Other relevant procedures	
	Maximum marks	12

		Marks
(b)	Audit procedures prior to inventory count attendance 0.5 for each procedure Procedures – Review prior year working papers for problems – Contact client – Book audit staff to attend the inventory counts – Obtain copy of inventory count instructions from client – Ascertain whether any inventory is held by third parties – Obtain last year's inventory count memo – Prepare audit programme for the count – Other relevant points **Maximum marks**	 **2**
(c)	Deficiencies in counting inventory 1 for each deficiency, 1 for explaining the reason for the deficiency and 1 for stating how to overcome deficiency. 3 max therefore per deficiency. Deficiencies – Inventory sheets stating the quantity of items expected to be found in the store – Count staff all drawn from the stores – Count teams allowed to decide which areas to count – Count sheets not signed by the staff carrying out the count – Inventory not marked to indicate it has been counted – Recording information on the count sheets in pencil – Count sheets for inventory not on the pre-numbered count sheets where only numbered when used – Other relevant points **Maximum marks**	 **12**
(d)	1 mark each for: Test of control aim Substantive procedure aim Stating test of control relevant to inventory count Stating substantive procedure relevant to inventory count **Maximum marks**	 **4** **30**

(a)

Audit procedure	Reason
(1) For a sample of emails filed on the store manager's computer match the details to a corresponding order filed on the order database.	To ensure that orders are completely and accurately recorded.
(2) For a sample of orders taken from the order database match the details to a corresponding paper delivery note and then to the entry in the perpetual inventory system.	To confirm that all goods ordered are subsequently received and then completely and accurately recorded in the inventory database.
(3) For a sample of purchase invoices agree the details to the corresponding order and confirmation of receipt on the order database.	To ensure that liabilities are only recognized in respect of goods ordered and received.
(4) For a sample of orders confirmed as received and invoiced on the order database trace and match the details to the corresponding entry in the payables ledger.	To confirm the completeness of the liability recorded in the payables ledger.

Audit procedure	Reason
(5) Review the order database for orders received but not yet invoiced.	To ensure that the year end accrual for goods received not invoiced has been calculated correctly.
(6) For a sample of purchase invoices trace the entry of the liability to the individual account in the payables ledger and confirm that the correct account has been credited.	To confirm that liabilities are allocated to the correct supplier account.

Top tips. In this case the answer only asked for six audit procedures. Other points which could have been mentioned include the following:

For a sample of orders agree the allocated supplier to the authorized supplier list	To ensure that goods are only purchased from suppliers authorized by management
For a sample of delivery notes seek evidence that the physical inventory has been agreed to the details on the delivery note eg a signature	To ensure that the goods delivered correspond to the goods actually received
For a sample of purchase invoices trace to the entry on to the purchases database	To ensure the completeness of purchases recorded on the purchases database

(b) Audit procedures performed prior to attending the inventory count

(i) Review prior year working papers and obtain an understanding of the nature and volume of inventory.

(ii) Obtain a copy of the inventory count instructions prepared by the client and discuss any significant issues arising from these with the client.

(iii) Assess the implications of the locations at which the inventory is held eg inventory held by third parties.

(iv) Book the necessary audit staff to attend the count.

Top tips. The answer only required four procedures, however the following additional points could have been made:

- Review internal control relating to inventory in order to identify potential problem areas eg cut-off
- Perform analytical procedures and discuss with management any significant changes in inventory
- Obtain last year's inventory count memo
- Prepare the audit programme for the count
- Consider the need for expert assistance

(c)

(i) Deficiency	(ii) Reason	(iii) Recommendation
The count sheets show the amount of inventory currently recorded on the perpetual inventory records.	This may encourage the counters to try to match the figure provided rather than to carry out the count as an independent exercise.	The count sheets should not show the perpetual inventory records balance. The count staff should record the number of items they have physically counted.
All count staff are drawn from the inventory warehouse.	These staff are not independent of the count. It would be possible for the counters to disguise errors or to cover up theft of inventory.	Count teams should consist of staff from other departments.

(i) Deficiency	(ii) Reason	(iii) Recommendation
The teams are allowed to choose which inventory they count within each area of stores.	This lack of detailed organisation may lead to certain inventory items being counted more than once whilst some items may not be counted at all.	Each team of counters should be given specific instructions regarding which area of the stores they are responsible for.
There is no system for marking items which have been counted.	Again this increases the risk that inventory will be double counted or omitted completely.	All inventory should be marked systematically to indicate that it has been counted eg by the use of stickers.
Information on the count sheets is recorded in pencil.	This increases the risk that the information could be amended after the count without authorisation, resulting in inventory being incorrectly stated.	Results of all counts on the count sheets should be recorded in ink.
Additional count sheets are not pre-numbered.	The pre-numbering of the count sheets allows control over the completeness of the information. If the staff using the separate sheets do not number them as they are used there is no means of identifying that all sheets issued have been returned. Lost count sheets may then go unnoticed.	All count sheets should be pre-numbered before they are issued.
Count sheets are not signed by the count teams.	It may be difficult to identify who is responsible for the count of specific items if subsequent questions arise. The signature also encourages the counters to take responsibility for the counting they have performed.	All count sheets should be signed by the members of the count team.

(d) (i) The aim of a test of control is to demonstrate that a control exists and operates effectively in preventing, or detecting and correcting material misstatements.

The aim of a substantive procedure is to detect material misstatements at the assertion level in the financial statements.

(ii) Test of control: Observation of the count teams to ensure that they are conducting the count in accordance with the inventory count instructions.

Substantive procedure: Identify and record details of damaged items of inventory to ensure that this is taken into account in the final valuation of inventory.

71 Evidence and written representations

Text references. Chapters 7, 8 and 18

Top tips. On question 2, which is the 10 mark question of the F8 paper, the key things to remember are the time you have to answer this relatively straightforward knowledge-based question and to resist the temptation to write down everything you know about the subject matters in question. Look at the requirements carefully – for example, part (b) asks you to 'list six items that could be included in a representation letter', so make sure you do indeed produce a list of six items.

Easy marks. This question on the F8 paper will allow you to pick up many easy marks as the questions are all knowledge-based. As long as you remember the points in 'Top tips' above, you should have no problems in securing the majority, if not all, of the marks available here.

Examiner's comments. In part (a) on audit evidence, although many candidates identified factors, they failed to explain them, thus not scoring the full marks available. Other criticisms included writing too much, not providing sufficient breadth of answer and, in a minority of cases, explaining the audit risk model which was not required. In part (b), on written representation letters, most candidates correctly provided a list, however some wrote far too much, some candidates were confused between written representation letters and the management letter, explaining the contents of an audit engagement letter and including items that would not be included in a written representation letter. In part (c), the main weaknesses were lack of explanation to answers, suggesting inappropriate actions (such as immediate resignation) and explaining every type of audit report modification.

Marking scheme

		Marks
(a)	Sufficiency of evidence	
	1 for each point	
	– Financial statement risk	
	– Materiality	
	– Accounting/internal control systems	
	– Auditor's knowledge	
	– Audit procedures	
	– Source and reliability	
	– Sampling method used	
	– Other relevant points	
	Maximum marks	4
(b)	Representation letter contents	
	0.5 mark per valid point	
	Maximum marks	3
(c)	1 for each point with explanation	
	– Increase tests of controls	
	– Discuss with management	
	– Substantive procedures	
	– Qualification of audit report	
	– Include in management letter	
	– Discuss with audit committee	
	Maximum marks	3
		10

(a) Audit evidence

Materiality

Material items will require more evidence to support them than immaterial items, which might be tested by comparative analytical review only.

Risk

The sufficiency of audit evidence required is affected by the level of risk in the area being audited.

Source and quality of evidence

If the evidence is high quality, then less may be required than if it were of poorer quality. In general, audit evidence from external third parties is more reliable than that from the client's records because it is independent. Similarly evidence generated by the auditor is more reliable than that from the client. Original documents are more reliable than copies which can be tampered with.

Internal control systems

Evidence obtained from the client's records is more reliable when the related control system is operating effectively (as tested by the auditor).

(b) Items to include in a written representation letter

- Acknowledgement from management that it has fulfilled its responsibility for the preparation and presentation of the financial statements as set out in the terms of the audit engagement and in particular, whether the financial statements are prepared and presented in accordance with the applicable financial reporting framework.
- Acknowledgement from management that it has provided the auditor with all relevant information agreed in the terms of the audit engagement.
- All transactions have been recorded and are reflected in the financial statements.
- Appropriateness of selection and application of accounting policies.
- Whether matters such as the following have been recognised, measured, presented or disclosed in accordance with the applicable financial reporting framework:
  - Plans or intentions that may affect the carrying value or classification of assets and liabilities.
  - Liabilities (actual and contingent).
  - Title to, or control over, assets, liens or encumbrances on assets, and assets pledged as collateral.
  - Aspects of laws, regulations and contractual agreements that may affect the financial statements, including non-compliance.
- No irregularities involving management or employees with a significant role in the accounting and internal control systems or that could have a material effect on the financial statements.
- Communication to the auditor of all deficiencies in internal control of which management is aware.
- Representations about specific assertions in the financial statements.
- Significant assumptions used by management in making accounting estimates are reasonable.
- Related party relationships and transactions have been appropriately accounted for and disclosed.
- All subsequent events requiring adjustment or disclosure have been adjusted or disclosed.
- The effects of uncorrected misstatements are immaterial, both individually and in aggregate, and a list of these is attached with this letter.

(*Note*: Only six were required.)

(c) Where tests of controls result in the auditor concluding that the audit evidence is not sufficient to support the audit opinion, he should then undertake detailed substantive testing to provide audit evidence as controls cannot be relied upon in this area.

He should also inform management and those charged with governance of the significant control deficiencies found as a result of the tests of controls by detailing them in the report to management and making recommendations to mitigate them.

If the additional audit work results in the auditor still concluding that the audit evidence cannot support the audit opinion, he should consider the impact on the audit report, once the errors have been quantified and materiality considered.

72 Ethics and going concern

Text references. Chapters 4 and 18

Top tips. This is a knowledge-based question covering ethical principles and going concern, both topics you should feel reasonably comfortable with. Make sure that you do not run over time on this question – be specific and answer the question set.

Part (a) asks you to explain the five fundamental principles of ACCA's *Code of Ethics and Conduct.* Bear in mind that to get the full 1 mark per principle you must provide an explanation rather than simply identifying the principle correctly.

Part (b) requires an explanation of the actions the auditors should carry out when assessing whether an entity is a going concern. This tests your knowledge of quite a specific part of ISA 570 *Going Concern* although a reasonable answer can be produced if you apply some common sense and have a good understanding of the principles of ISA 570. Think carefully about the requirement – you are not being asked to list the factors which might indicate that the company is not a going concern, but the actions the auditor would perform.

Easy marks. You should be able to pick up good marks in part (a) provided that you ensure that you explain the fundamental principles rather than simply listing them.

Examiner's comments. Part (a) on the fundamental principles of the ACCA's *Code of Ethics and Conduct* was answered well by most candidates. However, areas of weakness included stating that independence was a fundamental principle, stating threats (which were not required), and providing insufficient explanation of points made.

Part (b) was on going concern. Reasons for lack of marks included stating going concern indicators rather then actions to take, explaining actions that had no relevance to work on going concern, and explaining the process of and types of audit report relevant to the going concern assumption. Candidates must read and understand the question requirements before starting to write their answers.

Marking scheme

		Marks
(a)	1 mark for each principle. 0.5 for stating the principle and 0.5 for brief explanation	
	– Integrity	
	– Objectivity	
	– Professional competence and due care	
	– Confidentiality	
	– Professional behaviour	
	Maximum marks	5

Marks

(b) 1 mark per action

- Review management plans
- Additional audit procedures
- Written representations
- Loans from bank
- Receivables ageing
- Other relevant points – Allow 0.5 marks where candidate lists audit procedures such as review cash flow forecasts, review management accounts post year end, etc.

Maximum marks 5

10

(a) Fundamental principles

Integrity	Members should be straightforward and honest in all business and professional relationships.
Objectivity	Members should not allow bias, conflicts of interest or undue influence of others to override professional or business judgements.
Professional competence and due care	Members have a continuing duty to remain up to date with current developments in practice, legislation and techniques. Members should also act diligently and in accordance with technical and professional standards.
Confidentiality	Members should respect the confidentiality of information acquired as a result of providing professional services and should not disclose this information without the permission of the client to do so. Confidential information should not be used for personal advantage or the advantage of third parties.
Professional behaviour	Members should comply with the relevant laws and regulations and should avoid any action that discredits the profession.

(b) Audit actions to ascertain whether an entity is a going concern

When planning the audit the auditor must:

- Consider in particular whether there are any events, conditions and business risks which might cast doubt on the entity's ability to continue as a going concern
- Evaluate management's assessment of the entity's ability to continue as a going concern

When events or conditions have been identified which cast significant doubt on the viability of the business the following additional actions should be taken:

- Review management's plans for future actions based on its going concern assessment and ensure that these are feasible and that the outcome of these plans will improve the situation. (Specific procedures might include analysing and discussing cash flow, reviewing the terms of debentures and loan agreements)
- Gather sufficient appropriate audit evidence to confirm or dispel whether or not a material uncertainty exists regarding going concern. This will involve considering any additional facts or information which has become available since management's going concern assessment.
- Seek written representations from management regarding its plans for future actions and the feasibility of these plans
- Obtain information regarding the continuance of loan facilities from the company's bankers
- Identify indications of cash flow problems eg determine whether there has been an increase in receivables days by reviewing the receivables ageing analysis

73 LALD

Text references. Chapters 4, 18 and 19

Top tips. This question had some rather complicated points in it that you may not have seen in other questions, such as the section about the non-payment of an amount of sales tax. It is important not to get too bogged down in any one part of a question like this. If you had little to say about the sales tax point it's best to move on to the other sections and aim to pass by having some sort of attempt at all parts of the question.

Easy marks. Part (c) had the only really easy marks here. The basic legal procedures for removal of auditors are not often examined but when they are it is usually, like this, a straightforward test of knowledge.

Examiner's comments. This question was answered reasonably well. Weak answers focused on auditing the sales system and depreciation without reference to the errors found. In part (c), the professional etiquette on a change in auditor was not enough to give a full enough answer.

Marking scheme

		Marks
(a)	**Audit procedures – underpayment of sales tax. One mark per point**	
	Discuss with head of accounting department	1
	Perform additional tests	1
	Determine amount of underpaying	1
	Discuss with directors	1
	Note in management letter	1
	Breach of law	1
	Ask for response from directors	1
	Audit any further amount paid	1
	Provision for late payment	1
	Other relevant points	1
	Maximum marks	7
(b)	**1 mark for each value procedure**	
	Review working papers	1
	Determine extent of error	1
	Calculate new provision	1
	Material difference?	1
	Discuss with management	1
	Discuss with directors	1
	Management letter	1
	Potential need for qualification	1
	Other relevant points (each)	1
	Maximum marks	7
(c)	**1 mark per relevant point**	
	Notice to company – as shareholders – ask for removal	1
	Send to company within 28 days of meeting	1
	Write to members– with agenda – before meeting	1
	Send copy of auditor representations to members	1
	Attend meeting – organise votes	1
	Auditor remover – statement of circumstances	1
	Appoint new auditor	1
	Other relevant points	1
	Maximum marks	6
		20

(a) **Additional procedures re the underpayment of sales tax**

- Discuss with management how the payment was missed in order to assess whether it was indeed an 'accidental' error. If there are indications that it was deliberate it might cast doubt on the integrity of management and have implications for other areas of the audit.
- Enquire as to when the payment will be made.
- Review the cashbook for the post year-end period to identify if the payment has been made.
- Obtain an analysis of payables as at 30 September 20X5 and identify whether a liability has been recognised for the unpaid sales tax. Also determine whether a liability has been recognised for any penalty that may become due as a result of the late payment.
- Agree the liability to any sales tax return that has been prepared for the quarter ended 31 August 20X5.
- Review any correspondence between LALD and the tax authorities.
- Include details of the non-payment of sales tax in the management letter, drawing the directors' attention to the fact that this is a breach of law.
- Consider reporting the matter to the tax authorities.

(b) **Additional procedures re the under-provision of depreciation**

- Review the working papers prepared so far to assess whether the depreciation does appear to be understated.
- Carry out further substantive testing to determine the amount of the error. This could involve:
  - Analytical procedures such as proof in total calculations performed separately for each sub-class of plant and machinery at the appropriate rate.
  - Reperforming calculations of the depreciation charge on a sample (or extending the sample already tested) of individual assets from each sub class.
  - If errors are found in the sample these should be extrapolated to the population to assess if the total understatement is material.
- Irrespective of materiality, the error should be mentioned in the management letter, pointing out what deficiency in systems allowed it to happen, such as lack of review of depreciation rates as input to the non-current asset accounting system or lack of checking of year end manual journal adjustments.
- If the error is material, management should be asked to amend the financial statements and if they refuse this will lead to a qualified audit opinion on the grounds that the financial statements are materially misstated.

(c) **Procedures to remove auditors**

(*Note.* This answer is based on UK law. In this International paper, no specific legal framework is implied, so answers under a different framework, or with less detail, would also be acceptable.)

- The directors, as such, do not have the power to remove auditors. This power rests with shareholders, so the directors could only take this course of action if they were also shareholders or could persuade other shareholders to take steps to remove the auditors.
- (In their capacity as shareholders) they must send notice to the company asking for an extraordinary general meeting to be convened to consider a resolution to remove the auditors. This notice must be sent 28 days ahead of the meeting.
- (In their capacity as directors) they must send notice of this meeting and resolution to the shareholders and to the auditors.
- The auditors have a right to make written representations to the shareholders and the directors must send these to the members. The only exception to this is if the directors go to court and it is held that the representations are defamatory.
- The directors must allow the auditors to attend the extraordinary general meeting and speak to the shareholders.
- The resolution requires a majority vote of the shareholders.

- If the resolution is passed the directors must obtain a statement of circumstances form the auditors and deposit this along with the notice of the auditor's removal at Companies House within 14 days of the resolution being passed.

74 Tye

Text references. Chapters 4, 6, 13, 18 and 19.

Top tips. Part (a) highlights an inventory valuation issue arising at the finalisation stage. The requirement is to list actions and procedures in response to the directors wanting to adopt a policy which will result in a material error (based on the draft profit for the year). The audit work is complete apart from this matter and the procedures should be confined to this matter. Procedures at this stage of the audit will focus on the relevant accounting standard, discussions with the directors and the impact on the audit report.

Notice in part (b) you are told the valuation issue has been resolved. Instead you need to deal with both responsibilities relating to fraud (including reporting of fraud) and the ethical issue of the threat made by the finance director. In part (ii) think carefully about the different stakeholders and the auditor's relationship with each. This will help you discuss which groups it is appropriate to report to and why. Note that the scenario does not mention an audit committee directly, but the first paragraph does state the company follows best practice regarding corporate governance regulations. Therefore the company will have an audit committee and it is appropriate to report to the issue to them.

Easy marks. You should be familiar with the topical area of the auditor's responsibilities in relation to detecting fraud and so you should find (b) (i) relatively straightforward.

Examiner's comments. Part (a) was worth 6 marks. As the requirement verb was list, then including 6 relevant procedures in the answer would obtain full marks. The main weakness in many answers concerned the apparent need to go back and audit inventory from the beginning of the audit, even though the question requirement clearly stated that audit was complete apart from this issue.

In part (b) candidates were expected to state and discuss various responsibilities, reporting options and safeguards regarding fraud affecting the external auditor. In part (i), candidates were required to state the responsibilities of the external auditor regarding fraud. Many candidates managed to state 3 or sometimes 4 responsibilities to obtain a clear pass standard. In part (ii), candidates were required to discuss groups who could be informed regarding the fictitious inventory. Most candidates obtained marks for identifying groups, but few marks were obtained for stating why those groups were being reported. Almost all candidates found the discussion element of the question difficult. In part (iii) most candidates managed to mention key safeguards of resignation and qualifying the audit report anyway. However, other points such as discussion with the audit committee were not always mentioned.

ACCA examiner's answer. The ACCA examiner's answer to this question can be found at the back of this kit.

Marking scheme

		Marks
(a)	**Aviation fuel inventory**	
	1 mark each for each valid procedure or action:	
	– Any alternative treatments in GAAP	
	– Materiality calculation	
	– Review prior year working papers	
	– Discuss with directors	
	– Warn directors possible qualification	
	– Quantify amount	
	– Management representation	
	– Draft audit report	
	– Other relevant points	
	Maximum marks	6

		Marks
(b) (i) **Auditor and fraud**		
1 mark each for each valid responsibility:		
– Overall responsibility		
– Materiality		
– Approach to audit		
– Identification of fraud		
– Other relevant points		
Maximum marks		4
(ii) **Reporting options regarding fraud**		
Up to 2 marks each for each valid explained option – 0.5 for each body – then up to 2 if good reasons given for reporting to that body.		
– Audit committee		
– Government		
– Members		
– Professional body		
– Other relevant points		
Maximum marks		6
(iii) **Safeguards**		
Up to 2 marks per valid point. 1 for explaining the safeguard and 1 for the effectiveness of the safeguard		
– Audit committee		
– Second partner review		
– Resignation		
– Other relevant points		
Maximum marks		4
		20

(a) **Proposed valuation of inventory – procedures and actions**

1 Identify the relevant section of IAS 2 which prohibits the valuation of the inventory at market value (IAS 2 requires that inventory should be valued at the lower of cost and net realisable value) and ensure there are no exceptions permitted by the standard.

2 Calculate the magnitude of the misstatement which is clearly material in the context of the results for the year of \$500,000. The maximum misstatement is (\$120 – 15) × 6000 = \$630,000.

3 Ask the directors their reasons for wanting to value the inventory in this way.

4 Point out to the directors that the treatment is incorrect, the misstatement is material and any opinion on financial statements where inventory is valued in this way will be qualified.

5 Review findings last year to establish treatment in the past and, if this has occurred before, how it has been dealt with.

6 If the directors refuse to change the treatment, draft a suitable qualification.

(b) **Fraud**

(i) **Auditors responsibilities regarding the detection of fraud**

ISA 240 *The auditor's responsibilities relating to fraud in an audit of financial statements* provides guidance in this area.

The auditor is responsible for obtaining reasonable assurance that the financial statements are free from material misstatement including material misstatement caused by fraud.

The auditor is responsible for maintaining **professional scepticism** throughout the audit, considering the possibility of management override of controls, and recognising that audit procedures may need to be designed differently to detect fraud rather than error.

The audit team must discuss how and where the entity's financial statements may be susceptible to material misstatement due to fraud, including how fraud might occur.

If the external auditor does detect fraud, then the auditor must consider the implications for the audit as a whole. For example, the auditor will need to carry out additional testing as there could be a possibility of fraud in other areas. The auditor should also consider whether the suspected fraud casts doubt on any representations received to date.

(ii) **Reporting of fictitious inventory**

Shareholders

The auditor has a responsibility to modify the opinion if the financial statements are not free from material misstatement. If concluded the fraud is material (but not pervasive) the opinion will be qualified and the reason for the qualification given. Therefore the audit report to the members will state the misstatement occurred due to incorrect inventory quantities, but not necessarily state why the quantities were incorrect (ie due to fraud).

The Audit Committee

As the company follows best practice regarding corporate governance regulations, it will have an audit committee which strengthens the external auditor's position by providing a channel of communication and forum for issues of concern The issue should be disclosed the audit committee, who should then approach the board and ask them to revise the financial statements before making any other relevant recommendations (such as disciplining the financial director).

Government

Tye Ltd has a contract with the government. The incorrect inventory quantity turns a profit into a loss and constitutes a breach of contract. The auditor must consider whether there is a responsibility to report directly to the government. This will involve reviewing the contract between Tye Ltd and the Government.

(iii) **Possible safeguards in response to the intimidation threat**

Resigning from the engagement

Due to the unethical behaviour of the finance director, resignation may be considered necessary to eliminate the threat and avoid risking damage to the firm's reputation in the long term. The resigning auditor can normally require the directors to convene a general meeting to consider the circumstances of the resignation.

Second partner review

A second partner could be added to engagement team to review the engagement partner's judgements and conclusions, including the action taken in response to the fictitious inventory. This provides additional assurance the correct conclusions have been drawn because the second partner will not have been directly involved in discussions over this area.

Top tip. An additional valid safeguard is:

Communication with the audit committee
The audit committee is responsible for making recommendations to the board for it to put to the shareholders for their approval in the general meeting in relation to the appointment of the external auditor. Therefore the auditor should make the committee aware of the threat made and the reasons for it so they can take this into account when making their recommendation. If the board ignore the recommendation, the board will need to disclose why.

However discussion of two safeguards would be enough to gain full marks in this section.

75 Eastvale

Text references. Chapters 18 and 19

Top tips. This question tests your knowledge and application of audit reviews and reports. It's also important that you remember your financial reporting studies to apply to the two events that occur after the end of the reporting period. The best way to present your answer is to take each event in turn and answer the three requirements. This allows you to break the question down into more manageable chunks and gives more structure to your answers. Make sure that in (i), your answer is as specific as possible. In (ii), you must support your answer with good explanations. In (iii), you must justify your answer in order to score well.

Easy marks. There aren't easy marks as such in this question but if you take each situation in turn, and answer each of the requirements, you should be able to score reasonably well.

Note. The marking scheme has been revised to reflect any necessary amendments made to the question and/or answer.

Marking scheme

			Marks
(a)	**Fire at warehouse**		
	(i)	Audit procedures. 5 marks for fire 1 per well-explained point	
		Discuss the matter with the directors	1
		Letter of representation point	1
		Schedule of inventory destroyed – reasonable?	1
		Insurance	1
		Going concern status of company	1
		Other relevant points (each)	1
		Maximum marks	**4**
	(ii)	Amendment to financial statements 2 marks – 1 per well-explained point	
		Disclosure in FS – unlikely with reason	1
		No amendment to statement of financial position	1
		Other relevant points	1
		Maximum marks	**3**
	(iii)	Modification of audit report 3 marks – 1 per well-explained point	
		Modification of report	
		Going concern status?	1
		Inadequate disclosure by directors	1
		Other relevant points (each)	1
		Maximum marks	**3**
(b)	**Batch of cheese**		
	(i)	Audit procedures 5 marks for fire 1 per well-explained point	
		Discuss with directors	1
		Copy of damages claim	1
		Legal advice	1
		Press reports (or other third party) on cheese	1
		Going concern?	1
		Other relevant points (each)	1
		Maximum marks	**4**

		Marks
(ii)	Disclosure of event 2 marks – 1 per well-explained point	
	Disclosure event – because significant impact	1
	No adjustment	1
	Going concern issue – reputation	1
	May result in amendment to FS	1
	Other relevant points (each)	1
	Maximum marks	**3**
(iii)	Modification of audit report – 3 marks – 1 per well-explained point	
	Preparation of FS breakup basis	1
	Prepared going concern basis – emphasis of matter to note this	1
	Prepared going concern – but in doubt – emphasis of matter to note this	1
	Prepared going concern and disagree – adverse opinion	1
	Maximum marks	**3**
		20

(a) **Fire in warehouse**

(i) *Additional audit procedures*

- Discuss with management of EastVale to establish the date of the fire and exactly what happened
- Estimate the value of the inventory that was destroyed in the fire
- Inspect the insurance policy of the company to check that the company is covered adequately for the loss incurred and review any correspondence regarding this
- Discuss with the directors of EastVale whether the company can continue as a going concern given the high level of inventory that was destroyed in the fire
- Obtain written representations from management regarding the going concern status of the company

(ii) *Impact on financial statements*

As the fire is a non-adjusting event after the reporting period, providing the going concern basis is still appropriate no amendments are required to the financial statements for the financial year being audited. However, disclosure of the event is required by IAS 10 *Events after the reporting period* as the event is likely to be material. This disclosure should include the nature of the event and an estimate of its financial effect.

(iii) *Impact on audit report*

Providing the directors have properly disclosed the event the audit opinion would not be modified as this is a non-adjusting event after the period-end date and does not provide evidence of conditions that existed at the period-end date. However, an emphasis of matter paragraph could be included in the audit report to highlight the matter and draw it to the attention of users of the financial statements.

(b) **Cheese**

(i) *Additional audit procedures*

- Review legal correspondence regarding the claim to establish the amount of the claim
- Discuss the case with EastVale's solicitors to assess the likely outcome of the claim
- Review press reports regarding food poisoning to assess impact on the business
- Discuss the case with the directors, including their assessment of its impact on the going concern status of EastVale
- Obtain written management representations from the directors on the going concern status of the company

(ii) *Impact on financial statements*

This is a non-adjusting event after the reporting period. However, given its nature it should be disclosed in a note to the financial statements. If it impacts on the going concern status of the company, then the accounts would have to be prepared on a different basis and disclosures in accordance with IAS 8 *Accounting policies, changes in accounting estimates and errors* would be required.

(iii) *Impact on audit report*

If the directors consider that as a result of the food poisoning reports the company cannot continue as a going concern and they produce the accounts on a break-up basis, then the audit opinion would not be modified but the audit report would include an emphasis of matter paragraph to draw attention to users of this matter.

If the accounts are prepared on the assumption that the company is a going concern but the auditors do not agree with this then the audit report would include an adverse opinion on the financial statements.

76 OilRakers

Text reference. Chapter 18

Top tips. This is quite a technical question testing your knowledge of subsequent events both from the accounting and the auditing perspective. This was an optional question in the exam so sensible question selection would be important. If you are comfortable with this technical area you can pick up excellent marks. If your knowledge is less precise another question may be a better bet.

Part (a) asks for procedures that can be used to identify subsequent events. Here knowledge of ISA 560 would be extremely useful as this contains a list of procedures. Alternatively you could generate your own list by thinking about the sources of evidence eg discussion with management, board minutes, legal documents.

Part (b) (i) tests your knowledge of IAS 10. Again it is essentially a technical question. Remember, an adjusting event is one which provides more information about a condition existing at the period-end date. Adjusting events should be adjusted for. Non-adjusting events should be disclosed if they are significant to the understanding of the financial statements.

Part (b) (ii) is probably the trickiest part and relies on your knowledge of the auditor's responsibilities for subsequent events at different points in time. The key technical point to remember is that the auditor has a responsibility to perform procedures which will identify subsequent events up to the date that the audit report is signed. After this time he has no responsibility but if matters are brought to his attention he must consider the need for the accounts to be revised and for a new audit report to be issued.

Easy marks. These are available in parts (a) and (b)(i). Notice that these account for 11 out of a total of 20 marks so if you score well on these sections you are well on the way to passing the question overall.

Examiner's comments. Lots of candidates answered this question well. Part (a) was answered well although a minority of answers focused on explaining the accounting treatment of events after the reporting period, which was not required. In part (b), the following points arose:

- Stating that the company would no longer be a going concern as a result of the bad debt
- Stating that the fire was an adjusting event rather than non-adjusting
- Stating that the auditor was responsible for amending the financial statements, rather than the directors

Marking scheme

		Marks
(a)	**Audit procedures – one mark for each of the following (or 0.5 where the point is made briefly)**	
	Reviewing management procedures	1
	Reviewing minutes of meetings	1
	Interim accounts and cash flow forecasts	1
	Lawyers	1
	Going concern assumption	1
	Maximum marks	**5**
(b)	**Asking management for information – 0.5 for each of**	
	New borrowing commitments	0.5
	Asset sales	0.5
	New shares or debentures	0.5
	Assets destroyed or impounded	0.5
	Unusual accounting adjustments	0.5
	Any other valid point	0.5
	Allow other relevant points	1
	Maximum 5 marks per section	
	Bankrupt customer	
	Adjusting event + reason	2
	Audit responsible for detecting	1
	Procedures include	
	External evidence – receiver letter	1
	Internal evidence	1
	Audit accounting adjustment	1
	Chemical spill	
	Non-adjusting event but disclose + reason	2
	Audit responsibility for detecting – actually management	1
	Procedures include	
	Info on chemical spill	1
	Discuss accounting treatment/disclosure note	1
	Letter of representation	1
	Amend audit report – emphasis of matter paragraph	1
	Destruction of oil well	
	Non-adjusting event but disclose + reason	2
	Audit responsibility for detecting	1
	Procedures include	
	Evidence for destruction	1
	Check directors' actions – contact members?	1
	FS amended – audit amendment reissue report	1
	FS not amended – lawyer advice	1
	Maximum marks	**15**
		20

(a) **Audit procedures**

Reviewing procedures management has established to ensure that subsequent events are identified.

Reading minutes of board minutes and any minutes of meetings with shareholders.

Reading the latest available interim financial statements, budgets, cash flow forecasts and other related management reports.

Reviewing correspondence with solicitors regarding any litigation or legal claims.

Making inquiries of management as to whether events have occurred which might affect the financial statements. These inquiries would include:

- Updates on any ongoing issues already identified
- Whether new commitments, borrowings or guarantees have been entered into
- Whether sales or acquisitions of assets have occurred or are planned
- Whether the issue of new shares or debentures has been made or is planned
- Whether any assets have been destroyed eg by fire
- Whether there have been any developments regarding risk areas and contingencies
- Whether there are any events which call into question going concern

(b) (i) **Three events: IAS 10**

15 August 20X5

The bankruptcy of the major customer is an adjusting event after the reporting period. It provides additional information concerning the recoverability of the debt at the reporting date and as it represents 11% of receivables is likely to be material to the financial statements. An adjustment should be made in the financial statements reducing the receivables balance and profits.

1 November 20X5

The accidental release of the chemicals is a non-adjusting event. It occurred after the reporting date and does not provide further information about conditions at the year end. On this basis the adjustment made is not necessary. However the impact of the leak is likely to be significant as the company may incur penalties or fines due to the environmental damage. Disclosure of the event and an estimate of the financial effect should be made.

30 November 20X5

The fire at the well is a non-adjusting event. It occurred after the reporting date and does not relate to conditions which existed at the year end. Although there will be a loss of production and reduction in profits there is no indication that this is significant enough to call into question going concern. Disclosure should be made of the events surrounding the fire and an estimate of the financial effect.

(ii) **Auditor's responsibility and audit procedures**

15 August 20X5

The bankruptcy of the major customer takes place after the year end but before the audit report is signed. In accordance with ISA 560 the auditor is required to perform audit procedures designed to obtain appropriate evidence that all events up to the date of the auditor's report that may require adjustment of, or disclosure in, the financial statements have been identified.

These procedures would include the following:

- Confirming the details of the bankruptcy to documents received by OilRakers from the liquidator.
- Agreeing the balance outstanding to the confirmation received from the customer as part of the audit of receivables. If this is not available agree the outstanding balance to pre year-end invoices.
- Checking that the adjustment has been made correctly in the financial statements ie receivables are reduced in the statement of financial position and profits in the income statement.
- Confirming in the letter of representation that there are no further amounts due from this customer.

1 November 20X5

This event takes place after the audit report has been signed but before the financial statements have been issued. After the date of the audit report the auditor does not have any responsibility to perform audit procedures or make inquiries. However in this case as the auditor has been made aware of the chemical spill the situation should be discussed with management and an appropriate course of action decided.

Audit procedures would be as follows:

- Confirm the details included in the disclosure notes in the accounts by discussing the situation with management, looking at press reports and any other records which are available. Assess the adequacy of the disclosure in compliance with IAS 10.
- Check that no adjustment has been made in the accounts in respect of the spill.
- Review correspondence with legal experts regarding any liability for environmental damage.
- Obtain a revised version of the letter of representation confirming that there are no other events which should be brought to the auditors' attention.
- As the financial statements have been amended after the auditor's report has been signed a new audit report would need to be issued. This should be dated no earlier than the date of the revised financial statements. The revised report should include an emphasis of matter paragraph highlighting the events which are disclosed in the notes to the accounts.

30 November 20X5

The fire at the oil well takes place after the financial statements have been issued. The auditor has no obligation at all to make any inquiries regarding such financial statements by this date. When, as in this case, the auditor becomes aware of a fact which would have had an impact on the audit report, the auditor should consider whether the financial statements need revision, should discuss the matter with management and decide on the appropriate course of action.

Procedures would be as follows:

- Clarify the facts by discussion with management, reading minutes of board meetings and any reports submitted by experts on site.
- Check insurance documents to confirm that the damage caused to the well and any consequential damage eg environmental, is covered. Assess the basis on which the ten month time period has been calculated for drilling the new well to determine whether it is reasonable. Both of these factors may affect the viability of the business which should be assessed.
- Determine how management intend to deal with the issue. If the accounts are to be revised review the steps taken by management to ensure that anyone who had received the previously issued financial statements is informed of the situation.
- If management does not revise the financial statements and the auditor considers that revision is necessary, consider the means by which recipients of the initial financial statements can be contacted. Before any further action is taken legal advice should be sought.

77 ZeeDiem

Text references. Chapters 18 and 19.

Top tips. This question for 20 marks is about subsequent events. You need to be familiar with ISA 560 *Subsequent events* to score well in this question. There are several dates to bear in mind with this question so you might find it helpful to draw a timeline with the key dates on it while you are planning your answer, to help you get things into context.

Easy marks. Easy marks are available in part (a) (i) for four marks to explain whether the two events are adjusting or non-adjusting.

Examiner's comments. Common errors in (a) included listing lots of general procedures for subsequent events rather than linking those procedures to the scenario and explaining the going concern review in detail. While event 2 could potentially impact on going concern and mention of this was worth a mark, stating 5 or 6 going concern procedures was clearly inappropriate. In part (b) the main areas that was not fully considered was that the audit report had already been signed. Many candidates simply assumed that the auditor would issue a new report and management would accept this.

Note. The marking scheme has been revised to reflect any necessary amendments made to the question and/or answer.

Marking scheme

			Marks
(a)	(i)	Explanation of whether events adjusting or not. 2 marks for each event Destruction of inventory Release of dye **Maximum marks**	4
	(ii)	1 mark for each point regarding auditor responsibility and for each valid audit procedure Maximum 6 marks for each event Destruction of inventory Audit must identify material events post reporting period Need to check value of $225,000 is receivable Documentation from insurers Payment from third party Disclosure in financial statements Total inventory value end of year Other inventory affected? Management representation point Release of dye Ensure that material events is disclosed appropriately in financial statements Documentation of event Extent of disclosure in financial statements Action if disagree with amount of disclosure Possibility of modified audit opinion Written representation letter **Maximum marks**	12
(b)		1 mark for each audit procedure Discuss with directors Audit any amendment to financial statements Produce revised audit report Inform members in other methods – speak at meetings Resignation? Note not effective **Maximum marks** **Total marks**	4 20

(a) (i) *Adjusting and non-adjusting events*

Event 1

This is an adjusting event according to IAS 10 because it provides further evidence of conditions that existed at the year-end. Inventory at the year-end should be valued at the lower of cost and net realisable cost in accordance with IAS 2 *Inventories* and therefore in this case, inventory is currently overstated by $525k.

Event 2

This is a non-adjusting event as it does not provide further evidence of conditions that existed at the year-end, because the incident occurred after the year-end. It might require disclosure in the financial statements, but no adjustments are necessary.

(ii) *Auditors' responsibilities and audit procedures*

Event 1

ISA 560 *Subsequent events* requires that auditors perform audit procedures to obtain sufficient, appropriate audit evidence that all events up to the date of the auditors' report that may require adjustment or disclosure in the financial statements have been identified. Since the audit report will not be signed until the following week, the auditors must perform additional audit procedures for this event.

When the auditors identify events that require adjustment of, or disclosure in, the financial statements, they need to determine whether these events are appropriately reflected in the financial statements.

The auditors are required to request management to provide a written representation that all events occurring subsequent to the date of the financial statements and for which the applicable financial reporting framework requires adjustment or disclosure have been adjusted or disclosed.

The following audit procedures should be carried out:

- Inspect the insurers' report to confirm the value of inventory that is affected and to confirm the valuation of this inventory as a result.
- Consider whether the issue is material to the financial statements.
- If any of the defective mattresses have subsequently been sold, agree the amounts to supporting documentation and to the bank.
- Discuss the issue with the directors and inform them that the financial statements should be adjusted to reduce the value of year-end inventory by $525k.
- Obtain a written representation from management as to the value of inventory at the year-end.
- Review the amended financial statements to confirm that the inventory write-down has indeed been made.
- If the directors refuse to make the necessary amendments, the audit report may need to include a qualified 'except for' opinion on the grounds that the financial statements are materially misstated if this issue is material.

Event 2

As for event 1, ISA 560 requires auditors to perform audit procedures to obtain sufficient, appropriate audit evidence that all events up to the date of the auditors' report that may require adjustment or disclosure in the financial statements have been identified.

When the auditors identify events that require adjustment of, or disclosure in, the financial statements, they need to determine whether these events are appropriately reflected in the financial statements.

The auditors are required to request management to provide a written representation that all events occurring subsequent to the date of the financial statements and for which the applicable financial reporting framework requires adjustment or disclosure have been adjusted or disclosed.

The following audit procedures should be carried out:

- Inspect any reports from the Environmental Agency as to whether the release of dye was in breach of legislation and the outcome of this.
- Inspect the report from the insurers if it is available.
- Discuss the issue with the directors and inform them that the financial statements will need additional disclosure for this event.
- Obtain a written representation point from management about this event.
- Review the amended financial statements to confirm that the disclosure has been made satisfactorily.
- If the directors refuse to make the necessary disclosure, consider whether the audit report will need to contain a qualified 'except for' opinion.

(b) **Fine from Environmental Agency**

Since the financial statements and audit report have now been signed, it is the management's responsibility to inform the auditors of any issues that might affect the financial statements. The auditors have no obligation to perform any audit procedures regarding the financial statements after their report has been signed.

The auditor must consider whether the accounts need amendment as a result of the report from the Environmental Agency. They must discuss the matter with the directors of ZeeDiem and inquire how they intend to address the matter in the financial statements. In this case the fine is material so amendment is required to the accounts.

If management amends the financial statements, the auditor must carry out appropriate audit procedures and issue a new audit report on the amended accounts. The new report must be dated not earlier than the date the amended accounts are signed or approved.

Where management does not amend the financial statements, the auditors must express a qualified opinion or adverse opinion.

78 Green

Text references. Chapters 4 and 18

Top tips. In this question, the scenario is quite long so spend a bit of time going through it carefully and noting down potential issues arising. In part (a) be careful to make sure that your answer is full enough to score the available marks – the requirement asks you to 'identify and explain' so it's not sufficient to just produce a list of threats – you've got to explain them as well. First think about what the general threats are and then go through the scenario to identify whether any of these would be relevant in this situation. In part (c), you have to list the audit procedures you would undertake to determine whether the going concern basis is appropriate. Make sure the tests you describe are specific and sensible – vague answers won't score well.

Easy marks. You should be able to score well in part (b) on going concern as this requirement is knowledge-based and on a topic you should be very familiar with.

Examiner's comments. In part (a) many candidates demonstrated that they had a sound knowledge of ethical threats. However, problems included:

- Taking too long to explain the threats. A sentence or two was sufficient to obtain the marks for each
- Making general rather than specific comments

Answers to part (b) varied considerably. Many candidates still seemed to be confused by the concept of going concern. The main confusion related to describing going concern as a situation where the company would not be continuing in business rather than one where it would continue in business. In part (b) (ii) poorer answers provided long lists of directors' and auditors' responsibilities, which were not related to going concern.

Part (c) produced the best answers although only a minority of candidates related their comments to the scenario. Common errors included:

- Stating going concern indicators rather than work on the going concern concept
- Re-auditing historical information. Procedures needed to relate to going concern, which implied trying to determine how the company would perform in the future.

Marking scheme

			Marks
(a)	0.5 for identifying threat, 1 mark each for point (0.5 where not explained)		
	Self-review threat		
	Management threat		
	Advocacy threat		
	Familiarity threat		
	Fee income		
	Association threat		
	Other relevant points (each)		
	Maximum marks		**8**
(b)	Key points 1 for each point		
	(i)	State going concern (enterprise operational existence)	1
		Not used when liquidation or ceased trading	1
		Not used when directors will liquidate or cease trading	1
		Maximum marks	**3**
	(ii)	Directors responsibilities – prepare FS	1
		Evidence produce	1
		Auditor responsibilities – check GC concept	1
		Collect audit evidence	1
		Disclosure of going concern concept if necessary	1
		Maximum marks	**4**
(c)	Key points 1 for each point		
	Profit and cash flow forecasts		1
	Review order books		1
	Contact lawyers		1
	Review financial status – other GC indicators		1
	Correspondence organic certification		1
	Contact bank		1
	Representation letter		1
	Other good relevant points		1
	Maximum marks		**5**
			20

(a) **Ethical threats that could affect Lime**

Familiarity threat

A familiarity threat could arise since the audit partner of Lime has been friends with the managers of Green for the last fifteen years and has been providing informal advice to them. This may have the effect of reducing objectivity and independence when coming to a conclusion as to the truth and fairness of the financial statements of Green.

Undue dependence on fee income

The audit of Green will go out to tender, as well as the provision of other professional services. If Lime wins the tender, then it will have to consider whether the total fees from the provision of audit and other services are significant enough to cause a self-interest threat.

Advocacy threat

Green is considering court action against Black for loss of income and to stop it from growing GM crops. It may therefore require Lime to go to court to provide evidence on its behalf and this could give rise to an advocacy threat.

Self-review threat

If Lime wins the tender for the provision of audit and other professional services, a self-review threat may arise if for example, the firm is also providing a service to Green of preparing its financial statements or carrying out other review engagements.

Management threat

Again if the firm wins the tender for the provision of audit and other professional services, it may be in the position where it is providing a management function to Green. This could arise for example if it advises on the purchase of a new accounting system.

(b) **Going concern**

(i) Going concern relates to a company's ability to continue operating for the foreseeable future – this period is not defined but is generally assumed to be at least 12 months from the reporting date. It should not be applied to the preparation of financial statements when the company intends to cease trading or when it has intentions to file for bankruptcy.

(ii) Directors have a responsibility to make a specific assessment of the entity's ability to continue as a going concern. They must also satisfy themselves when preparing the financial statements that the going concern assumption is still appropriate. This applies even if there is no explicit requirement to do so in the financial reporting framework.

The auditors have a responsibility to consider the appropriateness of management's use of the going concern assumption in the preparation of the financial statements and to consider whether there are any material uncertainties about the entity's ability to continue as a going concern that need to be disclosed in the financial statements. They must also remain alert for evidence of events that may cast doubt on the entity's ability to continue as a going concern and must consider whether there are adequate disclosures in the financial statements regarding the going concern basis, so that the accounts give a true and fair view.

(c) **Audit procedures regarding going concern**

- Discuss with the managers of Green how they have concluded that the company can continue as a going concern
- Review profit forecasts and budgets of Green to assess whether the going concern assumption is relevant
- Review correspondence from legal advisers of Green concerning the potential court case against Black
- Discuss with legal advisers of Green the chances of Green being successful if this case is brought to court and potential costs involved
- Inspect relevant lending documentation issued by Green's bank to establish level of any borrowings/overdraft facilities and discuss with Green's bank manager
- Obtain a written representation point from the managers of Green to confirm that the company can continue as a going concern

79 Smithson

Text references. Chapters 18 and 19.

Top tips. This question for 20 marks is split into four parts. Therefore treat it as such – look at each part in turn, considering the mark allocation, and don't get overwhelmed by the question.

Parts (a) and (d) are knowledge-based and so you should be able to answer these well. Parts (b) and (c) relate to the question scenario – use this to generate ideas and help plan your answer. Part (b) is for eight marks on audit procedures to undertake – you must make sure that the procedures you describe are well-explained and specific – vague answers won't score well at all. Present your answers well – use short paragraphs for each point with spacing between them.

Easy marks. Easy marks are available in parts (a) and (d) of this question on going concern, provided of course that you are comfortable with this important area of the F8 syllabus. Again consider the mark allocation to help ensure that your answer does not include everything you know on this topic but does answer the specific question requirements.

Examiner's comments. Weaknesses for part (a) included saying that the auditor was responsible for producing cash flow forecasts, stating lots of audit procedures to carry out, and stating that it was the auditor's responsibility to produce financial statements on the going concern basis. Part (b) was not answered well overall. Key weaknesses included pproviding a list of going concern indicators rather than audit procedures, not providing sufficient detail on each procedure, and listing audit work on the financial statements. Part (c) proved to be difficult for some candidates, with many comments made being a repeat of the audit work already carried out in part (b), whilst other answers explained every possible type of audit report that could be produced. The main weakness in part (d) was using the term 'true and fair view' in the context of an assurance engagement with only a minority of candidates recognising that truth and fairness relate to statutory audit. Some candidates did not attempt this question, indicating poor time management for the paper as a whole.

Marking scheme

		Marks
(a)	Going concern meaning	
	1 mark each for:	
	– Definition	
	– ISA 570 explanation (don't need the ISA number)	
	– Audit procedures	
	– Realistic use of assumption	
	– Report to members	
	– Report to audit committee and/or directors	
	– Discussion with management on going concern	
	– Other relevant points	
	Maximum marks	4
(b)	Audit procedures on going concern	
	1 mark per procedure (0.5 if brief or unclear eg 'check the cash flow')	
	– Cash flow	
	– Directors' view going concern	
	– Other finance	
	– Interim financial statements	
	– Lack of non-current assets	
	– Reliance on senior employee	
	– Solicitor's letter	
	– Review order book	
	– Review bank letter	
	– Review other events after the reporting period	
	– Written representation	
	– Other relevant points	
	Maximum marks	8
(c)	Audit procedures company may not be a going concern	
	1 mark per action (0.5 if brief or unclear eg 'discuss with directors')	
	– Discuss with directors	
	– Need to modify audit report	
	– Possible emphasis of matter	
	– Possible qualification	
	– Letter of representation	
	– Other relevant points	
	Maximum marks	4

	Marks
(d) Negative assurance	
1 mark per action (0.5 if brief or unclear eg 'warning cash flow may be inaccurate')	
– Definition	
– Audit report = positive assurance	
– Level of reliance	
– Limited audit procedures	
– Other relevant points	
	4
Maximum marks	20

(a) Going concern

The going concern assumption is a fundamental principle in the preparation of financial statements. It assumes that an entity will continue in business for the foreseeable future with neither the intention nor the necessity of liquidation, ceasing trading or seeking protection from creditors. Assets and liabilities are recorded on the basis that the entity will be able to realise its assets and discharge its liabilities in the normal course of business.

Auditor's responsibilities

The auditor must consider the appropriateness of management's use of the going concern assumption in the preparation of the financial statements, through the review of future projections and discussion with management.

The auditor must also consider whether there are material uncertainties about the entity's ability to continue as a going concern, which need to be disclosed in the accounts.

The auditor must consider whether there are adequate disclosures regarding the going concern basis in the accounts for them to give a true and fair view.

The auditor must also report to the audit committee and members if he or she believes that the going concern assumption has not been used appropriately.

(b) Audit procedures to determine whether Smithson Co is a going concern

- Discuss with Smithson's managements to ascertain whether they consider that the company is able to continue as a going concern
- Review the cash flow forecast prepared, and consider the assumptions used in preparing it
- Review and discuss with management Smithson's latest available interim financial statements or management accounts
- Review board minutes for references to financial difficulties
- Review events after the year-end for issues that could affect Smithson's ability to continue as a going concern
- Discuss with Smithson's legal advisers what the outcome of the two court cases is likely to be and whether there are any other cases pending or likely to result
- Discuss with relevant management whether any new contracts have been awarded to the company, given that several contracts have been withdrawn as a result of the adverse publicity caused by the legal cases
- Obtain a written representation from management to confirm that Smithson can continue as a going concern
- Discuss with management the situation regarding the equipment and what their intentions are – will they be replacing machines in the near future?
- Discuss the requirement for additional finance by the company and how this will be acquired
- Review future cash flow projections and forecasts
- Review current borrowings of the company and repayment terms and consider whether the company will be able to repay these

(c) Audit procedures where Smithson Co considered not to be a going concern

The auditor should discuss with Smithson's management their opinion that the company cannot continue as a going concern and the reasons for coming to this conclusion.

The auditor should consider the impact of his findings on the audit report to be issued at the end of the audit and explain to the directors the effect on the opinion if any disclosures required are not made or if the accounts are prepared on an incorrect basis.

Where appropriate disclosure has been made, the opinion on the financial statements will not be modified but the report will include an emphasis of matter paragraph bringing readers attention to the material uncertainty that may affect the entity being able to continue as a going concern.

If the directors disagree and do not make additional disclosures that are required, the audit opinion will be qualified (except for) or adverse.

(d) Negative assurance' is when an auditor gives an assurance that nothing has come to his attention which indicates that the cash flow statement (in this case) is free from material misstatement. He therefore gives his assurance in the absence of any evidence to the contrary. The cash flow statement would have been prepared using forecast information which cannot easily be verified as correct as it is based on assumptions about the future. Therefore, the auditor can only provide limited, negative assurance on it.

The audit report, however, provides reasonable assurance that the financial statements present fairly, in all material respects the financial position of the company (or give a true and fair view). It does not guarantee the accounts are correct, but that they are true and fair within a reasonable margin of error. The financial statements are prepared using historical information and therefore the figures can be verified by the auditor, hence his ability to provide reasonable, positive assurance as to their truth and fairness.

80 Terms, evidence and modified reports

Text references. Chapters 4, 8 and 19

Top tips. This is a straightforward knowledge-based question for 10 marks on various aspects of the F8 syllabus. Make sure therefore that you do not run over time on this question – be specific and answer the question set.

In part (a), you are asked to state six items that could be included in an engagement letter. Bullet points for this question would be appropriate as there are three marks available so you could expect half a mark for each item. You therefore certainly will not have time to go into detail about the purpose of an engagement letter or ISA 210 *Agreeing the terms of audit engagements* – these are not required and will not score you any marks.

In parts (b) and (c), you are asked for brief explanations. Note that in part (b) you are asked for four types of audit evidence and in part (c) you are asked for three types of audit opinion modification. Giving more than the required number is a waste of your time and giving less than the required number will ensure you lose the straightforward marks available in this question.

Easy marks. This is a straightforward knowledge-based question on three areas of the syllabus. If your knowledge is sound, you will be able to score very well in this question.

Note. The marking scheme has been revised to reflect any necessary amendments made to the question and/or answer.

Marking scheme

		Marks
(a)	Contents of an engagement letter – 3 marks. 0.5 mark per point.	
	Objective of the audit of the financial statements	0.5
	Management's responsibility for the financial statements	0.5
	The scope of the audit with reference to appropriate legislation	0.5
	The form of any report or other communication of the results of the engagement	0.5
	The auditor may not discover all material errors	0.5
	Provision of access to the auditor of all relevant books and records	0.5
	Arrangements for planning the audit	0.5
	Agreement of management to provide a representation letter	0.5
	Request that the client confirms in writing the terms of engagement	0.5
	Description of any letters or reports to be issued to the client	0.5
	Basis of fee calculation and billing arrangements	0.5
	Maximum marks	**3**
(b)	Types of audit evidence – 4 marks. 0.5 only for stating the type and 0.5 for explanation. Maximum 2 marks for simply providing a list of types of evidence.	
	Inspection	1
	Observation	1
	Inquiry	1
	Confirmation	1
	Recalculation	1
	Reperformance	1
	Analytical procedures	1
	Maximum marks	**4**
(c)	Modification of audit opinion. 3 marks. 0.5 for the type of opinion and 0.5 for explanation.	
	Maximum marks	**3**
		10

(a) The following items would be included in the engagement letter:

- **Objective** of the financial statements
- **Management's responsibility** for the financial statements
- **Scope** of the audit
- Form of any **reports** or other communication of results from the engagement
- A **statement** that due to the test nature and inherent limitations of the audit and internal control, there is a risk that some material misstatements may remain undetected
- **Unrestricted access** to records and documentation requested for the audit
- **Arrangements** regarding planning and performance of the audit
- Expectation of receiving **written representations** on specific matters
- Request for client to confirm the **terms of the engagement** by acknowledging receipt of the letter
- Basis on which **fees** are calculated and any billing arrangements
- Description of **any letters or reports** the auditor expects to issue to the client

(*Note.* Only six were required.)

(b) Audit evidence that can be obtained by the auditor is described below:

Inspection

Inspection can encompass examining records, documents or assets. Looking at records and documents provides different levels of reliability depending on their nature and source. Inspection of assets can provide good evidence of existence but not of rights and obligations or valuation.

Observation

This consists of looking at a process or procedure being performed. An example would be observation of inventory counting.

Inquiry

Inquiry consists of seeking information from knowledgeable individuals, both from within and outside the organisation being audited. It can encompass both formal written inquiries or informal oral inquiries.

Confirmation

This is the process of obtaining a representation of information or of an existing condition from a third party, for example, a bank confirmation.

Recalculation

Recalculation is checking the mathematical accuracy of documents or records.

Reperformance

This is the auditor's independent execution of procedures or controls that were originally performed as part of the organisation's internal control, either manually or using CAATs.

Analytical procedures

Analytical procedures consist of evaluations of financial information made by a study of plausible relationships among both financial and non-financial data.

(*Note.* Only four were required.)

(c) Modified audit opinions

There are three types of modified opinion:

Qualified opinion

A qualified opinion will be issued due to either the auditor being unable to obtain sufficient appropriate audit evidence in respect of a material matter or because the auditor concludes the financial statements contain material misstatements. The opinion will be expressed as being '**except for** the effects' (or possible effects) of the matter that the qualification relates to. The misstatements (or possible misstatements) will be material but not pervasive.

Disclaimer of opinion

Where the auditor is unable to obtain sufficient appropriate audit evidence and the possible effects are both material and **pervasive**, the auditor is unable to express an opinion on the financial statements and a **disclaimer of opinion** will be expressed.

Adverse opinion

Where the auditor concludes the accounts are materially misstated and the misstatements are both **material and pervasive,** the financial statements are misleading, and an **adverse opinion** will be expressed.

81 Reporting

Text reference. Chapter 19

Top tips. This 10 mark short question is split into three parts and tests your knowledge of reporting. As with all the 10 mark questions, make sure you do not spend too long on this question overall and stick to the time allocations for each part. Note that the requirements in parts (a) and (b) are to 'list' and for part (c) to 'explain'.

Easy marks. This question should present you with no real problems as this is a key syllabus areas which you should be very comfortable with.

(a) Examples of other information

- A report by management or those charged with governance on operations
- Financial summaries or highlights
- Employment data
- Planned capital expenditures
- Financial ratios
- Names of officers and directors
- Selected quarterly data

(*Note.* Only six were required.)

(b) Audit report elements

- Title
- Addressee
- Introductory paragraph
- Description of management's responsibility for the financial statements
- Statement of auditor's responsibility
- Opinion paragraph
- Date of the report
- Auditor's address
- Auditor's signature

(c) Modified reports on review engagements

If there is a limitation on the scope of the work the auditor intended to carry out, he should describe the limitation in the report. If it is material to one area, he should express a qualified opinion of negative assurance due to amendments which might be required if the limitation did not exist. If it is pervasive, he should not provide any assurance.

If matters have come to the auditor's attention, he should describe them in the report. If the matter is material, he should express a qualified opinion of negative assurance. If it is pervasive, he should express an adverse opinion that the financial statements do not give a true and fair view.

82 Corsco

Text references. Chapters 18 and 19

Top tips. This question considers the issue of going concern and the potential impact on the audit report. This is primarily a technical question so the key will be to use your knowledge of ISA 570 and ISA 700/705/706. You do need to adopt a thorough approach, so for example in part (b) you need to consider **all** the possible scenarios where going concern might be called into question. Parts (c) and (d) are slightly trickier. For part (c) do not jump to conclusions but make sure you read all the information and weigh it up. Also remember that qualified opinions are issued relatively infrequently. In part (d) you need to think as practically as possible. Notice that you are asked to consider the difficulties which would be faced by both Corsco and the auditors.

Easy marks. There are no easy marks as such in this question although if you have a good knowledge of ISA 570 all the marks available are equally achievable. Parts (a) and (b) are slightly more straightforward as they do not involve application but you do need to give a reasonably detailed answer to score well.

Examiner's comments. Part (b) was not well answered. Answers were too general and few were able to properly describe the unqualified audit report with a paragraph referring to the significant uncertainty. In part (c) too many candidates assumed that a qualified audit opinion would be required. Going concern issues in practice are almost always dealt with by means of an unqualified (unmodified) opinion with a reference to the going concern issue. Part (d) was well answered. Please note that there is no verb to 'unqualify'.

Marking scheme

		Marks
(a)	External auditor responsibilities – going concern Up to 1 mark per point to a maximum of	5
(b)	Possible audit reports and circumstances Up to 1.5 marks per point to a maximum of	5
(c)	Report issued to Corsco Up to 2 marks per point to a maximum of	4
(d)	Difficulties associated with reporting on going concern Up to 1.5 marks per point to a maximum of	6
		20

(a) **External auditor's responsibilities and the work that the auditor should perform in relation to going concern**

(i) *Responsibilities*

According to ISA 570 the auditor must:

- Evaluate **management's assessment** of the entity's ability to continue as a going concern
- Consider whether there are, and remain alert throughout the audit for, events or conditions that may cast significant doubt on the entity's ability to continue as a going concern
- Enquire of management its knowledge of events or conditions beyond the period of the assessment that may cast significant doubt on the entity's ability to continue as a going concern
- Obtain sufficient appropriate audit evidence to determine whether a material uncertainty exists if events or conditions are identified that may cast significant doubt on the entity's ability to continue as a going concern

(ii) *Audit work*

- As part of the overall risk assessment the auditor must consider whether there are any events or conditions and related business risks which may cast significant doubt on the company's ability to continue.
- The auditor should evaluate the process by which management has assessed the viability of the company. The auditor should make enquiries of those charged with governance and examine supporting documentation such as cash flow forecasts and budgets.
- The auditor must consider whether the period used by management to assess the viability of the company is sufficient. If the period covers less than twelve months from the reporting date the auditor should ask management to extend the period to twelve months from the reporting date.
- The auditor should evaluate the assumptions used by management and determine whether they seem reasonable in the light of other known facts.
- Where events or conditions have been identified which may cast significant doubt on the entity's ability to continue as a going concern the auditor must review management's plans for future actions and gather sufficient appropriate audit evidence to confirm whether a material uncertainty exists. This will include:
  - Analysing and discussing the cash flow and interim financial statements
  - Reviewing the terms of debentures and loan agreements
  - Reading minutes of the meetings of shareholders and directors for reference to financing difficulties
  - Inquiring of the company's lawyers regarding litigation and claims

- Assessing the possibility of raising additional funds
- Reviewing events after the period end

- The auditor must seek written representations from management regarding its plans for future action.

(b) **Audit reports**

(i) Where the use of the going concern assumption is appropriate but a material uncertainty exists, provided that the auditor agrees with the basis of preparation of the accounts and the situation is adequately disclosed, an **unmodified opinion** is issued. The audit report will however include an **emphasis of matter paragraph** highlighting the uncertainty to the user and referring them to the details in the disclosure note.

(ii) Where the material uncertainty exists but the situation is not adequately disclosed the opinion should be **modified on the grounds that there is** insufficient disclosure and the financial statements are materially misstated. Depending on the specific circumstances this may be a qualified 'except for' or adverse opinion.

(iii) If in the auditor's judgement the company will not be able to continue as a going concern and the financial statements have been prepared on a going concern basis the auditor shall express **an adverse opinion**.

(iv) If the auditors are unable to form an opinion because they were not able to obtain sufficient appropriate audit evidence they shall issue **an 'except for' qualified opinion or a disclaimer**.

(v) If management is unwilling to extend its assessment where the period considered is less than twelve months from the reporting date the auditor shall consider **the need to modify** the opinion as a result of not obtaining this evidence

(c) **Report issued to Corsco**

Although the company is obviously experiencing some difficulties the evidence provided does not suggest that the business will cease to trade in the near future. The company has net assets and still appears to have options available to it in order to resolve its problems. The fact that the company has taken steps to restructure its finance and has been able to do so is also a positive sign.

On the basis that the situation is no worse than in previous years and that no reference has been made to going concern in the past it would not seem appropriate to refer to it this year. An audit report with an unmodified audit opinion would be issued.

(d) **Difficulties**

If the audit report mentions a going concern problem it is likely that Corsco will find it difficult to raise finance and customers and suppliers may be more cautious to do business with them. It is often said that it becomes a 'self-fulfilling prophecy' although this should not dissuade the auditor from modifying the audit opinion if the auditor feels there is genuine need.

The relationship between the auditor and the management of Corsco could become very strained particularly where the management of Corsco genuinely believe that no reference is required. This is particularly difficult as the matter is essentially one of judgement and will rarely be cut and dried. In extreme circumstances the auditors may lose the audit and fees from associated work.

As there has been no reference to going concern in the past to refer to it this year would suggest that the situation has deteriorated further (which contradicts the evidence) or that previous reports were not correct. This is a particularly contentious issue as there is ongoing public concern about the role of the auditor in warning shareholders about matters which will affect the value of their investment.

83 Hood Enterprises

Text reference. Chapter 19

Top tips. Parts (a) and (c) of this question should be reasonably straightforward as you should be familiar with directors' and auditors' responsibilities and with the difference between positive and negative assurance. In part (b), take a methodical approach and look at each sentence in turn.

Easy marks. Part (a) tests very basic knowledge so should have been reasonably easy. Part (b) was harder but there should have been a few easy marks for spotting some of the more obvious differences from what you will have seen in standard audit reports in your study material.

Examiner's comments. Part (a) focused on a relatively small area of knowledge. Candidates need to focus points on the published financial statements. This section was well answered. The main weaknesses occurred where candidates provided a list of duties of the directors that were not directly related to the financial statements.

The overall standard in part (b) was unsatisfactory. The main reason for this appeared to be the requirement word 'explain'. Most candidates managed to identify some of the errors in the report but answers contained very little explanation of why the point was an error. A minority of answers simply stated the contents of a normal unmodified report, which did not meet the question heading.

The overall standard in part (c) was high with most candidates correctly explaining positive and negative assurance and providing at least one benefit of negative assurance.

Marking scheme

		Marks
(a)	**Duties re financial statements**	
	Allow 1 mark for director responsibilities, and 1 for auditor responsibilities	
	Preparation of financial statements	2
	Fraud and error	2
	Disclosure	2
	Going concern	2
	Similar relevant points – each point	2
	Maximum marks	**6**
(b)	**Auditors' reports**	
	Up to 2 marks per relevant point	
	Use of term Auditing Standards	2
	Limitation on use of judgements and estimates	2
	Time limitation	2
	FS free from material error	2
	Directors' responsibilities	2
	Reference to annual report	2
	Allow other relevant points	2
	Maximum marks	**10**

		Marks
(c)	**Audit reports**	
	One mark per point	
	Meaning of positive assurance	1
	Meaning of negative assurance	1
	Advantages of negative assurance	
	Some comfort provided	1
	Credibility	1
	Cost effective	1
	Allow other relevant points	1
	Maximum marks	4
		20

(a) **Preparation of financial statements**

The directors have a legal responsibility to prepare financial statements giving a true and fair view. This implies that they have been prepared in accordance with the relevant IASs and IFRSs.

The auditor's duty is to carry out an audit (according to the International Standards on Auditing) and to give an opinion on whether a true and fair view is given (or whether the financial statements present fairly, in all material respects, the financial position of the entity). In doing this they will have to consider whether the relevant accounting standards have been properly followed.

Estimates and judgements and accounting policies

The directors have the responsibility for making the estimates and judgements underlying the financial statements and for selecting the appropriate accounting policies.

The auditor's responsibility is to assess the appropriateness of the directors' judgements and to modify the audit opinion in the case of any disagreement causing the auditors to conclude the financial statements are not free from material misstatement.

Fraud and error

The directors have a duty to prevent and detect fraud and error. This is a duty they owe to the shareholders and there is no 'materiality' threshold attached to their duty.

The auditor is responsible (under ISA 240) for obtaining reasonable assurance that the financial statements are free from material misstatement including material misstatement caused by fraud.

The auditor is responsible for maintaining **professional scepticism** throughout the audit, considering the possibility of management override of controls. The audit team must discuss how and where the entity's financial statements may be susceptible to material misstatement due to fraud, including how fraud might occur.

Disclosure

The directors are responsible for disclosing all information required by law and accounting standards.

The auditor's responsibility is to review whether all the disclosure rules have been followed and whether the overall disclosure is adequate. There are certain pieces of information, which, if not disclosed by the directors, must be disclosed by the auditor in his report. Examples of this are related party transactions and transactions with directors.

Going concern

The directors are responsible for assessing whether it is appropriate to treat the business as a going concern. In doing this they should look at forecasts and predictions for at least twelve months from the reporting date. They should also disclose any significant uncertainties over the going concern status of the company.

The auditors' responsibility is to consider whether there are any indicators of going concern problems in the company, and assess the forecasts made by directors and decide whether the correct accounting basis has been used and whether there is adequate disclosure of significant uncertainties.

The auditor must consider modifying the audit opinion in the auditor's report if:

(i) The directors have considered a period of less than twelve months from the reporting date (this could result in a qualified opinion due to an inability to obtain sufficient appropriate evidence)

(ii) The directors have used the going concern basis when the auditor believes that its use is not appropriate (this will be a result in an adverse opinion)

(iii) The auditor agrees with the basis chosen by the directors but feels that the disclosures are inadequate (this will probably result in a qualified 'except for' opinion)

(iv) The auditor agrees with the chosen basis, and that the disclosures are adequate but there are uncertainties over the going concern status of the company. In this case the opinion will be unmodified but an emphasis of matter paragraph will be added.

(b) **Errors in the report extract**

'Presentation of information in the company's annual report'

The auditor's legal responsibilities relate to the financial statements, which comprise the primary statements plus the supporting notes. They do not extend to any other information, for example a chairman's statement, or 5-year summary. To make this clear, this section should refer only to the financial statements.

Under ISA 720 *The auditor's responsibilities relating to other information in documents containing audited financial statements* the auditor has a responsibility to read the other information to identify whether there are any inconsistencies with the financial statements or anything that is misleading, but the primary opinion is given on the financial statements only.

'In accordance with Auditing Standards'

The report should specify exactly which auditing standards have been used so that there is no risk that readers misunderstand how the audit has been done. It should specify that the audit has been performed in accordance with **International Standards on Auditing**.

*'Evaluating ....the reasonableness of **all** accounting estimates'*

It is inappropriate to imply that the auditor has considered every estimate made by management. This is unlikely to be true because auditors do not look at every single transaction and item in the financial statements; it is the duty of the auditor to give assurance only on whether the financial statements are free from material misstatement.

'As much audit evidence as possible in the time available'

This phrase is inappropriate because it implies that the auditor has not had time to obtain all the evidence that is needed. The auditor is expected to obtain sufficient evidence on which to base conclusions. The auditor should have planned the audit so as to obtain sufficient evidence in the time available.

'Confirm'

This word should not be used because it implies a greater degree of certainty than is possible based on normal audit procedures. The certainty implied by the word *'confirm'* may expose the auditor to negligence claims if it turns out that there are any material errors in the financial statements. A more accurate description of the level of assurance given by an audit is 'reasonable assurance'.

'No liability for errors can be accepted by the auditor'

This disclaimer at first might appear to be useful in protecting the auditor against liability. However, the view of the ACCA is that general disclaimers should not be included in audit reports, as their use would tend to devalue the audit opinion.

'The directors are wholly responsible for the accuracy of the financial statements'

This statement should not appear in the auditor's responsibility section of the report. Details of management's responsibilities is differently worded and should appear in an earlier separate section of the report outlining the responsibility of management for the preparation of the financial statements.

(c) Positive assurance is the form of words used in a report where the auditor has obtained sufficient evidence to feel confident to give reasonable assurance that the information is free from material error. A normal audit opinion takes this form, ie 'In our opinion the financial statements present fairly, in all material respects, (or give a true and fair view of) the financial position of..'

Negative assurance is the form of words used where the auditor has obtained a lower level of evidence and can therefore give only a lower level of assurance. A review of a forecast would be an appropriate example of when this would be used. The auditor cannot be as confident about forward-looking information, based on the directors' assumptions.

A negative assurance opinion would be worded perhaps as ' nothing has come to our attention to suggest that the information is not based on reasonable assumptions…'

The advantages of the negative assurance would be:

- The bank will be able to place more reliance on the forecast as it has been subject to review by an independent professional. The level of comfort given will be less than that of an audit but forecast information cannot be verified to the same degree as historical information so the negative assurance is the best that could be expected in the circumstances.
- Negative assurance requires a lower level of work than a full scope audit so will be cheaper for the company.

84 MSV

Text reference. Chapter 19

Top tips. This is a question on audit reports. Part (a) is knowledge-based for six marks and should be straightforward, as discussed in more detail below in 'Easy marks'. You could answer this part in a tabular format, but it's not essential given it's a small, six mark question. In part (b), you have to apply your knowledge to two mini scenarios so take each one in turn and deal with it separately, noting the mark allocation against each. When explaining the impact on the audit report, make sure your arguments are clear and well thought out as this will maximise your chances of scoring a good mark in this part of the question. This part of the question is quite tricky so you need to approach it carefully. The audit report is a key topic area, given that it is the end-product of the external audit, so you should be confident and comfortable with a question on it that tests your knowledge and application skills.

Easy marks. Easy marks are available in part (a) of this question for identifying six elements of an audit report – you should be able to score full marks here, provided you explain the importance of each element you have identified.

Examiner's comments. This question was designed to check that candidates knew the elements of an audit report and, more importantly, the reason for each element. Common errors included:

- Listing the elements but not explaining them
- Not explaining the elements sufficiently clearly. For example stating 'Date of report: the date of the report' rather than the significance of the date – that the auditor had considered the effects of transactions on the financial statements to that date.

Part (b) provided a significant challenge to candidates and was not answered well. Many candidates did not realise that the audit was partly completed, issues had arisen that now had to be resolved and the auditor was into 'damage control' – gaining whatever evidence was possible to try and resolve the issues. Common errors included:

- Explaining how to audit sales and cash receipts and how to audit non-current assets. These procedures would normally have been completed
- Confirming systems notes. Again this would have happened much earlier in the audit

– Stating that the audit report would be qualified but not stating on what grounds or the type of qualification. Information was provided in the scenario to enable candidates to calculate materiality – only a minority used this information.

This question showed that while knowledge of the elements of audit reports was satisfactory an understanding of how to apply that knowledge was generally lacking.

Note. The marking scheme has been revised to reflect any necessary amendments made to the question and/or answer.

Marking scheme

			Marks
(a)	Elements of audit report. 1 mark for each of the following (being 0.5 for the element and 0.5 for explanation for that element).		
	Title of report		1
	Addressee of report		1
	Introductory paragraph		1
	Auditor's responsibilities		1
	Management's responsibilities		1
	Opinion		1
	Date of report		1
	Auditor's address		1
	Auditor's signature		1
	Maximum marks		**6**
(b)	Maximum 14 marks this section (8 for (1) and 6 for (2))		
	(i)	Additional audit procedure	
		Issue one – up to 6 marks	
		Additional audit work	1
		Discuss with directors	1
		Action against director	1
		Management letter	1
		Letter of representation	1
		Other relevant points (each)	1
		Issue two – up to 4 marks	
		Talk with director	1
		Asset transferred to director?	1
		Ask whether any payment made for yacht	1
		Check disclosure financial statements	1
		Check tax return	1
		Other relevant points (each)	1
	(ii)	Effect on audit report	
		Issue one – up to 3 marks	
		Amount is material	1
		Modify opinion qualified 'except for'	1
		Explain why modified	1
		Issue two – up to 3 marks	
		Modify opinion – qualified 'except for'	1
		Provide disclosure	1
		Maximum marks	**14**
			20

(a) **Audit report**

Title

The audit report should have a title which includes the wording 'independent auditor' to distinguish this report from others that may be prepared internally by the company.

Addressee

The report should be appropriately addressed as required by the engagement and local regulations. This is normally to the shareholders of the company or to those charged with governance.

Introductory paragraph

This section identifies the financial statements being audited, including the date and period covered. It also identifies the title of each statement that comprises the financial statements being audited.

Management's responsibility for the financial statements

This part of the report is included to describe the responsibilities of those who are responsible for the preparation of the financial statements including those in respect of internal control.

Auditors responsibility

This section describes the auditor's responsibility for expressing an opinion, notifies users that the audit was carried out in accordance with ISAs and explains what an audit involves.

Opinion

This indicates the financial reporting framework used to prepare the accounts and states the auditor's opinion as to whether the financial statements present fairly, in all material respects (or show a true and fair view of) the financial position of the audited entity in accordance with that framework.

Date

The audit report should be dated as at the completion of the audit, to show that the auditor has considered any events after the reporting period date up to the date of completion and how these might affect the financial statements. The report should not be dated earlier than the date on which the accounts are signed or approved by management.

Auditor's address

The audit report should name a specific location, which is normally the city or town where the auditor maintains the office that has responsibility for the audit.

Auditor's signature

The audit report should be signed in the name of the audit firm, the personal name of the auditor, or both, as appropriate. It is usually signed in the name of the firm because the firm assumes responsibility for the audit.

(Note. Only six were required.)

(b) **Issue 1 – understatement of sales income**

(i) *Audit procedures*

- Discuss the issue with the other directors of the company so that they are aware of the matter and its seriousness
- Perform further substantive audit work, such as detailed analytical review, to confirm the extent of the understatement
- Obtain a written management representation letter point of the estimate of the amount of the fraud

(ii) *Potential effect on audit report*

As this issue is material, the understatement of sales income representing 5% of total revenue for the year, it is likely to have a negative effect on the audit report. The report should include a qualified opinion on the basis of an inability to obtain sufficient appropriate audit evidence on sales for the year. The audit report should provide details of this matter giving rise to the qualified opinion in a 'Basis for qualified opinion' paragraph.

Issue 2 – personal use of boat

(i) *Audit procedures*

- Discuss the issue in more detail with the director concerned
- Through discussion, find out whether the director purchased the boat and if so, agree the amount to the cash book and bank statements and non-current asset register
- Review financial statements to ensure correct disclosure as a director's benefit within directors' emoluments

(ii) *Potential effect on audit report*

Non-current assets on the statement of financial position will be overstated since they include a boat that is used for personal use by one of the directors and not for the purposes of the business. Given that non-current assets are likely to be material to the statement of financial position, this issue may result in a qualified audit opinion on the basis that the overstatement of non-current assets has resulted in the accounts being materially misstated. The value of the boat should be taken off the statement of financial position and it should be reclassified as a benefit within the directors' emoluments notes.

85 Galartha

Text references. Chapters 18 and 19

Top tips. This question examines your understanding of the review stage of the audit and the audit report. It is important that you have a sound knowledge of the basic audit report and the circumstances in which the opinion will be modified. However, as with the majority of questions on this paper you also need to be able to apply this knowledge.

Part (a) asks you to state the additional procedures you would perform at the review stage where the directors have failed to comply with an accounting standard. In this instance there is no specific guidance in an ISA which you can refer to so you need to use your common sense and think practically. You will need to consider the implications for the audit report but there are other actions you need to think about too.

In part (b) you are provided with extracts from an audit report and are asked to explain the meaning and purpose of each of the extracts. Think about what each extract tells the reader and why you think it is important that this information is provided. The suggested answer below is presented in a columnar format but dealing with the meaning and purpose together would be equally acceptable.

Part (c) examines your knowledge of modified audit opinions. When stating the effect on the audit report, remember to consider both the grounds for modification and the degree of seriousness ('except for' or disclaimer/adverse). Make sure you justify the decision you have made.

Easy marks. Part (c) is the most straightforward part of the question. You should also score well in part (b).

Examiner's comments. In part (a), candidates had to explain how they would resolve an outstanding issue at the end of an audit. Errors and weaknesses included stating in detail how to audit buildings, not providing sufficient breadth of comments, confusion over the type of audit report to be provided, stating procedures/actions that could not be performed, and providing a lot of detail on the accounting treatment of depreciation. The overall standard of answers was satisfactory.

Part (b) was on the meaning and purpose of five extracts from an audit report. The main weaknesses were taking each extract as a separate opinion paragraph and explaining it in terms of different types of qualification, stating that the report was for the benefit of management and not explaining the meaning of each extract. Overall, the standard was satisfactory, but did identify a worrying lack of basic knowledge.

In part (c), the requirement was to explain the effect of two different situations on an auditors' report. Common errors were not stating the effect on the audit report, confusion regarding the terminology of the effect on the audit report, and suggesting additional audit work or amendments that could be made to the accounts. Answers varied in standard.

Marking scheme

		Marks
(a)	1 mark each for:	
	– Review of audit file	
	– Ensure true and fair override not required	
	– Meet with directors	
	– Warn directors about qualification	
	– Effect on audit report (material or pervasive materiality)	
	– Draft report	
	– Letter of representation	
	– Other relevant points	
	Maximum marks	6
(b)	1 mark per point	
	Para 1	
	Work in accordance with external standards	
	Work to identify material misstatements	
	May be other material misstatements	
	Para 2	
	Shows auditor disagrees with directors	
	Shows auditor view based on standards	
	Para 3	
	Quantifies effect of non-compliance	
	Shows what depreciation policy normally is	
	Para 4	
	Confirms quantification of effect on financial statements	
	Para 5	
	'Except for' = material qualification	
	Everything else OK in FS	
	Other relevant points	
	Maximum marks	10
(c)	1 mark per point	
	(i) Still disagree – modify report (+ reason)	
	Qualification = 'fundamental'	
	(ii) Uncertainty on one item only = modify report	
	Qualification = material 'except for adjustments that may be necessary'	
	Maximum marks	4
		20

(a) Additional procedures and actions

These would be as follows:

- Confirm the facts of the situation and ensure that appropriate audit evidence has been collected and recorded to date.
- Consider whether there are any legitimate reasons why depreciation has not been provided eg a departure from GAAP is required to give a true and fair view.
- Assess whether the potential adjustment is material to the financial statements. If it is not material no further action would be necessary.
- Discuss the situation with management and obtain an explanation as to why depreciation has not been provided.

- Explain to the management that in my opinion depreciation should be provided. Request that management adjust the financial statements and explain that failure to do so would result in a modified audit opinion.
- Assess the potential impact of the matter to determine whether the modified audit opinion ie material or pervasive.
- Obtain a written representation stating that depreciation will not be charged on buildings.
- Draft the relevant sections of the modified audit report.

(b) Meaning and purpose of extracts

Extract 1 **Meaning**	**Purpose**
International Standards on Auditing prescribe the principles and practices to be followed by auditors in planning, designing and carrying out various aspects of their audit work. Members are expected to follow these standards.	This confirms to the reader that best practice has been adopted by the auditor, assuring the reader that the audit has been properly conducted.
Ethical requirements refer to the professional code of conduct followed by the auditor.	This confirms that the auditor has acted professionally throughout the course of the audit.
Reasonable assurance means that, based on the judgement of the auditor, sufficient work has been performed in order to form an opinion within a reasonable margin of error.	This indicates however that not every balance and transaction has been considered in detail and as a result there could be additional errors apart from the non-depreciation of buildings.
Audit work identifies material misstatements ie those that would affect the reader's assessment of the financial statements.	This confirms that audit work is designed to identify significant issues, not necessarily all issues and therefore the identification of the issue concerning the non-depreciation of buildings is based on audit work carried out.
Extract 2 **Meaning**	**Purpose**
This explains that the accounting treatment of non-depreciation adopted by the company is not conducted in accordance with recognized practice as contained within the IASs.	The basis of the auditor's conclusion that the accounts contain a misstatement is highlighted ie the non-depreciation of buildings. The reference to the IASs gives authority to the auditor's opinion that the non-depreciation is incorrect.
Extract 3 **Meaning**	**Purpose**
The depreciation provision in the financial statements is understated by $420,000.	This explains the adjustment which should have been made in the financial statements and quantifies the effect of the non-depreciation so that the reader can assess the impact. It also indicates the depreciation policy so that the reader can understand the basis of the adjustment.
Extract 4 **Meaning**	**Purpose**
Non-current assets, profit for the year and accumulated reserves are all materially misstated.	This quantifies more specifically the effect of the adjustment on both the position statement balances and income statement.

Extract 5 Meaning	Purpose
Based on the professional judgement of the auditors the financial statements are factual, are free from bias and reflect the commercial substance of the business's transactions with the exception of the treatment of depreciation. This misstatement does materially affect the financial statements but does not render them meaningless overall.	This highlights that the audit report is modified due on the basis the financial statements are not free from material missatement. The phrase 'except for' indicates that the misstatement relates to one specific issue but that in other respects the financial statements give a true and fair view.

(c) (i) Impact on audit report

- The auditor would issue a modified audit opinion on the grounds that the accounts contain a material misstatement due to the continued non-depreciation of non-current assets.
- Due to the significant impact of the adjustment (a profit to a significant loss) the auditor may conclude that the effect is both material and pervasive and issue an adverse opinion. Otherwise a qualified opinion will be issued.

(ii)

- The auditor would issue a modified audit opinion on the grounds the auditor was unable to obtain sufficient appropriate audit evidence. The auditor has been unable to confirm the existence of inventory by attending the inventory count leading to uncertainty regarding the inventory valuation.
- The opinion is likely to be an 'except for the possible effects of..' opinion (rather than a disclaimer of opinion) indicating that whilst material adjustments may be required to the inventory balance in all other respects the financial statements give a true and fair view of the company's financial position.

Mock exams

ACCA
Paper F8
Audit and Assurance (International)

Mock Examination 1

Question Paper	
Time allowed	
Reading and Planning Writing	**15 minutes** **3 hours**
ALL FIVE questions are compulsory and MUST be attempted	
During reading and planning time only the question paper may be annotated	

DO NOT OPEN THIS PAPER UNTIL YOU ARE READY TO START UNDER EXAMINATION CONDITIONS

ALL FIVE questions are compulsory and MUST be attempted

Question 1

Viswa is a company that provides call centre services for a variety of organisations. It operates in a medium sized city and your firm is the largest audit firm in the city. Viswa is owned and run by two entrepreneurs with experience in this sector and has been in existence for five years. It is expanding rapidly in terms of its client base, the number of staff it employs and its profits. It is now 15 June 20X4 and you have been approached to perform the audit for the year ending 30 June 20X4. Your firm has not audited this company before. Viswa has had three different firms of auditors since its incorporation.

Viswa's directors have indicated to you informally that the reason they wish to change auditors is because of a disagreement about certain disclosures in the financial statements in the previous year. The directors consider that the disagreement is a trivial matter and have indicated that the company accountant will be able to provide you with the details once the audit has commenced. Your firm has explained that before accepting the appointment, there are various matters to be considered within the firm and other procedures to be undertaken, some of which will require the co-operation of the directors. Your firm has other clients that operate call centres. The directors have asked your firm to commence the audit immediately because audited accounts are needed by the bank by 30 July 20X4. Your firm is very busy at this time of year.

Required

(a) Describe the matters to consider within your firm and the other procedures that must be undertaken before accepting the appointment as auditor to Viswa. **(10 marks)**

(b) Explain why it would be inappropriate to commence the audit before consideration of the matters and the procedures referred to in (a) above have been completed. **(6 marks)**

(c) Explain the purpose of an engagement letter and list its contents. **(6 marks)**

(d) Briefly describe some of the audit risks that will be associated with the audit of Viswa, explaining why they are risks. **(8 marks)**

(Total = 30 marks)

Question 2

Towards the end of an audit, it is common for the auditor to seek a letter of representation (written representations) from the management of the client company.

Required

(a) Explain why auditors seek letters of representation. **(2 marks)**

(b) List the matters commonly included in the letter of representation. **(3 marks)**

(c) Explain why management is sometimes unwilling to sign a letter of representation and describe the actions an external auditor can take if management refuses to sign a letter of representation. **(5 marks)**

(Total = 10 marks)

Question 3

Professional ethics are relevant to both external auditors and internal auditors.

You work for a medium-sized firm of Chartered Certified Accountants with seven offices and 150 employees. Your firm has been asked to tender for the provision of statutory audit and other services to Billington Travel, a private company providing discounted package holiday services in the Mediterranean. The company is growing fast and would represent a substantial amount of fee income for your firm. The finance director has explained to you that the company would like the successful firm to provide a number of different services. These include the statutory audit and assistance with the preparation of the financial statements. The company is also struggling with a new computer system and the finance director considers that a systems review by your firm may be helpful. Your firm does not have much experience in the travel sector.

Required

(a) Explain why it is necessary for external auditors to be, and be seen to be, independent of their audit clients. **(3 marks)**

(b) With reference to the ACCA's *Code of Ethics and Conduct*, describe the ethical matters that should be considered in deciding on whether your firm should tender for:

(i) The statutory audit of Billington Travel **(4 marks)**

(ii) The provision of other services to Billington Travel **(4 marks)**

You are a student Chartered Certified Accountant and you are one of four assistant internal auditors in a large manufacturing company. You report to the chief internal auditor. You have been working on the review of the payables system and you have discovered what you consider to be several serious deficiencies in the structure and operation of the system. You have reported these matters in writing to the chief internal auditor but you are aware that none of these matters have been covered in his final report on the system which is due to be presented to management.

Required

(c) List the actions you might take in these circumstances. **(6 marks)**

(d) Explain the dangers of doing nothing in these circumstances. **(3 marks)**

(Total = 20 marks)

Question 4

You are the auditor of Fitta Co, whose principal activity is fitting out shops, hotels and restaurants. The company employs 180 weekly-paid employees and all employees are paid by direct transfer into their bank accounts.

Hours worked are recorded on timesheets which are completed by the site and workshop supervisors and submitted to Michelle, the payroll clerk, in the personnel department. Michelle checks the timesheets for completeness and to satisfy herself that they have been signed by the appropriate supervisor.

Michelle accesses the payroll system using a password which is known only to her and Carla, an accounts clerk, who covers for leave of absence. She then enters the hours worked, split between basic and overtime, into a computer and the program calculates the gross and net pay.

A printout of the current period's payroll is generated, detailing for each employee, hours paid, split between basic and overtime, gross pay, deductions, net pay, employer's tax and totals thereof. Michelle checks the hours paid on the computer printout to the timesheets and, if necessary, re-runs the payroll incorporating any amendments, and a printout of the revised payroll is obtained. The following reports are then generated:

Summary:	Cumulative details to date per employee
Payslips:	Details of gross pay, deductions and net pay
Autopay list:	Bank sort code, account number and net pay per employee, and total net pay.

The managing director, Mr Grimshaw, reviews the autopay list before Michelle uses a different password to transmit the details via direct transfer to the company's bank. Two days later a printout, listing bank and net pay details per employee together with the net pay total, is received from the bank and Michelle files it in date order.

On completion of payroll processing Michelle copies the payroll details onto a floppy disk which is stored in the fireproof safe in Mr Grimshaw's office.

Details of starters, leavers and amendments to employee details are recorded on standard forms by the site and workshop supervisors and passed to Michelle for input to the system. After updating the standing data, she obtains a printout and checks the details to the standard form which is filed with the personnel record of the respective employee.

Each month Michelle posts the weekly summaries to the nominal ledger accounts. She also extracts the tax details from the weekly payroll summaries and records the monthly figures on the taxation authorities payslip. The finance director, Mrs Duckworth, reviews the monthly figures for tax and prepares a cheque for the appropriate amount.

Required

(a) Identify the objectives of exercising internal controls in a wages system and discuss the extent to which the procedures exercised by Fitta achieve these objectives. **(10 marks)**

(b) Describe the procedures which would strengthen Fitta's wages system. **(10 marks)**

(Total = 20 marks)

Question 5

Your firm is the external auditor to two companies. One is a hotel, Tourex, the other is a food wholesaler, Pudco, that supplies the hotel. Both companies have the same year-end. Just before that year-end, a large number of guests became ill at a wedding reception at the hotel, possibly as a result of food poisoning.

The guests have taken legal action against the hotel and the hotel has taken action against the food wholesaler. Neither the hotel nor the food wholesaler have admitted liability. The hotel is negotiating out-of court settlements with the ill guests, the food wholesaler is negotiating an out-of-court settlement with the hotel. At the reporting date, the public health authorities have not completed their investigations.

Lawyers for both the hotel and the food wholesaler say informally that negotiations are 'going well' but refuse to confirm this in writing. The amounts involved are material to the financial statements of both companies.

Required

(a) Describe how ACCA's *Code of Ethics and Conduct* applies to this situation and explain how the external auditors should manage this conflict of interest. **(6 marks)**

(b) Outline the main requirements of IAS 37 *Provisions, contingent liabilities and contingent assets* and apply them to this case. **(7 marks)**

(c) Assuming that your firm continues with the audit of both companies, for each company describe the difficulties you foresee in obtaining sufficient audit evidence for potential provisions, contingent liabilities and contingent assets, and describe how this could affect your audit reports on their financial statements. **(7 marks)**

(Total = 20 marks)

Answers

DO NOT TURN THIS PAGE UNTIL YOU HAVE COMPLETED THE MOCK EXAM

A plan of attack

If this were the real Audit and Assurance exam and you had been told to turn over and begin, what would be going through your mind?

An important thing to say (while there is still time) is that it is vital to have a good breadth of knowledge of the syllabus because all the questions are compulsory. However, don't panic. Below we provide guidance on how to approach the exam.

Approaching the paper

Use your 15 minutes of reading time usefully, to look through the questions, particularly Question 1, to get a feel for what is required and to become familiar with the question scenarios.

Since all the questions in this paper are compulsory, it is vital that you attempt them all to increase your chances of passing. For example, don't run over time on Question 2 and then find that you don't have enough time for the remaining questions.

Question 1 is a 30 mark case-study style question on audit acceptance procedures and audit risks associated with the engagement. You must stick to time for this question as a whole and for each of the individual parts. Use the information in the scenario to help you and give you clues. For example, it states that the directors want the audit to be complete by a certain date so this will add to the audit risk.

Question 2 will always be a knowledge-based 10 mark question. You should be able to score well therefore. Look at the requirements of the question and the mark allocation carefully. For example, in part (b), you need to 'list' the matters included in the letter of representation, so make sure you do – don't be tempted to write down everything you know about letters of representation.

Question 3 is on ethics and professional matters. Again the question is split into several parts so take each in turn and don't run over time. There are lost of clues in the scenario so you should be able to generate enough points to score well. In part (b), use lots of sub-headings as this will give your answer more structure. Again, pay careful attention to the requirements for each part – 'list', 'explain' and so forth – these give you an idea of what your answer should look like.

Question 4 is a question on deficiencies in a payroll system. There is lots of information in the scenario so you need to work carefully through this first. A good way to set out your answer would be in a tabular format – in this way you can link the objectives to the potential improvements to the system. In this question, it is vital that you understand the difference between control objectives and the controls themselves. You need to set out your answer so that you are focussing on control objectives.

Question 5 is about events occurring after the reporting period and the potential impact on the audit report. You need to be sure of your financial reporting knowledge here, but there are also ethical and professional issues to address in this question so don't forget about those.

Forget about it!

And don't worry if you found the paper difficult. More than likely other candidates will too. If this were the real thing you would need to forget the exam the minute you left the exam hall and think about the next one. Or, if it is the last one, celebrate!

Question 1

Text references. Chapters 4 and 6

Top tips. This question looks at the procedures a firm should follow before taking on a new client. As such it should be a scenario that you feel reasonably well prepared for. Remember in broad terms that factors might include legal, ethical and practical considerations. In part (a) you are asked to describe matters to consider and other procedures that must be taken. The key here is to plan, as certain points could be mentioned under either heading. For example you could state that the level of fees is a matter you would consider. You could also say that discussion of fee levels with management is a procedure you would perform. You will not pick up marks for mentioning the same point twice. Mention it once and do not be too concerned about which point appears under which heading.

In part (b) notice that the structure of the question gives you the approach to take to the answer. Go back to the matters and procedures you have listed in part (a) and ask yourself why this was important. Try not to simply repeat the same point from part (a) again but explain its relevance, drawing on the specifics of the scenario as much as possible.

In part (d), use the clues in the scenario to help you to plan your answer. For example, it is a new client, there is a tight reporting deadline, potential lack of integrity of management etc.

Easy marks. These are available in part (c) of the question. You should be familiar with the basic purpose and content of the letter of engagement as set down in ISA 210 *Agreeing the terms of audit engagements.* However you need to answer both parts of the requirement (ie purpose and content). A list of contents alone will not pick up full marks.

Examiner's comments. Answers to part (a) tended to be very long although this did not necessarily detract from the number of marks scored. Many answers showed a lack of planning and poor structure resulting in the repetition of points. Common errors included a failure to make a connection between the point made and the scenario and discussing procedures that would apply after appointment such as deciding methods of testing.

In part (b) most candidates correctly focused attention on ethical issues and problems of not providing an appropriate level of service. Common errors included repeating the points from part (a) without additional explanation and a failure to consider the scenario.

Part (c) was generally well answered.

Marking scheme

		Marks
(a)	Internal matters and other procedures before appointment Up to 1 mark per point to a maximum of *Note.* There are many more details that could be provided for the 'professional etiquette' letter – credit may be given for these but not more than a maximum of 5 marks for internal matters	10
(b)	Starting the audit Up to 1 mark per point to a maximum of	6
(c)	Engagement letter Up to 1 mark per point to a maximum of	6
(d)	Audit risks Upto 1.5 marks per well explained point to a maximum of	8
		30

(a) **Matters to consider and other procedures before accepting appointment**

(i) *Matters to consider*

- The **risk** associated with the audit. The fact that the company has had three different auditors in five years increases the risk associated with accepting the appointment. It suggests that disputes are commonplace and are not necessarily as trivial as the directors have suggested.
- The size of the **fee** which the firm will be able to charge and whether this will lead to other work.
- Whether the firm has **staff available** with the relevant **expertise** who can perform the work to the required timescale. As the firm has other clients in this field it is likely that staff will have the relevant experience. However the firm may not have sufficient resources available as this is a particularly busy time of year.
- Whether there are any **conflicts of interest**. This is a potential problem as the firm has other clients that operate call centres. The firm needs to assess the extent of any risk and its ability to put suitable safeguards in place.
- Whether there are any other **ethical reasons** why the firm should not accept appointment. For example there may be independence issues if there is a close relationship or other connection between partners and staff and the directors.

(ii) *Other procedures*

- Seek the permission of the directors to obtain the details of the disagreement from the company accountant.
- Make independent enquiries if the directors are not personally known.
- Seek the permission of the directors to contact the outgoing auditors to confirm whether there are any matters that they should be aware of in making their decision as to whether they should accept the appointment or not. If permission is refused the appointment should not be accepted.
- Request the directors to notify the outgoing auditors of their possible appointment and to give the outgoing auditors permission to communicate with them. If this request is refused the appointment should not be accepted.
- Contact the outgoing auditors in writing, asking them to confirm the details of any matters relevant to their appointment. If there are no such matters this should also be confirmed.
- Review the communications received from the outgoing auditors and assess the impact of any matters noted.
- Discuss a more detailed timetable of events and the basis of the firm's fees.
- Obtain credit checks.

(b) **It would be inappropriate to commence the audit before consideration of the matters and procedures referred to above because:**

- **Audit risk needs to be managed**. Where there are significant questions over the integrity of management in their dealings with the auditors the firm may conclude that audit risk cannot be managed at an acceptable level and that therefore the appointment should not be accepted.
- The auditor will weigh up the fee that can be charged as the work would normally only be accepted on the basis that it would make **commercial sense** to do so.
- It is an **ethical requirement** that the work should be performed competently. This will not be the case if resources are insufficient or staff inexperienced. The firm would also want to reduce the risk of being sued for negligence.
- It is an ethical requirement to consider the effect of any conflicts of interest and the existence of any independence issues. The firm would be **in breach** of the ACCA's ***Code of Ethics and Conduct*** if it failed to do so. It may also find that other clients may object if they believe that a conflict exists between themselves and Viswa.
- The incoming auditors need to be able to evaluate **the integrity** of management. Communicating with the previous auditors is an important part of that process as well as any other independent enquiries which can be made.

- It is important that the auditor is fully aware of the expectations of the client so that he can assess his ability to satisfy these. An outline timetable of events aids this process.
- The audit firm is a commercial enterprise. It is important that the client is aware of the basis and size of the fee. This reduces the risk of subsequent disputes over payment.

(c) **Purpose and content of the engagement letter**

Purpose

The engagement letter should define clearly the extent of the **auditors' responsibilities** and so minimise the possibility of any **misunderstanding** between the client and the auditors. In this way it helps to reduce the expectation gap. It acts as a **contract** between the two parties and provides **written confirmation** of the auditors' acceptance of the appointment, the scope of the audit, the form of their report and the scope of any non-audit services.

Content

The form and content of the letter of engagement may vary for each client, but they would generally include reference to the following:

- The objective of the audit
- Management's responsibilities
- The applicable financial reporting framework
- The scope of the audit (including reference to applicable legislation, regulations or pronouncements of professional bodies to which the auditor adheres)
- The form of any reports or other communication of results of the engagement
- The fact that because of the test nature and inherent limitations of an audit, together with the inherent limitations of any accounting and internal control system, there is an unavoidable risk that some material misstatement may remain undiscovered
- Unrestricted access to records, documentation and other information requested in connection with the audit
- Basis on which fees are computed and billing arrangements

(d) **Audit risks associated with the audit of Viswa**

Viswa is rapidly expanding

The company is rapidly expanding. Rapid growth can lead to overtrading which in turn can result in the company going into liquidation as it cannot continue to finance itself. Ultimately this impacts on whether the company can continue as a going concern.

Integrity of directors

The previous auditors were dismissed on the basis of disagreements with the two directors. In fact, Viswa has had three different auditors since its incorporation five years ago. This may mean that the directors are prepared to bully the auditors to do as they wish and calls into question their integrity.

Tight reporting deadline for audit

The directors want the firm to start the audit immediately as audited accounts are required by the bank a month after the year-end. This increases the detection risk of the audit as the audit firm will be under time pressure and will also lack evidence of events occurring after the reporting period.

Reliance on financial statements by the bank

The directors of Viswa are meeting with the bank and will want to present a healthy set of accounts to them, in order to secure more borrowing for instance. This increases the risk that figures in the accounts are manipulated and hence misstated. There will also be increased risk of error in figures that are subjective such as provisions.

New audit client

Viswa will be a new audit client for the firm and although it does have other call centre companies in its portfolio, this increases the detection risk of the audit as the firm has had no previous experience of the company. This means it will be more difficult to identify areas of risk.

Question 2

Text reference. Chapter 18

Top tips. This question is quite structured so take each part in turn and deal with it, noting the mark allocation against each one and ensuring that you spend the appropriate time on each section of the question. Note the requirements in parts (a) and (d) to 'explain why' – this means that your answer should not just consist of a list of bullet points but that you must develop each point more fully. This question assumes a good knowledge of ISA 580 *Written representations* so make sure you are familiar with this area of the syllabus as it could come up in scenario-based questions about audit evidence or in a knowledge-based context, as in this case.

Easy marks. The requirements for this question are not difficult however so with sound technical knowledge you should be able to pick up good marks in part (a) and (b).

Examiner's comments. There were few good answers to this question with many candidates confusing this with the engagement letter or letter of weakness. Many thought that where the letter of representation could not be obtained the answer was to obtain other evidence. This demonstrated a failure to realise that by its very nature the letter of representation covers matters where there is little alternative evidence.

Marking scheme

		Marks
(a)	Letter of representation Up to 1 mark per point to maximum of	2
(b)	Common categories of matter included in the letter of representation ½ mark per point to maximum of	3
(c)	Management unwilling to sign and action if management refuses to sign Up to 1.5 marks per point to maximum of	5
		10

(a) **Letters of representation**

During an audit many representations are made to the auditor, usually in response to specific queries. Where the auditor considers that other **sufficient appropriate evidence is not expected to exist,** written confirmation is sought. This might include instances for example where knowledge of the facts is confined to management or where the matter is principally one of judgement. This reduces the possibility of misunderstandings arising.

Written representations should not however, be a substitute for other independent evidence.

The letter may also be used to obtain confirmations regarding more general matters. These are listed in points (i) – (iii) below.

(b) **Matters commonly included**

(i) Acknowledgement of directors' responsibility for the preparation and presentation of the financial statements

(ii) Confirmation that the transactions of the company have been recorded in the books and records and that all of these have been made available to the auditor

(iii) Opinion as to the expected outcome of any legal claims

(iv) Assumptions used in respect of tax treatments

(v) Confirmation as to the existence or otherwise of related party transactions

(vi) That there have been no events since the end of the reporting period which require revision of the accounts

(c) **Actions**

(i) In some instances the directors may be unwilling to sign the letter. This may be because they genuinely feel unable to confirm some of the information included. Alternatively it may be that they have not been entirely open with the auditor about some of the information provided and whilst they are willing to make statements orally, they are less prepared to confirm them in writing.

(ii) If the directors refuse to sign, the auditor must **discuss** the matter with the directors to determine the reason and attempt to come to a compromise which is acceptable to all.

If this is unsuccessful the auditor could **send a letter** setting out his understanding and ask for management confirmation. If management does not reply, the auditor should follow up to ascertain that his understanding is correct.

If this is still unsuccessful and the required representations cannot be obtained the auditor will need to consider the impact of being unable to obtain this evidence on the audit report. The auditor will need to consider whether the **audit opinion** will be qualified or a disclaimer issued due to the auditor being unable to obtain sufficient appropriate audit evidence.

Question 3

Text reference. Chapter 5

Top tips. This question examines ethics from the point of view of the external and internal auditors. You may find the second part of the question more difficult. Try to think logically, and apply what you know. As has been said a number of times already in this kit, it is important to be comfortable with internal audit issues. Remember, you are likely to be awarded a mark for each valid point you make. So, in part (a), three bullet pointed (relevant) reasons will be sufficient to obtain your marks. Apply this logic to each part you attempt.

Easy marks. These can be found in parts (a) and (b) of the question. Make sure you can explain the basic principle of independence. Application of the ACCA's *Code of Ethics and Conduct* is also a popular exam topic.

Marking scheme

				Marks
(a)	Independence of auditors			
	Up to 1 mark per point to maximum of			3
(b)	Ethical matters			
	(i)	Audit of Billington Travel		
		Skill and resources	2	
		Level of fee income	1	
		Conflict of interest	1	
				4
	(ii)	Other services	2	
		Independence	1	
		Skill and resources	1	
		Level of fee income		4
(c)	Actions to take			
	Up to 1 mark per point to a maximum of			6

		Marks
(d)	Risks of doing nothing Up to 1 mark per point to a maximum of	3 20

(a) **External auditor independence**

There are several reasons why external auditors need to be, and be seen to be independent.

(i) Auditors are required to give an **impartial view** as to whether accounts show a true and fair view to the owners of the company. They must be independent of management to do this.

(ii) The professional body, ACCA requires that firms are independent and may discipline firms that do not follow **ethical guidance**.

(iii) **Legislation** in many countries requires auditors to be independent of their clients.

(b) **Ethical matters**

(i) *Statutory audit considerations*

When deciding if the firm should tender for the statutory audit of Billington Travel, the ethical matters to consider are:

- Whether the firm has the **necessary skill** to undertake the audit. They do not have very much experience in the travel sector.
- Whether the level of the **fee income** (for the audit itself, and then combined with any other services undertaken), would make Billington's fees above 15% of total income.

  This would mean that the level of fees was higher than what is recommended by the ethical guide and would imply that the firm would not be sufficiently independent of the client to take the work.
- Whether undertaking the audit of Billington would cause a conflict of interest to arise with another client. This is unlikely, given their lack of experience in the travel sector.
- They must ensure that they have the staff available at the appropriate time to do the audit if their tender is successful.

(ii) *Other services considerations*

When deciding whether to tender to provide services other than audit to Billington Travel, the ethical matters to consider are:

- Whether the provision of services other than the audit will affect their **independence** to do the audit.

  This can be viewed in fee terms, and whether the other work will require them to make any management decisions, or review their own work. Preparing the accounts for a small private company is allowed by the ethical rules, if the directors accept responsibility for the accounting records.

  The firms will have to put some safeguards in place, however. They should ensure, where possible, that different staff prepare and audit the accounts. They should also discover why the client does not have the necessary skill to put together accounts and consider giving them assistance in this area.
- Whether they have **necessary skills** to undertake the work.

  A one-off review of a computer system should not affect independence. No management decisions would be made for the client. This could be seen as a systems review, adding value to the service of the auditor. It will also assist them to gain knowledge of the business to undertake the audit.

However, if they do not possess enough IT knowledge to do an appropriate review, they should not tender for the work.

- As noted above, whether the **additional fee income** will affect the independence of the firm to do the audit.

Internal audit issues

(c) **Actions to take**

The following actions are available to an internal auditor, in the order in which they are available.

- Discuss the problem with **other internal auditors** at the same level.

  Discussing the problem might reveal that the deficiency is not as serious as was feared. It might show alternative safeguards which counter-act the perceived deficiency and reveal that the senior internal auditor is right not to include it in the report.

  Discussion may also reveal that this problem is not isolated and that other staff at the same level may believe that there are other problems.

- Discuss the problem again with the **chief internal auditor**.

  It may be that the chief internal auditor has misunderstood the point being made or that the exclusion of the issue was an oversight. It may be possible for the chief internal auditor to be convinced of the problem. He might then amend his report.

- Make **notes** of the discussions.

  If the internal auditor cannot convince the chief internal auditor of the issue and feels that the system still has serious deficiencies, he will have to take his issue up with someone at a higher level in the organisation.

  It is therefore a good idea that he makes notes of all the discussions that he has had with the chief internal auditor on the issue, so that he can make his point fairly to those in authority over the chief internal auditor.

- Approach **senior management**

  Who exactly the senior management are will depend on the organisation. Often, organisations large enough to have a significant internal audit department will have an audit committee and such a problem might best be shared with a member of this committee.

  As members of audit committees are non-executive directors, they may show less bias towards the system than the chief internal auditor.

- **Further action**

  The concern is one internal to the organisation, so assuming that the issue does not involve any illegal activity (unlikely), no question of reporting to third parties arises.

  However, if the external auditors were later to seek to use internal audit's work, the internal auditor would be within his bounds to make his comments and concerns available to them as it is his duty as an employee of the company to give them explanations required for their audit.

(d) **Dangers of doing nothing**

A student chartered certified accountant is bound by the ethical code of the ACCA whichever sector he is working in. **Professional ethics** require accountants to be pro-active about such issues as this one. Ignoring this problem could result in the chief internal auditor perpetrating a fraud, for example.

In serious cases, doing nothing in a situation like this might result in the student being **disciplined by ACCA**.

In regard to the ongoing job prospects of the student accountant, if the problem later emerges, the blame for not discovering or reporting the problem may be laid with him. This will not look good on his **employment** record and might even lead to the **loss of his job**, should the systems fail to operate properly and problems arise.

Question 4

Text references. Chapters 9 and 10

Top tips. In this question you need to discuss the extent to which the company has achieved the control objectives of a wages system and then make recommendations for any improvements. The best way to set your answer out therefore would be in a tabular format, so that objectives and recommendations are linked together. This gives your answer much more structure. There are lots of clues in the question scenario so make sure you go through this carefully first and spend some time planning before launching straight into your answer. Look at the mark allocation and work out how many points roughly you need to raise to score well. Make sure your recommendations for improvement are sensible and pertinent to this company – in real-life you would be trying to add value to the client as a result of your audit work.

Easy marks. There aren't easy marks as such in this question but by careful consideration of the information in the scenario, together with your knowledge of controls, you should be able to pick up marks by your discussion points and sensible recommendations.

Marking scheme

		Marks
(a)	Objectives in the payroll system	
	Correct employees paid	2
	Paid the correct amount	2
	Ensure the deductions calculated correctly	2
	Correct accounting for the cost and deductions	2
	No fraud or error	2
	Maximum 2 points for each objective must be adequately explained	10
(b)	1 mark per sensible correction of a deficiency identified in section (a)	
	Restricted to a maximum	10
		20

(a)	(b)
Objective: To ensure the right employees are paid.	
Achieved?	**Improvements**
Amounts are paid directly into bank accounts via direct transfer, and this eliminates any cash mishandling problems. The autopay list is reviewed before transmission although it is not clear what for. Unusual amounts, employees, duplicate sort codes may not be identified.	Mr Grimshaw should perform the transmission of data by using a password known only to him and the review should cover the areas mentioned.
Mr Grimshaw reviews the list before Michelle transmits the details to the bank. This gives Michelle the opportunity to change the details before transmission.	Mr Grimshaw should also receive the printout from the bank, review to ensure accuracy of transmission, initial the form as evidence of review and then pass to Michelle for filing.

Objective: To ensure genuine employees only are paid and are paid correctly for all work done.

Achieved?	Improvements
Michelle reviews the timesheets for completeness which should ensure they are all received. Michelle ensures that the appropriate supervisor has authorised the hours worked.	
However she then enters the details and is the only one to check that the hours have been entered correctly. This could result in errors of numbers of hours processed.	An independent review using total hours and sample of employees should be performed after input to the system. Batch control totals may be sued to ensure completeness and accuracy of input.
Michelle does not appear to perform any review for reasonableness of the timesheets to ensure number of hours claimed are feasible.	A review of all timesheets independent of supervisors should be performed to ensure reasonableness of hours claimed. Total number of hours of overtime claimed should be reviewed for reasonableness. Reconciliation of basic hours claimed should be performed each week by an independent person (from Michelle and supervisor).
(a)	**(b)**

Objective: To ensure that net pay and deductions are calculated correctly.

Achieved?	Improvements
Amendments to be made to personnel records are detailed on a standard form by supervisors.	Amendment forms should be pre-numbered and breaks in the sequence should be investigated promptly.
There does not seem to be any check of completeness or accuracy of processing.	Printout obtained by Michelle should be reviewed by employee or supervisor or accountant as appropriate to check accuracy.
Michelle appears to have access to standing data and can therefore make unauthorised changes.	Master file changes should be made only by Mr Grimshaw who should periodically check sample of payslips for details back to source documentation.

Objective: To ensure that accounting for cost and deductions is accurate in the financial statement and in returns sent to the taxation authority.

Achieved?	Improvements
Cumulative details are stored on disc in a safe ensuring that returns can be filed even if data is last from the system.	Storage of the floppy disks could be more secure off-site (eg bank deposit box).
Mrs Duckworth reviews the monthly figures for tax and should identify any obvious errors.	The review could be more thorough and encompass all deductions with calculations of estimated costs and monthly reviews performed to identify fluctuations.

Objective: To ensure duties are adequately segregated.

Achieved?	Improvements
There is very little segregation of duties with Michelle performing most tasks.	More appropriate segregation has been noted above but generally more use of other personnel staff would achieve this objective.

Question 5

Text references. Chapters 4, 8 and 19

Top tips. The key with this question is to ensure that you apply your knowledge to the situation described. With part (a) and (b) in particular there is a danger that you could write everything you know about the ACCA's *Code of Ethics and Conduct* and IAS 37. Marks will be awarded for this (see below) but it is important that you show how the theory relates to the scenario.

In part (c) don't be afraid of suggesting more than one form of audit report. Where circumstances are uncertain there is likely to be a range of possible outcomes which will potentially affect the audit report issued.

Easy marks. The majority of the easy marks can be found in parts (a) and (b) of the question. In part (a) you can score well by demonstrating a basic knowledge of the ACCA's *Code of Ethics and Conduct*. In part (b) you are asked to outline the requirements of IAS 37. This is an opportunity to score marks for rote learned knowledge albeit Financial Reporting. The key is to use the definitions of a provision, contingent liability and contingent asset as a starting point.

Examiner's comments. Parts (a) and (c) were generally well answered.

In part (b) many candidates demonstrated a lack of basic understanding of IAS 37. Candidates must realise that provisions are provided for in the accounts but that contingent liabilities and contingent assets are disclosed at most.

Accounting standards are examinable for Paper F8 and must be learnt. (Those examinable in detail at this level are those examinable for Paper F3.)

Marking scheme

		Marks
(a)	Managing conflicts of interest Up to 1.5 marks per point to a maximum of	6
(b)	Main requirement of IAS 37 Up to 1.5 marks per point to a maximum of (No more than 4 marks for the requirements of IAS 37)	7
(c)	Sufficient audit evidence and audit reports Up to 1.5 marks per point to a maximum of	7
		20

(a) **Conflict of interest**

(i) The ACCA's *Code of Ethics and Conduct* states that on the face of it there is **nothing improper** in firms having two or more clients whose interests may be in conflict, provided that the work that the firm undertakes is not itself likely to be the subject of the dispute. In the case of Tourex and Pudco the conflict has arisen as the result of food poisoning which is in no way related to the work of the auditors. On this basis there is no reason why the auditors should not continue to act for both parties.

(ii) The Code states that the firm's work should be managed so as to avoid the interests of one client adversely affecting those of another. This could be achieved by the auditors of Tourex and Pudco by putting adequate **safeguards** in place.

(iii) The audit firm should **notify** Tourex and Pudco that they are acting for both and ask for consent to continue. Tourex and/or Pudco may decide to seek alternative representation although if the audits have already commenced this may be difficult.

(iv) The impact of the potential conflict of interest would be reduced if **different engagement partners** were appointed and different staff made up the audit team. It may be possible to use teams from different offices of the same firm.

(v) Depending on the size of the audit firm it may have specific procedures and monitoring in place to prevent confidential information being passed on. This is sometimes referred to as a '**Chinese wall**'.

(b) **IAS 37**

Requirement

IAS 37 states that a provision is a **liability of uncertain timing or amount**. It should be recognised as a liability when:

- An entity has a **present obligation** (legal or constructive) as a result of a past event
- It is **probable** that a transfer of economic benefits will be required to settle the obligation
- A **reliable estimate** can be made of the obligation

Application

In this case it appears that both Tourex and Pudco have an **obligation** to compensate for the food poisoning. As the talks are out-of-court this seems to be a constructive rather than a legal obligation. As negotiations are on-going it seems more likely than not (ie probable) that both companies will have to pay some compensation. If a reliable estimate of the amounts involved can be made then the accounts of both Tourex and Pudco would include a provision. However as lawyers for both the hotel and the food wholesaler refuse to confirm the state of affairs in writing there may not be sufficient evidence to support an estimate of the obligation. If this is the case no provision would be included.

Requirement

IAS 37 defines a contingent liability as:

- A **possible obligation** that arises from past events and whose existence will be confirmed only by the occurrence or non-occurrence of one or more uncertain future events not wholly within the entity's control; or
- A **present obligation** that arises from past events but is not recognised because:
  - It is **not probable** that a transfer of economic benefits will be required to settle the obligation; or
  - The amount of the obligation **cannot be measured with sufficient reliability**.

Contingent liabilities should **not be recognised** in the financial statements but they should be **disclosed**. Required disclosures are:

- A brief description of the nature of the contingent liability
- An estimate of the financial effect
- An indication of the uncertainties which exist
- The possibility of any reimbursement

Application

If it is not probable that Tourex and/or Pudco will be required to pay compensation or if it is not possible to estimate the amounts involved a contingent liability should be disclosed in the accounts as described above.

Tourex and Pudco would also need the consider the need for a contingent liability in respect of any fines that they may incur as a result of the public health authority investigations.

Requirement

A contingent asset is a **possible asset** that arises from past events and whose existence will be confirmed by the occurrence or non-occurrence of one or more uncertain future events not wholly within the entity's control. A contingent asset **must not be recognised**. Only when realisation of the related economic benefits is **virtually certain** should recognition take place (ie when it is no longer contingent.)

Disclosure is required in the accounts if it is **probable** that economic benefit will be realised. A brief description should be provided along with an estimate of its likely financial effect.

Application

Tourex has a potential contingent asset in respect of its counter claim against the food wholesaler. The treatment will depend on the likelihood of the claim being successful. At this stage it would not be reasonable to conclude that receipt of payment from Pudco is virtually certain therefore an asset would not be recorded. If sufficient evidence is available to confirm that receipt is probable then the contingent asset should be disclosed as described above.

Requirement

IAS 37 states that where some or all of the expenditure needed to settle a provision may be expected to be recovered from a third party the reimbursement should be recognised only when it is **virtually certain** that it will be received. The reimbursement should be treated as a separate asset and the amount recognised should not exceed the liability to which it relates. The provision and the reimbursement may be **netted off** in the income statement.

Application

It is possible that Tourex and/or Pudco have insurance to cover them in these circumstances. Only if the success of any insurance claim is virtually certain should an asset be recognised. If success is probable the reimbursement should be disclosed as a contingent asset, otherwise no reference to this should be made.

(c) **Difficulties and audit report implications**

Difficulties

The main problem is going to be the **availability of evidence** regarding the outcome of the litigation and the public health authority inspection and the amounts which are involved. This affects the decision as to whether or not provisions need to be recognised or contingent assets and liabilities need to be disclosed. The lack of evidence is caused by the following:

The out-of-court settlements are still on-going

- The lawyers have refused to confirm the state of affairs in writing. Informal oral representations are less reliable than written evidence.
- The public health authority investigation is not complete. This could result in fines being incurred or if severe breaches of regulations are identified could lead to the businesses being shut down.

Audit report implications

- The lawyers refusal to provide written evidence could result in the auditors being unable to obtain sufficient appropriate audit evidence. Unless alternative evidence is available the audit opinion would be modified. Given that the effect is unlikely to be pervasive, a qualified 'except for' opinion would be issued.

  (In the light of this possibility the lawyers may be persuaded to provide the evidence required.)
- The outcome of the various legal proceedings constitute a significant uncertainty as resolution is dependent upon circumstances outside the control of the companies involved and the amounts are material to the accounts. Provided that all the evidence expected to be available supports the treatment adopted by management the opinion would not be modified but the report would include an emphasis of matter paragraph highlighting the situation for the readers.
- If there is an indication that the public health authority inspection could lead to the closure of either business significant doubts could surround the issue of going concern. Provided that the auditors agree with the treatment of this situation and the level of disclosure provided by management the matter would also be referred to as an emphasis of matter without modifying the audit opinion.

ACCA

Paper F8

Audit and Assurance (International)

Mock Examination 2

Question Paper	
Time allowed	
Reading and Planning Writing	15 minutes 3 hours
ALL FIVE questions are compulsory and MUST be attempted	
During reading and planning time only the question paper may be annotated	

DO NOT OPEN THIS PAPER UNTIL YOU ARE READY TO START UNDER EXAMINATION CONDITIONS

ALL FIVE questions are compulsory and MUST be attempted

Question 1

Fizzipop manufactures and distributes soft drinks. Its inventories are controlled using a real-time system which provides accurate records of quantities and costs of inventories held at any point in time. This system is known within the company as the 'Stockpop' system and it is integrated with the purchases and sales system. Fizzipop has an internal audit department whose activities encompass inventories.

No year-end inventory count takes place. Inventories are held in several large warehouses where non-stop production takes place.

Your firm is the external auditor to Fizzipop and you have been asked to perform the audit of inventories. Inventories include finished goods and raw materials (water, sugar, sweeteners, carbonating materials, flavourings, cans, bottles, bottle tops, fastenings and packaging materials).

Your firm, which has several offices, wishes to rely on the 'Stockpop' system to provide the basis of the figure to be included in the financial statements for inventories. Your firm does not wish to ask the company to conduct a year-end inventory count.

Required

(a) Describe the principal audit risks associated with the financial statement assertions relating to inventory. **(4 marks)**

(b) Describe the audit tests that you would perform on the 'Stockpop' system during the year in order to determine whether to rely on it as a basis for the raw materials and finished goods figures to be included in the financial statements. **(12 marks)**

Note. You are not required to deal with work in progress.

(c) Describe the audit tests you would perform on the records held by Fizzipop at the year-end to ensure that raw materials and finished goods are fairly stated in the financial statements. **(10 marks)**

(d) Explain the factors you should consider before placing reliance on the work undertaken by internal audit on the inventory at Fizzipop. **(4 marks)**

(Total = 30 marks)

Question 2

There are similarities and differences between the responsibilities of internal and external auditors. Both internal and external auditors have responsibilities relating to the prevention, detection and reporting of fraud, for example, but their responsibilities are not the same. Both internal and external audit are part of an organisation's overall corporate governance arrangements. Sometimes, the responsibilities of internal auditors are outsourced to external organisations.

Required

(a) Explain the difference between the responsibilities of internal auditors and external auditors for the prevention, detection and reporting of fraud and error. **(5 marks)**

(b) Outline the issues that should be considered when an organisation decides to outsource the internal audit function. **(5 marks)**

(Total = 10 marks)

Question 3

You have been presented with the following draft financial information about Hivex, a very successful company that develops and licences specialist computer software and hardware. Its non-current assets mainly consist of property, computer hardware and investments, and there have been additions to these during the year. The company is experiencing increasing competition from rival companies, most of which specialise in hardware or software, but not both. There is pressure to advertise and to cut prices.

You are the audit manager. You are planning the audit and are conducting a preliminary analytical review and associated risk analysis for this client for the year ended 31 May 20X3. You have been provided with a summarised draft income statement which has been produced very quickly and certain accounting ratios and percentages. You have been informed that the company accounts for research and development costs in accordance with IAS 38 *Intangible assets.*

INCOME STATEMENT

	Year ended 31 May	
	20X3	*20X2*
	$'000	$'000
Revenue	15,206	13,524
Cost of sales	3,009	3,007
Gross Profit	12,197	10,517
Distribution costs	3,006	1,996
Administrative expenses	994	1,768
Selling expenses	3,002	274
Profit from operations	5,195	6,479
Net interest receivable	995	395
Profit before tax	6,190	6,874
Income tax expense	3,104	1,452
Net profit	3,086	5,422
Retained profits	1,617	3,983
Dividends paid	$1,469,000	$1,439,000

Accounting ratios and percentages

Earnings per share	0·43	1·04
Performance ratios include the following:		
Gross margin	0·80	0·78
Expenses as a percentage of revenue:		
Distribution costs	0·20	0·15
Administrative expenses	0·07	0·13
Selling expenses	0·20	0·02
Operating profit	0·34	0·48

Required

(a) Using the information above, comment briefly on the performance of the company for the two years. **(8 marks)**

(b) Use your answer to part (a) to identify the areas that are subject to increased audit risk and describe the further audit work you would perform in response to those risks. **(12 marks)**

(Total = 20 marks)

Question 4

You are an audit manager in an audit firm with ten offices and 250 staff. Your firm is the auditor of Calva, a chain of supermarkets. Your firm has been the auditor of this client for many years.

All of the planning work and tests of controls have been completed for Calva for the year ended 31 December 20X3. Staff are still working on substantive procedures. The company operates a continuous inventory checking system with good records and you have tested this system and will be relying on the records for the year-end figure.

The company is intending to invest a substantial amount in opening new stores during the next year and it has been negotiating with both banks and property companies in relation to leases.

Required

(a) Describe the objectives of the following and how these objectives will be met in the audit of Calva:

(i) Overall review of financial statements; **(4 marks)**

(ii) Review of working papers. **(6 marks)**

(b) Describe the:

(i) Auditor's responsibilities with regard to subsequent events; **(6 marks)**

(ii) Procedures that should be applied during the subsequent events review at Calva. **(4 marks)**

(Total = 20 marks)

Question 5

Homes'r'Us is a large listed construction company based in the north of the country, whose activities encompass housebuilding and development. Its annual revenue is $550 million and profit before tax is $70 million.

You are the audit senior involved with the audit of Homes'r'Us for the year ended 31 December 20X7. The following matters have come to your attention during the review stage of the audit in April 20X8.

(i) Customer going into liquidation

One of Homes'r'Us' major commercial customers has gone into liquidation shortly after the year-end. As at the year-end, the customer owed the company $7.5 million.

(ii) Claim for unfair dismissal

One of the company's construction workers, Basil Evans, was dismissed in November 20X7 after turning up to work under the influence of alcohol. In December 20X7, Mr Evans began a case against the company for unfair dismissal. Lawyers for the company have advised that it will be highly unlikely that he will be successful in his claim.

(iii) In March 20X8 a fire was started by vandals at one of the company's ten storage depots, destroying $1 million worth of building materials.

Required

For each of the three events at Homes'r'Us mentioned above:

(a) Describe the additional audit procedures you will carry out. **(7 marks)**

(b) State whether the accounts will need to be amended and explain your reasoning. **(7 marks)**

(c) Discuss the potential impact on the audit report, fully explaining your answers. **(6 marks)**

(Total = 20 marks)

Answers

DO NOT TURN THIS PAGE UNTIL YOU HAVE COMPLETED THE MOCK EXAM

A plan of attack

If this were the real Audit and Assurance exam and you had been told to turn over and begin, what would be going through your mind?

An important thing to say (while there is still time) is that it is vital to have a good breadth of knowledge of the syllabus because all the questions are compulsory. However, don't panic. Below we provide guidance on how to approach the exam.

Approaching the paper

Use your 15 minutes of reading time usefully, to look through the questions, particularly Question 1, to get a feel for what is required and to become familiar with the question scenarios.

Since all the questions in this paper are compulsory, it is vital that you attempt them all in order to increase your chances of passing. For example, don't run over time on Question 2 and then find that you don't have enough time for the remaining questions.

Question 1 is a 30 mark case-study style question on audit procedures on inventory. You must stick to time for this question as a whole and for each of the individual parts. Use the information in the scenario to help you and give you clues.

Question 2 will always be a knowledge-based 10 mark question. You should be able to score well therefore. Look at the requirement of the question and the mark allocation carefully. For example, in part (b), you need to outline the issues to consider for outsourcing, so make sure you do – don't be tempted to write down everything you know about outsourcing in general.

Question 3 is a scenario-based question on audit risk using analytical procedures. Don't be daunted by all the figures. Go through them line-by-line and note down areas that you could comment on. Your answer to part (a) should help you with part (b) but note the two requirements in part (b) – to identify the risk areas and to describe the audit work you would do.

Question 4 is on the review stage of the audit. The question has been broken down into four parts, so take each in turn and deal with it. In parts (a) and (b) (ii) remember to relate your answer to the company in the scenario – don't just produce a general answer on audit review and subsequent events.

Question 5 is on subsequent events and their potential impact on the audit report. There are three situations in this question so take each in turn, making sure you take materiality and accounting treatment into consideration.

Forget about it!

And don't worry if you found the paper difficult. More than likely other candidates will too. If this were the real thing you would need to forget the exam the minute you left the exam hall and think about the next one. Or, if it is the last one, celebrate!

Question 1

Text reference. Chapter 13

Top tips. The key to this question is to appreciate that the scenario deals with the issue of a perpetual inventory system. Remember that in this case there is no year end count to determine inventory quantities but inventory records are maintained instead. When you think about the tests that you would perform in part (a) think about what will affect the accuracy of the inventory records. What you are really being asked for are tests of controls with the emphasis on confirming the **quantity** of inventory. Your tests need to consider the accuracy with which movements in inventory are recorded (ie sales and purchases) and whether the regular counts which are performed will pick up any discrepancies between book records and actual inventory. In part (b) which considers the year end tests, assuming that you can rely on the system to provide the correct figure for the quantity of inventory the other main issue will be valuation. Here you can use your basic knowledge of IAS 2 to provide you with ideas. Note that in part (b) you are being asked for substantive procedures with the emphasis on valuation.

Easy marks. Easy marks are available in parts (a) and (b). The other parts are quite demanding so don't run over time.

Examiner's comments. The distinction between tests to be carried out during the year and at the year end seemed to confuse students. Many did not appreciate the need for inventory checks to be carried out during the year and described year end counts in spite of the fact that the question said these were not performed. Where candidates explained how the real-time inventory system would be agreed to physical inventory in part (a) they obtained high marks.

Common errors in part (b) included:

- Explaining valuation tests which would have been appropriate for the year end
- Providing extensive details of general controls over the writing of the computer program which was not the main focus of the question.

Answers to part (c) were of a higher standard. Most were aware of the relevant accounting standard and then applied this to tests to confirm cost and net realisable value. Some good comments were made regarding the storage of soft drinks showing that candidates were attempting to use the scenario.

Common errors in part (c) included:

- Explaining year-end inventory counts
- Explaining tests on the payables system which, whilst affected by inventory movements, was not the focus of the question.

Marking scheme

		Marks
(a)	Risk associated with inventory	4
(b)	Audit tests on 'Stockpop' system during the year Up to 1.5 marks per point to a maximum of	12
(c)	Audit tests on records at year-end Up to 1.5 marks per point to a maximum of	10
(d)	Factors to consider to rely on internal audit work Upto 1 mark per point to a maximum of	4
		30

(a) **Principal risks associated with the financial statement assertions for inventory**

One of the risks associated with inventory is its appropriate **valuation**. Inventory should be valued at the lower of cost and net realisable value per IAS 2 *Inventories*. Inventory can be a material figure in the financial statements of many entities, particularly manufacturing companies, and therefore appropriate valuation of inventory is very important, particularly for obsolete and slow-moving items. The valuation can also be a matter of judgement and this increases the risk associated with inventory.

Inventory in the statement of financial position must **exist** - this is another key assertion. Inventory can be subject to theft and misappropriation, and is often held at more than one location, and so controls to safeguard it are very important.

Cut-off is another key issue for inventory. All purchases, transfers and sales of inventory must be recorded in the correct accounting period as again inventory can be a material figure for many companies. Incorrect cut-off can result in misstatements in the financial statements at the year-end and this can be of particular concern where inventory is material. Auditors therefore need to consider whether the management of the entity being audited have implemented adequate cut-off procedures to ensure that movements into and out of inventory are properly identified and reflected in the accounting records and ultimately in the financial statements.

(b) **Audit tests during the year**

The key issues during the year will be to confirm that the system forms a sound basis for recording the **quantity** of inventory and that unit costs are recorded accurately. As a result the following tests will be performed:

- Discuss with management the procedures for inventory checking during the year to ensure that all items are **counted at least once**.
- Obtain a **copy of the inventory count instructions** and review them to establish whether procedures are adequate and will result in reliable information.
- A sample of counts would be **observed** during the year. The sample would be selected on the basis of warehouses where material inventory balances are held and those where the risk of error is increased. The procedures would be observed to ensure that they comply with the instructions. Staff from other offices may be asked to visit warehouses local to them.
- **Test counts** would be performed and the results traced through the sales and purchases system.
- Any reports produced by internal audit regarding the procedures adopted at the inventory count and the 'Stockpop' system design would be **reviewed** and their **conclusions evaluated** (providing that it is appropriate to place any reliance on internal audit).
- For a sample of goods received and goods despatched I would **trace the entries** through the 'Stockpop' system. These transactions would also be checked to the purchases and sales system to ensure that costs are correctly recorded.
- Review all **exception reports** and confirm that exceptions have been dealt with and any necessary adjustments made.
- As the validity of the inventory balance is dependent on the system it may be appropriate to consider the use of **CAATs**. For example test data could be used to confirm the controls over the incorrect input of unit cost data.

(c) **Audit tests at the year-end**

Obtain a breakdown of the inventory quantity and costs and agree these figures to the figures produced by the 'Stockpop' system.

Discuss with management any recent problems experienced with the system particularly those occurring between the last count attended by the auditors and the year end. Confirm the action taken by management to resolve any problems.

Compare inventory levels with those of the previous year and discuss any significant differences with management.

Perform cut-off tests. Despatch notes and goods received notes before and after the year end should be traced to the sales and purchases account to ensure that they have been accounted for in the correct period. Entries in the sales and purchases accounts should also be agreed back to source documentation

Obtain schedule of inventory valuation and confirm it is in accordance with IAS 2 *Inventories* ie at the lower of cost and net realisable value.

For raw materials check a sample of items to suppliers invoices.

For finished goods review and test the system for identifying slow-moving and out of date products. The company should be able to provide information showing the ageing of inventory by reference to sell by dates.

Review the basis for any adjustment made by management for slow-moving/obsolete items. Compare the level of adjustment with previous years and discuss with management.

Review quantities of products sold after the year end to determine that year end inventory has or will be realised.

(d) **Factors to consider before relying on the work of internal audit**

- Whether the work has been performed by staff with adequate technical training and proficiency as internal auditors
- Whether the work of internal audit assistants has been properly supervised, reviewed and documented
- Whether sufficient, appropriate audit evidence has been obtained in order for reasonable conclusions to be drawn
- Whether the conclusions reached are appropriate
- Whether any report produced is consistent with the results of work undertaken
- Whether any exceptions or unusual matters identified and disclosed have been adequately resolved

Question 2

Text references. Chapters 1 and 5

Top tips. This question covers corporate governance and the role of the internal auditor. It also covers another important issue, fraud, and the role of both internal and external auditors in relation to it. It is important in this question that you do not get the timing wrong. This is critical on this question of the paper, especially, as it is very tempting to write down everything you know about fraud and outsourcing.

Easy marks. This question is wholly knowledge-based so should be straightforward, proving your knowledge is sound. As stated above, make sure you stick to the time allocation so that lack of time does not affect your performance in subsequent questions.

Examiner's comments. Parts (a) and (b) were generally answered well, although many candidates spent far too long on part (a) at the expense of the rest of the paper.

Marking scheme

		Marks
(a)	Prevention, detection and reporting of fraud and error 1.5 marks per point to maximum of	5
(b)	Outsourced internal audit issues 1 mark per point to maximum of	5
		10

(a) **Prevention, detection and reporting of fraud and error**

External auditors

Prevention and detection

The external auditors are bound by the requirements of ISA 240. This requires that auditors recognise that **fraud and error may materially affect the financial statements** and design procedures to ensure that the risk is minimised. The auditors have no specific requirement to prevent or detect fraud. However, they must maintain **professional scepticism** throughout the audit, recognising that circumstances may exist that cause the financial statements to be materially misstated. By conducting the audit in accordance with ISAs the auditor obtains reasonable assurance that the financial statements are free from material misstatement caused by fraud or error. However, due to the nature of fraud the risk of not detecting fraud is higher than the risk of not detecting error.

Reporting

ISA 240 also sets out the requirements in relation to reporting fraud. If auditors suspect or detect a fraud, they must report it on a **timely basis** to the **appropriate level of management**. If management are implicated the matter must be communicated to **those charged with governance**, unless the fraud necessitates immediate reporting to a **third party**.

The matter should only be referred to in the audit report if the opinion is modified on those grounds. It may also be that the matter is one which needs reporting to a relevant authority in the public interest. If the auditors feel that this is so, they should seek **legal advice** before taking any action, and request that the entity reports itself. If the directors refuse to make any disclosure in these circumstances, the auditors should make the disclosure themselves.

Internal auditors

Prevention and detection

It is likely that the internal auditors will have a role both in the prevention and detection of fraud. Indirectly, they play a role in their involvement with the **internal controls** of a business, which are set up to limit risks to the company, one of which is fraud. Directly, they may be engaged by the directors to carry out tests when a fraud is suspected, or routinely to discourage such activity. However, if a serious fraud was suspected, a company might bring in **external experts**, such as forensic accountants or the police.

Reporting

If internal auditors discovered issues which made them suspect fraud, they would **report it immediately** to their superiors, who would report to those charged with governance. In the event that an internal auditor suspected top level fraud, he might make disclosure to the relevant authority in the public interest.

(b) **Outsourcing internal audit**

There are various matters to consider:

(i) A major matter to consider is **cost**. It is possible that a fee to a service provider might be lower than the fixed cost of maintaining an internal department. This must be assessed.

(ii) **Independence**. A key aim of an internal audit department is to provide an objective look at the company's operations. An external provider will be more independent.

(iii) **Understanding of the business**. Conversely, however, an external provider is likely to have less knowledge of the business and its staff, particularly at the outset of the relationship.

(iv) Another important matter is **control**. When an internal audit department is truly internal, the directors have control over what work is carried out. To an extent, they may be able to still control what work is done under the terms of their contract with the service provider, but the control over day to day work will inevitably be less. On the other hand, however, an external team may be able to see the bigger picture, and provide an excellent service the directors might not have envisaged.

(v) **Change issues**. When considering outsourcing a department, the firm will have to consider carefully what happens to the staff previously involved in that department, for legal reasons.

(vi) **Choice**. There is much choice of service provider on the market, and the company will have to ensure that it purchases the correct blend of skill, qualification, value and service.

Question 3

Text references. Chapters 6 and 7

Top tips. This question looks much more daunting than it actually is. In part (a) you are asked to assess the performance of a company based on information provided. The key is not to panic but to work systematically through the information noting the key changes. Use the ratios provided but don't be afraid to do your own basic calculations, for example calculating the % rise in revenue. Try to avoid simply stating that figures have gone up or down. Instead you should be evaluating the situation ie is this good or bad, is there any information in the question which might explain this change, is this in line with expectations? These are the sorts of questions which you need to be asking.

Part (b) then asks you to identify the risk areas and to describe the audit work you would perform. Note that the emphasis is on the audit work rather than risk. The examiner is expecting you to identify the areas which need more attention but is not looking for a detailed explanation of the risk itself.

Easy marks. In this question it is probably fair to say that there are no easy marks. That does not mean that you are not capable of passing the question but you do need to think carefully about your approach. In part (a) the examiner is looking for comment supported by basic calculations, ie an appraisal of the situation set out by the income statement.

In part (b) the most effective way to pick up marks is to target the right areas for further work. One way to achieve this is to ensure that you use your results in part (a) to provide the structure for part (b) of your answer.

Examiner's comments. Most candidates made a good attempt at analysing the performance of the company but too many made basic calculation errors. A common mistake was to approach the question from the point of view of a management consultant rather than an auditor. Many candidates ignored the audit work requirement in part (b) and provided business advice instead. Whilst many of the suggestions were valid they did not score marks as this was not the requirement of the question. Those who did address the audit work often used vague and unspecific terms for example, 'further testing should be undertaken'. Candidates also showed a basic lack of understanding in key areas. Too many stated that they would perform substantive procedures on tests of controls and thought that earnings per share was calculated using retained earnings as the numerator. Also note that costs are often 'misposted' (but rarely 'misappropriated').

Marking scheme

		Marks
(a)	Performance Up to 1 mark per point to a maximum of	8
(b)	Higher risk areas and audit procedures Up to 1.5 marks per point to a maximum of	12
		20

(a) **Performance**

(i) Revenue and gross profit have both **increased significantly**, revenue by 12% and gross profit by 16%. In addition the gross profit margin has increased from 78% to 80% which seems high. These figures indicate **strong performance** but could also be the result of errors particularly in the light of the fact that we are told that the information has been produced quickly. This issue will affect all of the figures in the draft income statement.

(ii) Operating profit has **fallen** by 20% as compared to the previous year and the operating profit margin has fallen from 48% to 34%. This appears to be due to the **increase in distribution and selling expenses**.

(iii) Distribution costs **have increased** by over 50% and represent 20% of revenue as compared to 15% of revenue last year. This could be the result of a significant **change in sales mix** (hardware is likely to be comparatively more expensive to distribute than software) or **inefficiencies**. Alternatively costs may not have been allocated on a consistent basis between distribution costs and administrative expenses.

(iv) Selling expenses have **increased** substantially now representing 20% of revenue. This could be explained by the **need to increase advertising**.

(v) The increase in distribution and selling costs has been slightly offset by a decrease in administrative expenses of 43%. This could be the result of misclassification of expenses or effective economies. Overall it **does not have a significant impact** on the results.

(vi) Net interest receivable has increased by 151%. This has slightly offset the effects of the increased operating expenses on profit before tax, however profit before tax still represents a fall of nearly 10%.

(vii) Net profit has **fallen** by 43% largely due to the **significant increase in the income tax expense**. In spite of this dividend payments have seen a slight increase.

(viii) Without additional information it is not possible to explain fully the fall in the EPS ratio. It will have been affected by the fall in profits but it may also have been affected by a change in the number of shares.

(b) **Risks areas and further work**

Revenue	• Obtain a breakdown of sales on a monthly basis and discuss significant fluctuations with management. Any explanations should be corroborated. • Check the accounting policy for revenue recognition particularly in respect of software licences to ensure that it has been applied consistently and in accordance with accounting standards. • Perform tests of controls on controls over the processing of sales orders and invoicing. Sample sizes should reflect the increased risk. • For a sample of sales transactions perform substantive procedures tracing the transaction from the initial order to the posting in the ledgers. The sample size would be affected by the results of the tests of controls. • Check cut-off at the year end to ensure that revenue has only been recognised in relation to sales genuinely made in the accounting period.
Gross margin	• The gross margin of 80% seems high in spite of the nature of the business. Obtain industry information to establish an industry average. • Compare the gross profit margin on a quarterly basis and compare with the results of the previous year. Discuss the reasons behind significant variations with management. • Obtain a breakdown of costs included in cost of sales and compare with previous year to establish any change in the way that costs have been allocated to the expense categories. • Check the basis on which costs have been capitalised as development costs. Those which do not meet the conditions of IAS 38 *Intangible assets* should be expensed. • For a sample of expenses trace the transaction from source documentation to posting in the accounts. • Agree opening inventory to previous years accounts. The position statement audit should provide evidence regarding the quantity and valuation of closing inventory. In particular cut-off should be confirmed to ensure that it is in line with sales cut-off.

Operating expenses	• Obtain a breakdown of distribution costs, administrative expenses and selling costs. Compare the nature of the expenditure with that included in the previous year to highlight any misclassification. • Compare monthly levels of expenditure with previous year and obtain explanations for any significant changes. • Review the impact of depreciation on the operating expenses figures. Obtain a schedule of non-current assets and recalculate depreciation charged based on the company's policy. Confirm that this is consistent and reasonable in the light of the nature of the asset. • Perform tests of controls on controls over the processing of expenses from initiation of the transaction to posting in the ledgers. • For a sample of expenses trace the transaction from its source eg invoice to its recording in the ledgers. • Review expenses incurred after the year end to ensure that all expenses relating to the current period have been correctly accrued for.
Interest	• Obtain an analysis of interest payable/receivable. • Agree interest payable to bank statements/loan agreements. • For interest receivable perform a proof in total calculation based on the interest rates applicable to the different categories of investment. • For a sample of investments agree the interest actually received and accrued for to the terms of the investment.
Tax	• Obtain a copy of the tax calculation to establish why it has increased so significantly. Discuss the calculation with management and confirm any explanations. • Obtain and review any correspondence with the tax authorities.
Dividends	• Discuss the rationale behind the dividend payment with management, particularly regarding sustainability. • Confirm that the payment of the dividend is minuted. • Check that the payment does not breach legislation regarding distributable profits.
Earnings per share	• Confirm the basis on which the calculation has been performed. If additional shares have been issued confirm that the legal procedures have been complied with and establish the purpose of the share issue. • Reperform the EPS calculation.

Question 4

Text reference. Chapter 18

Top tips. This is an example of a question which is easy if you know the answer! In other words if you have a good understanding of ISA 560 it is very straightforward but if you don't it will be a struggle. This type of question serves as a reminder that for this paper there is often no substitute for simply learning the basics of the auditing standards.

Easy marks. Overall this is a reasonably straight forward question. Easy marks are available particularly in part (b) but this depends on a sound knowledge of ISA 560.

Examiner's comments. This was essentially a knowledge based question. Those who were familiar with the material scored well. Those who were not performed badly.

Marking scheme

			Marks
(a)	(i)	Objectives and how they are met: overall review of financial statements Up to 2 marks per point to a maximum of	4
	(ii)	Objectives and how they are met: review of working papers Up to 2 marks per point to a maximum of	6
(b)	(i)	Responsibilities Up to 2 marks per point to a maximum of	6
	(ii)	Subsequent events review procedures Up to 2 marks per point to a maximum of	4
			20

(a) **Objectives and how they are met**

(i) *Overall review of the financial statements*

The objective of the review of financial statements in conjunction with the conclusions drawn from other audit evidence obtained is to provide a **reasonable basis** on which to form the audit opinion. Due to the skill involved in making this assessment this review would normally be carried out by the engagement partner or senior manager.

The auditor should consider whether the information presented in the financial statements is **in accordance with local/national statutory requirements**. This will vary depending on whether the company is listed or not. This work would normally be performed by the completion of a checklist.

The auditor should consider whether the **accounting policies** employed are in accordance with accounting standards, properly disclosed, consistently applied and appropriate to the company. This can be confirmed by performing a review of the accounting policies adopted, comparing them with previous years and discussing any changes with management. In the case of Calva there is no information to suggest that any changes have been made.

The auditors should consider whether the financial statements are **consistent** with their knowledge of the company's business and with the results of other audit procedures. In the audit of Calva this can be achieved by:

- Assessing whether analytical procedures applied when completing the audit confirm that information is consistent
- Whether the presentation adopted in the financial statements may have been unduly influenced by the directors' desire to present matters in a more favourable light

- Assessing the potential impact of the aggregate of uncorrected misstatements identified in the course of the audit.

(ii) *Review of working papers*

The objectives of the review of working papers is to ensure that:

- The work has been **properly planned** and **executed**
- **Key issues** have been identified and that **sufficient evidence** has been obtained particularly in risk areas.
- **Outstanding matters** are highlighted and that conclusions drawn are supported by facts.

In the audit of Calva this can be achieved as follows:

All working papers should be reviewed by a member of the audit team who is senior to the individual who has performed the work. Audit seniors will review the work of audit juniors, and audit managers will review the work of audit seniors. This type of review would normally take place as the audit progresses to ensure that the work performed is of good quality and to deal with any issues as they arise.

The review would normally be evidenced by a signature or initial. Review comments or follow up procedures would be noted. These are often written in red to highlight them. Significant matters would be referred to the engagement partner.

The extent of the review will depend on the materiality of the balances involved and the associated risk. In the case of Calva, a supermarket, these are likely to be non-current assets, cash and inventory. These would normally be reviewed in detail by the audit manager.

At the end of the audit the engagement partner would perform a final file review. This is less detailed than the audit manager review but concentrates on key risk areas and outstanding matters. It is essential that these are resolved satisfactorily before the audit opinion is issued and that there is documentary evidence of the partner's conclusions.

(b) (i) **Auditor's responsibilities with regard to subsequent events**

- The auditor is required by ISA 560 to perform procedures designed to obtain sufficient appropriate audit evidence that all events **up to the date of the auditor's report** that may require adjustment or disclosure have been identified.
- The auditors do not have any obligation to perform procedures or make enquiries regarding the financial statements **after the date of the report**.
- If after the date of the auditor's report but before the financial statements are issued the auditor becomes aware of a fact that might materially affect the financial statements, the auditor must consider the need to amend the accounts, discuss the matter with management and take appropriate action.
- If the financial statements are amended the auditors must extend their procedures to the date of their new report which should be dated the day it is signed.
- The auditor cannot insist that financial statements are amended. It is up to the management to make this decision. If the auditor believes that amendment is required but management refuse to do so the auditor shall express a qualified opinion or an adverse opinion provided the audit report has not already been released. If the audit report has been issued to the company the auditor should take steps to prevent it from being circulated and seek legal advice.
- If facts are discovered after the financial statements have been issued the auditor would need to consider the need for these to be revised and for a new audit report to be issued.

(ii) **Procedures**

- The auditors would consider the procedures by which management identify subsequent events.
- The auditors would read board minutes of meetings held after the year end for evidence of substantial transactions taking place shortly after the reporting date for example entering into commitments for new leases.

- The auditors would review the latest accounting records and financial information including cash flow forecasts and budgets. They would also review any post year end correspondence with the bank and property companies to assess the impact of the outcome of the negotiations.
- The auditors would make enquiries of management particularly regarding new borrowings or issues of shares and debentures which may have been necessary in order to finance the expansion plan.

Question 5

Text references. Chapters 18 and 19

Top tips. This question looks at events occurring during the review stage of the audit. There are three events so take each in turn and deal with it separately. Use sub-headings in your answer so that you address each of the requirements in the question – audit procedures, accounting treatment and effect on audit report. You need to be familiar with your financial reporting knowledge on events after the reporting period and on provisions. You have to explain the effect on the audit report, if any. Make sure your explanations are succinct and to the point.

Easy marks. These are available in the part of the requirement on audit procedures, but make sure the procedures you describe are specific and well-explained, otherwise you won't score well.

Marking scheme

			Marks
(i)	Customer going into liquidation		
	Up to 2 marks for additional audit procedures	2	
	Explanation of any amendments to accounts	2	
	Impact on the audit report	3	
			7
(ii)	Unfair dismissal		
	Up to 2 marks for additional audit procedures	2	
	Explanation of any amendments to accounts	2	
	Impact on the audit report	3	
			7
(iii)	Fire		
	Up to 2 marks for additional audit procedures	2	
	Explanation of any amendments to accounts	2	
	Impact on the audit report	2	
			6
			20

(i) **Customer going into liquidation**

Audit procedures

- Assess the likelihood of recovery of this amount by discussion with the directors of Homes'r'Us
- Confirm the amount of the amount outstanding as at the year-end by inspection of the receivables ledger and correspondence with the customer
- Review any correspondence between the company and the customer to assess the likelihood of recovery of any amounts
- Obtain a written representation point regarding the amount outstanding from the customer from the directors of Homes'r'Us
- Confirm the details of the bankruptcy to documents received by Homes'r'Us from the liquidator

Impact on accounts

The financial statements will need to be amended as this is an example of an adjusting event after the reporting period. It provides additional information concerning the recoverability of the debt at the reporting date.

Revenue, profit and net assets will all be overstated by $7.5 million if the accounts are not adjusted. The amount represents 10.7% of profit before tax and 1.4% of revenue so is clearly material.

An adjustment is required in the financial statements to reduce the receivables balance and profits.

Effect on audit report

The effect of the matter on the financial statements is clearly material. If the adjustments required are made, then there would be no effect on the audit report.

If the directors refused to make the adjustment required, the audit opinion would be modified on the basis that the accounts are not free from material misstatement and a qualified 'except for' opinion would be issued, as the matter is material but not pervasive.

(ii) **Claim for unfair dismissal**

Audit procedures

- Discuss the case for unfair dismissal with the directors of Homes'r'Us to find out background of case, date when claim was lodged and assessment of success
- Review lawyer's correspondence regarding this case as it may have an impact for next year's audit
- Review any press reports in the local or national papers about this claim against the company
- Review minutes of board meetings regarding this case and any other claim cases against the company
- Obtain written representations on this matter from the directors of Homes'r'Us

Impact on accounts

A provision for this claim is not required since the requirements for recognising a provision under IAS 37 *Provisions, contingent liabilities and contingent assets* are not met. Under IAS 37, a provision should be recognised when there is a present obligation as a result of a past event, it is probable that a transfer of economic benefits will be required to settle it and a reliable estimate can be made.

In this case, it appears unlikely that Mr Evans will be successful in his claim and so no provision should be recognised in the financial statements for the year ended 31 December 20X7.

Disclosure of a contingent liability is also unlikely to be required since the possibility of any transfer in settlement appears to be remote.

Effect on audit report

There would be no effect on the audit report as a result of this matter as no amendment would be required to the financial statements. An unmodified report on the financial statements could therefore be issued.

(iii) **Fire**

Audit procedures

- Discuss fire with management of Homes'r'Us to clarify facts of the situation
- Read minutes of board meetings and any reports submitted by insurers
- Review insurance documents to confirm that damage cause by the fire is covered

Impact on accounts

The fire at the storage depot is a non-adjusting event after the reporting period – it does not relate to conditions which existed at the year-end. It is unlikely that the fire is significant enough to impact on the going concern of the company. Disclosure of the event surrounding the fire should be made, together with an estimate of the financial effect.

Effect on audit report

Provided that adequate disclosure has been made of the event and its financial impact, there would be no need to modify the audit opinion as a result of this incident. An emphasis of matter paragraph drawing attention to this issue is probably not likely to be required, provided adequate disclosure has been made in the notes to the financial statements.

Effect on audit report

Provided that adequate [illegible] made of the events as [illegible] there will be no need to modify the audit opinion [illegible] matter paragraph [illegible] attention to the [illegible] going concern [illegible] the accounts [illegible] financial statements.

ACCA

Paper F8

Audit and Assurance (International)

Mock Examination 3

December 2009

Question Paper	
Time allowed	
Reading and Planning Writing	15 minutes 3 hours
ALL FIVE questions are compulsory and MUST be attempted	
During reading and planning time only the question paper may be annotated	

DO NOT OPEN THIS PAPER UNTIL YOU ARE READY TO START UNDER EXAMINATION CONDITIONS

ALL FIVE questions are compulsory and MUST be attempted

Question 1

(a) Explain the importance of audit planning and state TWO matters that would be included in an audit plan. **(6 marks)**

Redburn Co, a publisher and producer of books of poetry, has been a client of your firm of Chartered Certified Accountants for a number of years. The manager in overall charge of the audit has been discussing the audit plan with the audit team, of which you are a member, prior to commencement of the work. The audit manager has informed the team, among other things, that there has been a growing interest in poetry generally and that the company has acquired a reputation for publishing poets who are still relatively unknown.

During your audit you determine:

(i) Contracts with the poets state that they are given a royalty of 10% on sales. Free copies of the books are provided to the poets and to some organisations such as copyright libraries and to others, such as reviewers and university lecturers. No royalties are given on these free copies.

(ii) The computerised customer master file contains a code indicating whether a despatch is to earn a royalty for the author. This code is shown on the sales invoice and despatch note when they are prepared.

(iii) A computerised royalties file is held, all entries therein bearing the invoice number and date.

(iv) The company keeps detailed statistics of sales made, including trends of monthly sales by type of customer, and of colleges where its books are recommended as part of course material, based on reports from sales staff.

(v) Bookshops have the right to return books which are not selling well, but about 10% of these are slightly damaged when returned. The company keeps similar records of returns as it does for sales.

Required

(b) Describe TWO procedures used to ensure that the sales statistics kept by the company may be relied upon. **(4 marks)**

(c) Describe THREE substantive tests you should perform to ensure that the royalties charge is accurate and complete, stating the objective of each test. **(6 marks)**

(d) A material figure in the statement of financial position of Redburn Co is the amount attributed to inventory of books.

Required

State TWO inherent risks that may affect the inventory figure and suggest ONE control to mitigate each risk. **(4 marks)**

(e) The management of Redburn Co have told you that inventory is correctly valued at the lower of cost and net realisable value. You have already satisfied yourself that cost is correctly determined.

Required

(i) Define net realisable value; **(2 marks)**

(ii) State and explain the purpose of FOUR procedures that you should use to ensure that net realisable value of the inventory is at or above cost. **(8 marks)**

(Total = 30 marks)

Question 2

(a) ISA 500 *Audit Evidence* requires audit evidence to be reliable.

Required

List FOUR factors that influence the reliability of audit evidence. **(4 marks)**

(b) ISA 260 *Communication with Those Charged with Governance* deals with the auditor's responsibility to communicate with those charged with governance in relation to an audit of financial statements.

Required

(i) Describe TWO specific responsibilities of those charged with governance; **(2 marks)**

(ii) Explain FOUR examples of matters that might be communicated to them by the auditor. **(4 marks)**

(Total = 10 marks)

Question 3

ISA 315 *Identifying and Assessing the Risks of Material Misstatement Through Understanding the Entity and Its Environment* requires auditors to obtain an understanding of the entity and its environment, including its internal control.

Required

(a) Explain why obtaining an understanding of the entity and its environment is important for the auditor. **(4 marks)**

Letham Co is a large engineering company with ten manufacturing units throughout the country in which it is located. The manufacturing process is capital intensive and the company holds a wide variety of plant and equipment.

The finance director is responsible for the preparation of a detailed non-current assets budget annually, which is based on a five-year budget approved by the whole board of directors after consultation with the audit committee. This annual budget, which is also approved by the full board, is held on computer file and is the authority for the issue of a purchase order.

When the item of plant and equipment is delivered to the company, a pre-numbered goods received note (GRN) is prepared, a copy of which is sent to the accounting department, and used to update the non-current assets budget to reflect the movement. The equipment is carefully inspected by production personnel and tested for proper operation. An operational certificate is prepared by the production department and this is used by the accounting department, together with the GRN, to check against the purchase invoice when it is received.

At the same time as the purchase invoice enters the purchasing system, a computerised non-current assets register is updated. Access to the non-current assets register is restricted to personnel in the accounting department. On a rolling basis throughout the year the non-current assets register is compared to plant and equipment on site by accounting department personnel, using identification numbers in the register and permanently marked onto each item in the factory.

The internal audit department also tests on a sample basis the operation of the system from budget preparation to entry in the non-current assets register. Internal audit staff also compare a sample of entries in the non-current assets register with equipment on the shop floor.

Required

(b) Identify SIX STRENGTHS in Letham's control environment in respect of non-current assets and explain why they may reduce control risk. **(12 marks)**

(c) As part of your work as external auditor you are reviewing the non-current assets audit programme of the internal auditors and notice that the basis of their testing is a representative sample of purchase invoices. They use this to test entries in the non-current assets register and the updating movements on the annual budget.

Required

(i) Explain why this is not a good test for completeness;

(ii) State a more appropriate test to prove completeness of the non-current assets records, including the non-current assets register.

(4 marks)

(Total = 20 marks)

Question 4

(a) Explain the difference between the interim audit and the final audit. **(4 marks)**

You are the senior in charge of the audit of Brampton Co for the year ending 31 January 2010 and are currently planning the year-end audit. Brampton specialises in the production of high quality bread of various kinds.

During the interim audit you noted that, in the present economic down-turn, the company has suffered as its costs are increasing and its prices have been higher than its competitors because of lower production runs. One indicator of the problems facing the company is that it has consistently used a bank overdraft facility to finance its activities.

At the time of the interim audit you had discussed with company management what actions were being taken to improve the liquidity of the company and you were informed that the company plans to expand its facilities for producing white bread as this line had maintained its market share. The company has asked its bank for a loan to finance the expansion and also to maintain its working capital generally.

To support its request for a loan, the company has prepared a cash flow forecast for the two years from the end of the reporting period and the internal audit department has reported on the forecast to the board of directors. However, the bank has said it would like a report from the external auditors to confirm the accuracy of the forecast. Following this request the company has asked you to examine the cash flow forecast and then to report to the bank.

Required

(b) Explain whether you would be able to rely on the work of the internal auditors. **(6 marks)**

(c) Describe THREE procedures you would adopt in your examination of the cash flow forecast. **(6 marks)**

(d) Explain the kind of assurance you could give in the context of the request by the bank. **(4 marks)**

(Total = 20 marks)

Question 5

(a) Identify and explain FOUR assertions relevant to accounts payable at the year-end date. **(6 marks)**

You are the audit senior responsible for the audit of Have A Bite Co, a company that runs a chain of fast food restaurants. You are aware that a major risk of their sector is that poor food quality might result in damage claims by customers.

You had satisfied yourself at the interim audit that the company's control risk as regards purchases of food and its preparation in the kitchen was low. However, during your final audit it comes to your attention that one month before the year-end, a customer has sued the company for personal injury caused by food poisoning, claiming an amount of $200,000 in compensation. This amount is material to the stated profit of the company, but management believes that it has good defences against the claim.

Required

(b) (i) State TWO controls that the company should have in place to reduce the risk associated with purchases of food and its preparation in the kitchen; and

(ii) State TWO audit procedures you should carry out during controls testing to satisfy yourself that control risk in this area is low. **(4 marks)**

(c) In respect of the potential claim state THREE items of evidence you should obtain and explain how they might enable you to form a conclusion on the likelihood of the claim being successful. **(6 marks)**

Following your audit you have concluded that there is a possibility, but not a probability, that the claim will be successful. However, management have decided not to make a provision or disclosure in the financial statements in respect of this matter.

Required

(d) Describe how the matter should be reported in the financial statements and explain the effect on your audit report. **(4 marks)**

(Total = 20 marks)

Answers

DO NOT TURN THIS PAGE UNTIL YOU HAVE COMPLETED THE MOCK EXAM

A plan of attack

If this were the real Audit and Assurance exam and you had been told to turn over and begin, what would be going through your mind?

An important thing to say (while there is still time) is that it is vital to have a good breadth of knowledge of the syllabus because all the questions are compulsory. However, don't panic. Below we provide guidance on how to approach the exam.

Approaching the paper

Use your 15 minutes of reading time usefully to look through the questions, particularly Question 1, to get a feel for what is required and to become familiar with the question scenarios.

Since all the questions in this paper are compulsory, it is vital that you attempt them all to increase your chances of passing. For example, don't run over time on Question 2 and then find you don't have enough time for the remaining questions.

Question 1 is a 30 mark case-study style question on planning, risk assessment and audit procedures relating to inventory and royalties charges. You must stick to time for this question as a whole and for each of the individual parts. Use the information in the scenario to help you and give you clues. For example you are told that royalties are 10% of related sales, so you should be able to use this fact to aid you in thinking of substantive tests to ensure the royalties charge is accurate and complete.

Question 2 will always be a knowledge-based 10 mark question. You should be able to score well therefore. Look at the requirement of the question and the mark allocation carefully. You are told in (b) to provide two responsibilities of those charged with governance and four examples of matters that might be communicated to them, so don't waste time providing more information than is asked for. Describe and explain the two responsibilities and four examples you are most certain of and move on.

Question 3 starts by asking why it is important for and auditor to obtain an understanding of the entity and its environment. The remainder of the question is based on a scenario which describes the control environment in respect of non-current assets. Use the clues in the scenario to generate the strengths in the control environment. When answering the questions relating to completeness, remember that when you are testing for completeness you are looking for assets that have not been recorded in the records being tested.

Question 4 includes a straightforward knowledge based requirement where you are asked to contrast the interim and final audit, and three further parts based on a scenario. Stick to your time allocation for each part and try and relate your answers in (b) and (c) to the scenario where possible. Remember how the uncertainties involved in future cash flow predictions will affect the level of assurance that can be given when answering (d).

Question 5 is a scenario based question and one of the most important things for you to do is to remember that the food industry has its own particular risks. Standard controls and procedures won't get you full marks here. When addressing the requirements relating to the potential claim, you will need to draw on your financial reporting knowledge.

Forget about it

And don't worry if you found the paper difficult. More than likely other candidates will too. If this were the real thing you would need to forget the exam the minute you left the exam hall and think about the next one. Or, if it is the last one, celebrate!

Question 1

Text references. Chapters 7, 8 and 13.

Top tips. Part (a) is largely knowledge based and you should know why planning is important and the matters included in an audit plan from your studies. Remember, only two matters are required, so don't state more than you are asked for. Because there are only two marks allocated to audit plan matters, four points are needed to demonstrate the importance of planning to gain full marks.

Do not be fazed by part (b) just because the procedures are not in respect of information in the accounting records. Here the sales statistics are potentially a useful analytical review tool as they provide monthly trends, but before the auditor can use this information, he or she must confirm the integrity of this data. Therefore you needed to describe procedures which achieve this objective.

Part (c) requires a description of three substantive tests and asks you to state the associated objectives. Using a tabular approach will help you maintain focus when answering this question. Part (d) also lends itself to a tabular approach.

Part (e)(ii) is quite tricky. Although stating the procedures is straightforward, you must add sufficient explanation to gain full marks. Because there are eight marks available you will need to include sufficient detail in respect of each of the general procedures.

Easy marks. You should be able to obtain the majority of the marks in part (a), which can be answered from a basic knowledge of audit planning. There are also easy marks available in part (e)(i) for defining net realisable value.

ACCA examiner's answer. The ACCA examiner's answer to this question can be found at the back of this kit.

Marking scheme

			Marks
(a)	Audit planning		
	Up to 1 mark for any of the following, but maximum 4.		
	Important areas of the audit		
	Potential problems		
	Effective and efficient audit		
	Selection of engagement team members and assignment of work		
	Direction, supervision and review		
	Coordination of work	4	
	Two matters		
	Up to 1 mark for relevant matters, but maximum 2.		
	Risk assessment generally		
	Assessment of control environment		
	Decision to test controls		
	Scope of substantive testing		
	Procedures to comply with ISAs	2	
	Maximum marks		6
(b)	Sales statistics		
	Up to 1 mark each for each relevant procedure, but maximum 4.		
	Reconcile to recorded sales		
	Compare trends		
	Discuss with management		
	Customer codes		
	Reports from sales staff		
	Maximum marks		4

(c) Substantive tests on royalties

Up to 1 mark for description of test and up to 1 mark for stating objective, but maximum 6.

Compare royalties with sales income
Compare budgeted and actual royalties
Review sales statistics
Check whether royalties due and correctly calculated
Agree royalty payments to supporting documentation
Check cut-off
Compare expected and actual royalties
Maximum marks 6

(d) Inventory risks

Up to 1 mark for each identifi ed risk and up to 1 mark for mitigating control, but maximum 4.

Deterioration
Unsaleable – lack of demand
Unsaleable – defective
Theft likely
Poor inventory counting
Poor cut-off
Sale or return
Maximum marks 4

(e) (i) Define net realisable value

½ mark for reference to IAS 2 and 1/2 mark for each element of definition.

IAS 2
Selling price
Less estimated costs to completion
Less estimated costs to make the sale
Maximum marks 2

(ii) Four procedures

Up to 1 mark for stating procedure and up to 1 further mark for explanation, but maximum 8.

On sales price
On costs to completion
On selling and distribution cost
Discussion with management
Maximum marks 8

10

30

(a) **The importance of audit planning**

ISA 300 *Planning an audit of financial statements* covers the general planning process. This requires the auditor to plan the audit so that the engagement is performed in an effective and efficient manner. Proper audit planning can:

- Help the auditor devote appropriate attention to important areas of the audit
- Help the auditor identify and resolve potential problems on a timely basis
- Assist in the selection of appropriate team members and assignment of work to them
- Facilitate the direction, supervision and review of work.

Top tips. You could also have validly stated that planning helps the auditor to properly organise and manage the audit so it is performed in an effective manner, and that it assists in the coordination of work done by experts.

Matters included in the audit plan

Two matters that would be included in an audit plan are as follows:

- A description of the nature, timing and extent of planned risk assessment procedures
- A description of the nature, timing and extent of planned further audit procedures at the assertion level.

Top tips. There are a number of other matters that would be included, but only two were required. Other matters you might have come up with include:

- Assessment of inherent and control risk and an understanding and assessment of the control environment
- Whether the auditor will undertake controls or substantive testing or a combination of both (along with details of how this was decided)
- Other planned procedures required to be carried out to comply with ISAs.

(b) **Procedures used to ensure the sales statistics may be relied upon**

- Perform a reconciliation of the sales figures in the sales statistics to the sales recorded in the accounting system.
- Inquire of management how they use the sales statistics, and whether they form the basis of management decisions (if the statistics play an important part in decision making, management have an incentive to ensure it is accurately compiled).

Top tips. Other valid procedures include:

- Comparing trends in the current year with previous years to ensure they appear reasonable
- Checking customer codes on the customer master file are properly input to make sure the customer type is properly identified.
- Reviewing reports from sales staff to ensure information on university take-up of books is accurate.

(c) **Substantive tests to ensure the royalties charge is accurate and complete**

Substantive test	Objective of test
Compare actual royalties with the budgeted figures for royalties and investigate significant differences by obtaining explanations from management and obtaining corroborative evidence.	To assure the auditor that actual royalties are in line with management expectations, and there is a valid reason for any variances.
Consider whether the royalties charge represents a reasonable proportion of stated sales income and obtain explanations from management if this is not the case.	To satisfy the auditor the royalties charge appears reasonable when compared to stated sales income.
Select a sample of sales entries and check whether royalties had been correctly recorded in respect of these sales (that is, if they are due, a royalty charge is recorded at 10% of the sales value).	To provide the auditor with evidence on the completeness and accuracy of the royalties charge, and to confirm that royalties were due on despatches.

Top tips. You could have validly stated other procedures and related objectives, but only three of each was required. Other procedures which could have been included are set out below.

Agree a sample of royalty payments to supporting sales and despatch documentation, checking that despatches are to individuals/organisations attracting royalties.	To prove that royalty payments have come from a sale and despatch that royalties should have been paid on.
Select sales for an appropriate number of days before and after the year end and check against despatch notes.	To check that the proper cut-off treatment has been applied and only royalties on sales on or before the year end are included.
Review the sales statistics to establish which despatches attract royalties.	To provide evidence the royalties charge was based on reliable information (as proved in (b)).
Using the sales data on monthly sales by type of customer, calculate the expected level of royalties paid by multiplying the sales by 10%. Compare with actual royalties and investigate significant differences by seeking explanations from management and obtaining corroborative evidence.	To gain evidence over the completeness and accuracy of royalties paid.

(d) **Inherent risks and mitigating controls**

Inherent risks that may affect Redburn Co's inventory and mitigating controls are set out below:

Inherent risk	Mitigating control
There may be insufficient demand for books of relatively unknown poets and therefore books may not be saleable.	A record should be kept of inventory movements on a line by line basis to identify slow moving book titles.
There is a risk that the poetry books will deteriorate over time.	Books should be stored in dry conditions and materials should be sourced which do not deteriorate in the short term.

Top tips. Other valid inherent risks and related mitigating controls which could have been stated include those given below (but only two were required).

Books are damaged or defective and therefore not saleable.	Active inspection at inventory counts to identify books in poor condition.
Books are relatively small removable items and therefore susceptible to theft.	Books should be stored in a secure location, preferably with CCTV if this is cost effective.
Books held on sale and return but still in the return period are not included within inventory.	A separate record of books on sale on return should be maintained, reviewed and compared with inventory records to ensure all books still owned by Redburn Co are included.
Inventory counts are not properly carried out.	Independent and experienced counters should be used during inventory counts. Clear counting instructions should be issued and counters should count in pairs using numbered sheets, with one individual counting and the other checking.
Movements in and out of inventory near the year end cause incorrect cut off treatment.	Movement of books in and out is prohibited during the inventory count.

(e) **Net realisable value (NRV)**

(i) **Definition of NRV**

IAS 2 *Inventories* defines NRV as 'the estimated selling price in the ordinary course of business, less the estimated costs of completion and the estimated costs necessary to make the sale'.

(ii) **Procedures**

Procedures appropriate to assess that NRV is at or above cost are as follows:

(1) Develop an estimate of (or obtain actual) sales prices and proceeds in respect of inventory held at the year end. This is done to provide the sales price for the NRV calculation and should involve the following:

- Inspecting post year end sales invoices to obtain actual sales prices for year end inventory
- If there are no sales of the inventory line being tested, obtain management's estimated sales price. The auditor should assess the reasonableness of this, for example by inspecting current price lists or looking at the sales reports from sales staff.
- Having identified slow moving or damaged items from the sales reports and results of inventory counts, the auditor should ensure that these are assigned a nil value.

(2) Establish an estimate of costs to completion (to include in the NRV calculation). This will involve the following:

- The books may be complete, but if not (for example the books are unbound) the auditor must determine the cost to completion using actual post year end cost records or budgeted costs. Any further costs for returned books to make them saleable should also be taken into account.

(3) Determine directly attributable selling, distribution and marketing costs (to form part of the NRV calculation).

- Estimate these costs for the books being tested and whether any apportionment of costs to inventory lines is reasonable (for example apportionment by weight or size for distribution costs).

(4) Combine the three elements above (1 less 2 and 3) to arrive at NRV and compare with the cost. Discuss your findings and estimates with management and other informed staff to gain comfort that conclusions are reasonable.

Question 2

Text references. Chapters 3 and 8.

Top tips. In (a), remember that only factors affecting reliability are needed. Do not be tempted to write about, for example, sufficiency.

Easy marks. This is a knowledge based question and if you are familiar with the two relevant ISAs, you should obtain the majority or all of the marks here.

ACCA examiner's answer. The ACCA examiner's answer to this question can be found at the back of this kit.

Marking scheme

				Marks
(a)		Reliability of audit evidence		
		Up to 1 mark for identification of factors, but maximum 4.		
		Independent source Effective controls Evidence obtained directly by auditor Written evidence Original documents Normal course of business Informed management Evidence about the future		
		Maximum marks		4
(b)	(i)	Responsibilities of those charged with governance		
		½ mark for identification of responsibility and a further ½ if adequately described, but maximum 2.		
		Strategic direction Accountability obligations Financial reporting process		
		Maximum marks	2	
	(ii)	Matters to be communicated		
		1/2 mark for identification of matter and a further 1/2 mark if explanation is adequate, but maximum 4.		
		Matters under the following headings – Auditor's responsibilities – Planned scope and timing – Significant findings from audit – Independence issues		
		Maximum marks	4	
				6
				10

(a) **Reliability of audit evidence**

Reliability is influenced by the source and nature of the information, including the controls over its preparation and maintenance. Four specific factors that influence reliability are:

- Audit evidence from **external sources** is more reliable than that obtained from the entity's records because it is from an independent source.
- Evidence obtained **directly by auditors** is more reliable than that obtained indirectly
- Evidence in the form of **documents (paper or electronic)** or **written representations** are more reliable than oral representations, since oral representations can be retracted.
- **Original documents** are more reliable than photocopies or facsimiles, which can easily be altered by the client.

Top tips. Only four factors were needed other valid factors would be:

- Evidence created in the **normal course of business** is more reliable than evidence created specifically for the audit.
- Original Evidence obtained from the entity's records is more reliable when the related **control system operates effectively.**

(b) **Those charged with governance**

(i) **Responsibilities**

Those charged with governance are responsible for overseeing the strategic direction of the entity and obligations related to the accountability of the entity. The obligations relating to accountability will include overseeing the financial reporting process.

(ii) **Matters communicated to those charged with governance by the auditor**

Matters to be communicated to those charged with governance by the auditor include the following:

The auditor's responsibilities in relation to the financial statement audit

This is communication that the auditor is responsible for forming and expressing an opinion on the financial statements and that the audit does not relieve management or those charged with governance of their responsibilities.

Planned scope and timing of the audit

An overview of the planned scope and timing of the audit will be communicated, including the timing of the interim and final audits, reporting deadlines and the audit approach (for example the reliance to be placed on internal control).

Significant findings from the audit

These could include:

- The auditor's views about significant qualitative aspects of the entity's accounting practices, including accounting policies, accounting estimates and financial statement disclosures
- Significant difficulties encountered during the audit and significant matters arising from the audit that were discussed or subject to correspondence with management
- Written representations requested by the auditor.

Auditor independence

The auditors will state that the engagement team and others in the firm have complied with relevant ethical requirements regarding independence and that safeguards that have been applied to eliminate any identified threats to independence.

Question 3

Text references. Chapters 6, 10 and 12

Top tips. Part (b) is slightly unusual because you are being asked to identify strengths rather than deficiencies in a control environment. However you should be able to apply your knowledge and gain the majority of the marks. In fact half of the marks are available for essentially stating facts already given in the scenario which you consider to be strengths. Ask yourself, what controls in general would be expected over non-current assets? Is there a specific example of this general control in the scenario? If so then you have identified a strength. Don't forget to also answer the second mini-requirement and explain why each strength may reduce control risk. This requirement lends itself to a tabular answer.

Easy marks. Part (a) offers some easy marks for a basic knowledge of the importance to an auditor of understanding the entity being audited and its environment.

ACCA examiner's answer. The ACCA examiner's answer to this question can be found at the back of this kit.

Marking scheme

		Marks
(a)	Understanding entity and environment	
	1 mark for identification of reason and a further 1 mark for explanation, but maximum 4.	
	Risks of material misstatement	
	Design and performance of audit procedures	
	Identification of assertions	
	Maximum marks	4
(b)	Strengths in control environment	
	Up to 1 mark for identification of strength and a further 1 mark for impact on control risk, but maximum 12.	
	Approval of budgets	
	Updating of budget	
	Matching operation adequate	
	Assessment of operation of equipment	
	Independent updating and holding of non-current assets register	
	Independent tests on non-current assets register	
	Internal audit tests on existence	
	Internal audit review of whole system	
	Maximum marks	12
(c)	Test for completeness	
	Up to 1 mark for what the current test does and a further 1 mark for an adequate explanation.	
	1 mark for identification of a more appropriate test and a further 1 mark for an explanation why it is more appropriate.	
	What the test does	
	Why it is inadequate	
	More appropriate test	
	Why more appropriate	
	Maximum marks	4
		20

(a) **Importance of understanding the entity and its environment**

Understanding the entity and its environment (including the entity's internal control), is important to the auditor because it allows the auditor to:

- Identify and assess the risks of material misstatement, whether due to fraud or error, at both the assertion and the financial statement level.
- Assess the reliance that can be placed on internal control
- Design and perform further audit procedures in response to the assessed risks such that detection and audit risk can be reduced to an acceptable level.
- Establish a frame of reference for exercising audit judgement, for example, when setting audit materiality.

(b) **Strengths in Letham's control environment and impact on control risk**

Strength	Why this may reduce control risk
Detailed annual budgets and five-year budgets are approved by the full board.	This gives the auditor comfort that non-current asset purchases are properly authorised because purchase orders are only issued for budgeted assets.
When plant and equipment is delivered, the GRN triggers an update of the budget to reflect the new asset.	This prevents the purchase of duplicate assets.
Equipment is carefully inspected and tested for proper operation by production staff.	This will help ensure the equipment operates effectively and any loss of capability during re-delivery will be foreseen if there is a fault.
The accounts department have access to the GRN and operational certificate and can compare purchase invoices against these as they are received.	This will prevent the accounts department paying for equipment not received or assets which are not operational.
Only the accounts department has access to the non-current asset register and they initiate the updates of the register as they enter the purchase invoices.	This segregation of duties helps prevent production personnel making fraudulent entries on the non-current asset register, a document used for control purposes.
On a rolling basis, the assets on the register are compared to on-site equipment by accounting department personnel to ensure there are no discrepancies	This will reduce the risk of loss and theft because missing assets will be identified on a timely basis. This should act as incentive for production personnel to assist in safeguarding the assets and deter them from misappropriating assets.

Top tips. The testing and comparisons by internal audit are also strengths in the control environment. Their increased independence and work to ensure controls operate effectively would help to reduce control risk. However only six were included above as this was enough to gain full marks.

(c) **Completeness testing**

(i) **Purchase invoice based testing**

Comparing a representative sample of purchase invoices to non-current assets register and the annual budget proves only that those particular invoices are accurately recorded and gives little evidence over completeness.

Purchase invoices form the basis of the entries on the asset register (they are updated simultaneously) and testing one to the other will not detect missing purchase invoices.

Similarly testing from the invoices to the budget will only aid in highlighting an asset not recorded on the budget if that asset was delivered **and** the invoice was received. However it will not identify missing asset entries for items that have been delivered but no purchase invoice has received.

(ii) **Appropriate completeness test**

In order to test completeness of non-current asset records effectively, any sample should be selected from the goods received notes (GRNs) because:

- This document is used to update the annual budget
- GRNs will include equipment delivered even if no purchase invoice has been received
- At the point of delivery you would expect acceptance of a corresponding liability.

To test completeness, GRN's should be traced to the purchase invoices to make sure initially that there are not related missing purchase invoices. Then the GRNs and invoices should be traced to the budget and non-current asset register to ensure none have been omitted.

Top tips. An equally valid test would involve tracing visible assets to entries in the non-current assets register and budget movements (i.e. checking on the budget that they are noted as purchased).

Question 4

Text references. Chapters 1, 7 and 11.

Top tips. In part (b) you can use the requirements in ISA 610 *Using the work of internal auditors* (relating to assessing the adequacy of internal audit work) to structure your answer. It states that auditors must evaluate internal audit's objectivity, technical competence, whether the work is carried out with due professional care and whether there is likely to be effective communication between internal and external audit. However you must remember to fully explain each point to gain full marks.

In part (c) think of how cash forecasts are constructed; they start with an opening balance and future cash flows are projected based on assumptions and plans. This should give you ideas for procedures. For example you will need to assess the validity of the assumptions somehow, and you need to check the correct opening balance has been used.

Easy marks. Part (a) on explaining the difference between the interim audit and the final audit is relatively straightforward. In part (d) you should not have much difficulty in deciding the kind of assurance to be given. You should know that when reporting on cash flow forecasts there is likely to be considerable uncertainty over the predicted cash flows and only a limited level of assurance can be given.

ACCA examiner's answer. The ACCA examiner's answer to this question can be found at the back of this kit.

Marking scheme

		Marks
(a)	Difference between interim audit and final audit	
	Up to 1 mark for each relevant explanation and example of procedure at interim and final audit, but maximum 4.	
	Interim audit and final audit parts of whole audit	
	Interim audit performed during year but final audit at or after the year-end	
	Interim audit performs procedures that cannot be performed at the final audit	
	Interim audit forms interim conclusion, but final audit results in audit opinion	
	Typical work at interim audit	
	Typical work at final audit	
	Maximum marks	4

(b) Work of internal audit

1/2 mark for identification of each factor and up to 11/2 marks for full explanation, but maximum 6.

Independence – to whom report; links to audit committee
Competence – qualifications and experience
Effective communication – between internal and external auditors
Professional care – properly planned and performed
Maximum marks 6

(c) Examination of forecast

Up to 1 mark for identification of a relevant procedure and a further 1 mark if adequately described, but maximum 6.

Opening balance
Accuracy of past forecasts
Assumptions
Sales budgets
Non-current assets required
Increased working capital required
Maximum marks 6

(d) Kind of assurance

1 mark for each relevant point and a further 1 mark for a proper explanation, but maximum 4.

Not possible to give a report on accuracy and why
Limited assurance or negative assurance
What this kind of assurance means
Testing assumptions and reporting on validity
Forecast properly prepared on basis of assumptions
Maximum marks 4

20

(a) **Difference between the interim audit and the final audit**

Auditors usually carry out their audit work for a financial year in one or more sittings. These are referred to as the **interim audit(s)** and the **final audit**. The final audit opinion will be a result of conclusions based on evidence obtained during both the interim and final audit.

The interim audit

Interim audit visits are carried out during the period of review and work typically carried out includes:

- Re-assessing the risk assessment made at the planning stage
- Tests of controls and systems, although substantive audit procedures may also be carried out.

The final audit

The final audit visit is at the year-end or shortly after and work focuses on the audit of the financial statements. Some audit procedures can only be performed at the final audit visit, such as:

- Agreeing the financial statements to the accounting records and examining adjustments made during the process of preparing the financial statements.
- A subsequent events review.

The auditor will also carry out testing to ensure any conclusions from interim audit are still valid at the year end.

(b) **Relying on the work of internal auditors**

The external auditor has sole responsibility for the audit opinion expressed on the financial statements. However the work of internal audit may be used for the purposes of the external audit as long as the internal auditors are:

- **Independent** of the accounts department and have no conflicting responsibilities, constraints or restrictions. It seems that internal audit are reporting straight to the board, but this may include the finance director supervising the accounts department. Ideally internal audit would report to an audit committee.
- **Technically competent** and have had adequate training. Past experience of any internal audit work reviewed previously and knowledge of staff holding relevant professional qualifications should aid in the assessment of the competence of internal audit.
- Able to **communicate effectively** with external audit. Internal audit should be able to communicate openly with the external audit.
- Exercising **due professional care**. In order to rely on the work, the auditor must establish whether it was properly planned, supervised, documented and reviewed.

(c) **Examination of the cash flow forecast**

When examining the cash flow forecast, procedures undertaken would include the following:

- Agree the opening balance of the cash forecast to the closing cash book balance to ensure the correct opening balance has been used in the forecast.
- Consider how accurate previous company forecasts have been by comparing actual cash flows with previous forecasts. If previous forecasts are shown to have been accurate, it is more likely the current forecasts will be reliable.
- Review the assumptions made in preparing the forecasts and consider whether they are consistent with what is known about the business and its environment. For example costs have been increasing recently, so a decrease in costs in the forecasts would need to be investigated.

Top tips. There are other valid procedures, but only three were required to gain full marks. Other valid procedures include:

- Obtain evidence that the cash outflows for non-current assets needed to expand white bread facilities are included and the included investment is sufficient to generate any additional sales inflows projected. Ask production personnel what level of machinery investment is needed to expand production by a given proportion and then corroborate to current prices of this machinery (using supplier quotes if available).
- Consider the adequacy of the proposed working capital increase. Increased working capital would result in cash outflows so determining its adequacy is important.

(d) **Level of assurance**

It is not possible for the external auditors to confirm the accuracy of the forecast as requested by the bank. The forecast will be based on assumptions made by management and it would be impossible to gain enough evidence to confirm these are completely accurate.

Due to the uncertainties of the future cash flows included in the forecast, the bank should be informed that only a limited level of assurance can be provided in any report, expressed in the form of **negative assurance**.

The report will set out the types of procedures undertaken and the assumptions made by management. If no irregularities were found during the work performed, the report will state that nothing had come to the attention of the auditors that would cause them to believe that management's assumptions do not provide a reasonable basis for the cash forecast.

The auditor could also conclude in the report on whether the forecast has been properly prepared on the basis of the assumptions.

Question 5

Text references. Chapters 10, 16 and 18

Top tips. Three of the four requirements clearly state the number of items you need to state and/or explain (whether it be assertions, controls etc.). This should help you to keep to time and give you an idea of how the marks are allocated; therefore helping you decide how much detail to go into for each aspect you need to explain.

Easy marks. A basic understanding of assertions will gain you full marks in part (a) as long as you 'explain' and don't just 'identify' assertions relevant to payables.

ACCA examiner's answer. The ACCA examiner's answer to this question can be found at the back of this kit.

Marking scheme

		Marks
(a)	Accounts payable assertions 1/2 mark for identification of assertion and up to 1 mark for each explanation of assertion, maximum 6. Rights and obligation Valuation and allocation Existence Completeness	
	Maximum marks	6
(b)	Control risk and audit procedures Up to 1 mark for each control identified, but maximum 2. Up to 1 mark for each audit procedure, but maximum 2. Overall authority Approved suppliers Inspection on receipt Storage of food Use-by dates	
	Maximum marks	4
(c)	Evidence on claim Up to 1 mark for identification of each item of evidence and up to a further 1 mark for explanation. Written claim Review controls Inspection reports View of lawyer Representations	
	Maximum marks	6
(d)	Reporting in financial statements Up to 1 mark for assessing meaning of probable and possible and a further mark for showing how the matter should be disclosed, but maximum 2. Meaning of possibility Therefore contingent liability Note disclosure Audit reporting Up to 1 mark noting that modification (except for) would be necessary and a further 1 mark for disclosures.	
		4
		20

(a) **Assertions relevant to accounts payable**

The assertions relevant to accounts payable at the year end date include:

- **Existence** – Trade payables are valid liabilities and exist.
- **Rights and obligations** – Trade payables are the obligations of the entity (services or goods have been provided resulting in an obligation to transfer economic benefits in the future).
- **Completeness** – All liabilities in respect of trade payables have been recorded in the accounting records.
- **Valuation and allocation** – All trade payables are included in the accounts at appropriate amounts.

(b) **Food purchase and preparation – controls and procedures**

Controls that the company should have in place to reduce the risk associated with purchases of food and its preparation are set out in the table below along with related procedures to be carried out during controls testing.

Control	Procedure
Only pre-approved suppliers should be used and a list of these suppliers should be provided to purchasing staff along with instructions prohibiting the use of other suppliers.	Inspect the approved supplier list and ensure only these are used by interrogating purchases data for evidence of use of other suppliers.
Food purchases should be inspected or tested where necessary on arrival. Staff inspecting should evidence this by signing the goods received note or a formal inspection document.	Examine a sample of the document used to evidence inspection/testing and ensure they are all signed.

Top tips. There are other valid controls (including keeping the food stored in a refrigerated and clean place and adherence to use-by dates) and related procedures (examination of the storage area and checking no food is past its use-by date), but only two of each was required in order to gain full marks.

(c) **Evidence and conclusion in respect of potential claim**

Evidence should be collected which will enable a conclusion to be formed on the likelihood of the claim being successful. Once this has been established, it is possible to apply IAS 37 *Provisions, contingent liabilities and contingent assets* to determine whether any provision is necessary. Evidence obtained should include the following:

- Obtain and inspect the written claim by the customer. This should give details of the claim including
  - The reason for the claim
  - Which food is involved and where it was consumed
  - When the incident took place.
- Request and obtain written representations from management on their view of how likely it is the claim will succeed. Although this is internal evidence and not as good as third party evidence, it can be used together with other evidence in forming an overall conclusion on the claim.
- Communicate with the company's legal advisers using a specific letter of enquiry which includes:
  - Management's assessment of the outcome of the identified claim and its estimate of the financial implications
  - A request that the entity's external legal advisers confirm the reasonableness of management's assessments and provide the auditor with further information if they consider the list to be incomplete or incorrect.

This will provide third party evidence from professional legal advisers on the likelihood of the claim being successful.

Top tips. Other valid evidence could be obtained by:

- Reviewing the controls in operation over purchases and food preparation to make sure they were effective
- Obtaining any reports from previous inspections of the food areas to provide details of any problems arising in the past.

(d) **Reporting the claim in the financial statements and effect on the audit report**

The likelihood of the claim being successful is considered possible (rather than probable). Therefore IAS 37 requires the company to disclose details of the contingent liability in a note to the financial statements. The note should include:

- A brief description of the nature of the contingent liability
- An estimate of its financial effect (a maximum of $200,000)
- An indication of the uncertainties about the amount and timing of the outflow
- The possibility of any reimbursement.

Management have decided not to comply with IAS 37 and have not disclosed details of the claim in the financial statements. Because of this and because the amount is material, the financial statements will not be free from material misstatement.

The auditors should request that management include the appropriate disclosure, but if management refuse the auditor's opinion will be modified. A qualified 'except for' opinion will be issued on the grounds that the financial statements contain a material misstatement.

ACCA examiner's answers: June and December 2009 papers

June 2009 paper question references

June 2009 paper question number	Kit question reference
1	30
2	44
3	26
4	8
5	74

The December 2009 answers are the answers to the questions in Mock exam 3.

1 (a) Audit strategy document

Section of document	Purpose	Example from B-Star
Understanding the entity's environment	Provides details of the industry area that the company is in along with specific information about the activities and strategies of the individual client.	Size of the theme park sector and expected growth over the next few years.
Understand the accounting and internal control systems	Details of accounting policies of the client and previous assessments of internal control systems indicating the expected extent of reliance on those systems.	Accounting policy for sales – sales are stated net of sales taxes. Reliance on control systems in B-Star may be limited due to lack of documentation of controls.
Risk and materiality	The assessment of risk for the client and risk of fraud and error and the identification of significant audit areas. The materiality level for audit planning purposes.	Materiality for sales to be 5% of turnover. B-Star receives cash sales – audit work required to determine the completeness of sales.
Consequent nature, timing and extent of audit procedures	Details of the focus on audit work on specific areas. Detail on the extent of use of audit software and possible reliance on internal audit.	Audit software could be used to provide analytical procedures on the sales of B-Star.
Co-ordination, supervision and review of audit work	Details the extent of involvement of experts, client locations and staffing requirements for the audit.	B-Star has only one location – audit staff will be required to work there for X weeks.

(b) (i) Risk affecting completeness

- The computer system does not record sales accurately and/or information is lost or transferred incorrectly from the ticket office computer to the accounts department computer.
- Cash sales are not recorded in the cash book; cash is stolen by the accounts clerks.
- Tickets are issued but no payment is received – that is the sale is not recorded.
- Cash is removed by the ticket office personnel, by the security guards or by the account clerks.
- The account clerks miscount the amount of cash received from a ticket office.

(ii) Use of tests of controls and substantive procedures

Tests of controls

Tests of control are designed to ensure that documented controls are operating effectively. If controls over the completeness of income were expected to operate correctly, then the auditor would test those controls.

In B-Star, while controls could be in operation, e.g. the account clerks agreeing physical cash to computer summaries, there is no indication that the control is documented; that is the computer summary is not signed to show the comparison has taken place. The auditor could use the test of inquiry – asking the clerks whether the control has been used, and observation – actually watching the clerks carry out the controls. As noted above though, lack of documentation of the control does mean relying on tests of control for the assertion completeness of income has limited value.

Substantive procedures

Substantive procedures include analytical procedures and other procedures.

Analytical procedures include the analysis of significant ratios and trends and subsequent investigation of any trends or relationships that appear to be abnormal. These procedures can be used effectively in B-Star as an approximation of income that can be obtained from sources other than the cash receipt records.

Other procedures, or tests of detail, are normally used to verify statement of financial position assertions and include obtaining audit evidence relevant to specific assertions. However, they could be used in B-Star to trace individual transactions through the sales/cash systems to ensure all ticket sales have been recorded (completeness assertion). The use of other procedures will be time consuming.

(c) (i) Substantive analytical procedures – completeness of income for one day

- Obtain proof in total. Tickets sold times price should equal day's income.
- Compare daily sales to budgeted daily sales (for example weekends and bank holidays would expect more income).
- Compare sales with previous days and account for changes such as variations for weather.

- Compare sales to souvenirs sales (more people in park means more souvenir sales).
- Compare ticket offices day-by-day and staff rotation to see if sales lower some day/some staff (attempt to identify fraud also).
- Compare the expected sales from ticket numbers to the total sales amount from cash and credit sales for each ticket office.

(ii) Substantive analytical procedures – completeness of income for the year

- Obtain the sales income from the previous year. Multiply this by 115% to provide a rough estimate of the income for this year.
- Obtain information on the number of days with rain during the last year. Where this is more or less than 30, adjust the income estimate by 1/730 down for each day of rain above 30 or 1/730 up for each day of rain less than 30. (Note: B-Star only attracts 50% of the normal number of customers on a rainy day; hence one day of rain decreases total customers by 1/730 in the year.)
- Compare actual income to budgeted income for the year. Ask the directors to explain any significant deviations.
- Obtain industry information on the popularity of theme parks, and change in customer numbers. Compare these trends to the results obtained by B-Star. Where B-Star performed significantly better or worse than average, obtain explanations from the directors.

(d) Audit of year end credit card receivable

- Agree the balances on each credit card company's ledger account to the list of receivables.
- Cast the list of receivables and agree the total to the total on the receivables ledger control account.
- For the last day of the financial year and the first day of the new financial year, agree total sales income from ticket office records to the cash book and receivables ledger ensuring they are recorded in the correct period.

For a sample of material balances and a random sample of immaterial items,

- Obtain direct confirmation from the credit card company of the amount due to B-Star using a receivables confirmation letter.
- Where direct confirmation is not possible, obtain evidence of cash receipt after the end of the financial year. Agree the amount on the bank statements post year end of B-Star to the amount due in the receivables ledger (less any commission due).
- Review after date sales day book for debit notes indicating that sales may have been overstated in the prior year.
- Obtain the financial statements of B-Star and ensure that the receivables amount is disclosed as a current asset net of commission due to the credit card companies.

2 (a) Sampling methods

Methods of sampling in accordance with ISA 530 *Audit Sampling and Other Means of Testing*:

Random selection. Ensures each item in a population has an equal chance of selection, for example by using random number tables.

Systematic selection. In which a number of sampling units in the population is divided by the sample size to give a sampling interval.

Haphazard selection. The auditor selects the sample without following a structured technique – the auditor would avoid any conscious bias or predictability.

Sequence or block. Involves selecting a block(s) of continguous items from within a population.

Tutorial note: *Other methods of sampling are as follows:*

Monetary Unit Sampling. *This selection method ensures that each individual $1 in the population has an equal chance of being selected.*

Judgemental sampling. *Selecting items based on the skill and judgement of the auditor.*

(b) Assertions – classes of transactions

Occurrence. The transactions and events that have been recorded have actually occurred and pertain to the entity.

Completeness. All transactions and events that should have been recorded have been recorded.

Accuracy. The amounts and other data relating to recorded transactions and events have been recorded appropriately.

Cut-off. Transactions and events have been recorded in the correct accounting period.

Classification. Transactions and events have been recorded in the proper accounts.

(c) Audit report term

Modified. An auditor modifies an audit report in any situation where it is inappropriate to provide an unmodified report. For example, the auditor may provide additional information in an emphasis of matter (which does not affect the auditor's opinion) or qualify the audit report for limitation of scope or disagreement.

3 (a) (i) **Benefits of using audit software**

Standard systems at client

The same computerised systems and programs as used in all 25 branches of Tirrol Co. This means that the same audit software can be used in each location providing significant time savings compared to the situation where client systems are different in each location.

Use actual computer files not copies or printouts

Use of audit software means that the Tirrol Co's actual inventory files can be tested rather than having to rely on printouts or screen images. The latter could be incorrect, by accident or by deliberate mistake. The audit firm will have more confidence that the 'real' files have been tested.

Test more items

Use of software will mean that more inventory records can be tested – it is possible that all product lines could be tested for obsolescence rather than a sample using manual techniques. The auditor will therefore gain more evidence and have greater confidence that inventory is valued correctly.

Cost

The relative cost of using audit software decreases the more years that software is used. Any cost overruns this year could be offset against the audit fees in future years when the actual expense will be less.

(ii) **Problems on the audit of Tirrol**

Timescale – six week reporting deadline – audit planning

The audit report is due to be signed six weeks after the year end. This means that there will be considerable pressure on the auditor to complete audit work without compromising standards by rushing procedures.

This problem can be overcome by careful planning of the audit, use of experienced staff and ensuring other staff such as second partner reviews are booked well in advance.

Timescale – six week reporting deadline – software issues

The audit report is due to be signed about six weeks after the year end. This means that there is little time to write and test audit software, let alone use the software and evaluate the results of testing.

This problem can be alleviated by careful planning. Access to Tirrol Co's software and data files must be obtained as soon as possible and work commenced on tailoring Cal & Co's software following this. Specialist computer audit staff should be booked as soon as possible to perform this work.

First year audit costs

The relative costs of an audit in the first year at a client tend to be greater due to the additional work of ascertaining client systems. This means that Cal & Co may have a limited budget to document systems including computer systems.

This problem can be alleviated to some extent again by good audit planning. The manager must also monitor the audit process carefully, ensuring that any additional work caused by the client not providing access to systems information including computer systems is identified and added to the total billing cost of the audit.

Staff holidays

Most of the audit work will be carried out in July, which is also the month when many of Cal & Co staff take their annual holiday. This means that there will be a shortage of audit staff, particularly as audit work for Tirrol Co is being booked with little notice.

The problem can be alleviated by booking staff as soon as possible and then identifying any shortages. Where necessary, staff may be borrowed from other offices or even different countries on a secondment basis where shortages are acute.

Non-standard systems

Tirrol Co's computer software is non-standard, having been written specifically for the organisation. This means that more time will be necessary to understand the system than if standard systems were used.

This problem can be alleviated either by obtaining documentation from the client or by approaching the software house (with Tirrol Co's permission) to see if they can assist with provision of information on data structures for the inventory systems. Provision of this information will decrease the time taken to tailor audit software for use in Tirrol Co.

Issues of live testing

Cal & Co has been informed that inventory systems must be tested on a live basis. This increases the risk of accidental amendment or deletion of client data systems compared to testing copy files.

To limit the possibility of damage to client systems, Cal & Co can consider performing inventory testing on days when Tirrol Co is not operating e.g. weekends. At the worst, backups of data files taken from the previous day can be re-installed when Cal & Co's testing is complete.

Computer systems

The client has 25 locations, with each location maintaining its own computer system. It is possible that computer systems are not common across the client due to amendments made at the branch level.

This problem can be overcome to some extent by asking staff at each branch whether systems have been amended and focusing audit work on material branches.

Usefulness of audit software

The use of audit software at Tirrol Co does appear to have significant problems this year. This means that even if the audit software is ready, there may still be some risk of incorrect conclusions being derived due to lack of testing, etc.

This problem can be alleviated by seriously considering the possibility of using a manual audit this year. The manager may need to investigate whether a manual audit is feasible and if so whether it could be completed within the necessary timescale with minimal audit risk.

(b) Reliance on internal audit documentation

There are two issues to consider; the ability of internal audit to produce the documentation and the actual accuracy of the documentation itself.

The ability of the internal audit department to produce the documentation can be determined by:

- Ensuring that the department has staff who have appropriate qualifications. Provision of a relevant qualification e.g. membership of a computer related institute would be appropriate.
- Ensuring that this and similar documentation is produced using a recognised plan and that the documentation is tested prior to use. The use of different staff in the internal audit department to produce and test documentation will increase confidence in its accuracy.
- Ensuring that the documentation is actually used during internal audit work and that problems with documentation are noted and investigated as part of that work. Being given access to internal audit reports on the inventory software will provide appropriate evidence.

Regarding the actual documentation:

- Reviewing the documentation to ensure that it appears logical and that terms and symbols are used consistently throughout. This will provide evidence that the flowcharts, etc should be accurate.
- Comparing the documentation against the 'live' inventory system to ensure it correctly reflects the inventory system. This comparison will include tracing individual transactions through the inventory systems.
- Using part of the documentation to amend Cal & Co's audit software, and then ensuring that the software processes inventory system data accurately. However, this stage may be limited due to the need to use live files at Tirrol Co.

4 (a) Role of internal and external auditors – differences

Objectives

The main objective of internal audit is to improve a company's operations, primarily in terms of validating the efficiency and effectiveness of the internal control systems of a company.

The main objective of the external auditor is to express an opinion on the truth and fairness of the financial statements, and other jurisdiction specific requirements such as confirming that the financial statements comply with the reporting requirements included in legislation.

Reporting

Internal audit reports are normally addressed to the board of directors, or other people charged with governance such as the audit committee. Those reports are not publicly available, being confidential between the internal auditor and the recipient.

External audit reports are provided to the shareholders of a company. The report is attached to the annual financial statements of the company and is therefore publicly available to the shareholders and any reader of the financial statements.

Scope of work

The work of the internal auditor normally relates to the operations of the organisation, including the transaction processing systems and the systems to produce the annual financial statements. The internal auditor may also provide other reports to management, such as value for money audits which external auditors rarely become involved with.

The work of the external auditor relates only to the financial statements of the organisation. However, the internal control systems of the organisation will be tested as these provide evidence on the completeness and accuracy of the financial statements.

Relationship with company

In most organisations, the internal auditor is an employee of the organisation, which may have an impact on the auditor's independence. However, in some organisations the internal audit function is outsourced.

The external auditor is appointed by the shareholders of an organisation, providing some degree of independence from the company and management.

(b) Benefits of audit committee in Conoy Co

Assistance with financial reporting (no finance expertise)

The executive directors of Conoy Co do not appear to have any specific financial skills – as the financial director has recently left the company and has not yet been replaced. This may mean that financial reporting in Conoy Co is limited or that the other non-financial directors spend a significant amount of time keeping up to date on financial reporting issues.

An audit committee will assist Conoy Co by providing specialist knowledge of financial reporting on a temporary basis – at least one of the new appointees should have relevant and recent financial reporting experience under codes of corporate governance. This will allow the executive directors to focus on running Conoy Co.

Enhance internal control systems

The board of Conoy Co do not necessarily understand the work of the internal auditor, or the need for control systems. This means that internal control within Conoy Co may be inadequate or that employees may not recognise the importance of internal control systems within an organisation.

The audit committee can raise awareness of the need for good internal control systems simply by being present in Conoy Co and by educating the board on the need for sound controls. Improving the internal control 'climate' will ensure the need for internal controls is understood and reduce control errors.

Reliance on external auditors

Conoy Co's internal auditors currently report to the board of Conoy Co. As previously noted, the lack of financial and control expertise on the board will mean that external auditor reports and advice will not necessarily be understood – and the board may rely too much on external auditors

If Conoy Co report to an audit committee this will decrease the dependence of the board on the external auditors. The audit committee can take time to understand the external auditor's comments, and then via the non-executive director, ensure that the board take action on those comments.

Appointment of external auditors

At present, the board of Conoy Co appoint the external auditors. This raises issues of independence as the board may become too familiar with the external auditors and so appoint on this friendship rather than merit.

If an audit committee is established, then this committee can recommend the appointment of the external auditors. The committee will have the time and expertise to review the quality of service provided by the external auditors, removing the independence issue.

Corporate governance requirements – best practice

Conoy Co do not need to follow corporate governance requirements (the company is not listed). However, not following those requirements may start to have adverse effects on Conoy. For example, Conoy Co's bank is already concerned about the lack of transparency in reporting.

Establishing an audit committee will show that the board of Conoy Co are committed to maintaining appropriate internal systems in the company and providing the standard of reporting expected by large companies. Obtaining the new bank loan should also be easier as the bank will be satisfied with financial reporting standards.

Given no non-executives – independent advice to board

Currently Conoy Co does not have any non-executive directors. This means that the decisions of the executive directors are not being challenged by other directors independent of the company and with little or no financial interest in the company.

The appointment of an audit committee with one non-executive director on the board of Conoy Co will start to provide some non-executive input to board meetings. While not sufficient in terms of corporate governance requirements (about equal numbers of executive and non-executive directors are expected) it does show the board of Conoy Co are attempting to establish appropriate governance systems.

Advice on risk management

Finally, there are other general areas where Conoy Co would benefit from an audit committee. For example, lack of corporate governance structures probably means Conoy Co does not have a risk management committee. The audit committee can also provide advice on risk management, helping to decrease the risk exposure of the company.

5 (a) Valuation of aviation inventory

- Review GAAP to ensure that there are no exceptions for aviation fuel or inventory held for emergency purposes which would suggest a market valuation should be used.
- Calculate the difference in valuation. The error in inventory valuation is $105 * 6,000 barrels or $630k, which is a material amount compared to profit.
- Review prior year working papers to determine whether a similar situation occurred last year and ascertain the outcome at that stage.
- Discuss the matter with the directors to obtain reasons why they believe that market value should be used for the inventory this year.

- Warn the directors that in your opinion, aviation fuel should be valued at the lower of cost or net realisable value (that is $15/barrel) and that using market value will result in a modification to the audit report.
- If the directors now amend the financial statements to show inventory valued at cost, then consider mentioning the issue in the weakness letter and do not modify the audit report in respect of this matter.
- If the directors will not amend the financial statements, quantify the effect of the disagreement in the valuation method – the sum of $630,000 is material to the financial statements as Tye Co's income statement figure is decreased from a small loss to a loss of $130,000 although net assets decrease by only about 0·3%.
- Obtain a management representation letter from the directors of Tye Co confirming that market value is to be used for the emergency inventory of aviation fuel.
- If the directors will not amend the financial statements, draft the relevant sections of the audit report, showing a qualification on the grounds of disagreement with the accounting policy for valuation of inventory.

(b) (i) External auditor responsibilities regarding detection of fraud

Overall responsibility of auditor

The external auditor is primarily responsible for the audit opinion on the financial statements following the international auditing standards (ISAs). ISA 240 (Redrafted) *The Auditor's Responsibilities Relating to Fraud in an Audit of Financial Statements* is relevant to audit work regarding fraud.

The main focus of audit work is therefore to ensure that the financial statements show a true and fair view. The detection of fraud is therefore not the main focus of the external auditor's work. An auditor is responsible for obtaining reasonable assurance that the financial statements as a whole are free from material misstatement, whether caused by fraud or error.

The auditor is responsible for maintaining an attitude of professional scepticism throughout the audit, considering the potential for management override of controls and recognising the fact that audit procedures that are effective for detecting error may not be effective for detecting fraud.

Materiality

ISA 240 states that the auditor should reduce audit risk to an acceptably low level.

Therefore, in reaching the audit opinion and performing audit work, the external auditor takes into account the concept of materiality. In other words, the external auditor is not responsible for checking all the transactions. Audit procedures are planned to have a reasonable likelihood of identifying material fraud.

Discussion among the audit team

A discussion is required among the engagement team placing particular emphasis on how and where the entity's financial statements may be susceptible to material misstatement due to faud, including how fraud might occur.

Identification of fraud

In situations where the external auditor does detect fraud, then the auditor will need to consider the implications for the entire audit. In other words, the external auditor has a responsibility to extend testing into other areas because the risk of providing an incorrect audit opinion will have increased.

(ii) Groups to report fraud to

Report to audit committee

Disclose the situation to the audit committee as they are charged with maintaining a high standard of governance in the company.

The committee should be able to discuss the situation with the directors and recommend that they take appropriate action e.g. amend the financial statements.

Report to government

As Tye Co is acting under a government contract, and the over-statement of inventory will mean Tye Co breaches that contract (the reported profit becoming a loss), then the auditor may have to report the situation directly to the government. The auditor of Tye Co needs to review the contract to confirm the reporting required under that contract.

Report to members

If the financial statements do not show a true and fair view then the auditor needs to report this fact to the members of Tye Co. The audit report will be qualified with an except for or adverse opinion (depending on materiality) and information concerning the reason for the disagreement given. In this case the auditor is likely to state factually the problem of inventory quantities being incorrect, rather than stating or implying that the directors are involved in fraud.

Report to professional body

If the auditor is uncertain as to the correct course of action, advice may be obtained from the auditor's professional body. Depending on the advice received, the auditor may simply report to the members in the audit report, although resignation and the convening of a general meeting is another reporting option.

(iii) Intimidation threat – safeguards

In response to the implied threat of dismissal if the audit report is modified regarding the potential fraud/error, the following safeguards are available to the auditor.

Discuss with audit committee

The situation can be discussed with the audit committee. As the audit committee should comprise non-executive directors, they will be able to discuss the situation with the finance director and point out clearly the auditor's opinion. They can also remind the directors as a whole that the appointment of the auditor rests with the members on the recommendation of the audit committee. If the recommendation of the audit committee is rejected by the board, good corporate governance requires disclosure of the reason for rejection.

Obtain second partner review

The engagement partner can ask a second partner to review the working papers and other evidence relating to the issue of possible fraud. While this action does not resolve the issue, it does provide additional assurance that the findings and actions of the engagement partner are valid.

Resignation

If the matter is serious, then the auditor can consider resignation rather than not being re-appointed. Resignation has the additional safeguard that the auditor can normally require the directors to convene a general meeting to consider the circumstances of the resignation.

1 **(a)** Audit planning is addressed by ISA 300 (Redrafted) *Planning an Audit of Financial Statements*. The standard notes that an audit plan will be developed after the overall audit strategy has been established and then states that adequate planning benefits the audit of financial statements in several ways, including the following:

- Helping the auditor to devote appropriate attention to important areas of the audit.
- Helping the auditor identify and resolve potential problems on a timely basis.
- Helping the auditor properly organise and manage the audit engagement so that it is performed in an effective and efficient manner.
- Assisting in the selection of engagement team members with appropriate levels of capabilities and competence to respond to anticipated risks and the proper assignment of work to them.
- Facilitating the direction and supervision of engagement team members and the review of their work.
- Assisting, where applicable, in coordination of work done by experts.

The following are examples of matters that would be included in the audit plan:

(i) A description of the nature, timing and extent of planned risk assessment procedures sufficient to assess the risks of material misstatement.

(ii) This would include assessment of inherent risk and control risk at both the entity and assertion level. An important element of the plan would be the understanding and assessment of the control environment of the organisation.

(iii) A description of the nature, timing and extent of planned further procedures at the assertion level for each material class of transactions, account balance, and disclosure.

(iv) This would include an explanation of the decision
   - whether to test the operating effectiveness of controls (an important decision is whether reliance is to be placed on controls).
   - on the nature, timing and extent of planned substantive procedures (this would depend on the decision as to the level of control risk).

(v) Audit procedures required to be carried out for the engagement in order to comply with ISAs, for example, the use of external confirmations to obtain sufficient appropriate evidence at the assertion level.

(b) Appropriate procedures would include:

- Reconcile the sales statistics to the recorded sales in the accounting records. *(Tutorial note: Other audit procedures should already have proven the validity of the recorded sales.)*
- Compare trends this year to those of prior years to ensure they are reasonable.
- In this connection consider any changes in client circumstances and exercise professional scepticism as these statistics are produced internally.
- Discuss with management the analyses they have made and the actions they have taken as a result of the statistical information available to them. They would probably use them, for example, in deciding whether reprints of books are necessary.
- On a test basis check that the customer codes on the customer master file are properly entered to ensure that the type of customer is properly identified.
- Review reports from sales staff to ensure that information on college take-up of books is accurate.

(Tutorial note: As a general rule statistics that are kept on a day-to-day basis for the company's own purposes, will be much more reliable than those prepared especially for the auditor. However, the auditor should carry out procedures to ensure that they are accurate enough for audit purposes.)

(c) Appropriate substantive tests to satisfy the auditor that the royalties charge is accurate and complete include:

	Test	Objective
(i)	Compare the royalties charge with stated sales income and obtain explanations from management if the figures do not appear reasonable.	To satisfy the auditor that the royalties charge in the income statement is reasonable in relation to stated sales income.
(ii)	Compare budgeted royalties figure with actual figures. If variations are significant, obtain explanations from management.	To satisfy the auditor that the actual figures had been anticipated by management, thus providing evidence as to their reliability.
(iii)	Review the sales statistics (proven in (b) above) to ascertain those despatches that attract royalties.	This would be evidence that the royalties charge was soundly based.
(iv)	Take a sample of recorded sales entries and check: – whether royalties are due in respect of the customer. – if they are, that the entry in the computerised royalties file has been calculated at 10% according to the contracts agreed with the published poets.	These are detailed tests to prove that royalties were due on despatches and that the calculation of the royalty was accurate.
(v)	Take a sample of royalty payments and agree to supporting despatch and sales documentation, checking in particular that all despatches are to individuals and organisations attracting royalties.	This is a test to prove that recorded royalty payments have resulted from despatches and sales attracting royalties.
(vi)	Select sales for 15 days before the year end and 15 days afterwards and compare with the dates of despatch notes.	This is to check that cut-off is accurate. The royalties charge should only include royalties on sales up to the cut-off date.
(vii)	Calculate the expected level of royalty payments based on monthly trend information for type of customer. Obtain sales figures and multiply by 10%. Compare expectation to actual royalties and obtain explanations from management for any significant variations.	This test should provide the auditor with evidence as to the completeness and accuracy of royalties paid.

This list is not exhaustive and other procedures may be appropriate.

(d) There are many inherent risks that may affect the inventory of books and some of these are set out below, together with controls that would mitigate each risk.

Inherent risks	Mitigating controls
Risk of deterioration.	Books should be stored in a location with air conditioning to keep them in saleable state.
Some books may not be saleable because of lack of demand.	Maintenance of movement records to identify slow-moving items.
Books may be defective and therefore not saleable.	Inspection of books returned from customers to identify those that are not in good condition. Identification of defective items at interim or period-end inventory counts.
Books may be attractive and easily transportable, making attempted theft likely.	Books to be kept in a secure location with restriction of entry to authorised personnel.
Poor counting of inventory at the period end.	The use of independent and experienced inventory counters. The use of teams to cover specific areas of the locations where inventory is held. The use of pre-numbered inventory count sheets. And other inventory count procedures.
Poor cut-off as there may be movements of goods during the inventory count.	Movement of books out stopped during the count or only allowed by permission of authorised official in charge of the count. Book returns received during count held in separate area. Identification of last movements in and out.
Goods on sale or return are held by customers but should be included within inventory until the return period is passed.	Detailed records should be maintained of goods on sale or return and this should be reviewed at the year end to ensure that any goods within the return period have been included in inventory.

(e) (i) Net realisable value is defined in IAS 2 *Inventories* as: 'the estimated selling price in the ordinary course of business less the estimated costs of completion and the estimated costs necessary to make the sale.'

(ii) Appropriate procedures to determine that net realisable value of book inventory is above cost would include:

(1) Assessment of estimated proceeds from the sale of items of inventory. Sales price in the period following the year-end is one important element of net realisable value. Procedures to determine sales prices include:

- Obtain actual sales prices by reference to invoices issued after the year-end and determine that the sales were genuine by vouching sales invoices to orders, despatch notes and subsequent receipt of cash.
- If actual sales prices are not available, the auditor should obtain estimated sales prices from management. It would be necessary to assess how reasonable these estimated prices were. The auditor might be aided in this respect by reviewing the reports from sales staff backed up by discussions with management.
- Particular attention should be paid to sales prices of books identified as slow-moving. *(Tutorial note: Slow-moving books might be identified by obtaining lists of sales made in the preceding (say) six months and reviewing reports from sales staff. The sales statistics would also be useful in this respect.)*
- For damaged books disposal price may be nil or very low and the auditor should examine records of disposal of such books in the past. *(Tutorial note: Damaged books should have been identified during the inventory count.)*

(2) Determine estimated costs to completion. These costs represent another important element of net realisable value. Relevant procedures include:

- Some books may still be in production and will initially be included in inventory at cost to date; for example, they may have been printed but not bound. The auditor should examine production budgets and actual costs (for binding, for example) to determine actual costs to completion. *(Tutorial note: It is not uncommon for publishers to print books but leave them unbound until sales in the immediate future are expected.)*
- Books returned may incur extra costs before they can be made ready for resale and the auditor should examine cost records to obtain a reasonable estimate of such costs.

(3) Determine costs to be incurred in marketing, selling and distributing directly related to the items in question.

- In general terms the auditor may determine the percentage relationship between sales and selling and distribution expenses.
- However, the distribution costs of heavy books are likely to be higher than for (say) light paperback books and the auditor should assess whether the cost weighting is reasonable.

(4) All of the above matters should be discussed with management bearing in mind that, although they represent an internal source of evidence, they are the most informed people regarding the saleability of books on hand and regarding determination of the various elements of net realisable value.

2 (a) The following five factors that influence the reliability of audit evidence are taken from ISA 500 *Audit Evidence*:

(i) Audit evidence is more reliable when it is obtained from independent sources outside the entity.
(ii) Audit evidence that is generated internally is more reliable when the related controls imposed by the entity are effective.
(iii) Audit evidence obtained directly by the auditor (for example, observation of the application of a control) is more reliable than audit evidence obtained indirectly or by inference (for example, inquiry about the application of a control).
(iv) Audit evidence is more reliable when it exists in documentary form, whether paper, electronic, or other medium. (For example, a contemporaneously written record of a meeting is more reliable than a subsequent oral representation of the matters discussed.)
(v) Audit evidence provided by original documents is more reliable than audit evidence provided by photocopies or facsimiles.

Other examples are:

(vi) Evidence created in the normal course of business is better than evidence specially created to satisfy the auditor.
(vii) The best-informed source of audit evidence will normally be management of the company (although management's lack of independence may reduce its value as a source of such evidence).
(viii) Evidence about the future is particularly difficult to obtain and is less reliable than evidence about past events.

(b) (i) Those charged with governance are responsible for overseeing:

- the strategic direction of the entity
- obligations related to the accountability of the entity. This includes overseeing the financial reporting process.

(ii) General audit matters that might be communicated to those charged with governance are addressed in ISA 260:

(1) The auditor's responsibilities in relation to financial statement audit.

This would include:

- A statement that the auditor is responsible for forming and expressing an opinion on the financial statements.
- That the auditor's work is carried out in accordance with ISAs and in accordance with local laws and regulations.

(2) Planned scope and timing of the audit.

This would include

- The audit approach to assessing the risk of serious misstatement, whether arising from fraud or error.
- The audit approach to the internal control system and whether reliance will be placed on it.
- The timing of interim and final audits, including reporting deadlines.

(3) Significant findings from the audit.

This heading could include:

- Significant difficulties encountered during the audit, including delays in obtaining information from management.
- Material weaknesses in internal control and recommendations for improvement.
- Audit adjustments, whether or not recorded by the entity, that have, or could have, a material effect on the entity's financial statements. For example, the bankruptcy of a material receivable shortly after the year-end that should result in an adjusting entry.

(4) A statement on independence issues affecting the audit.

This would include:

- That the audit firm has ensured that all members of the audit team have complied with the ethical standards of IFAC.
- That appropriate safeguards are in place where a potential threat to independence has been identified.

(Tutorial note: The lists of examples listed under the above headings are not exhaustive and in practice many more specific matters would be communicated to those charged with governance.)

3 **(a)** The auditor obtains an understanding of the entity, its control environment and its detailed internal controls:

(i) to identify and assess the risks of material misstatements, whether due to fraud or error, at the financial statement and assertion levels. Risks would include inherent risk and control risk. An important objective would be to determine the extent to which the auditor would rely on the internal control system.

(ii) to provide a basis for designing and implementing responses to the assessed risks of material misstatement in the financial statements. This would involve the design and performance of the audit procedures required to form an opinion on the truth and fairness of the financial statements. An important objective would be to determine the extent and nature of audit procedures to reduce detection risk, and therefore audit risk, to an acceptable level.

(iii) to set the scene for identifying assertions and collecting sufficient appropriate evidence to prove that the assertions are reasonable.

(b) Strong points in the control environment of Letham Co in respect of non-current assets are set out below, together with explanations as to their impact on control risk:

	Strengths	**Impact on control risk**
(i)	Approval of the five-year and annual budgets by the board of directors.	The annual budget is the 'trigger' for placing orders for equipment. Its approval by the board will ensure that only authorised non-current assets are purchased.
(ii)	The budget is updated when the order for new equipment is placed.	The company can use the updated budget at any time to anticipate cash outflows. It will also ensure that there is no duplication of assets purchased.
(iii)	Pre-numbered goods received notes and operational certificates are available to the accounting department for comparison with the purchase invoice.	Only goods that have been received and are operating effectively will be paid for.
(iv)	Informed people in the production department carefully assess the proper operation of the equipment.	This will help to ensure the operational effectiveness of plant and equipment.
(v)	The accounting department, independent of the production facility, updates the non-tangible assets register and only the accounting department has access to it.	The potential for fraudulent entries to cover theft/unauthorised purchases will be reduced and the non-current assets register, an important non-current assets control document, cannot be manipulated by the people who hold the assets.

	Strengths	Impact on control risk
(vi)	Accounting department personnel, independent of production, perform rolling tests to ensure that the non-current assets register and non-current assets on hand are in agreement with each other.	The risk of theft and loss of plant and equipment is reduced and the likelihood that all items in the register existing increased.
(vii)	The internal audit department tests on a sample basis that recorded non-current assets are in existence, but see (c) below.	The internal auditing department will be more independent than the accounting department and hence will provide further comfort that the non-current assets register is not overstated.
(viii)	Internal audit test the operation of the entire non-current assets recording system.	Any controls which are not operating effectively are likely to be identified and rectified before significant errors can occur.

(c) **(i)** Great care must be taken in selecting the starting point for audit testing. The test that the internal auditors performed, namely, selecting a representative sample of purchase invoices for testing to the non-current assets register and to the updating movements on the annual budget, proves merely that register and budget are in agreement with the purchase invoices issued. It is therefore not a good test to prove the completeness of purchase invoices and therefore of the entries in the register and budget. In addition, the purchase invoices are issued by many different suppliers and there is no common serial number to enable the company to ensure that all purchases are accounted for.

(ii) A more appropriate test would be to make the selection from goods received notes (GRNs), as the issue of a GRN is normally the point at which liability is accepted and is in any event the document used to update the non-current assets budget. In other words, it is important to identify your audit objective and then to decide on what sample will be the most appropriate to aid you in meeting that objective. The GRNs would be traced to the recorded purchase invoices to ensure that the latter were complete and then to the entries in the non-current assets register and to the updating entries in the budget to ensure that these too were complete.

An additional appropriate test would be to select a sample of plant and equipment visible on the shop floor and trace them to the non-current assets register to identify whether they have been:

- included in the register
- noted against the budget as purchased
- paid for by tracing purchase invoice through to payment.

(Tutorial note: The auditor would of course wish to prove that the GRNs are complete and might select a sample of purchase orders and trace them to the GRNs to ensure GRNs have been prepared in each case or the order rejected for good reason. Another appropriate test on the GRNs would be to prove that the numbering sequence was complete.)

4 **(a)** The interim audit, as its name suggests, is that part of the whole audit that takes place before the year-end. The auditor uses the interim audit to carry out procedures that would be difficult to perform at the year-end because of time pressure. The final audit, on the other hand, will take place after the year-end and concludes with the auditor forming and expressing an opinion on the financial statements for the whole year subject to audit. It is important to note that the final opinion takes account of conclusions formed at both the interim and final audit.

Typical work carried out at the interim audit includes:

- consideration of inherent risks facing the company. *(Tutorial note: risk would be initially considered at the planning stage, but is, in fact, reassessed at all audit stages.)*
- recording the system of internal control.
- carrying out tests of control on the company's internal control system and evaluating its effectiveness to determine the level of control risk.
- performing sufficient substantive testing of transactions and balances to be satisfied that the books and records are a reliable basis for the preparation of financial statements.
- identification of potential problems that may affect the final audit work. A basic aim is to ensure as far as possible that there are no undetected problems at the year-end.

Typical work carried out at the final examination includes:

- Follow up of items noted at the inventory count.
- Obtaining confirmations from third parties, such as bankers and lawyers.
- Analytical reviews of figures in the financial statements.
- Reviews of events after the reporting period.
- Consideration of the going concern status of the organisation.

(Tutorial note: At the final audit the auditor would carry out tests to ensure that the conclusions formed at the interim audit were still valid.)

(b) The external auditors would normally be able to use the work of the internal auditors provided that:

– they are independent (in this case, of the accounting department and finance director to whom the accounting department reports). It appears that they have reported to the whole board, which would be a factor increasing their independence. It would be even better if they had strong links with the audit committee (if applicable).

– they are competent. Your firm would have formed a view in past years of their reliability by considering the background (including qualifications and experience, particularly as regards forecasting) of the internal audit staff and by examining their reports and working papers. You may also have reviewed some aspects of their work in the current year to the same end.

– effective communication, whether there is likely to be effective communication between the internal auditors and the external auditor.

– they have exercised due professional care, the work would need to have been properly planned including detailed work programmes, supervised, documented and reviewed.

You would still take full responsibility for any report that you issue.

(c) Audit procedures adopted in the examination of the cash flow forecast would include:

(1) Check that the opening balance of the cash forecast is in agreement with the closing balance of the cash book, to ensure the opening balance of the forecast is accurate.

(2) Consider how accurate company forecasts have been in the past by comparing past forecasts with actual outcomes. If forecasts have been reasonably accurate in the past, this would make it more likely that the current forecast is reliable.

(3) Determine the assumptions that have been made in the preparation of the cash flow forecast. For example, the company is experiencing a poor economic climate, so you would not expect cash flows from sales and realisation of receivables to increase, but either to decrease or remain stable. You are also aware that costs are rising so you would expect cost increases to be reflected in the cash forecasts.

(4) Examine the sales department detailed budgets for the two years ahead and, in particular, discuss with them the outlets that they will be targeting. This would help the auditor determine whether the cash derived from sales is soundly based.

(5) Examine the production department's assessment of the non-current assets required to increase the production of white bread to the level required by the sales projections. Obtain an assessment of estimated cost of non-current assets, reviewing bids from suppliers, if available. This would provide evidence on material cash outflows.

(6) Consider the adequacy of the increased working capital that will be required as a result of the expansion. Increased working capital would result in cash outflows and it would be important to establish its adequacy.

(d) You would inform management that it would not be possible to give a report on the accuracy of the cash flow forecast. The forecast is an assessment of cash flows in the future which is uncertain, particularly in the second year.

The bank should be informed that the kind of report that you could give is a limited assurance or negative assurance report. You would be able to state in your report the kind of work you had carried out, the assumptions that management had made and then to give a negative form of assurance in which you would state, among other things, that nothing had come to your attention that would cause you to believe that the assumptions do not provide a reasonable basis for the cash forecast. You could then go on to say that the forecast has been properly prepared on the basis of the assumptions.

This is assuming that this kind of opinion is appropriate in the light of the work you have performed.

5 (a) As regards accounts payable there are many different assertions that have to be addressed. Some relevant assertions are set out below:

(i) Rights and obligations – Accounts payable represent amounts actually due by the company, that is, there is an obligation, taking into account:
  – the actual performance of services for the company; or
  – transfer of title in goods transferred to the company; and
  – cash payments or other genuine debit entry.

(ii) Valuation and allocation – Accounts payable have been correctly valued taking into account original transaction amounts and such matters as trade discounts and local sales tax.

(iii) Existence – The original transaction amounts are valid and the liability exists.

(iv) Completeness – All accounts payable are recorded in the accounting records.

(Tutorial note: The importance of assertions lies in the fact that they provide objectives for the auditor and enable the evidence search to be carried out in a logical fashion. The auditor will determine the assertions that are made about a particular figure appearing in the financial statements. This provides a series of objectives about that audit area and then the auditor searches for evidence to prove that each objective is met and that the assertion is valid or invalid.)

(b) Controls that the company has in place to reduce the risk associated with purchases of food and its preparation in the kitchen, together with relevant audit procedures on controls testing, would include the following: *(Tutorial note: For a restaurant it is important that food quality is good and in particular that it does not present any danger to the customer arising from deterioration or poor practices in its preparation.)*

	Controls	Audit Procedures
(i)	Overall authority for food purchasing should be in the hands of a designated person to ensure that the food purchased is of the desired quality. This is often in the hands of the head chef.	Review the company's organisation chart and identify the person with overall responsibility for food purchasing. Discuss with management his or her background and expertise.
(ii)	There should be a list of approved suppliers to ensure that the food comes from sources known for their quality.	Examine the list of approved suppliers of food and check that there are no purchases of food from other parties.
(iii)	On receipt of food, whether meat, fish, or vegetables and fruit, it should be carefully inspected by informed people, including those responsible for food preparation. This would be to ensure that it was of the desired quality (as well as quantity). A goods received note (GRN) should be signed to provide evidence of receipt and inspection.	Examine a sample of GRNs to ensure that all bear an approved signature indicating that food has been inspected for quality on receipt.
(iv)	Food purchased should be kept in a clean place and refrigerated, if necessary. This would be to ensure that it has kept its quality.	Examine the food storage areas, including refrigerators, on a surprise basis to ensure they are clean and tidy. Ensure that the refrigerators are maintained at the correct temperature. Another test in this area might be to examine reports of local authority and other inspectors to ensure they were happy that the food was being properly stored.
(v)	Strict adherence to use-by dates to ensure that no poor quality food is prepared.	Check that there is no food on the premises which is past its use-by date. Discuss with management what happens to food which is past its use-by date, that is, how it is disposed of.

(c) Evidence collected by the auditor to enable a conclusion to be formed on the likelihood of the claim being successful (that is, whether a provision would be necessary according to IAS 37 *Provisions, Contingent Liabilities and Contingent Assets*) includes:

	Evidence	Explanation
(i)	Obtain the written claim by the customer.	This would tell you the reason why the claim was being made and provide other relevant details, such as whether the customer dined in the restaurant or purchased carry-out food, and the date when the alleged food poisoning took place.
(ii)	Review the controls in force over purchases and food preparation (see (b) above).	This would be to ensure that the company controls appeared to be effective.
(iii)	Obtain written reports concerning any inspections that had been carried out by company staff or third parties in the food store and food preparation areas.	This would provide evidence about any problems that had arisen affecting food quality. Discuss with management the actions that were taken to correct any problems that had arisen.
(iv)	Discuss the matter with the company's lawyers to obtain their view on the likelihood of the claim being successful.	This would provide evidence from a professional third party as to the likelihood of the claim succeeding and the reasons why the lawyers had reached their conclusion.
(v)	Obtain management representations regarding the likelihood of the claim succeeding.	This is internal evidence and should be approached with professional scepticism, but it would provide the auditor with the views of an informed group of people.

(d) As you have concluded that the likelihood of the claim being successful is only possible, it would be appropriate for the company to explain the contingent liability by way of note as required by IAS 37, giving a description of the nature of the contingent liability, an estimate of its financial effect, an indication of the uncertainties relating to the amount and timing and the possibility of any reimbursement.

If the company includes a note of this nature, there would be no need to modify your audit opinion. However, if the contingency is not disclosed, the auditor would modify the audit opinion on the grounds of an 'except for' disagreement and include in the report the required details of the contingent liability. The auditor should try to persuade management to include the disclosure before issuing the modified opinion. *(Tutorial note: An 'except for' qualification would be appropriate as the contingent loss is material only, that is, the uncertainty is not major.)*

BPP LEARNING MEDIA

Notes

Review Form & Free Prize Draw – Paper F8 Audit and Assurance (International) (1/10)

All original review forms from the entire BPP range, completed with genuine comments, will be entered into one of two draws on 31 July 2010 and 31 January 2011. The names on the first four forms picked out on each occasion will be sent a cheque for £50.

Name: ______________________ **Address:** ______________________

____

____

How have you used this Kit?
(Tick one box only)

☐ Home study (book only)
☐ On a course: college ____________
☐ With 'correspondence' package
☐ Other ____________

Why did you decide to purchase this Kit?
(Tick one box only)

☐ Have used the complementary Study Text
☐ Have used other BPP products in the past
☐ Recommendation by friend/colleague
☐ Recommendation by a lecturer at college
☐ Saw advertising
☐ Other ____________

During the past six months do you recall seeing/receiving any of the following?
(Tick as many boxes as are relevant)

☐ Our advertisement in *Student Accountant*
☐ Our advertisement in *Pass*
☐ Our advertisement in *PQ*
☐ Our brochure with a letter through the post
☐ Our website www.bpp.com

Which (if any) aspects of our advertising do you find useful?
(Tick as many boxes as are relevant)

☐ Prices and publication dates of new editions
☐ Information on product content
☐ Facility to order books off-the-page
☐ None of the above

Which BPP products have you used?

Text	☐	*Success CD*	☐	*Learn Online*	☐
Kit	☑	*i-Learn*	☐	*Home Study Package*	☐
Passcard	☐	*i-Pass*	☐	*Home Study PLUS*	☐

Your ratings, comments and suggestions would be appreciated on the following areas.

	Very useful	*Useful*	*Not useful*
Passing ACCA exams	☐	☐	☐
Passing F8	☐	☐	☐
Planning your question practice	☐	☐	☐
Questions	☐	☐	☐
Top Tips etc in answers	☐	☐	☐
Content and structure of answers	☐	☐	☐
'Plan of attack' in mock exams	☐	☐	☐
Mock exam answers			

Overall opinion of this Kit *Excellent* ☐ *Good* ☐ *Adequate* ☐ *Poor* ☐

Do you intend to continue using BPP products? *Yes* ☐ *No* ☐

The BPP author of this edition can be e-mailed at: paulsutcliffe@bpp.com

Please return this form to: Lesley Buick, ACCA Publishing Manager, BPP Learning Media, FREEPOST, London, W12 8BR

Review Form & Free Prize Draw (continued)

TELL US WHAT YOU THINK

Please note any further comments and suggestions/errors below.

Free Prize Draw Rules

1 Closing date for 31 July 2010 draw is 30 June 2010. Closing date for 31 January 2011 draw is 31 December 2010.

2 Restricted to entries with UK and Eire addresses only. BPP employees, their families and business associates are excluded.

3 No purchase necessary. Entry forms are available upon request from BPP Learning Media. No more than one entry per title, per person. Draw restricted to persons aged 16 and over.

4 Winners will be notified by post and receive their cheques not later than 6 weeks after the relevant draw date.

5 The decision of the promoter in all matters is final and binding. No correspondence will be entered into.